ENGLISH G

LIGHTHOUSE

Lehrerfassung

5

Vokabeltrainer-App

Verfügbar für: iOS, Android und Windows Phone

Dieses Buch gibt es auch auf
www.scook.de
Buchcode: **okay4-3t7xq**

Es kann dort nach Bestätigung der Allgemeinen Geschäftsbedingungen genutzt werden.

English G · Lighthouse · Band 5
Lehrerfassung

Im Auftrag des Verlages herausgegeben von
Wolfgang Biederstädt, Köln
Frank Donoghue, Nenagh, Irland

Konzepterarbeitung von
Susan Abbey, Nenagh, Irland
Wolfgang Biederstädt, Köln
Frank Donoghue, Nenagh, Irland

Erarbeitet von
Susan Abbey, Nenagh, Irland
Frank Donoghue, Nenagh, Irland

unter Mitarbeit von
Joachim Blombach, Herford
Annette Bondzio-Abbit, Bielefeld
Hartmut Bondzio, Bielefeld
Uta Franke, Leipzig
Marc Proulx, Berlin
Martina Schroeder, Stedtlingen
Udo Wagner, Voerde
Herbert Willms, Herford

in Zusammenarbeit mit der Englischredaktion
Klaus Unger (Projektleitung); Annegret Hauser (koordinierende Redakteurin); Doreen Arnold, Jutta Seuren, Kathrin Spiegelberg, Silvia Wiedemann *sowie beratend* Irja Fröhling, Mara Leibowitz, Olivia Wintgens; Stefanie Tamke (bildrechtliche Unterstützung)

Vokabelanhänge
Ingrid Raspe, Düsseldorf; Uwe Tröger

Beratende Mitwirkung
Birgit Estabillo, Berlin; Verena Flocke, Düren; Alexander Kraft, Guldental; Jürgen Lohmann, Dinslaken; Jörg Rademacher, Mannheim; Andrea Rohoff, Hannover; Dr. Daniela Schirmer, Kiel; Berit Schaarschmidt, Aschaffenburg; Konstanze Stöckermann-Borst, Leimen; Herbert Willms, Herford sowie Ulrike Rath, Aachen

Layoutkonzept und technische Umsetzung
Klein & Halm Grafikdesign, Berlin

Umschlaggestaltung
Cornelsen Verlag Design unter Verwendung der Entwürfe von Klein & Halm Grafikdesign, Berlin, und kleiner & bold, Berlin

www.cornelsen.de

Soweit in diesem Lehrwerk Personen fotografisch abgebildet sind und ihnen von der Redaktion fiktive Namen, Berufe, Dialoge und Ähnliches zugeordnet oder diese Personen in bestimmte Kontexte gesetzt werden, dienen diese Zuordnungen und Darstellungen ausschließlich der Veranschaulichung und dem besseren Verständnis des Inhalts.

Die Internetadressen und -dateien, die in diesem Lehrwerk angegeben sind, wurden vor Drucklegung geprüft. Der Verlag übernimmt keine Gewähr für die Aktualität und den Inhalt dieser Adressen und Dateien oder solcher, die mit ihnen verlinkt sind.

Dieses Werk berücksichtigt die Regeln der reformierten Rechtschreibung und Zeichensetzung.

Alle Drucke dieser Auflage sind inhaltlich unverändert und können im Unterricht nebeneinander verwendet werden.

© 2016 Cornelsen Schulverlag GmbH, Berlin

Das Werk und seine Teile sind urheberrechtlich geschützt.
Jede Nutzung in anderen als den gesetzlich zugelassenen Fällen bedarf der vorherigen schriftlichen Einwilligung des Verlages.

Hinweis zu den §§ 46, 52 a UrhG: Weder das Werk noch seine Teile dürfen ohne eine solche Einwilligung eingescannt und in ein Netzwerk eingestellt werden. Dies gilt auch für Intranets von Schulen und sonstigen Bildungseinrichtungen.

Druck: Firmengruppe APPL, aprinta Druck, Wemding

1. Auflage, 1. Druck 2016
ISBN 978-3-06-032714-0

PEFC zertifiziert
Dieses Produkt stammt aus nachhaltig bewirtschafteten Wäldern und kontrollierten Quellen.
www.pefc.de

Dein Englischbuch enthält folgende Teile:

Unit 1–4	Die vier Kapitel des Buches
Diff-Bank	Weitere Aufgaben – unterschiedlich schwer
Wordbank	Zusätzliche Wörter und Wendungen zu bestimmten Themen
Text file	Interessante Texte, passend zu den Units
Exam file	Aufgaben zur Vorbereitung auf die Abschlussprüfung
Language file	Zusammenfassung wichtiger Sprachregeln
Skills file	Beschreibung wichtiger Lern- und Arbeitstechniken
Vocabulary	Wörterverzeichnis zum Lernen der neuen Wörter
Dictionary	Alphabetisches Wörterverzeichnis (*English-German*)

Die Units bestehen aus diesen Teilen:

Lead-in	Einstieg in die neue Unit
Theme 1 / Theme 2	Neue Themen mit vielen Aktivitäten und Übungen
Focus on language	Entdecken von Regeln und Üben wichtiger Strukturen
Text	Eine Geschichte zum Lesen
Skills training	Hören: *Listening* – Lesen: *Reading* – Sprechen: *Speaking* – Schreiben: *Writing* – Sprachmittlung: *Mediation* – Hör-/Sehverstehen: *Viewing*
STOP! CHECK! GO!	Üben, Vertiefen, Lernfortschritte feststellen (Von der Lehrperson kannst du ein Lösungsblatt erhalten. Hörtexte findest du auf der Audio-CD im Workbook.)

In den Units findest du diese Symbole:

👥 👥	Partnerarbeit / Gruppenarbeit
🎧 🎧	Nur auf CD / Auf CD und im Schülerbuch
▶️	Filme auf der DVD
○	Leichtere Übungen
●	Schwierigere Übungen
○ // ● p. 104	Parallelaufgaben: die leichtere in der Unit – die schwierigere in der Diff-Bank
More help p. 102	Hilfen zu einer Aufgabe in der Diff-Bank
More practice 3 p. 104	Weitere Übungen in der Diff-Bank
More challenge 4 p. 107	Weitere Übungen mit höherem Schwierigkeitsgrad

INHALT

	Lerninhalte	Your task (Lernaufgabe)	Texte
Unit 1 Life down under	• Geografie und Sehenswürdigkeiten Australiens kennen lernen • über Besonderheiten von Land und Leuten sprechen • sich mit der Geschichte und Kultur der australischen Ureinwohner/innen befassen • sich in Notfallsituationen verständigen • Zeitformen korrekt verwenden • eine Präsentation vorbereiten, halten und auswerten	**A presentation about Australia** selbstständig für eine Präsentation recherchieren, sie erstellen und vortragen; dazu Feedback geben und erhalten (p. 23)	**Magazine articles** *Ban on climbing Uluru …* (p. 10) *Australia welcomes its new citizens* (p. 10) *Teenagers help fight bush fires* (p. 11) *Camels in the outback* (p. 11) *Australia's deadliest animals* (p. 11) *First Australians* (p. 15) **Website** *Royal Flying Doctor Service* (p. 12) **Teens' real life stories** *Living in the Kimberley* (p. 16) *I'm a mud racer* (p. 16) *Beach culture* (p. 16) *One day changed my life* (p. 16) **Text** adapted from the novel **Swerve** (pp. 18–21, *easier version* pp. 103–104)
*MORE CHALLENGE 1 Understanding idioms	• eine Geschichte über einen japanischen Gastschüler in Tasmanien erschließen • mit idiomatischen Wendungen umgehen		**Text** adapted from the novel **The Spare Room** (p. 28) **Cartoons** *English idioms* (p. 29)
Unit 2 Respect	• über *cyberbullying* sprechen und mögliche Auswege diskutieren • sich über den Umgang mit *peer pressure* austauschen • ein Experiment zum Thema Diskriminierung durchführen und reflektieren • berichten, was jemand gesagt hat • lernen und üben, wie Konversationen gelingen	**Do something!** in Gruppenarbeit ein Projekt gegen Diskriminierung erarbeiten und präsentieren (p. 37)	**Online article** *Is peer pressure a problem for you?* (p. 32) **Article** *Racism: It stops with me* (p. 35) **Text** adapted from the novel **Watching you, watching me**: "Natasha's side of the story" (pp. 41–43), *easier version*: "Matt's side of the story" (pp. 115–116)
*MORE CHALLENGE 2 Living with disability	• zwei authentische Texte über das Leben mit Behinderungen erschließen • eigenes Verhalten reflektieren		**Blog entry** *The kid in a wheelchair* (p. 50) **Online article** *A fashion model and a role model* (p. 50)

Die hier (und auf S. 5–7) aufgeführten Angebote sind nicht obligatorisch abzuarbeiten. Die Auswahl der Übungen und Übungsteile richtet sich nach den Schwerpunkten des schulinternen Curriculums. (*) = optionale Angebote

Kompetenzen	Sprache	Seite
Listening: advert *The Flying Doctors* (p. 12) conversations *Emergencies on the beach* (p. 13) teens' audio stories for a competition (p. 16) **Speaking course (1)** *Giving a presentation* (pp. 22–23) silent dialogue *Getting help* (p. 13) **Reading:** articles *What makes Oz special?* (pp. 10–11) *Tips from the RFDS website* (p. 12); *First Australians* (p. 15) **Writing:** Kommentar *Australia – a place to visit?* (p. 11) einen Artikel schreiben *Tips for tourists in Australia* (p. 13) zusammenfassen, was man einem Text entnommen hat (p. 15) **Mediation** (+ intercultural competence): Teile eines Songtexts analysieren und sprachmitteln (p. 14) **Viewing** (+ intercultural competence): *An Australian road trip* (p. 9); *The Burdekin Crew* (p. 14) *How to improve your presentations* (p. 22)	**Wortschatz** und **Strukturen** describing places and activities; avoiding emergencies; getting help, talking about a difficult history; teens' everyday life in Australia; useful phrases for presentations **using tenses correctly** revision: **simple present**, **simple past**, **going to-*future***, ***past progressive*** (p. 17) ***STOP! CHECK! GO!** (pp. 24–27) Üben und vertiefen; Lernfortschritte erkennen	8
Listening: dialogues *Fun with idioms* (p. 29) **Reading:** *Akira's first morning* (p. 28) **Mediation:** English and German idioms (p. 29)	**Wortschatz** und **Strukturen** talking about cultural differences **dealing with idioms** (p. 29)	28
Listening: dialogues *Come shopping with me!* (p. 34); *Guess what happened last night* (p. 38) **Speaking course (2)** *Successful conversations* (pp. 44–45) Auswege aus *cyberbullying*-Situationen diskutieren (p. 31) sprechen über rassistisches Verhalten (p. 35) role-plays *Why don't you go out with us?* (p. 34) *Badges – a group experiment* (p. 35) **Reading:** article *Is peer pressure a problem for you?* (p. 32) **Writing:** Kommentar *Peer pressure is a big problem …* (p. 33) **Study skills:** einen Slogan erschließen (p. 36) **Viewing** (+ intercultural competence): *I thought we were friends* (pp. 30–31) *'What you say matters' by Brothablack* (p. 36) *Dos and don'ts in conversations* (p. 44)	**Wortschatz** und **Strukturen** speculating about a conflict; giving advice; supporting an opinion with arguments; reflecting on feelings and interactions; planning and presenting a project; useful phrases for conversations ***indirect speech*** in statements, questions and commands (pp. 39–40) **more on backshift in *indirect speech*** (p. 114) ***STOP! CHECK! GO!** (pp. 46–49) Üben und vertiefen; Lernfortschritte erkennen	30
Reading: blog entry; article (p. 50) **Speaking:** Reaktionen auf Texte verbalisieren und eigene Haltungen reflektieren (p. 50)	**Wortschatz** und **Strukturen** talking about feelings and attitudes **-ing-*forms (participles)* instead of subordinate clauses** (p. 51)	50

INHALT

	Lerninhalte	Your task (Lernaufgabe)	Texte
Unit 3 **Looking forward**	· über *life skills* und die eigene Zukunft sprechen · persönliche Stärken, Schwächen und Vorlieben beschreiben · Stellenangebote verstehen · über den persönlichen Idealberuf sprechen · *CV* und *cover letter* verfassen lernen · Fragen formulieren · sich auf *job interviews* vorbereiten	**Who will get the job?** Bewerbungsgespräche durchführen und evaluieren (p. 67)	**Quiz** *Are you ready for the real world?* (p. 52) **Adverts** *Internet job ads* (pp. 56–57) **Official documents** *CV* (p. 58) *Cover letter* (p. 59) **Text** *adapted from the short story* **Seashell Motel** (pp. 62–64, *easier version* pp. 123–125)
***MORE CHALLENGE 3** Creative writing	· kreatives Schreiben in unterschiedlichen Genres · *question tags* verwenden		**Example texts** (p. 72) a self-description, a story, a dialogue and a poem
Unit 4 **Generation** *like*	· sagen, was man *cool* oder *uncool* findet · eigene digitale Gewohnheiten reflektieren · über Selbstdarstellungen sprechen (*profiles*, *selfies*, *tattoos*) · mit Werbestrategien umgehen lernen · sagen, was passieren wäre, wenn … · sich an Diskussionen beteiligen	**A survey in your class** eine Klassenumfrage zum Thema *What's (not) cool and why?* durchführen und die Ergebnisse präsentieren (p. 75)	**Articles** *Being a screenager* (p. 76) *Your kind of profile picture?* (p. 78) *Are you ad-savvy?* (p. 80) *Hundreds of teenagers gatecrash party* (p. 82) **Text** *adapted from the novel* **Gamer** (pp. 84–87, *easier version* pp. 136–138)
***MORE CHALLENGE 4** Street art	· über Kunst im öffentlichen Raum sprechen · einen Film über Banksy kennen lernen		**Film review** *Exit through the gift shop* (p. 95)

Anhang

PARTNER-B-Seiten		96
DIFF-BANK		98
*WORDBANK		142
*TEXT FILE		146
TF 1	Oz: Facts for visitors (Unit 1)	146
TF 2	Waiting for something to happen (Unit 2)	148
TF 3	Job description: Cleaner of the world's oceans (Unit 3, Bilinguales Modul Geography)	152
TF 4	Music in your life (Unit 4)	154
*EXAM FILE		156

SKILLS FILE		162
SF 1–4	STUDY AND LANGUAGE SKILLS	162
SF 5–6	LISTENING SKILLS AND READING SKILLS	166
SF 7	SPEAKING COURSE	170
SF 8	WRITING COURSE	172
SF 9	DESCRIBING PHOTOS AND PICTURES	179
SF 10	MEDIATION SKILLS	180
LANGUAGE FILE		182
LF 1–2	TALKING ABOUT THE PRESENT	182
LF 3–7	TALKING ABOUT THE PAST	183
LF 8–9	TALKING ABOUT THE FUTURE	187
LF 10	Using tenses	187
LF 11–12	Word order (statements, questions)	188

Kompetenzen	Sprache	Seite
Listening: interviews *Ideas for the future* (p. 55) **Speaking course (3)** *Doing well in job interviews* (pp. 66–67) über *life skills* sprechen (p. 53) sich selbst beschreiben und mit anderen über Stärken und Schwächen austauschen (p. 55) über geeignete Stellenangebote sprechen (p. 57) **Reading**: scanning; reading for details (job ads pp. 56–57) **Writing**: *CV* und *cover letter* verfassen (pp. 58–59) Figurencharakterisierungen verfassen (p. 65) a diary entry (p. 65) **Mediation**: ein Ferienjob für eine kanadische Freundin in Deutschland (p. 59) **Viewing** (+ intercultural competence): *Strengths and weaknesses* (p. 54); *Interview stress* (p. 66)	**Wortschatz** und **Strukturen** describing people and job requirements; structures and phrases for CVs and cover letters; characterization of literary figures; evaluating job interviews revision: **question words**, **word order in questions** (p. 61) *subject and object questions* (p. 126) *questions with prepositions* (p. 126) ***STOP! CHECK! GO!*** (pp. 68–71) Üben und vertiefen; Lernfortschritte erkennen	52
Writing: creative writing (p. 72); writing a conversation (p. 73)	**Wortschatz** und **Strukturen** *question tags* (p. 73)	72
Listening: interviews *Teens react* (p. 74); *Digital habits* (p. 77) **Speaking course (4)** *Taking part in discussions* (pp. 88–89) describing photos and speculating about situations (p. 77) **Reading**: reading for details and note-taking (pp. 76–77) finding the main points of a text (pp. 80–81) **Writing**: a written discussion *For and against tattoos* (p. 79) keeping an ad diary; writing an ad report (p. 81) *An email to the author* (p. 87) **Mediation**: talking about the ad industry (p. 81) **Viewing** (+ intercultural competence): *Shocking news!* (p. 88)	**Wortschatz** und **Strukturen** talking about digital habits, describing photos, talking about advertising strategies, taking part in discussions, argumentative writing **conditional sentences type 3** (p. 83) **-ing-form (gerund)** or **to-infinitive** (p. 131) ***STOP! CHECK! GO!*** (pp. 90–93) Üben und vertiefen; Lernfortschritte erkennen	74
Listening: presentation *An outdoor art gallery* (p. 94) **Speaking**: *Talking about street art* (p. 94) **Reading**: review *Exit through the gift shop* (p. 95) **Writing**: einen *film review* verfassen (p. 95)	**Wortschatz** und **Strukturen** describing and analysing art and giving one's personal reaction; reviewing a film	94

LF 13–15	Questions	189
LF 16	The comparison of adjectives	191
LF 17–19	Adverbs	191
LF 20	Indirect speech	192
LF 21	Modal verbs and *be allowed to, have to, be able to*	195
LF 22–24	Conditional sentences: types 1, 2, 3	196
LF 25–26	Relative clauses, contact clauses	198
LF 27	Participle clauses instead of subclauses	199
LF 28	Reflexive pronouns	200
LF 29	The *-ing*-form (the gerund)	200
LF 30	The passive	202
LF 31	Question tags	203
GRAMMATICAL TERMS		204

VOCABULARY	206
DICTIONARY (English–German)	235
IRREGULAR VERBS	264
LIST OF NAMES	266
ENGLISH SOUNDS · THE ENGLISH ALPHABET	267
ENGLISH-SPEAKING COUNTRIES	268
COUNTRIES AND CONTINENTS	269
QUELLENVERZEICHNIS	270
TYPICAL INSTRUCTIONS IN TESTS AND EXAMS	272

Unit 1 — Life down under

▶ KV 1 ▶ INKL p. 8–9

Uluru – an important place for Aboriginal Australians

A °sheep station near Perth in Western Australia

On the Stuart Highway in the °outback

1 What do you know about Oz?

a) **Think:** Work alone. Answer these questions.
The map and the photos can help you. Make notes.
1. Can you find at least one nickname for Australia?
2. Where do most people live in Australia – inland or on the coast?
3. What are Australia's biggest cities?
4. What kinds of landscape can you find in Australia?
5. What wild animals can you find in Australia?
6. What do you think the Australian climate is like?
7. Which side of the road do they drive on in Australia?
8. What are the First Australians called?
9. When it's winter in Europe, what season is it in Australia?

! You can find more information in ▶ Text file 1, pp. 146–147.

b) **Pair:** Compare your answers.

c) **Share:** Talk about your answers in class. What else would you like to know?

▶ KV 2   ▶ INKL p. 8–9

Christmas on the beach

Diving at the Great Barrier Reef

Sydney – not the capital, but Australia's biggest city

2 VIEWING   An Australian road trip

Young people often make films about their road trips in Australia.

a) Watch this road trip film. What do we learn about Australia? Make notes in a table like this. 👥 Then compare your notes.

climate	kinds of landscape	roads and driving	other details
…	…	…	…

b) Watch the film again. What activities and places do you see? Make a list in class – as many as you can.   More help p. 98

– swimming in …
– surfing …

c) Talk about these questions in class:
- Would you like to do a road trip in Australia? Why (not)?
- Where would you like to go? Why?
- Who would you go with?
- What activities would you like to do?

More practice 1 p. 98   More challenge 1 p. 98

▶ Workbook 1, p. 4

1 THEME 1

▶ KV 3 ▶ INKL p. 10–11

Articles from around Australia

1 °**JIGSAW** What makes Oz special?

a) 👥 Make groups of five. Each member of the group should read one of the articles (A–E).
b) Work alone. Make notes on anything in your article that makes Australia special.
c) 👥 Compare your notes with someone who has read the same article.

A

Ban on climbing Uluru comes nearer

Together with Sydney Harbour Bridge and the Great Barrier Reef, Uluru is probably the best-known tourist sight in Australia. 200,000 visitors travel there every year, and at the moment they are allowed to climb the rock. But for how long?
Uluru is the name that the local Aboriginal people give to the rock. People travel miles across the flat, empty landscape of central Australia to see it. Most visitors want to see the rock when the sun goes up, or in the evening as the sun goes down. That's because it changes colour and becomes burning red. Others want to climb it and to see the view from the top.
But Uluru is more than a tourist sight. For the local Anangu people Uluru is °sacred, and they don't climb it. According to their law, only a few people are allowed to go up the rock at special times. That's why they politely ask visitors not to climb the rock.
In the past most visitors went up on the rock. Today more and more people decide not to do it, but still about one in five visitors climb the rock. How much longer will they be allowed to do it?

B

Australia welcomes its new citizens

Like thousands of other people, Nikki Li became a new Australian citizen on Australia Day (26 January). Originally from Hong Kong, Nikki has decided that she wants to make her life in Australia, like many other immigrants before her.

"When we first moved to Australia, my brother and I didn't want to leave our friends and family. But there were lots of other Chinese people here and we felt at home. Now I love my life here in Sydney. I'm so happy and proud to be an °Aussie," Nikki says.

Since the arrival of the British in 1788, Australia has been a country of immigrants, and this tradition continues. Today °one in four Australians were born outside the country. That means that 25% of Australians out of a population of over 23.6 million are not originally from Australia. That compares with 13% in the US and 9% in the EU. Like Nikki, the °majority of these immigrants settle in the large cities on the coast, especially Sydney, Melbourne and Perth.

10

▶ KV 3 ▶ DFF 1.1 ▶ DFF 1.2 ▶ INKL p. 10–11

1

C Teenagers help fight bush fires

Volunteers fighting a bush fire in the Blue Mountains

Students from Berowra, north of Sydney, took time off their school work to help fight bush fires in the Blue Mountains. They are all doing their final school exams at the moment, but the °Rural Fire Service volunteers wanted to help. For many of the students this was their first time to go into action. Bush fires are a big problem in Australia. Every year houses are destroyed in bush fires, and large areas of land are burned.

D Camels in the outback

They were first °imported to Australia in the 1800s, and then they went wild. The number of camels has since °exploded, and there are now more than a million across the states of Western Australia, South Australia and Queensland, which makes it the largest °herd on earth.

The camels are a big problem for farmers as they drink water – there isn't much of that in some parts of Australia – and they destroy fences. Experts are afraid that native animals such as °kangaroos and °emus will suffer if the camels are not controlled.

E Australia's deadliest animals

Australia is home to some of the most dangerous animals in the world. Sharks, spiders and snakes are the things people worry about most. But now experts at the Australian Museum in Sydney have made a list of dangerous animals °based on how deadly they are and how likely you are to meet them. There are snakes, spiders and sharks on the list, but at the top are – °jellyfish. Bees are at number two on the list, which may also seem a bit surprising. But lots of people are allergic to bee stings. At number six on the list are salt water crocodiles, which are common in the north, including tourist hot spot Kakadu National Park.

d) Go back to your group and tell them what you have found out.
Together choose the top three things that make Australia special for you, and rank them 1 to 3. Report to the class.

More practice 2 | p. 98

2 WRITING Australia – a place to visit?

▶ Skills file 8.2, p. 174

In your opinion, what are the things that make Australia interesting and different for visitors? Would you like to visit Oz? Write a short comment and explain your answer.

More practice 3 | p. 99   More challenge 2 | p. 99

1 THEME 2
▶ DFF 1.3 ▶ INKL p. 12–13

Emergencies in Oz

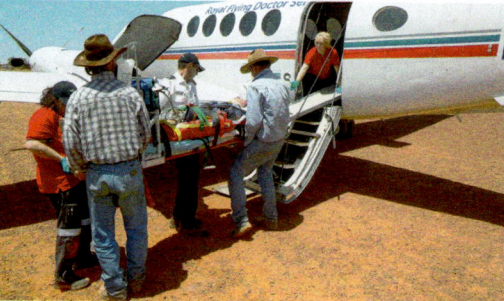

The Royal Flying Doctor Service (RFDS)

1 LISTENING   The Flying Doctors

a) Look at the photo. Talk to a partner.
What do you think the RFDS does?

b) Now listen to the advert and make notes.
1.01
- Where do the Flying Doctors work?
- Why are they important?
- What do they need?
 Then compare your notes.

2 READING   Tips from the RFDS website

a) Scan these tips and find out: ▶ Skills file 6.2, p. 167
- What problems can you have in the outback?   - What kind of climate can you *expect* there?

Royal Flying Doctor Service

Outback travelling   Here are some tips to help you to stay safe:
- Always bring lots of water with you – 10 *litres* per person, per day.
- If your car *breaks down*, never leave your vehicle. Use it for *shade*.
- If you are walking in the outback and get lost, go to high ground and *light* a small fire.
  At night, use your torch and your whistle.

Heat stress   If you suffer from *heat* stress and *feel sick*, this is what you should do:
- Get out of the sun and get into the shade.   - Drink lots of water.
- *Cool down* with wet towels.   - Call a doctor.

Snake *bites*   Australia has about 21 different dangerous snakes. If a snake bites you,
here's some advice:
- Don't try to catch or kill the snake. It can bite again.
- Stay calm and *still*.
- Try to °*identify* the snake, so the doctor can find an °*anti-venom* more quickly.
- Get to a hospital or a doctor as soon as you can – or call the emergency services.

---

b) Put the words in the boxes together to make 'emergency phrases' – as many as you can.

| break • call • cool • get (5x) • light • stay (2x) • use |

| a doctor • a small fire • calm and still • down (2x) • into the shade • into trouble • lost • out of the sun • safe • to a hospital • your torch and your whistle |

c) Match these phrases with words or phrases from the text in a).
1 keep out of danger (paragraph 1)   *stay ...*
2 lose your way (paragraph 1)
3 go under a tree (paragraph 2)
4 make yourself feel cooler (paragraph 2)
5 don't get excited (paragraph 3)
6 *phone for an ambulance* (paragraph 3)

More practice 4 | p. 99

▶ KV 4A ▶ DFF 1.4 ▶ DFF 1.5 ▶ INKL p. 12–13

3 LISTENING   Emergencies on the beach

a) Listen to conversations 1–3. Match them to these signs (A, B, C).

> **!** Some Australian phrases:
> Aussie (Australian) • bloody (very) •
> g'day (hello) • °mate (friend) •
> see ya later (goodbye)

A

B RIP CURRENTS – SWIM WITH CARE

C Protect your skin — °SLIP, °SLOP, °SLAP, °SLIDE, °SEEK

b) Complete the sentences. Choose from these verbs. Listen again and check.   p. 100

have • help • hurt • look •
swim • take • think

1 "G'day. I don't ... you should swim here. It's dangerous."
2 "If I were you, I'd ... between the flags – it's safer over there."
3 "G'day. Can you ... us? My mate has hurt his foot."   Box: Voc., p. 209
4 "It isn't bleeding, but I see some redness. Does it ... now?"
5 "I feel a bit sick and I ... a headache."
6 "Let me ... your temperature. It's quite high and you ... a bit red."

▶ Skills file 5, p. 166

c) Explain the signs to a partner in your own words.

4 SPEAKING   Getting help

a) °Silent dialogue: Decide who's partner A and who's partner B.
Partner A: Look at the picture. You are on a beach, and you have a problem. Your arm hurts. You see a lifeguard. Write the first line of your dialogue on a piece of paper. Then give it to B. Don't speak. Continue.
Partner B: You are a lifeguard on this beach. You see a young person with a problem. Try to help. Read what A wrote and write your answer. Give it to A. Don't speak. Continue.

b) When you've finished the silent dialogue, practise saying it with your partner.

c) Act your dialogue for the class.   More practice 5 p. 100

▶ Wordbank 1, p. 142

5 WRITING   Tips for tourists in Australia   ▶ Skills file 8.1, pp. 172–173

a) Write a short article (80–100 words) about how to avoid problems in Australia.
Begin like this: *Australia is a great country for a holiday. But you have to be very careful there ...*

b) Reading circle: Put all the articles on the wall. Read them and write comments.

1 THEME 3
▶ INKL p. 14–15

Pride in my people

1 VIEWING The Burdekin Crew

a) ⃝ The Burdekin Crew are a group of Aboriginal Australian high school kids from the town of Ayr. They wrote a song and made a video about who they are and where they're from. Watch the video.

b) Watch the video again and look out for these symbols of Aboriginal culture.

A **body painting**   B  the colours of the Aboriginal flag   C **traditional** dance steps

c) Work in groups of three. Each student should pick one question. Watch the video again and talk about your question.
1. What kind of music and dancing do they use? Do you like it?
2. What kind of place is Ayr?
3. What do you notice about the Burdekin Crew (how many, age, what clothes, etc.)?

d) Discuss in class: What is the message of the video? Give reasons for your answer.
A Life in a small town is boring.
B It's great to be Australian.
C Be proud of who you are.
D Things are difficult for young people.

2 Eyes wide open

a) ° **MEDIATION** Pick one of these verses (A or B) from the song. What do you think the message is? Explain it in one or two sentences.

A
Can you believe how far we've come?
The journey is long, but it has just begun.
Eyes **wide** open, walking into the sun,
Pride in my people, °**roll as one**.

B
Remember where you come from, °**stay on track**,
Look to the future, don't look back.
Stay positive, °**stand tall** like my °**pop**,
Burdekin from the bottom all the way to the top.

b) Discuss in class: What things can you be proud of?

▶ DFF 1.6 ▶ INKL p. 14–15

3 READING First Australians

a) 👥 Skim this text (the headings and the pictures). What do you think it's about?

▶ *Skills file 6.1, p. 167*

A difficult past
For almost 50,000 years Aboriginal Australians have lived in this huge country. They are often called Indigenous Australians – or sometimes First Australians – because they were the first people here. They lived a simple life and they were mostly °nomadic – they moved around a lot, °gathered food and hunted wild animals. But in the 1700s it all changed when Europeans came to Australia. The Europeans took the lands of the Aboriginal Australians to farm and to build towns – mostly on the coast. There was a lot of trouble and many Aboriginal people were killed or put in prison. They had to move into the outback where the land wasn't so good and where there wasn't much food. Another problem was that the Europeans brought diseases to the continent and many Indigenous Australians died.

Problems today
Today there are about 670,000 Indigenous Australians in Australia – less than 3 % of the °total population (23.6 million). So they are a small °minority in their own country. Some Indigenous Australians have taken on the modern Australian way of life, but many haven't. Many young Indigenous Australians leave school early, are unemployed, or have problems with alcohol. Many have bad health and don't live long. Lots of Indigenous Australians are very poor.

A special culture
Aboriginal culture is strong. It has no written language. That means Aboriginal Australians tell their stories in dances and in paintings – 'dot paintings'. The painter uses a °stick and makes thousands of dots in different colours. These stories are secret, so only Aboriginal people really understand them.
But if you look at a painting long enough, you might see the stones, plants, trees, tracks and animals of the outback. Other things that you find in Aboriginal culture are °boomerangs and °didgeridoos. Boomerangs were used to hunt animals, to °dig in the ground or as a knife. The didgeridoo is an instrument that makes a fantastic deep sound.

a dot painting

a boomerang

a didgeridoo

the emu dance

b) 👥 Read the text and find the two paragraphs that match the following descriptions.
- This paragraph describes the terrible things that happened when settlers came to Australia.
- In this paragraph we discover some of the fantastic things that Aboriginal Australians can make.

c) 👥 Describe in one sentence what the other paragraph is about.

More practice 6 | p. 100

d) ⦿ **WRITING** Write a text about this topic:
I've learned some interesting things about Aboriginal Australians, e.g. …

More challenge 3 | p. 101

Some ideas: painting • flag • dance • proud • history • hunting • the land • diseases • jobs • the Europeans • school • health • money • …

1 FOCUS ON LANGUAGE
▶ INKL p. 19

1 A window on your life

a) These texts (A–D) were sent into a competition. Imagine you are part of the jury. Choose at least one print story and one audio story, and take notes about things you find fascinating or different in the stories.

> **Give us a window on your life!**
> Enter our competition. Send us a short personal story about yourself, your hobby, family or area. The story must be real, and it must be short – about 200 words or 2 minutes of audio or video.

A Living in the Kimberley
by Aaron

This is probably the most °remote place that you can live in Australia. My parents have a million-°acre cattle station, over 300 km from the nearest town. I do my school work on the computer with School of the Air. That means that I can be at home, and when school work is finished, I can do my jobs on the station, like feeding the cattle and horses, repairing fences, etc. I don't have much contact with other kids, so I look forward to school camp in Broome. That happens once a year for a week. It's 700 km each way. But it's worth it.
In the dry season the weather is great here – that's from May to November. But in the wet season – from December to April – it rains a lot, and the roads are often closed. So by the end of October we have to order everything we need for the next six months. You have to think of everything – food, coffee, toothpaste, toilet paper – because if the roads are closed, you can't get any more.
Life here is sometimes hard, but I don't want to live anywhere else.

B I'm a mud racer by Ella

It was the day before my 16th birthday. I was so excited. The track was wet, and the car was going everywhere. Then I hit the side, and my car turned over. I was hanging upside down in my seat, and I was °freaking out.
Yes, I drive cars. I'm a mud racer. I'm a 16-year-old girl and I have an awesome car. It's white and it's got tractor tyres, and it's waterproof, so it can go through a metre of mud. The idea is that two cars race around in a figure of eight and the fastest wins.
You might think I'm too young to drive, but in mud racing you can start from the age of 15. Dad did most of the work on the car, but I've learned a lot about cars too. The best part is that dad gave me the car. So now I'm going to °stick with it and have as much fun as I can.

C 1.03 Beach culture by Ava

A °dreamy day in the life of a teen who lives in a town on the coast ...

D 1.04 One day changed my life by Ethan

Sport came first for him, then something happened ...

b) Which story is the most fascinating? Discuss, then vote for your favourite.

▶ DFF 1.7   ▶ INKL p. 19

2 REVISION   Using tenses
Look at the FOCUS box and answer the questions.

> **FOCUS**
>
> 1 In Text A, Aaron writes about his life and the things he does regularly. He only uses one tense. Which one – the **simple present** or the **simple past**?   ▶ *Language files 1, p. 182; 3, p. 183*
>
> 2 In Text B, Ella writes about her hobby and she uses different tenses.
>   a) In one paragraph she only uses the **simple present**. In which one? Why does she use it?
>   b) In the first paragraph she doesn't use the present tense at all. Why not?   Box: Voc., p. 211
>   c) In the last paragraph Ella uses different tenses. Find examples of something her dad did (**simple past**), something she has learned (**present perfect**) and something she plans to do (**going to-future**).   ▶ *Language files 3, p. 183; 5, p. 185; 8, p. 187*
>
> 3 ● Ella uses the **simple past** and the **past progressive** in paragraph 1. Find examples of both. Why does she use the **past progressive**?   ▶ *Language files 3, p. 183; 4, p. 184*

▶ *Language file 10, p. 187*

3 Living in the Gong
O Complete the text with the correct form of the *simple present*.

Mmmmm. I *love* (love) that smell. … you … (1 like) it? That … (2 be) the smell of my mum's cooking. She … (3 cook) traditional Lebanese food: kebabs, hummus and awesome Lebanese bread. But sometimes I … (4 feel) like something different, and where we … (5 live) that's no problem. I live in the Gong. … you … (6 know) what that … (7 mean)? It … (8 be) short for Wollongong. It's a pretty big town that … (9 not be) too far from Sydney. It's a great place because people from so many different cultures … (10 live) here. There … (11 be) people from Britain, Greece, Bosnia, Croatia, Serbia, Germany, Turkey, India and China. We all … (12 get on) well together.

4 It was my 18th birthday    p. 101
Complete the sentences with the correct form of the *simple past*.

1 It *was* (be) my 18th birthday and I was travelling with my mate Simon in the outback.
2 One day we … (come) to a river. Two tourists were waiting there.
3 We … (not try) to cross because the water was moving very quickly. But we … (not panic).
4 So we … (decide) to make camp for the night.
5 When we … (get up) the next morning, it was raining hard. The river … (be) even higher than the night before.
6 We … (start) to panic when we saw that the water was getting closer and closer to our tent.

5 ● NOW YOU   A window on your life
a) Decide what kind of personal story you would like to write.   More help p. 102
b) Write a text for the competition. You can put your text in your DOSSIER.

> ! - Keep your text short and simple.
> - Don't be too general. Try to think of moments or events that are special to your life.
> - You could record your story, or even make a slide show.   ▶ *Skills file 8.1, pp. 172–173*

1 TEXT
▶ INKL p. 16–18

Swerve is a book about a boy who loves muscle cars, a grandfather who has never met his grandson, and a girl who is in danger. These three people do a trip together – into the heart of Australia. You can read some of their story here. If you want to read a simpler version of the story, go to pages 103–104.

The Holden Monaro – a °muscle car

1 Before you read

Skim the pictures and the headings to find the answers to these questions. ▶ *Skills file 6.1, p. 167*

1. What are the names of the three main characters in the story?
2. How many kilometres did they plan to drive?
3. Where did the trip start and finish?
4. What kind of countryside did they travel through?
5. What's special about a muscle car?

Swerve (adapted from the novel by Phillip Gwynne)
1.05

1 Sydney School

A skinny old guy with a long grey ponytail and a °waistcoat °turned up
5 at the school gate one afternoon.
"Hugh," he said as I walked past.
"Yes," I said, wondering
10 how he knew my name.
"I want to talk to you."
Stranger danger! Stranger danger! I thought. But there was something °familiar about him. So I stopped.
15 "About what?"
"About you and me."
Stranger danger! Stranger danger! I thought.
"Your name is Hugh Twycross. You were born on the seventeenth of February. Your mother's
20 name is Carol Hughes. She was born on the third of May …"
I stopped. "How do you know all this stuff?"
"Because I'm your grandfather."
"No, you're not!"
25 "Your mother is my daughter."
"My mum's real father is dead."
"Then you're looking at a ghost, kiddo[1]!" he said to me.

Poppy

He did look familiar. He had my mother's nose
30 and chin – my nose and chin.
That night I told mum that her father had come
35 to the school.
"My father is dead!" she said.
"He's dead to me!"
I rang grandma.
40 "It's best if your mother explains," was all she could say.
Mum said that I should have nothing to do with the old man. She phoned the school.
45 She phoned the police. But he wasn't °threatening me, so there was nothing they could do.
Every day he came to the school. At first I ignored him. But on the third day I stopped
50 and talked to him. Looking at him was like looking in a funny mirror. He was my grandfather – my 'Poppy'.
One day Poppy phoned me at school.
"How's your driving?" he asked.
55 "I'm learning," I said. "But it's difficult to get the hours of practice."

Hugh and Poppy

---

[1] kiddo (*infml.*) [ˈkɪdəʊ] Kleine/r

"I have an answer to the problem," Poppy said. "You can drive me to the Big Rock."
"You mean Uluru?" I asked.
60 "°You got it – Uluru!"

Uluru – the 'Big Rock'

2 Plans

I visited Poppy at his apartment. He had a map of Australia open on the table. "We're here," he said, pointing a finger at Sydney.
65 "And Uluru is here," he said, pointing at the centre of Australia.
"Two thousand, eight hundred ks² away."

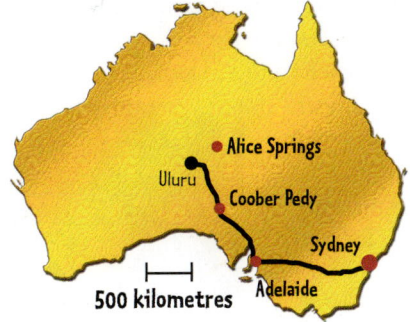

He looked at me. "It's a fair bloody hike³. So do you want to do it?"
70 "But why?" I asked.
"Because I always wanted to go there, and now is the time to do it. But I can't drive."
Then he said, "I'd like to show you something."
I followed him to an old garage behind the
75 building.

"Are you ready?" he asked when he opened the door. There was a car in the garage – but it wasn't just any car. It was the best muscle car – a 1969 Holden Monaro. I had only seen
80 pictures of these cars before.
Yellow and black stripes – it looked like a tiger. It looked amazing.
"Whose is this?" I asked. It was his.
"So are you up for it?" he asked.

85 I thought about my school, my music exam next week, my parents, my future …
Then I thought of driving 2800 ks to Uluru in a Holden HT Monaro GTS 350 V8.
"I'm up for it," I said.

3 The Million Star Motel

So Hugh and Poppy begin their trip to Uluru in the Holden muscle car. It has a very big engine. So it's very fast. But it's almost 40 years old and it isn't very easy to drive.

95 We were on the highway °heading west towards the Blue Mountains. As the city's skyscrapers got smaller and smaller in the mirror, my excitement got bigger and bigger.
I looked over at Poppy and smiled. He smiled
100 back at me.

It was getting dark, so we left the highway and we drove onto a track.
"If you see a roo⁴ on the road, don't swerve," Poppy said. "It's better to hit the roo than risk
105 your life."
After an hour we came to a clearing. We stopped the car and got out beside a river – the Darling. Poppy opened the °boot and took out cooking equipment, two camping chairs and
110 two swags⁵. He put the swags – our beds – on the ground.
Then he made a fire and got the billy⁶ to make tea. Poppy pointed to the sky.
"They call this the Million Star Motel."

At the Million Star Motel

4 South Australia

115 We were driving through the desert at 80 ks an hour. It was 415 ks to Port Augusta and 1700 to the Big Rock.
"Can't I go a bit faster?" I asked Poppy.
"No, you can't," Poppy answered.

---

² k (Abkürzung, *infml.*) *Kilometer*   ³ a fair bloody hike [feə blʌdi ˈhaɪk] *eine ganz schöne Strecke*   ⁴ roo (*infml.*) [ruː] *Känguru*
⁵ swag (AustE [swæg], infml) *Bettrolle (Gepäckrolle, die man auf der Schulter trägt)*   ⁶ billy [ˈbɪli] *Kochgeschirr*

1 TEXT
▶ INKL p. 16–18

A road train

120 A road train °appeared behind us suddenly and wanted to °overtake. So I °pulled over to let it pass.
"Don't let them °bully you," Poppy said.
There were also animals on the highway. This
125 was the world's longest zoo. There were horses, cattle and sheep, kangaroos and emus, and thousands of goats.
I saw a °hooded figure standing by the road.
"Look, a hitchhiker," I said and I pulled over.
130 The hitchhiker was short, thin, wearing jeans and a hoodie with the hood up, hiding his face.
"Where are you going?" Poppy asked.
"Adelaide," he answered in a little voice. His name was Jimmy and he was from Broken Hill.
135 After about half an hour a big black car °flew past us.

A Typhoon – another muscle car

"Hey," Poppy said. "What was that?"
"A Typhoon – with a four-litre °turbo-charged engine – very fast," I said.
140 I noticed that the hitchhiker had °sunk down in the seat.
We stopped at a roadhouse[7] for fuel.
"You hungry?" Poppy asked. – "A bit," I said.
"I'll stay here in the car," the hitchhiker said.

5 In the roadhouse
I ordered a cheese and tomato sandwich.
"Do you have any brown bread?" I asked the woman.
"It's all brown when you toast it, darl[8]," she said.
150 Poppy went to the toilet. A man and a woman came into the roadhouse. The man was short, but big – like a bodybuilder. The woman was kind of glamorous. They came to the °counter.
"We're looking for our daughter," the woman
155 said, taking out a photo.
"I haven't seen her," the woman behind the counter said.
"Can I have a look?" I asked. "I saw a hitchhiker this morning."
160 The glamorous woman showed me the photo – a girl about my age, blue hair, small face, big eyes.
"Have you seen her or not?" the bodybuilder asked.
165 "No, it was somebody else. A boy," I said.
The man and the woman talked to some truckies[9] at another table.
Poppy came back, and we left the roadhouse.
I couldn't see the hitchhiker in our car.
170 "He's gone," I said to Poppy. But when I got into the car I could see he was asleep.
The bodybuilder and the glamorous woman came out of the roadhouse.
Suddenly, I turned round to look at the hitch-
175 hiker. On his finger nails there was pink nail polish.
"Hey, your parents are looking for you,"
180 I said.
"They aren't my parents," she answered.

Bella

"Then why do they have your photo?" I asked.
185 "Please don't say anything. Those people, they're really dangerous," she said.
The couple got into their car – the Typhoon muscle car that had °rocketed past us earlier – and left.
190 "They've gone now," I said.
She °sat up and pulled her hood back. Short messy hair. Nose °stud. Big eyes. She said her name was Bella and she was seventeen.

6 At Yulara, near Uluru
200 *Hugh, Poppy and Bella drive to Coober Pedy together. Hugh really likes Bella, and he thinks that she likes him. But at Coober Pedy Bella meets another guy. She decides to travel to Uluru with him. Hugh is disappointed. Hugh*

---

[7] roadhouse [ˈrəʊdhaʊs] *Raststätte*   [8] darl (infml. [dɑːl], kurz für darling) *Liebling; freundliche Anrede, auch bei Unbekannten*
[9] truckie (AustE [ˈtrʌki], infml) *LKW-Fahrer/in*

▶ KV 5 ▶ INKL p. 16–18

205 and Poppy go on without Bella, and they arrive at a campground in Yulara, a small town near the Big Rock – Uluru.

I woke to the sound of my phone. It was Bella. "Hello," I said. But there was no answer, just
210 the sound of a car engine and voices.
Bella: "Where are we going?"
Bodybuilder: "To °teach you a lesson."
We heard the sound of someone hitting someone else.
215 Bella screaming: "You °arsehole!"
It took me a °while to understand what was happening. They had Bella. Her phone must be in her pocket and she had °pressed 'redial' to call me.
220 Bella: "Help! We just passed *The Brain*. Please help!"
Then the phone °went dead.
"What's the problem?" Poppy asked.
"Bella's in trouble," I said, getting into the car.
225 "I'm coming," he said, jumping out of his swag.
"Where's *The Brain*?" I asked Poppy.
"It's at this end of the Big Rock," he said.
We drove out of Yulara campground to the Uluru road, and I °put my foot down ...

2 True, false or not in the text?

1 Poppy was Hugh's grandfather. (part 1)
2 Hugh thought Poppy's car was terrible. (2)
3 Hugh saw a kangaroo and swerved. (3)
4 They stopped for a hitchhiker near Uluru. (4)
5 Poppy ate a sandwich in the roadhouse. (5)
6 Hugh was worried about Bella. (6)

More practice 7 | p. 105

3 Retell the story

a) Use the ideas in the boxes. In boxes 4–6 use the correct form of the verbs.

1 Hugh was a student at ...	2 Hugh visited Poppy at ...	3 Hugh and Poppy left Sydney
One day Poppy ...	They looked at a map of ...	and drove through ...
Hugh was surprised because ...	Then Poppy showed Hugh a ...	They camped beside ...
Poppy said he wanted to ...	Hugh decided to ...	They made ...
		In the sky they saw ...

| 6 Bella phone Hugh because / man and woman have ... / they be at / Hugh and Poppy get into / they want to ... | 5 In roadhouse / Hugh have / man and woman come / look for ... / hitchhiker say that they ... | 4 Hugh and Poppy drive through / pull over for a ... / he wear a / at a roadhouse they stop for ... |

b) Compare your texts.

4 At the Million Star Motel

Look at the picture in part 3 of the story. Then do task a) or task b).

a) Write a message from Hugh to his mum.
b) Write a dialogue between Poppy and Hugh.

5 The end of the story

What do you think happens next? Tell a partner. Then listen and find out.

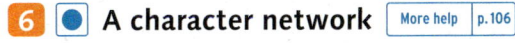

6 A character network

Make a character network for the people in the text.

More practice 8 | p. 107   More challenge 4 | p. 107

▶ Workbook 19–20, p. 13

1 SPEAKING COURSE (1) Giving a presentation
▶ INKL p. 20–21

1 VIEWING How to improve your presentations

a) Watch part 1 – Oh no! A presentation for Friday!
- Why does Tim want to do a good presentation?
- How can the students help each other?

b) Watch part 2 – Practising the presentation.
Did you enjoy the presentation? Do you think Tim will impress Milly? Give reasons.

c) Look at the checklist with a partner.
- What things did Tim do well?
- What things could he do better?

Take notes. Then watch part 2 again and check.

d) Watch part 3 – Feedback for Tim.
Do the group say the same things about Tim's presentation as you did?

e) Watch part 4 – Amy's presentation.
- First say what she did well.
- Then say where she could improve.

f) Watch part 5 – Feedback for Amy.
Do the group say the same things about Amy's presentation as you did?

▶ Skills file 7.1, p. 170

2 NOW YOU What to work on?
Think: Choose three things from the checklist that you need to work on to improve your own presentations.
Pair: Agree on a list of four things that both of you need to work on.
Share: Agree on a list of (maximum five) things that you all need to work on. These are the important things for your feedback on other presentations.

CHECKLIST: Preparing a presentation

Make your presentation interesting.
Don't just copy from the internet or from books – use your own words.
Keep your notes short.

Give your presentation a clear structure.
Use good phrases:
- for the introduction
- when you move from part to part
- at the end

Prepare your materials.
Make sure your visuals (photos, pictures, charts, etc.) are clear and interesting. Make sure the audience can read them. Check your equipment before you start.

Practise giving your presentation.
Don't just read from your notes – look up.
Speak slowly and clearly.
Look at the audience and smile.
Ask for questions at the end.

! When you're giving feedback, be positive!
- First pick out at least one good thing about the presentation – more if you can.
- Then pick out one thing that the °presenter could do better.

▸ KV 6   ▸ DFF 1.8   ▸ INKL p. 20–21

3 YOUR TASK   A presentation about Australia

Step 1: Choose your topic and do some research

a) You have to give a presentation about an aspect of Australia that interests you.
Look at the network. Choose a topic for your presentation.

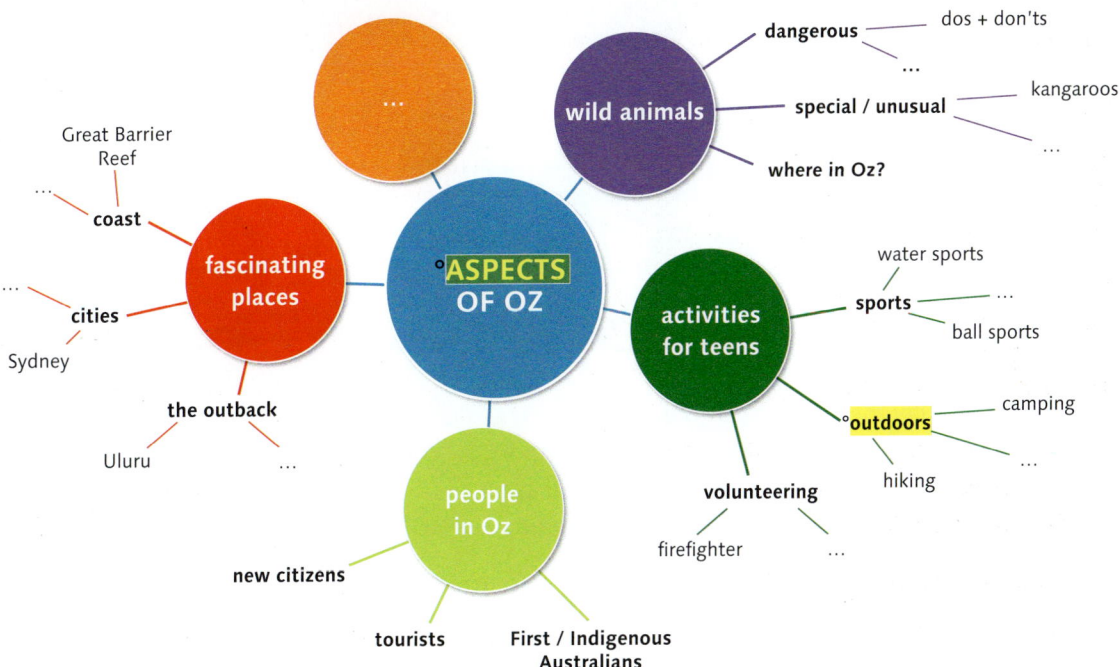

b) Make your own network for your topic.
Do some research and find out more.

> ! Use good websites and check on more than one site.
> ▸ Skills file 4, p. 165

Step 2: Prepare your notes and materials   ▸ Skills file 7.1, p. 170

Step 3: Practise your presentation

Today I'm going to talk about …	Now I'm going to	I hope you enjoyed
First …	explain / tell you about / …	my presentation.
Next …		
Finally …	Let's look at the screen.	Any questions?

Step 4: Give your presentation / Prepare your feedback
While listening, the other students should prepare their feedback with a feedback sheet.

More help   p. 107

Step 5: Give each other feedback and learn from it
Think about how you can improve your presentation.

- The first part was great.
- I liked the part where you …
- Try to look up from your notes.
- Don't forget to look at the audience.

▸ Workbook 21–25, pp. 14–16

STOP! CHECK! GO!
▶ KV 9 ▶ DFF 1.3 ▶ DFF 1.7 ▶ INKL p. 22–25

1 LISTENING
Planning a trip

Listen to Sophie (17) and Rani (18) from London. They want to get to know Oz, meet people and have fun.

a) Look at the pictures. Discuss which activity Sophie and Rani will choose and why.

b) Listen again. Choose endings for 1–6.

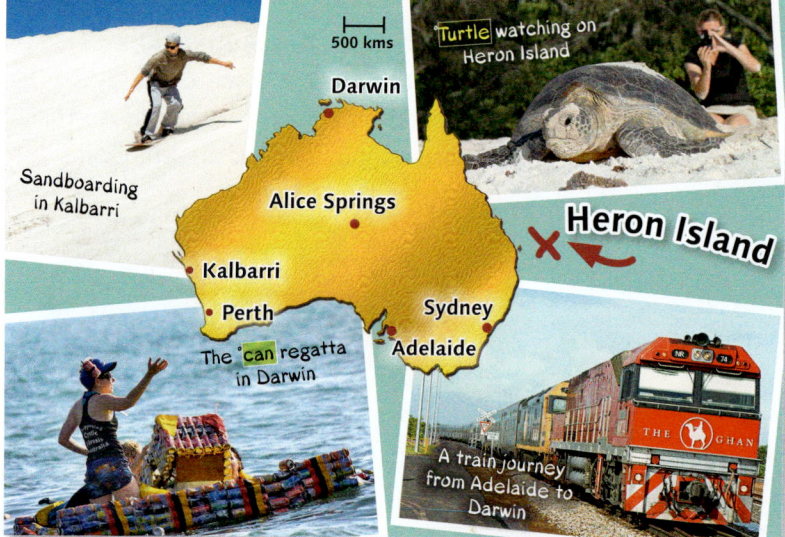

1 The turtles °lay their eggs …
A in July.
B all year round.
C from November to March.

2 Staying on Heron Island …
A costs a lot of money.
B °isn't allowed.
C isn't expensive.

3 Sandboarding is …
A a dangerous sport.
B a sport for all ages.
C a sport for young people.

4 The Ghan train journey goes …
A from south to north.
B from east to west.
C from north to south.

5 Darwin is famous for …
A a special °soft drink.
B an unusual boat race.
C a big parade.

6 The art in Kakadu is …
A in a very old book.
B °indoors, in an art °gallery.
C outdoors, on rock.

2 LANGUAGE Rani's Oz Travel Blog

Complete the sentences with the correct verb forms.  p. 108

> Use the **simple present**, **simple past**, **going to-future** or **infinitive**.

July 1st: We're still at the airport. When we … (1 arrive), the °pilots were just beginning to °strike. But we're lucky and in about an hour our plane for Australia … (2 be) ready for °take-off.

July 3rd: We … (3 get to) our hostel in Darwin early in the morning and met our tour guide, Tony, who was waiting for us. Tomorrow we … (4 see) Aboriginal rock paintings in Kakadu National Park. It's 10 pm now and we … (5 need) some sleep.

July 4th: It was amazing to see the ancient rock paintings. You can still … (6 find) traditional Aboriginal art all over Oz. While I was enjoying the art, Sophie was °chatting with the tour guide ;-))

July 6th: Yesterday we … (7 spend) a lazy day. Tonight we … (8 visit) Mindil Beach Sunset Market. The market … (9 start) at 5 pm every Thursday. It's famous for live music.

July 7th: When we were having breakfast and making plans for the day, Tony arrived and … (10 invite) us to Crocosaurus Cove. There we … (11 swim) with crocodiles – well, we were in a cage and the crocodiles were swimming all around us. It was an awesome experience – the highlight of an amazing first week in Oz.

▶ Language file 10, p. 187

▶ KV 9 ▶ DFF 1.1 ▶ INKL p. 22–25

3 READING   Aussies – crazy about sports

a) Skim texts 1–4 and match one of the headings A–E to each text. (There's one extra.)

▶ Skills file 6.1, p. 167

A Car Racing
B Horse Racing
C Australian Rules Football
D Water Sports
E Rugby Union

1 Australia has a great climate, and most Australians live near the coast, so it's no surprise that beaches are an important part of the Australian way of life. The Aussies love to be in, on or next to water, and they enjoy many different activities, from swimming to windsurfing. If you want to °enter a new and fascinating world of °colourful reefs and reef fish, you can try diving. Or try surfing at some of the world's most beautiful beaches. There are hundreds of top surf beaches, and Australia is a paradise for surfing °beginners and for experts. You want to be active, but you don't want to suffer in the summer heat? Jump in, cool down and have fun.

2 This much-loved sport was one of the first in Australia: the first horses arrived in 1788, and since then this sport has been an important part of Australian culture. Today it is the third most watched sport in the country, and there are more than 19,000 races a year. The day of the famous Melbourne Cup race is a national holiday – it is known as 'the race that stops a nation'. All over the country, towns and cities are very quiet from 2 pm to 4 pm as people find the nearest TV to watch the big race. And it isn't just about the horses. A big race is like a carnival with colourful clothes and glamorous fashions. Have you ever heard of Black Caviar? She has won every race in her six years of racing.

3 Australians have had a long °love affair with these sports, including F1 Grand Prix, and desert °rally racing, but they especially love V8 supercars. A nickname for the fans is 'petrolheads'. If you aren't from this continent, V8 supercars may be new to you. For a long time, a V8 supercar was °either a Ford (blue) °or a Holden (red), so fans were either blue or red. Since 2013 there have been new rules. Now you can see other cars, such as Nissan and Mercedes. All cars use a 5-litre V8 engine and they go as fast as 300 °kph. On a normal race weekend, 100,000 to 250,000 fans turn up and cheer for their team. Some drivers are real superstars – like Jamie Whincup and Craig Loundes.

4 This national sport is the most popular sport in the country. It was °invented in Australia in 1858 and some of its rules come from an Aboriginal game, Marn Grook. There are 22 players in a team: 18 on the field and four extra players who can change with any other player as often as the coach wants. Players can kick or °hand-pass the ball, but they are not allowed to throw it. It's a °powerful game because players can make body contact when they bump into and °tackle each other to try to win the ball. In a typical game, you are likely to see lots of °goals, so it's a fast and exciting sport to watch. Sometimes people compare this sport to °Gaelic Football (from Ireland) or rugby, but there are a lot of differences.

b) Find words or phrases that mean:
1 how people live in Australia ①
2 people who know a lot or have a lot of experience ①
3 become less hot ①
4 a funny name used instead of the real name ③
5 a big region of the world ③
6 say that things are similar to (or different from) other things ④

c) Answer these questions:
1 Name four different water sports.
2 Why is Australia a good place for water sports? (Give two reasons.)
3 What is the oldest organized sport described in the texts?
4 Where does Australian Rules Football originally come from?
5 Find three adjectives that describe Australian Rules Football.

More challenge 6 p. 109

STOP! CHECK! GO!
▶ KV 7 ▶ DFF 1.2 ▶ INKL p. 22–25

4 SPEAKING Talking about a picture

Partner B: Go to page 96.
Partner A:
a) Describe to your partner what you can see in your picture. These questions can help you: Who? What? Where? When? Why?
▶ *Skills file 9, p. 179*

b) Listen to your partner.

c) Together find out what the pictures have in common and what is different.

5 WRITING Slip, slop, slap, seek and slide

Ant (16) is from Australia. He's visiting Europe with his family. This is part of his travel blog.

Do they need a new health slogan in Germany?
Here in Germany you see a lot of people °lying or playing in the sun in the middle of the day. The problem is that they don't always protect their skin. That's not healthy! I think maybe it's because they think a °suntan is cool. In Australia skin °cancer is a big topic. We always cover our arms and shoulders, use sunscreen, put on a hat, stay under a tree or an °umbrella between 11 am and 3 pm and put on sunglasses. To help Australians to remember the rules, the government has a slogan.
The slogan is five short words beginning with 's': "Slip, slop, slap, seek, slide". It means you should slip on a shirt, slop on sunscreen, slap on a hat, seek shade and slide on sunglasses.
I think there should be a similar slogan here in Germany too. What do you think of this idea?

SLIP SLOP SLAP SEEK SLIDE

Protect yourself in five ways from cancer

a) Read Ant's post. Explain what "Slip, slop, slap …" means and why it's important.

b) ● Write a comment. If you agree with Ant, think of a good slogan for Germany. It can be in English or German. If it's in German, explain it in English.

More help | p. 109

▶ *Skills file 8.2, p. 174*

▸ KV 8   ▸ DFF 1.4   ▸ DFF 1.9   ▸ INKL p. 22–25

6 MEDIATION   Understanding signs and advice in Australia

a) Here are five signs that you can find at the beach or at the roadside in Australia. Explain in German what they mean.

▸ Skills file 10, pp. 180–181

b) You are in a pharmacy. Your mother has been stung by a bee. Her hand is red and it hurts. Help her to talk to the pharmacist.

°Pharmacist	G'day. What can I do for you?
Your mum	Erkläre bitte, was passiert ist.
(1) You	…
Pharmacist	Is she allergic to bee stings?
(2) You	*Sie möchte wissen, …*
Your mum	Nein, bin ich nicht.
(3) You	…
Pharmacist	Has she pulled out the sting?
(4) You	…
Your mum	Ja, habe ich.
(5) You	…
Pharmacist	Put this cream on the sting once or twice a day. Keep it away from your eyes, nose and mouth. It will feel better pretty quickly, but it may be red for a few days. It will feel better if you put ice on it. Use a towel between the ice and your skin – you shouldn't put the ice °directly on your skin. And don't let the ice stay on the skin for longer than 20 minutes.
(6) You	*Du sollst diese … Sie darf nicht … Du kannst …*
Pharmacist	Your hand should be fine in two or three days. If it isn't better by then, you should see a doctor.
(7) You	*Wenn es in …, sollst du …*
Your mum	Thank you.

MORE CHALLENGE 1

Understanding °idioms

> Den Wortschatz von diesen Seiten findest du im Vocabulary auf S. 232.

1 The Spare Room

a) Read the blurb about the book. What kind of things do you think are new and different for Akira in Australia? Compare your ideas.

> The °*Spare Room*, by Kathryn Lomer, is about Akira, a 19-year-old Japanese boy who is in Tasmania (Australia) to learn English. He lives with the Moffat family – Alex, Jess and their daughters Angie and Daisy. Akira stays in their spare room. This is a journey into a world that is very different to Akira's own world. He has to deal with lots of things that are very new and strange for him.

b) Imagine waking up on your first morning in a strange room, in a strange house, in a strange country. How would you feel? Now read the text below and find out how it was for Akira.

🎧 1.09

I can still remember the strangeness of waking up in that room. The sounds around the house. A dog °barking somewhere. Exotic bird calls. As I lay there I thought about how
5   many mornings I'd woken up on my own futon at home … and never thought about my °surroundings, what I could hear, smell.

I wondered what I should do first. What was appropriate – to go out to the kitchen for
10 breakfast in my *yukata*? Did the family eat breakfast together? When did people °shower? Or perhaps they had °baths? I had noticed that the shower was above the °bathtub, which seemed strange. In Japan we have a bath in
15 the evening after showering. So many questions about such a simple thing as getting out of bed and starting the day. I °realized how much I would have to learn.

When I got to the kitchen, there was no one
20 there. I looked around and found the kettle, filled it up and switched it on. I didn't know what else to do. I didn't want to go looking in the °cupboard for cups or tea. What kind of tea, °anyway? … I sat down at the table,
25 wondering what to do, and just as I did a growl came from under the table. I jumped. Under the table there was a little white dog! Next minute, Daisy burst into the room. "*Ohaiyo-gozaimasu*!" she said.
30 "*Ohaiyo-gozaimasu*!" I answered. She was so sweet, wanting to °put me at ease. "But I want to speak English, Daisy," I said. "Oh yes, I know. But just a little Japanese too. Please? For me? Pretty please?" she said.
35 Pretty please! I was lost. What did that mean? It was going to take me a long time to learn this language, I thought.

2 READING   Akira's first morning

Answer these questions.
1. What things does Akira find different?
2. What would he like to know?
3. Does Akira feel comfortable in his new home? Give at least one example.
4. What Japanese words do we find in the text? What do you think they mean?
5. How would you describe Akira? Explain.
6. Akira doesn't understand 'Pretty please'. It's an idiom. What do you think it means?

> An **idiom** is a special phrase that can be difficult to understand. The meaning of the whole phrase is different from the meaning of the individual words.

28

3 LISTENING Fun with idioms

Akira hears lots of idioms, but he doesn't always understand them. Listen. Match each idiom (1–7) with the correct meaning (A–G).

1 I'm the °chief bottle-washer.
2 Can you give me a hand, please?
3 That should do the trick.
4 What's your °poison?
5 What's the °damage?
6 I'm on cloud nine!
7 I'm like a fish out of water.

A I'm very happy.
B How much does that cost?
C That will be fine.
D I °feel uncomfortable.
E I need some help.
F I do all the jobs.
G What would you like to drink?

> ! It's important to understand idioms. But it's risky to use them.
> ▶ *Skills file 2, p. 163*

4 MEDIATION More English idioms

a) What do you think the underlined idioms mean? Explain them in German.

1 How do you feel?
– I'm over the °moon!"

2 I'm going to pass my test.
– Yeah! Pigs might fly!

3 I know a good joke.
– I'm all ears!

4 Do you like my new phone?
– Wow! It's the bee's knees.

5 You're talking too fast.
Hold your horses!

6 How was the driving test?
– A piece of cake!

b) Can you think of idioms in German that match these English idioms?

5 MEDIATION German idioms

Explain these idioms to an English-speaking visitor.
1 Ich habe Schwein gehabt.
2 Ich verstehe nur Bahnhof.
3 Du hast nicht alle Tassen im Schrank!
4 Das Leben ist kein Ponyhof.
5 Das ist mir Wurst!
6 Ich habe die Nase voll.

> ! Say **when** you'd use these idioms, **who with** and **what they mean** in English.

Unit 2 Respect

▶ INKL p. 26–27

1 Six scenes from a film

a) Think: Look at the six pictures.
Guess what's happening in this film.
Make notes.
These questions can help you:
- Who are these teens and where are they?
- What are they doing or saying or feeling?

b) Pair: Compare your ideas.
Use phrases like these:
- I think the teenagers are ...
  Perhaps they ...
- One boy looks ...
- Maybe the others ...

c) Share: Tell the class what you think this film is about.

2 VIEWING   I thought we were friends ... (part 1)

a) Watch part 1 of the film. Look at your notes. What did you guess right?

b) Watch part 1 again and finish these sentences:
1 We can see that the four teens are friends because ...
2 Perhaps Shaz is a bit jealous of Patrick because ...
3 Patrick deleted the messages from his phone because ...
4 The teacher talked to Patrick because ...
5 Patrick's dad knew something was wrong because ...

30

▶ DFF 2.1   ▶ INKL p. 26–27

3 VIEWING   I thought we were friends … (part 2)

a) Before you watch, guess what will happen next. [More help p. 109]

b) ○ Watch part 2 of the film.
Who said what?
1 "That's no big deal – everybody does it."
2 "We thought it was just a bit of fun."
3 "But in the lunch break, that was °kinda stupid."
4 "We didn't think about how you were feeling."
5 "I hoped that the problem would just go away."
6 "I feel bad because I didn't say stop."

c) Now talk in class about these questions:
1 Do you think that it's a good ending? Why (not)?
2 Can the four teens be friends again? Why (not)?
3 ● What is the main message of the film?   [More help p. 109]

Patrick

Shaz

Simone
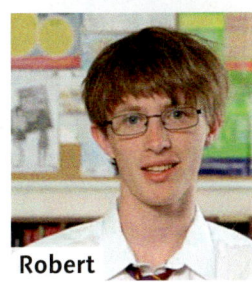
Robert

4 NOW YOU   About cyberbullying
What advice would you give …
- to the victim?
- to the bystander (who sees the bullying)?
- to the bully?

If you think someone is bullying someone else, you should …

If you get horrible messages, you should …

Before you write a mean message, think about …

… [More challenge 1 p. 110]

▶ Workbook 1–2, p. 19

2 THEME 1
▶ KV 10   ▶ INKL p. 28

Dealing with peer pressure

1 ⓞ Under pressure
Skim the online article below. Who do you think it is written for – teens or adults?

▶ Skills file 6.1, p. 167

Home >> pressure   contact

Is peer pressure a problem for you?

What is peer pressure?
Your peers are people who are similar to you – people who are your age, who are in the same groups, or who have the same interests. So your peers are your classmates, the people on your sports team, or members of your youth group. Do you sometimes do something just because everybody else is doing it? That's peer pressure.

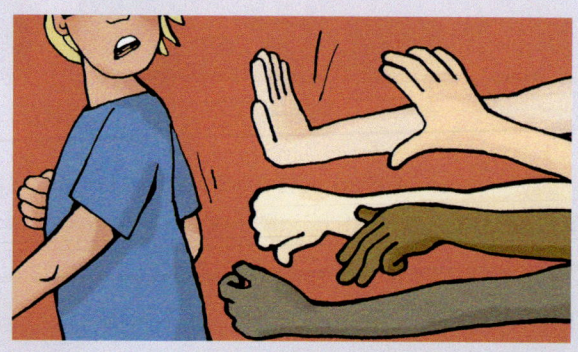

Who is influenced by peer pressure?
The short answer is everybody. Everybody likes to fit in. We all like to feel part of a group. It's normal.

Why is peer pressure such a big issue for teens?
Because when you're a teenager, what your friends think is important. That's why you want to do what your friends are doing, and wear what they are wearing. You're afraid that you'll look silly if you don't do the same. Even worse, you might lose your friends.

So is peer pressure always a bad thing?
No, it can be a great thing! Your peers can give you great ideas. They can °motivate you to do cool things. On the other hand, sometimes people can feel under pressure to try illegal or risky things like cigarettes, alcohol, drugs or shoplifting. And that can get you into trouble.

How can teens deal with peer pressure?
- Think for yourself. Just because 'everybody is doing it', doesn't mean that 'it' is a good thing. If you don't feel comfortable with something, don't do it!
- Be strong. Good friends won't stop being your friends just because you have a different point of view. You don't have to agree on everything. Good friends respect different opinions.
- Talk to your friends. They've probably had a similar problem at some point, so they will understand how you feel.   Box: Voc., p. 214
- Be there for your friends. Support them if they are feeling under pressure to do things they don't want to do. Help them to say no.

▶ KV 10   ▶ KV 11   ▶ DFF 2.2   ▶ INKL p. 29

2 READING   Understanding the text

a) Are these sentences true or false? Give the line numbers from the text.
1 Peer pressure is when people do things just because other people are doing them. 4–11
2 Only teenagers feel peer pressure, not adults. 13–14
3 Peer pressure is always a bad thing. 20–21

▶ Skills file 6.4, p. 168

b) Choose the right answer.
1 What's the main message of the text?
   A You shouldn't join a group because if you do, you'll be influenced by peer pressure.
   B Peer pressure is normal, you have to deal with it. ✗
   C You should always do what your friends do, because if you don't, you might lose them.

2 The text says that your friends can be very important because …
   A they help you when you're under pressure. ✗
   B they always have the same opinion as you.
   C life would be very boring without them.

3 If you feel under pressure to do something that you think is wrong, …
   A don't talk about it.
   B you shouldn't do it. ✗
   C you should do it – or you'll look silly.

▶ Skills files 6.3, p. 167; 6.5, p. 168

c) Find words or phrases in the text for …
1 people who are like you (paragraph 1) peer group
2 a problem (paragraph 3) issue
3 **stealing** things from shops (paragraph 4) shoplifting
4 **accepting** other points of view (paragraph 5) respecting

d) Read the text again and find …
1 two reasons why teenagers don't like to be different from their friends.
2 two negative things that teenagers might do because of peer pressure.
3 at least two things that good friends do for each other.

3 ● WRITING   Now you: "Peer pressure is a big problem for teenagers"

Do you agree? Write a comment (about 100 words). Give reasons and examples.   More help   p. 110

Step 1: Before you write, think of situations where teenagers can feel peer pressure. Make notes.
   👥 Compare your ideas with a partner.
Step 2: So what do you think? Is peer pressure a big problem for teens? Now start your comment. First give your opinion.
Step 3: Choose two examples of peer pressure from your notes in step 1. Describe them °**briefly** in the next part of your comment.
Step 4: Write a conclusion. You can put your comment in your DOSSIER.

Useful phrases:
- In my opinion, …
- In my experience, …
- I (definitely) think …
- I (really) don't think …
- On the one hand, …
- On the other hand, …
- Firstly, / Secondly, / …
- For example, …
- To sum up, …

▶ Skills files 8.1, 8.2, pp. 172–174

▶ Workbook 3–4, p. 20

2 THEME 1
▶ DFF 2.3   ▶ INKL p. 30

4 LISTENING   Come shopping with me!

1.11

a) Listen to part 1, then complete these sentences:
1. Megan is talking to Ava because …
2. Megan wants Ava to …   ▶ *Skills file 5, p. 166*

b) Compare your answers to a). Then discuss:
Do you think it was a good idea for Ava to say yes? Why (not)?

1.12
c) Listen to part 2, then complete these sentences:
1. Ollie thinks that Megan is …
2. Ollie's advice to Ava is …

d) Compare your answers to c). Then discuss:
What should Ava say to Megan next time she sees her?

1.13
e) Listen to part 3 and find out what Ava does.
What do you think? Did she find a good solution to the problem?

f) Choose one of the pictures, and write your own version of that scene. Perform the dialogue for the class.

5 ROLE-PLAY   Why don't you go out with us?

a) Choose one of the role cards and think about what you can say.

Partner A	Partner B
Your friend (partner B) hasn't gone out with you **lately**. You want to know why. Ask him / her some questions.	You haven't gone out with your friends lately. One of them (partner A) wants to know why. Answer his / her questions.
1 come out with us?	1 when go out / some people in group / drink too much alcohol / not comfortable with that
2 understand / not everybody drinks / it's OK if you don't want to	2 but feel silly / people say things / don't like it
3 maybe / could go out / **just the two of us**	3 nice idea/ where?
4 What about / cinema?	4 sure / what film?
5 what about …?	5 agree or suggest a different film
6 agree / when / where / meet?	6 what about …?
7 agree / look forward to it!	7 fantastic! / say goodbye

b) Double circle: Perform the dialogue with at least two partners. Then swap roles.

▶ *Text file 2, pp. 148–151*   ▶ *Workbook 5–6, p. 21*

THEME 2

▶ KV 12 A–C   ▶ INKL p. 31

Think before you speak

1 ACTIVITY   **Badges** – a group experiment

a) Everybody gets a badge: red, green, blue, orange. Sit with your colour group. Read your role card on these pages (red – page 111; green – page 117; blue – page 101; orange – page 102).

b) Walk around. Ask the question on your role card. Note the answers and the badge colour of your partners.

c) Sit in your colour group again and answer these questions:
1. How many people did you talk to?
2. How many green people, red people etc.?
3. What interesting things did you learn?
4. Was everybody friendly and helpful?
5. Did everybody answer your question?
6. Did you enjoy the survey? Why (not)?

d) Make new groups of four with one of each colour in every group. Answer c) again.

e) Now talk about these questions in class:
1. Which colour was most popular? Which was least popular? Why?
2. How did you find the activity: fun / fair / frustrating / …? Why?
3. Give examples of discrimination in real life.

2 Dealing with discrimination

a) Read the article and imagine how Adam Goodes felt. Discuss in class.

Racism: It stops with me

At a big football game between Sydney and Collingwood, an indigenous player was called a racist name by a young fan.

Adam Goodes is one of Sydney's biggest stars. When he heard what the 13-year-old girl said, he stopped and told security staff that the girl had called him a racist name.

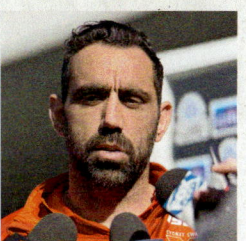
Adam Goodes

The girl was taken from the stadium and questioned by the police. Later the teenager phoned Goodes and said that she was sorry and that she would never use racist names again. Goodes said that he didn't blame the girl. He said that she was only 13 years old and still innocent. He added that society was to blame for prejudice and racism. That's why the girl thought it was OK to call people names.

Adam Goodes is now taking part in a new anti-racism campaign. It's called *Racism: It stops with me*.

b) Finish these sentences about the article.
1. Sydney and Collingwood are …
2. Adam Goodes is a …
3. At a game, a teenage girl called …
4. The police questioned …
5. The girl said …
6. Adam Goodes thinks …

▶ Workbook 7, p. 22

2 THEME 2
▶ KV 13 ▶ INKL p. 32

3 VIEWING 'What you say matters' by Brothablack

a) Watch the video. What do you think the song is about? Discuss.

b) Complete these sentences about the four scenes in the video.
Then watch the video again and check your answers.

1 Kat thinks that Jane is good at maths because she looks
Ⓐ Australian Ⓑ Asian.

2 The two girls don't think that Sarah is Aboriginal because she looks too Ⓐ white Ⓑ black.

3 The Aboriginal boy thinks that he should get on the bus first because the Aboriginal people came to Australia Ⓐ last Ⓑ first.

4 One boy says that the other boy is fast only because he's
Ⓐ white Ⓑ black.

c) Think about this slogan from the song:
Face the racism, kick the racism.
1 Read the dictionary **entries** and pick the right meaning for *face* and for *kick*.
2 Say what the slogan means in German.

d) Say what these phrases from the song mean. Check the new words in a dictionary.
1 You're not better than me, you're **equal** to me.
2 Stop the **negativity** in your **vicinity**.
3 Excuse me, your **ignorance** is showing.
4 Stand up for **unity**.

e) Discuss: What's the message of the video? Does the video work for you? Give reasons. More help p. 112 More challenge 3 p. 112

---

face¹ /feɪs/ *Substantiv* Gesicht
face² *Verb*
1 (*einer Person / Sache*) gegenüber sein
2 vor etwas stehen
3 (*einer Sache*) entgegentreten
4 **Let's face it!** Machen wir uns nichts vor!

kick¹ /kɪk/ *Substantiv*
1 (*mit dem Fuß*) Tritt, Stoß
2 (*Sport*) Schuss, Kick
kick² *Verb*
1 (*mit dem Fuß*) treten
2 (*Sport*) schießen, kicken
3 (*Gewohnheit, Idee*) aufgeben, sich davon befreien

! Always look at **all** the words in an entry in the dictionary. Pick the best meaning.
▶ *Skills file 2, p. 163*

▶ KV 14   ▶ DFF 2.4   ▶ INKL p.33

4 YOUR TASK — Do something!

No racism, discrimination or bullying in our schools! You can do something in your school. Here are some ideas:

Step 1: Pick a project Read through the projects below, and pick one that you like.
👥 Find two or three other students who want to do the same project.

Step 2: Organize your project Meet in your groups and decide how much time you need for your project and who does what. Then work on your project.

Project A
Scenes of discrimination

1. Look at the four scenes on page 36.
2. Choose one scene or more and write your own texts and dialogues for a short play. Use your own words. [More help p. 112]
3. Check your texts with your group and with your teacher.
4. Learn your texts and practise your scene.

Project C
A campaign

1. Collect lots of good English slogans for an anti-discrimination campaign.

Anti-bullying	Anti-racism
No place for bullying!	Racism: It stops with me!

2. Then agree on your favourite slogans. Check your slogans with your teacher.
3. Make badges, posters and postcards with your slogans.

Project B
Immigrants' stories

1. Find people in your school or in your family who have come from other countries and who °are happy to talk about it.
2. Think of good questions and then °interview the people. [More help p. 113]
3. Write short texts about these people's experiences. Add maps, flags, pictures, etc.
4. Ask the people to read your text – make sure they agree with it. Check with your teacher too.

Project D
Songs about discrimination

1. Find another song about discrimination, racism, bullying, etc. Or write your own song.
2. °Pick out the important words and slogans. If they are new, first guess what they mean. Make notes and check in a dictionary.
3. Prepare to talk about your song and to explain it (including the difficult words). Put important parts of the text on the board.

Step 3: Present your project

Project A: Act your scenes.
Project B / C: Put your stories, posters, etc. on the wall.
Project D: Present, explain and play your song.

2 FOCUS ON LANGUAGE
▶ KV 15   ▶ INKL p. 37

1 Guess what happened last night

a) Kai is telling his friend about what happened last night. Listen. Then answer these questions:
1. Where did Kai meet Emily?
2. Why did Kai start the conversation?
3. Why was Emily interested in him?

b) Match these sentences to the speech bubbles.
A Are you new?
B Can you introduce me to him?
C Don't be a pain!
D Yes, this is my first time at the club.
E It's great.
F OK. Just for a minute.
G Can you say hello to that girl, please?
H Sure, no problem.
I The singer is my brother.
J What do you think of the music?
K Your brother has an amazing voice.

c) What exactly does Kai say when he's telling the story to his friend? Listen and complete the sentences.
1. I asked her if she ... new.
2. She said that she ... at the club for the first time.
3. I asked her what she ... of the music.
4. I told her that the singer ... my brother.
5. I asked my brother to ... hello to her.
6. He told me not to ... a pain.

2 Indirect speech: statements

Look at the FOCUS box and answer the questions.

FOCUS

In both these sentences we find out what Emily said.
- Ⓐ She said, "This is my first time at the club." ➜ Ⓑ She said that this was her first time at the club.

1 Which sentence (Ⓐ or Ⓑ) gives exactly the words that she said (= **direct speech**)?
2 Which sentence (Ⓐ or Ⓑ) reports what she said (= **indirect speech**)?
3 Write down the two sentences. Mark all the differences. What has changed?

Ⓐ	Ⓑ
This	?
is (simple present)	?
my	?

▶ Language file 20, p. 192–193

3 What were their exact words?

○ Complete the speech bubbles. p. 113

1 The girl told Kai's brother that her name was Emily.
2 He said that his name was Dan.
3 Dan told Emily that he often came to the club.
4 She told him that she didn't come very often.
5 She explained that she played soccer, and practice was usually on the same night.
6 He suggested that she should come to the talent show on Saturday night if she was free.
7 She thought that was a great idea.

Speech bubbles (Emily):
1 My name is Emily.
4 I ... come very often.
5 I ... soccer, and practice ... usually on the same night.
7 That ... a great idea.

Speech bubbles (Dan):
2 My name ... Dan.
3 I often ... to the club.
6 You should come to the talent show on Saturday night if you ... free.

4 I didn't believe him

Dan told Emily a lot about himself. What did she tell her friend? Use the *simple past*.

1 I met this boy, Dan.
   He told me that he was ...
2 He also said that ...
3 He added that ...
4 He told me that ...
5 Then he said that ...
6 Next he told me ...
7 And finally he said that ...
But to be honest, I didn't believe anything he said.

1 "I'm great at sport."
2 "I play in my school rugby team."
3 "I'm captain of the soccer team too."
4 "I can play six different instruments."
5 "My favourite instrument is the didgeridoo."
6 "My parents are famous actors."
7 "My dad lives in Hollywood."

2 FOCUS ON LANGUAGE
▶ DFF 2.5   ▶ DFF 2.6

5 Indirect speech: questions

FOCUS

1 What's different here? Complete the sentences below.
  A Kai asked Emily, "Are you new?" ➔ **B** Kai asked Emily if she was new.
  - A word has been added: …
  - The word order has changed from verb + subject to …
  - The direct question **A** ends with a **?** The indirect question **B** ends with a …

2 Compare these examples:
  C I asked her, "What music do you like?" ➔ **D** I asked her what music she liked.

▶ Language file 20, p. 193

6 Are you OK?

Eric had an accident and a woman stopped to help. What did he tell his dad?

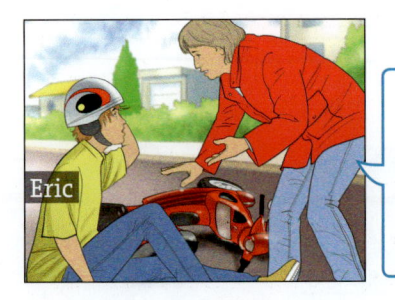

1 "Do you need an ambulance?"
2 "Are you OK?"
3 "How do you feel?"
4 "Do you have a headache?"
5 "Can you move your leg?"
6 "Do you want some water?"

1 A woman asked me …
2 She wanted to know …
3 Then she asked …
 …

7 Indirect speech: commands, requests, advice

FOCUS

Finish the sentences below:
Kai asked Dan, "Can you say hello to the girl, please?" ➔ Kai asked Dan to say …
Dan told Kai, "Don't be a pain." ➔ Dan told Kai not to …
Kai's friend told him, "You should phone Emily." ➔ Kai's friend told him to …

▶ Language file 20, p. 194

8 Good advice?

Josh is very nervous before his first date. He's reading his friends' advice. Complete the sentences.

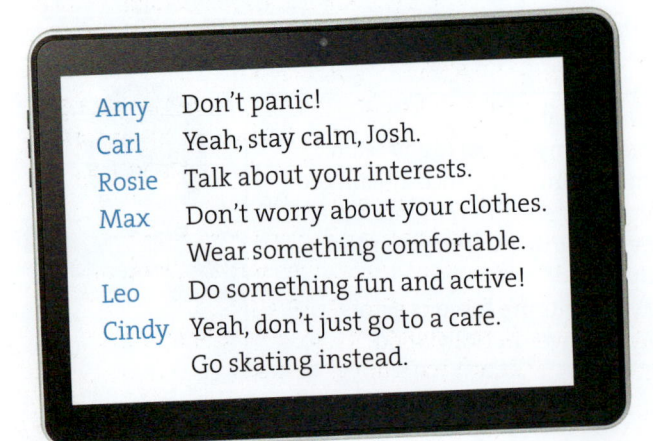

Amy	Don't panic!
Carl	Yeah, stay calm, Josh.
Rosie	Talk about your interests.
Max	Don't worry about your clothes.
	Wear something comfortable.
Leo	Do something fun and active!
Cindy	Yeah, don't just go to a cafe.
	Go skating instead.

Amy told me …, but I'm very nervous!
Carl told me … Rosie told me …
Max had some interesting advice. He …
Leo had a good idea. He …
Cindy agreed. She …

More challenge 4 | p. 114

▶ Workbook 11–12, p. 25

TEXT

▶ KV 16 ▶ INKL p. 34–36

Watching you, watching me

This story has two sides – a boy's side and a girl's side. The boy's side of the story is shorter and it's on pages 115–116. The girl's side of the story is longer and it starts on this page. You can read one part – or both parts. Happy reading!

1 While you read

a) Think about these questions. Then compare with students who have read the same side.
1 Who is the hero of the story?
2 Where does he or she live?
3 Who does he or she live with?
4 What's he or she interested in?
5 What does he or she think about the neighbour from across the road?

b) Find a partner who has read the other side. Compare your answers to the five questions.

Natasha's side of the story …

1.15 (adapted from the novel *Watching you, watching me* by Chloe Rayban)

1 There it was again – that funny feeling. I turned around and looked back down the road.
5 I could feel someone watching me. But where from? The street was empty – not even a car. I looked at number twenty-five.
10 It had been empty for a long time. Jamie and Gemma called it the °spooky house because sometimes I had told ghost stories about it to keep them quiet.
Number twenty-five really did look spooky.
15 It was a tall house. The windows were °boarded up and there were lots of °weeds in the front garden.

Later that evening Jamie was hiding behind a curtain because he had to go to bed.
20 He called me.
"Tasha!" He ran and put his arms around me.
"They're there," he said. "They're really there."
"What are where?"
"At number twenty-five – the °spooks!"
25 "Don't be silly. There's no such thing as spooks."
"Come and look. There are lights in the house …"

He took me to the window and we waited in the darkness, staring out. I looked at number
30 twenty-five. And then I °froze. He was right. A small light was moving through the rooms. It was moving upstairs now …
"What are you two doing?" Mum pulled the curtains back and found us sitting there.
35 "We've found a spook," Jamie said.
"Tasha," mum said with a warning look.
"No, it isn't me this time. But there is someone or something in number twenty-five. °See for yourself."
40 The three of us stood behind the curtain … and then mum said, "Squatters! I knew this would happen if that house was left empty like that." Then she went downstairs to find dad.
"What are squatters?" Jamie asked.
45 I put my arms around him.
"Squatters are people who haven't got houses °of their own. So they find empty houses and they squat in them. They live there without paying any money."

50 Dad came through the door at that moment. He stared out of the window.
"It isn't spooks, it's squatters," Jamie said.
"I can't see a thing," he said.

We stood there together.
55 "See ... there it is in the top room," I said.
"Yeah," dad said. "It must be a candle."
"Right, I'm going to phone the police," mum said.
"No, wait," dad said. "Let's think about this for a
60 moment. It's probably some poor guy who sleeps in the street or something."
"Dad's right, Mum," I said. "There could be some poor old homeless guy in there ..."
"This is a °respectable street. Families, children
65 ... the last thing we need is squatters," she answered.
Then she looked at Jamie.
"Bed for you, Jamie. Look at the time!"
She went off with him.
70 "I was a squatter once," dad said.
"You? You were a squatter?" I said, surprised.
"Not for long. When I was a student. We had no money ..."
"So what do you think we should do?" I asked.
75 "I guess I should visit our new neighbour. Bring the phone in here and if you see a problem, ring 999. Oh ... and don't tell mum, OK?"

I stood at the window with the phone in my hand. I had a sick feeling in my throat. What if
80 there were violent people in number twenty-five?
I watched dad as he crossed the road.

He hammered on the front door. Nothing happened for °a while. Dad hammered again –
85 harder this time. Number twenty-five was quiet. Then I saw the light, and it was moving down through the house. I waited, expecting the Incredible Hulk to come out. But it didn't. Dad stood there. He was talking through the door.
90 I couldn't hear what he was saying. Then he °shook his head and came back across the road. I heard our door and I went down the stairs.
"He said that he had every right to be there. He told me I was an old busybody. And he told
95 me to °piss off!"
I wanted to laugh, but I didn't.
"What did he sound like?" I asked.
"Quite young."
"How young?"
100 "Hard to say – seventeen ... eighteen ..."

"What does he look like?" Gemma asked from the kitchen. My little sister loved romances, love stories ...
"I haven't met him yet. We talked through the
105 door," dad said.
"Gemma, listen," I said. "This is like some tramp ... he probably smells."
"Hey Gem – °bedtime. °Off you go," dad said.

Later that night, when I went up to bed,
110 I opened my window as usual. I stared out of the window. The light was still there – in the top room now.
I just watched. Nothing was happening – the light was moving around.
115 "What's going on?" Gemma was beside me.
"Sssssh," I said. "Nothing."
"I guess he's cool," she said.
"What would you know?" I said.

▶ KV 16   ▶ DFF 2.7   ▶ INKL p. 34–36

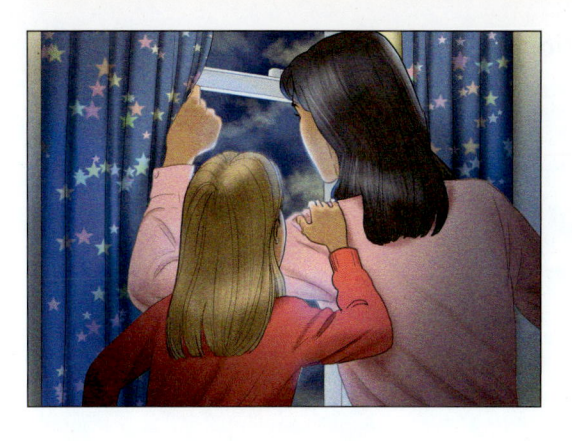

Gemma was only nine. I was fourteen and
120 I had never had a boyfriend.
Other girls at school had boyfriends – they
°teased me. But mum and dad were strict
about pubs and clubs – parties too. It really
wasn't fair.
125 "Look, the light has gone out," Gemma said.
After that I closed the curtains and went to
bed. But I couldn't sleep for hours. I kept
thinking of the squatter in number twenty-five
– our °mysterious new neighbour. Then I guess
130 I fell asleep.

2 Paragraph headings
Match these headings (A–E) to the five paragraphs of Natasha's story.
A Dad the detective
B An interesting new neighbour
C Jamie sees a ghost
D Somebody is watching
E Dad the squatter

3 Talking about the text   ▶ Skills file 6.7, p. 169
a) Answer the questions and finish the sentences about the story.
1 The **characters**: Who is the story about?
   - The main character in this story is …   She's …   It's also about her family, …

2 The **setting**: Where does the story happen?
   - The story happens in a street in …   We're in Natasha's …   We also learn about number …

3 The **plot**: Say what happens in the story – in a few sentences.
   - First Natasha thinks that …   Then her brother sees …   He thinks it's …
   Natasha's mum says that it's a …   Natasha's dad goes …   Then …

4 The **mood**: How do you feel when you read this story? Why?
   - I think that it's scary when …   It's funny when …   It's exciting when …   It's …

b) 👥 Now find a partner who has read Matt's side of the story. Compare your notes.

More practice 2 | p. 117

4 A book **recommendation**?
a) 👥 Discuss in class: Did you like Natasha's story? What did you like? What didn't you like? Would you like to read the book? Vote in class.

b) ● Write a review of the story. Write about the plot, the setting, your favourite characters and the mood of the story. Say if you would like to read the book and why (not).

More help | p. 117   More challenge 5 | p. 118

▶ Workbook 14–16, p. 27

2 SPEAKING COURSE (2) Successful conversations
▶ INKL p. 38–39

1 VIEWING Dos and don'ts in conversations

a) Watch part 1 of the film: What does Jan say about saying hello in English and German? Do you agree with what he says about saying hello in German?

b) Watch part 2 of the film and spot Jan's mistakes. Make notes.
👥 Compare your notes.
Have you spotted all the mistakes?

c) Before you watch part 3 of the film, think of useful tips for someone who is going to England on an exchange.
👥 Agree on your top three tips.

❗ Look at the box below for ideas. Careful! Some of these are good tips. Others are not helpful.

- Only speak when you're spoken to!
- When people ask you questions, say as much as you can.
- Be careful. Don't make too many mistakes.
- Don't worry about making mistakes.
- Try to sound as English as you can.
- It's OK to sound German. – The important thing is to talk!
- Be polite. Use words like *please*, *thank you* and *sorry* often.
- ...

d) Watch part 3 with no sound. What do you think Jan and Sarah say this time?
👥 Discuss in class and collect your suggestions on the board.

e) Watch part 3 again, this time with sound. Compare your suggestions from d) with what Jan and Sarah say in the film.

f) Compare Jan and Sarah's tips with your tips from c). Would you change any of your tips now?

▶ KV 17 ▶ DFF 2.8

2 NOW YOU   Your conversation, step by step

A **B** **C**

Step 1: Starting off
a) How can you start the conversation? Choose a suitable phrase from the box for each scene or come up with your own ideas.

> Excuse me, is this seat free?
> Hi, I love your T-shirt / shoes / …
> Hello. How are you?
> …

b) How would you introduce yourself? There are some ideas in the box.

> I'm …, by the way.
> My name is … and I'm from …
> Nice to meet you.
> …

Step 2: Keep the conversation going
a) Think of at least two things you could say to each of the people in the scenes above.

b) 👥 Compare your ideas.

> Where are you from?
> Do you like …?
> Have you been to …?
> I'm really enjoying my stay here.
> What class are you in?
> The weather is great today.
> …

Step 3: A good ending
Choose phrases from the box for each scene, or come up with ideas of your own.

> It was really nice talking to you.
> See you around sometime.
> Have a good day!
> Bye. See you later.
> I hope we meet again.
> What are you doing tomorrow evening?
> …

Step 4: Have a conversation
a) 👥 Pick one of the scenes A–C. Make a dialogue.

b) 👥 Perform your dialogues for the class.
👥 Give feedback. Did the people talk a lot? Did they sound friendly?

> ❗ Be friendly. Smile!
> Listen carefully. Give full answers.
> If you don't know a word, paraphrase.
> ▶ Skills file 7.2, p. 170

More practice 3 | p. 118

▶ Workbook 17–21, pp. 29–30

STOP! CHECK! GO!
▶ KV 18 ▶ DFF 2.5 ▶ DFF 2.6 ▶ INKL p. 40–43

1 LANGUAGE — How to talk to your parents

a) What exactly did Jay and her mum say? Complete the dialogue:

I said I wanted to meet Amy after school. Mum said it was a school night. She asked me how much homework I had. I told her that I didn't have very much.
Mum wanted to know where Amy lived. I said I didn't know. I told her we wanted to go to the mall. I asked her if she could pick me up from there.
Mum asked if I had any money. I told her I didn't, but I reminded her that it was nearly my birthday. Mum asked if I °was serious. Then she said I couldn't go.

Jay	I … to meet Amy after school.
Mum	But it'… a school night. How much homework … you …?
Jay	Oh, I … … very much.
Mum	Where … Amy …?
Jay	I … know. We … to go to the mall. … you pick me up from there?
Mum	… you … any money?
Jay	No, I …. But it'… nearly my birthday…
Mum	… you serious? You … go.

b) Jay wants to go to a concert next week. Complete what she says about her friends' advice.

Meg	Choose a good time to ask your parents.
Max	Stay calm and don't get angry.
Elli	Finish all your homework before you ask.
Tia	Tell them that you really want to go.
Meg	Don't ask for money for the tickets.
Max	Use your birthday money.

1 Meg told me …
2 Max told me …
3 Elli had a great idea. She told me …
4 Tia told me …
5 Meg told me …
6 Max …

c) What did Jay tell her friends about this discussion with her parents? p. 118

Jay	Mum and dad, can I talk to you about the concert? I really want to go.
Dad	Do you have any homework to do?
Jay	No, I don't. It's all finished.
Mum	How much do the tickets cost?
Jay	They are expensive but I have the money from my birthday.
Dad	What time does the concert end?
Jay	Ten o'clock.
Dad	It's a bit late for a school night.
Mum	Yes, I don't want you to be tired at school.
Jay	It's just one night. But OK, I respect your opinion.
Mum	I really like your °attitude, Jay.
Dad	I agree. You can go to the concert, Jay.

I asked my parents if I *could* (1) talk to them about the concert.
I told them I really … (2) to go.
Dad asked if I … (3) any homework.
I said that it … (4) all finished.
Mum wanted to know how much the tickets … (5).
I told them that they … (6) expensive but I … (7) the money from my birthday.
Dad asked what time the concert … (8).
I said ten o'clock.
Dad said it … (9) a bit late for a school night.
And mum agreed with him. She said she … (10) want me to be tired at school.
I said it … (11) just one night, but I … (12) her opinion.
Mum said she really … (13) my attitude.
Dad said that I … (14) go!
Wow! Great advice, guys!

▶ Language file 20, pp. 192–194   More challenge 6 p. 119

46

▶ KV 18 ▶ DFF 2.7 ▶ INKL p. 40–43

2 READING Volunteering

Lily and Mike are volunteers. They've written about their work (in Texts A and B). Their notes for a presentation about the advantages of volunteering are in Text C.

A I'm Lily and I'm a volunteer lifeguard in LA. Every weekend our group meets and we learn about water safety and organizing beach games and competitions for hundreds of visitors. We're also taught first aid and °life-saving °techniques. Because a lifeguard has to be an excellent swimmer, I'm in a swimming program. The swimming has even helped me to do better in PE. And last month I became the leader of our school first aid crew.
What do I like most? I like informing visitors about the safest places to swim and learning to use life-saving equipment. But I also enjoy just having fun with my friends on the beach. Also, this volunteer job keeps me fit.

B My name is Mike and I'm at East High School. A friend asked me to volunteer to teach °children with special °needs how to swim. Doing this volunteer work once a week has made a big difference in my life. I've learned about the different needs of all these children and how to help them to improve their skills. The highlight of every lesson is the water polo game we all play together. At school I used to have problems with keeping appointments and being on time. These children look forward to seeing us each week, and I don't want them to be disappointed. Since I started, I've never been late or missed a lesson. It makes my °fellow students and me happy to help these kids to feel pride, improve their self-respect and have fun.

C Volunteering has lots of advantages:
1. You learn to communicate with people, to organize activities and to °lead groups.
2. Volunteering teaches you time management skills.
3. Volunteers often do better at school.
4. Volunteering can help you to stay healthy.
5. You learn to be patient and to respect other people.

a) Find words/phrases meaning: p. 119
1. very good (A, line 10)
2. team of people who work together (A, line 14)
3. things you need to rescue someone (A, line 17)
4. kids who have disabilities (B, lines 4–5)
5. feel unhappy because something you hoped for doesn't happen (B, line 16)
6. organizing your own time (C, number 2)
7. able to deal with a difficult situation without getting fed up (C, number 5)
8. be polite and kind to others (C, number 5)

b) Match a final sentence to each text. (There's one more than you need.)
1. Everyone has the right to take part in sports activities, and that's why we think our work is important.
2. To sum up, volunteering – even if it's just once a week – can make a real difference to your life.
3. Volunteers need more help and support to do their important work.
4. I'm thinking of applying for a job as a professional rescue worker.

▶ Skills files 6.3, p. 167; 6.5, p. 168

c) For each of the five statements in Text C find examples from Texts A and B.
Example: (1) organizing beach games and competitions ...   More challenge 7 p. 119

STOP! CHECK! GO!
▶ KV 18 ▶ DFF 2.1 ▶ DFF 2.2 ▶ INKL p. 40–43

3 LISTENING   Tell your story

a) Listen to four stories from the radio programme *Your Story*. Find out what each story is about and match it to one of these signs. (There's one more sign than you need.)

A RACISM   **B** CAUTION PEER PRESSURE   **C** Cyber-bullying   **D** STOP BULLYING NOW!   **E** VIOLENCE

b) Read these questions. Listen again and answer each question in fewer than 10 words.

1. Why was the website so terrible for Joshua?
2. Who made the website?
3. How did Sheila bully Karen?
4. What is Karen's message?
5. What examples of racism are there in Gorodema's life in Germany?
6. In what way did the two friends put pressure on Jessica? (Name two things.)
7. How did Jessica feel in the end?

4 MEDIATION   SOR–SMC

Your British exchange partner Dave wants to know more about SOR–SMC.
Answer his questions using information from this text:

SCHULE OHNE RASSISMUS
SCHULE MIT COURAGE

Die Idee für eine „SOR – SMC" wurde 1988 von Lernenden in Belgien entwickelt. Sie wollten praktisch etwas tun gegen Diskriminierung aller Art.

Inzwischen beteiligen sich hunderttausende Schülerinnen und Schüler in Belgien, Spanien und Deutschland an dem Projekt. Bundesweit wurden bereits über 1.700 Schulen mit dem Titel „Schule ohne Rassismus – Schule mit Courage" ausgezeichnet. Courage (Mut) ist wichtig, um sich mit Diskriminierungen auseinanderzusetzen.

SOR – SMC ist ein Projekt von und für Schüler und Schülerinnen. Jede Schule kann den Titel erwerben, wenn sie folgende Voraussetzungen erfüllt: Mindestens 70 % aller in einer Schule Lernenden und Arbeitenden verpflichten sich durch Unterschrift, sich künftig gegen jede Diskriminierung an ihrer Schule aktiv einzusetzen, bei Konflikten einzugreifen und einmal im Jahr Aktionen zum Thema durchzuführen (z.B. Theater, Musik, Filmtage, Feste, Info-Stände). Zudem muss jede Schule einen oder mehrere prominente Paten bzw. Unterstützer finden.

Dave   What is SOR-SMC?   *You ...*
Dave   What do schools have to do to be part of the project?   *You ...*
Dave   How many schools in Germany are part of the project?   *You ...* ▶ Skills file 10, pp. 180–181

5 WRITING   Schools against racism

Your school is taking part in „Schule ohne Rassismus – Schule mit Courage". Think of an interesting project for your school. Describe it in an article. These questions can help you:

- What is your project about?
- Why do you want to do it?
- What do you need?
- Who is it for?
- What might be the effects?
- How do you want to present your project?

More help   p. 120

▶ DFF 2.8   ▶ INKL p. 40–43

6 LISTENING   Friendly conversations

a) Listen to dialogues 1–3 and match a picture (A–C) to each dialogue. Say whether the German student in each dialogue sounds friendly.

b) Listen again. Write down as many friendly and polite phrases as you can.

c) Write down three tips to help Robert from Dialogue 3 to be more polite and friendly.

d) Complete the dialogue and help Robert to have a more friendly conversation with Amanda.

Robert   …
Amanda   Oh, that's OK! It was my mistake. I haven't seen you before. Are you new?
Robert   …
Amanda   Oh, cool, Germany? How interesting! I spent a week in Füssen last year. I was there with my °orchestra. It was beautiful.
Robert   …
Amanda   Well, my next class is in a few minutes. What do you have next?
Robert   …
Amanda   I'm not really into math and science. I like music and drama. What are your favourite subjects?
Robert   …
Amanda   Well, OK, see you later. It was nice meeting you. Oh, by the way, I'm Amanda.
Robert   …

7 SPEAKING   Role-play

Partner B: Go to page 96.
Partner A: Read your role card and prepare a role-play with your partner.
Start your conversation very politely. Don't forget to introduce yourselves to each other.
You have 7 minutes to prepare.

> You've just arrived at Green Valley High School for an exchange programme. You're at a welcome party for exchange students. Maybe you can find somebody who can show you the most interesting places in town tomorrow?
> You go over to the °buffet table to get a drink when you see somebody making eye contact with you.
> Keep a conversation going with him / her for at least three minutes.

MORE CHALLENGE 2

Living with disability

> Den Wortschatz von diesen Seiten findest du im Vocabulary auf S. 233.

1 READING Two opinions

a) Britain and Jack both have to cope with disability. Compare their experiences and their feelings, and give examples from the texts (line numbers).
▶ Skills file 6.4, p. 168

'The kid in a wheelchair' by Britain R.

My life is happy and normal, but it isn't always easy, because of my disability. I have difficulty walking because I have a disease called muscular dystrophy, and over the years it has got worse.

When I was very young, I could still °keep up with my peers, although it took me longer to do some things. During °elementary school, however, things like standing and climbing stairs became difficult. When other kids rode bikes or played sports, I couldn't. By °middle school, I needed to use a wheelchair. My older brothers traveled °abroad with a student program, but I couldn't. More recently, I wasn't allowed to get a driver's license or a job.

Believe me, there is prejudice against people with disabilities. I have been called names like "cripple". For some people I'm "the kid in the wheelchair". They can't see °beyond my disability.

I have experienced many °hardships in my life because of my disability. I have also learned there are more important things in life than walking. Perhaps some °able-bodied people could learn from my experiences.

A fashion model and a role model

Jack Eyers is a personal trainer and has also worked as a fashion model, walking the catwalk at New York Fashion Week.

Eyers was born with a °rare °condition that meant that his right leg didn't grow °properly, and at the age of 16 he chose to have the leg amputated. He doesn't try to hide his prosthetic leg, °displaying it proudly and preferring to wear shorts °rather than trousers.

Being a sporty child, Eyers was frustrated by his disability – and by the °taunts of some of his classmates – but then he realized he could channel his frustration into weightlifting, boxing and, later, his career.

"If I had seen more °disabled models when I was growing up, maybe I would have felt more °confident about myself," °admits Eyers, who hopes he can now be as much a role model as a fashion model.

b) Do the following tasks.
1 Why do you think that Britain wrote his article? Discuss.
2 Explain how Jack can be a role model for disabled people and others.
3 Describe your response to the texts. Do they make you think about the way you react to people? How?
▶ Skills file 6.5, p. 168

▶ DFF 2.9

2 LANGUAGE   Understanding *-ing*-forms *(participles)*
a) Complete the FOCUS box.

> **FOCUS**
>
> You sometimes find *-ing*-forms *(participles)* in written texts.
> They can be used to make a sentence shorter:
>
> Example: 'Jack has worked as a fashion model, <u>walking</u> the catwalk ...'
> This is a short way of saying: ➔   '... and he has walked the catwalk'
>
> How could you replace the *-ing*-forms *(participle)* in this sentence?
> '<u>Being</u> a sporty child, Eyers was frustrated by his disability.'
>
> Ⓐ When he was ...   Ⓑ Because he was ...   Ⓒ Although he was ...

▶ *Language file 27, p. 199*

b) Replace the *-ing*-forms *(participles)* in these sentences.
Use words like 'and', 'while', 'because', 'when'.
 1 Kelly got onto the boat, <u>shouting</u> goodbye to her parents.
 2 <u>Feeling</u> tired, she went to find her °cabin.
 3 <u>Sitting</u> down in her cabin, she suddenly realized that she didn't have her phone.
 4 <u>Hoping</u> someone had found it, she spoke to one of the crew.
 5 Back on deck, she could see her parents on the harbour wall, <u>waving</u> her phone in the air.
 6 She waved back, <u>thinking</u>: How do I get my phone now?

3 LANGUAGE   Using *-ing*-forms *(participles)*
Combine the sentences. Replace the underlined verb forms with *-ing*-forms *(participles)*.
 1 <u>I was</u> an energetic child. I enjoyed all kinds of sports, but I wasn't very good at them.
 2 My parents encouraged me. <u>They thought</u> it was good to do sport.
 3 I joined a soccer club and went every week.
    <u>I hoped</u> that I would soon be in the team.
 4 But the coach didn't pick me. <u>She said</u> I wasn't good enough.
 5 <u>I felt</u> °rather fed up. I decided to look for a different sport.
 6 <u>I was walking</u> through the park one day.
    I saw a game of tag rugby.
 7 <u>I joined in</u>. I discovered to my surprise that I was good at it.

Unit 3 — Looking forward

▶ INKL p.44–45

1 QUIZ Are you ready for the real world?

a) Do this magazine quiz.

In the near future your life will change. Perhaps you'll go to a new school or **college**. Perhaps you'll start training, or even start a job. And many of you will leave home. You'll have to be more independent. Are you ready for that?

1 If you had to make a meal, what would you do?
- Ⓐ I'd look for a recipe, buy the **ingredients** and cook them.
- Ⓑ I'd cook pasta with tomato **sauce**. It's easy.
- Ⓒ I'd get a **takeaway** or order something online.

2 Imagine you had to do the shopping for a week. What would you do?
- Ⓐ I'd make a shopping list, go to cheap shops and buy only what I need.
- Ⓑ I'd go to the nearest supermarket and **pick up** the things that I see.
- Ⓒ I'd probably buy lots of crisps and sweets, etc.

Box: Voc., p. 218

3 What chores do you do at home?
- Ⓐ I often empty the dishwasher and use the **vacuum cleaner** and the **washing machine**. Sometimes I **iron** my clothes.
- Ⓑ I do some chores, e.g. I tidy up, set the table, etc. But I don't know how to use the washing machine and I hate using the vacuum cleaner.
- Ⓒ I never do chores. That's for parents!

4 Do you **earn your own pocket money?**
- Ⓐ Yes, I have a part-time job and I can buy my own stuff.
- Ⓑ I have a part-time job, but I don't earn a lot of money.
- Ⓒ No! When I need money I ask mum or dad, or my grandparents.

5 Do you **manage your own money?**
- Ⓐ I **budget** – I plan how much I can spend on going out, hobbies, etc.
- Ⓑ I try not to **overspend**. But I don't really budget.
- Ⓒ I often **run out** of money, so I have to borrow.

Box: Voc., p. 219

6 Do you save any money?
- Ⓐ Yes, I try to save a little every week.
- Ⓑ Sometimes. But then I spend it!
- Ⓒ No. I like to enjoy my money.

▶ INKL p. 44–45

7 Are you looking forward to living with other people?
- Ⓐ Yes, but we'll have to plan well, share the chores, clean often, etc.
- Ⓑ I've never really thought about it. I think I'll miss home.
- Ⓒ Yippee! I can't wait to leave home. It'll be party, party, party!

8 Are you a responsible student?
- Ⓐ I think I am. I work hard at school and I don't stay out late in term time.
- Ⓑ I'm quite responsible. I do my school work, but I sometimes go to bed very late, especially at weekends.
- Ⓒ Well … I like to go out a lot and to do things with friends, even in the week. I do my school work when I have time.

9 If you lost your bus ticket, what would you do?
- Ⓐ I'd buy another one.
- Ⓑ I'd sit down and cry … or I'd phone home for help.
- Ⓒ I'd go on the bus without a ticket.

10 Are you good at deciding things?
- Ⓐ Yes, but I sometimes get advice.
- Ⓑ Most of the time. Sometimes it's hard to decide.
- Ⓒ I usually do the same thing as my friends.

b) Did you pick mostly A, B or C? Read the results below.

Mostly Ⓐ
Great! You manage your money well and you have the life skills you need to be independent. But life is more than work and money. Don't forget to enjoy yourself.

Mostly Ⓑ
You're quite independent, but you still need to learn a few important life skills before you leave home. Decide which skills are important for you and get some advice.

Mostly Ⓒ
You know how to have fun, but you're not ready for the real world. You need to be more independent. Make plans to change. Learn one new skill every week.

2 Life skills

a) Think: What are the six most important life skills for a young person – and why? Look at the quiz for ideas and add your own ideas. Make a list.

b) Pair: Compare your lists and agree on the top three skills. Give reasons.

c) Share: Tell the class what you and your partner think. Give your reasons.

▶ Workbook 1–3, p. 33

3 THEME 1
▶ DFF 3.1 ▶ INKL p. 46–47

What are you like?

1 VIEWING Strengths and weaknesses

a) Watch the two scenes without sound and think about these questions:
1 Where are the people?   2 What do you think is happening?

b) Read the statements below. Then watch the scenes with sound. Are they true or false?

1 This isn't the first time that Neil has been late for a match.
2 Neil says sorry, and the coach says it's no problem.
3 Neil isn't allowed to play in the match.

4 Maggie is cross with Julie and talks to her rudely.
5 Maggie doesn't think that Julie's clothes are appropriate for her work experience.
6 Julie understands that Maggie is giving her some good advice.

Neil

Maggie   Julie

2 Describing people

a) How would you describe Neil (scene 1) and Julie (scene 2)?
Watch the scenes again if you need to. Make notes. Then compare.

| Neil Julie | is isn't | confident • energetic • enthusiastic • helpful • polite • punctual • reliable • … | He She | is isn't | good at OK at | • talking to people • working in a team • reacting to criticism |

b) ⊙ Use your notes to complete this description of Neil.
In scene 1 Neil is polite and he's … He isn't punctual and he isn't …
On the other hand, he's good at … and he's OK at …

c) Write a description of Julie in the same way.

d) ● Write a description of a friend or someone in your family.
Let them read it (or explain it to them in German). Do they agree with it?

▶ KV 19   ▶ INKL p. 46–47

3 LISTENING   Ideas for the future

a) You're going to hear five young people talking about their ideas for the future. Read the statements below. Then listen and choose the correct statement (A–F) for each person. (There is one more than you need.)
Example: 1 Charlotte: …   2 Tom: …   3 …

Charlotte   Tom   Max   Ruby   Summer

A I'm sporty and I like teamwork. I know what job I want to do.
B I like looking after people. I'd like to work with children or old people.
C I'm good at art. I'd like to study at university, but I don't know what job I want to do.
D I'd like to leave school and start work as soon as I can.
E I'm not very patient, so I can't imagine working with children.
F I'm good at finding solutions to problems. I like science.

▶ Skills file 5, p. 166

b) Can you add to these descriptions of the five young people? Listen again. Note down at least one more thing about each of them – more if you can.

4 ACTIVITY   Identity card

a) Make notes about yourself on a card like this.   ▶ Wordbank 2, p. 143

What you are like	Your strengths
Choose three adjectives to describe yourself.	Mention at least two things you're good at or quite good at.
Your weaknesses	**Your hopes and plans**
Mention one or two things you're not so good at.	Say something about your hopes and plans for the future, even if you don't have any real ideas yet.

b) 👥 Make appointments with three students. Tell each partner about yourself, and listen to what they have to say about themselves.

c) Use your notes to write a text about yourself, your strengths and weaknesses, and your plans for the future. You can put your text in your DOSSIER.

▶ Workbook 4–5, p. 34

3 THEME 2
▶ DFF 3.2 ▶ INKL p. 48–49

What's next?

1 Internet job adverts

Scan the job adverts and find as many jobs as you can. Compare your lists.

▶ Skills file 6.2, p. 167

1 CHANDLERS UK

We are looking for °apprentices for our business in London. This is a great chance for you to become a qualified painter and °decorator. You will work 4 days a week and go to college 1 day.

Hours: Monday to Thursday, 8 am to 5 pm.
You need to be able to work carefully. You sometimes need °a good head for heights

APPLY NOW

2 Elite Stylists, Liverpool

We are a leading make-up, fashion and hair stylist company for TV shows, fashion shows, film studios and °red carpet events. This is your chance to become a celebrity stylist, so start your new °career now.
You should be energetic and reliable.

Full training on the job.
°Salary: Up to °£20K, plus travel costs.
Send us your CV and photo today.

Box: Voc., p. 220

3 LOLA Events Management

We need:
• bar staff
• cooks
• waiters

To work in our team, you must have some experience and excellent communication skills.
Pay: £6.75 to £10 per hour

We also need a trainee manager:
Qualifications: A °university degree
Salary: £20 – £25,000 per year

Please apply now – we can't wait to meet you.

4 Jobs in Canada

If you are 18 to 30 years of age, you can apply for a °visa to live and work in Canada for up to one year.

- **Camp assistants:** We are looking for confident and fun young people from around the world who are great with children. Come and help in one of 800 camps across Canada.
Earn up to $1700 for 10 weeks' work.

- **Hotel workers:** Work in a hotel in the ski season as a cleaner, receptionist or waiter. You have to be friendly, polite and helpful. You'll work 5 days per week and get 2 days free to ski and °snowboard. You can earn C$10 per hour. No experience is needed.

▶ KV 20 ▶ DFF 3.3 ▶ DFF 3.4 ▶ INKL p. 48–49

5

Pet Care Business, Bedworth, UK
Animal Care Assistant

Pay: £6.50 per hour   Job: Full-time
Hours: 40 hours per week

You would be responsible for:
- dog walking and feeding
- office work
- taking animals home

You need:
- a full driving licence
- to be enthusiastic and friendly
- to be hard-working

If you are an °animal lover and have some experience, please apply today.

6

Ever thought of becoming a pilot?

You need to:
- be able to work shifts
- have good communication skills
- be calm at all times
- be fit
- be a team player
- be responsible

For more information, go to the LONDON CITY AIRPORT website.

2 Different jobs – different duties

a) Look at the job adverts again. Find at least one job where you have to:
1 work with your hands   4 work with kids   7 work in a team
2 go to school / college   5 work outdoors   8 work at night
3 work with food   6 work with famous people   9 work with animals

b) 👥 Compare your answers.

3 Different jobs – different skills and qualities

a) Match each of the skills and personal qualities with at least one job in the adverts:
1 be calm in all situations   4 have a qualification   7 have a feeling for colour
2 be energetic and reliable   5 be adventurous and fun   8 be enthusiastic
3 be polite and helpful   6 have some experience   9 have good communication skills

b) 👥 Compare your answers.   [More practice 1 p. 120]

4 NOW YOU   A job for me?

👥 Pick the most interesting job advert. Then talk about these questions:
1 Do you have the right qualities for this job?   2 What skills do you need to learn?   [More practice 2 p. 120]

5 Your ideal job

🔵 Imagine your ideal job. Do some research and write a short text about it.   [More help p. 121]

▶ Wordbanks 3–4, pp. 144–145

▶ Text file 3, pp. 152–153   ▶ Workbook 6–8, pp. 35–36

THEME 3
▶ INKL p. 50–51

Selling yourself

1 Are you **dynamic**?
Look at this job advert and talk about these questions:
- What do you have to do in this job?
- What skills do you need?

5th Ave Fashions – new Frankfurt store
We're looking for dynamic part-time **sales** assistants! You'll **work** on the sales floor, in the **fitting rooms**, at the **cash desks** and you'll **answer the phone**. You **need** to be a team player, have good communication skills and be able to work **flexible** hours. And you need good English to speak to our international customers. Email us your CV – in English – today.

Box: Voc., p. 221

2 Paul's CV
Do you think that Paul is a good candidate for the job? Why (not)?

- CVs in English are different to CVs in German.
- A personal statement is a short paragraph to describe yourself. ▶ Wordbank 2, p. 143
- Begin with your present school.
- Give examples of the kind of work you have done.
- Write a short paragraph with <u>interesting</u> details.
- Give two names and addresses as references.

Paul Schulz
Address: Rehstraße 95, 65933 Frankfurt am Main
Mobile: 0151 321 50717   Email: paulschulz23@gerlink.de

Personal statement
I am a confident and enthusiastic student with good communication and telephone skills. I have some work experience and I'd like to learn new skills.

Key skills
- Strong team member   – Good computer skills
- Friendly and polite   – Good English and Italian

Education
2012 to present: Sophie-Scholl Gesamtschule, Frankfurt
2008 to 2012:   Gaisenthal Grundschule, Ulm

Work experience
Supermarket: Filling shelves, cleaning (summer job)
Petrol station: Working at cash desk (work experience)

Interests and **achievements**
I am interested in clothes and have my own fashion blog. I am a **keen** footballer and am captain of the under-18s team.

References
Dieter Lutz (English teacher)   Monika Bold (manager)
Fontanestraße 42   Lindenallee 108

3 NOW YOU   Your CV
a) Write a CV for yourself like Paul's. You can put it in your DOSSIER.
▶ Skills file 8.5, p. 176

b) Compare your CV with other students. Who is most suitable for the job at 5th Ave Fashions?

More challenge 1 p. 121

▶ KV 21 ▶ KV 22 ▶ DFF 3.5 ▶ DFF 3.6 ▶ INKL p. 50–51

4 Cover letters

a) Lisa is also applying for the job. Do you think that she's a good candidate? Why (not)?

Waldstraße 279
61449 Steinach

The Manager
5th Ave Fashions
Zeil 94
Frankfurt am Main   28th February 20..

Dear Sir / Madam

I am writing about the job of part-time sales assistant at your store. I saw the **advertisement** on your website yesterday, and I would like to apply for this job.

I am a student and last year I had a Saturday job in a department store for five months. I worked on a cash desk in the shoe department, so I think that I would be very **suitable** for the job.

I am energetic and reliable. I enjoy working with people and I am very keen on sales because you meet lots of people. I speak good English. It's my favourite subject at school. I am available on Saturday afternoons and on one evening every week – Thursdays if possible.

I **enclose** my CV and I look forward to hearing from you.
Yours faithfully   Box: Voc., p. 222

Lisa Freund
Lisa Freund

! Don't use short forms:
I'm = I am   it's = it is
ad = advertisement

! If you don't know a name, write **Dear Sir / Madam**.

! Always start your first sentence with a capital letter.

! Say where you saw the advertisement.

! Write about **relevant** experience and say why you're suitable.

! If you start with *Dear Sir / Madam*, finish with **Yours faithfully**.
If you start with a name, finish with **Yours sincerely**.

b) Write a cover letter for Paul Schulz. Use ideas and language from Lisa's letter. ▶ Skills file 8.6, p. 177

5 MEDIATION   A job for a friend

A 16-year-old friend (Ella) from Canada is coming to Berlin for the summer, and she'd like a job. She loves gardening and her German isn't great. You've found this ad.
Write an email to Ella and give her the most important details about the job. Explain why you think it would be a suitable job for her.
Write about 120 words.   More practice 3   p. 121

▶ Skills files 8.3, p. 174; 10, pp. 180–181

Park- und Gartenhilfen gesucht (m/w)

Tätigkeit: Gartenjobs im Grünen für junge Leute (m/w) aus aller Welt. Frische Luft, angenehme Atmosphäre und ein sympathisches internationales Team erwarten dich.

Vorkenntnisse: nicht erforderlich, wir arbeiten dich ein. Gartenarbeit und Pflanzen solltest du mögen. In unseren Teams wird Englisch gesprochen.

Anforderungen: Du bist zuverlässig und fleißig? Interessiert an Parks und Gärten? Dann bewirb dich bitte mit Lebenslauf und schreibe uns, warum du zu uns passt.

Alter: 16 bis 30 Jahre   **Start:** 1. Juli
Arbeitsorte: in Berlin   **Bewerbung bitte auf Englisch**

▶ Workbook 9–10, p. 37

3 FOCUS ON LANGUAGE
▶ INKL p. 55

1 Questions about Emma

a) Do you know why Emma Watson is famous? Skim the text and look at the photos to find out.

All about Emma

1. Emma Watson was ten years old when she played Hermione in the first Harry Potter film. That was in 2000.
2. Emma worked on the Harry Potter films for 10 years. She finished work on the last film in 2010.
3. In real life Emma is good friends with the actors who play Harry and Ron in the films.
4. Emma was born in Paris in 1990. She isn't French though! She's English. (She speaks French, but not very well.)
5. She moved to England with her mum and her younger brother when she was five.
6. The name of her first school in England is very appropriate for a Harry Potter actor. It was called the Dragon School!
7. Since the end of the Harry Potter films Emma has done lots of things. She has acted in more films, and she has worked as a model. She loves fashion and many people admire her style.
8. She went to university in the US and studied English.
9. She's a great role model for young people. She gave a speech at the United Nations in New York about equal rights for women.
10. Who knows what Emma will do next? One thing is for sure. We will definitely hear more about her in the future!

---

b) Work in groups. Read the article. What questions do you think the interviewer asked to get this information? Write at least one question for each point in the article. [More help p. 121]

c) Then listen to the interview. How many of your questions does the interviewer ask?

d) Listen again. What other interesting or surprising questions does the interviewer ask?

2 REVISION Question words

Complete the questions with a question word. Then try to answer the questions. (Check your answers on p. 122.)

1. ... played Harry in the Harry Potter films?
2. ...'s the name of the school that Harry, Hermione and Ron went to?
3. ... didn't Harry Potter live with his parents?
4. ... Harry Potter books are there?
5. ... Harry Potter films are there?
6. ... are there more films than books?
7. ... wrote the Harry Potter books?

▶ DFF 3.7

3 REVISION — Word order in questions

a) ⭕ Answer the questions in the FOCUS box.

> **FOCUS**
>
> **1** What are the missing words?
> Where __ Emma born? – She was born in Paris.
> __ Emma French? – No, she is English.
> __ you seen all the Harry Potter films? – Yes, I have.
>
> **2** Look at the word order in the questions and in the answers. What comes first:
> the subject (Emma / she / I / ...)? Or the verb (was / is / have / ...)?

▶ Language files 11–12, pp. 188–189

b) ⭕ Read the statements and ask follow-up questions to find out more. 🎧 p.122

1 My role model is my teacher, Mrs Smith.
 – Why *is she* your role model?
2 My friend Kadir wasn't born in Germany.
 – Where …… born?
3 Last year I was on work experience.
 – How long …… on work experience?
4 I'm worried about my next work experience.
 – Why …… worried about it?
5 I want a weekend job. I've sent out lots of CVs.
 – How many CVs …… sent out?

4 REVISION — Making questions with *do / does* and *did*

a) Answer the questions in the FOCUS box.

> **FOCUS**
>
> **1** Look at the questions and answers. When do you use *do*, *does*, or *did*?
> **Does** Emma speak French? – She speaks French, but not very well.
> When **did** Emma move to England? – She moved there when she was five.
> **Do** you think that Emma is a good actor? – Yes, I think that she's a very good actor.
>
> **2** 🔵 What do you notice about the **word order** in these questions and the answers?
> Look at the subjects and the verbs.

▶ Language file 12, p. 189

b) Complete the questions. 👥 Then interview a partner.

1 Where … you … (live) now? … you … (live) in the same place when you were a child?
2 How many languages … you … (speak)?
 … your friend … (speak) more than you?
3 What sports … you … (like) watching?
 … you … (enjoy) doing sport?
4 What kind of music … you … (enjoy)?
 … you … (have) a favourite band or singer?
5 What people … you … (admire)? Why … you … (think) they are good role models?

| More practice 4+5 | p.122 | | More challenge 2+3 | p.126 |

5 👥 NOW YOU — Great interviewers need great questions

a) Who would you like to interview? Agree with a partner.

b) What questions would you like to ask? Together agree on your top five questions.

c) Report to the class. Which pair has the most interesting questions? Give reasons.

d) Do some research. Then perform the interview for the class. ▶ Language file 14, p. 190

▶ Workbook 11–15, pp. 38–39

3 TEXT

▶ KV 23   ▶ INKL p. 52–54

1 Before you read: Look at the blurb

The 'blurb' is the short text on the back cover of a book. It tells the reader what the text is about.

a) Read the blurb and finish these sentences:
1. The writer's name is …
2. The main character is …
3. The story happens in …
4. The main character wants a job in a …
5. But she's too young – only …
6. So she says she's …

> 'Seashell Motel' by Lois Metzger: Sixteen-year-old Cindy from New York pretends she's nineteen in order to work for the summer in a motel in Atlantic City. But she soon realizes that what she has done is far more complicated than to turn a six upside down …

b) Compare your answers. Then read the story. You can read an easier version on pp. 123–125.

Seashell Motel   (adapted from a short story by Lois Metzger)

1 Cindy Fisher, age sixteen, lied to get her summer job.
Before the summer, Mrs. Karpinsky, a teacher at
5 Cindy's high school in New York City, told all the °tenth graders that a summer job was a good
10 idea. She talked about jobs in neighborhood restaurants, °bakeries, small offices and city parks. (Cindy had done those kinds of jobs before – boring!)
Then Mrs. Karpinsky °mentioned the Seashell
15 Motel down in Atlantic City, New Jersey. They were looking for a front desk °clerk. Cindy °immediately put up her hand and said, "I'll take that one."
Mrs. Karpinsky walked over to Cindy and °handed
20 her the application form. Then she looked at Cindy and said, "Sorry, you must be nineteen."
"I can do it," Cindy said.
"I'm sure you could, dear," the teacher said. "But for this job you have to live °on your own
25 in a strange city."
But Atlantic City's not strange, Cindy thought. When she was younger, she had gone there every summer with her family for two weeks. She remembered the beautiful boardwalk
30 along the ocean. She loved going on the rides, eating candy and hearing the ocean all the time. In Atlantic City, the ocean seemed to be everywhere.

Cindy couldn't give the application form back
35 to Mrs. Karpinsky.
"I'll give it to my older sister," she said. "She's nineteen."
"That's a fine idea," Mrs. Karpinsky said.
"Your baby sister is nineteen? Since when?"
40 said Charlotte, 'a friend of Cindy's, who was sitting next to her. Cindy smiled.
When she got home, Cindy told her parents that there was a new summer program at school and that lots of sixteen-year-old girls
45 would be going to hotels all along the east coast.
"The teacher said that it would be good for me," she told them. Her parents looked impressed.

62

So Cindy filled out the application form and wrote down her age as '19', not '16'.
How easy, she thought. You just turn a six upside down!

2 Cindy read the Seashell Motel brochure on the bus to Atlantic City. 'Ocean view' it said, but when she got to the boardwalk there was no Seashell Motel there. Then she saw the sign for the motel – it was °several °blocks from the sea. As she walked along, she thought that the city seemed sadder than she remembered, with many stores closed. Finally, on Arctic Avenue, there it was – the Seashell Motel. Only three °storeys high, modern, °unattractive, beige. No ocean view! Cindy couldn't even hear the waves.
At the front desk there was a young man with short brown hair, a blue jacket and a tie – about twenty-two years old.
"Welcome," he said and smiled. "A room for the weekend?"
"My name is Cynthia Fisher," Cindy said. Cynthia sounded much more °mature, she thought.
"I'll be working here – with you, I guess."
"You look a little young," he said.
It's my clothes and my hair, Cindy thought. I have to look older. "I'm nineteen. This is °actually my third job," she lied.
"Fine," he said. "I'm Tim Chamberlain. I'm studying hotel management in Louisiana."
Cindy heard his accent. She had never met a boy from the South before.
"Are you in college too?" he asked.
"High school … I mean I finished high school last year … now I'm at Queens College," she lied. I'll have to tell lies all summer, Cindy thought.

3 Cindy stood behind the front desk, her hair pulled back, in a white blouse, a dark blue skirt and °pumps with °heels. The make-up on her skin and the lipstick on her lips felt funny. Get used to it, she told herself.
Munny, the manager, was a tall, cheerful guy with curly brown hair.
"You can work the morning shift – from eight in the morning to four in the afternoon. Or the evening shift – from four in the afternoon until midnight. Or the °graveyard shift – from midnight to eight."
There were also a couple of guys in the kitchen, two °bellhops and two °ladies who did the cleaning. They were very sweet – but didn't speak much English.
Then there was Cal. He came to the motel every Thursday afternoon to fill up the drinks machine in the lobby. He had long dark hair, sea-green eyes and always wore a neon T-shirt. He was nice – he gave Cindy a couple of cans of *Orange* before he filled the machine.
He was sixteen and a half and lived in Atlantic City. Sometimes, when Cindy went to the beach in her time off, she imagined romantic walks with Cal.
And there were the guests. Cindy gave them their rooms, accepted their credit cards, answered their phone calls and sometimes made °wake-up calls.
One night, when she was on the graveyard shift, Tim told her that the man in Room 111 wanted a wake-up call at 5 am.
"Good morning," Cindy said cheerfully on the phone.
"This is your wake-up call."
"Are you crazy?" the man said and he °slammed down the phone.
It was Tim's joke.
"You'll get me fired!" Cindy complained to Tim.
"Munny won't care. He likes a good joke," Tim answered.

4 One afternoon Cal gave Cindy three cans of *Orange* and said, "Hey Cynthia, want to go to the boardwalk tonight?"
"Yes, sure, that sounds like fun," she answered.
Later, when they were on the boardwalk, Cal asked Cindy, "Want to go to the Hall of Mirrors?"
It was dark in there and Cindy saw Cal and

3 TEXT
▶ KV 23   ▶ INKL p. 52–54

herself thousands of times in the mirrors. Cal
145 took Cindy's hands and he wanted to kiss her,
but she pulled back. Cal liked Cynthia.
But would he like Cindy? she thought.
"I get it," he said, "I'm too young. Hey, it's OK,
Cynthia."
150 Cindy felt terrible. This Atlantic City summer
was a bad idea. She hadn't just turned a
number upside down, she had turned herself
upside down!
"Don't look so sad," Cal told her. "We can still
155 take a walk together sometimes."
"Let's just go," she said. Cindy wanted to leave
the Hall of Mirrors, but she couldn't find the
door.
She felt trapped – trapped in her lies …

5 The next week a hurricane hit Atlantic City.
Cindy had never heard anything like it.
She lay in her bed listening to the wind and the
rain. Then the phone rang. It was Cal.
"I'm downstairs," he said. "I thought you might
165 like to go for a walk."
"You mean now?" Cindy said, °shocked.
"Walk in the hurricane?" she asked.
"You'll see, it's so beautiful," he said.
"It's so crazy!"
170 "I've lived here my whole life. I know what I'm
doing," he said.
Cindy wanted to go … but did Cynthia?
"Put on a °swimsuit and °sandals," Cal said. "I'll
wait for you in the lobby."
175 Down in the lobby Cal was wearing dark
shorts and sandals. He took Cindy's hand.
Outside the wind was much louder. They
walked towards the boardwalk and they got
very wet.
180 The streets were flooded. It was dangerous,
but Cindy felt calm and safe with Cal.
At the boardwalk the sky and the sea were the
same dark grey.
You couldn't see where the sea ended and the
185 sky began.
"What do you think, Cynthia?" Cal said.
"I told you the truth, didn't I?"

6 "Cal," Cindy suddenly said. "I haven't told
you the truth. I'm not who you think I am."
190 "You're not?" Cal said.
"I'm only sixteen years old. So the way I dress,
the way I act, the way I feel … it's just one big
lie!"   Box: Voc., p. 224
Cindy could see that Cal was trying to
195 understand this. Finally he smiled at her.
"You're so brave. I'm sixteen and I've never
been away from home – not even for a night,"
he said.
"I don't feel brave, I just feel trapped. I told lies
200 to the motel, I told lies to my parents and I told
lies to you."
"So you're brave, and also a little °foolish. When
will you tell your parents?" Cal asked.
"I'll tell them everything, but not just yet,"
205 Cindy said.
The hurricane was getting louder.
"Let's go back," Cal said.

Back at the motel a window had broken and
sea water was coming into the motel.
210 Look! Cindy thought, the brochure wasn't
lying, Seashell Motel does have an ocean view.

▶ KV 24 ▶ INKL p. 52–54

2 Questions for you

a) Answer these questions about part 1.
1. Why do you think Cindy wanted the job at the Seashell Motel?
2. Cindy lied to her teacher. What did she lie about?
3. Cindy lied to her parents. What did she lie about to them?

b) Pick one part of the story (parts 2–6) and read it.
Then make two or three questions for your part, and agree on the answers.

c) Make groups of 5 students – with one student for each part (2 – 6). Ask and answer all your questions.

More practice 6 | p. 126

3 The characters in the story

a) Copy this table and make notes about one of the characters in the story (Cindy, Tim or Cal). Use words and phrases from the story – and your own ideas.

NAME	FROM	AGE	PERSONALITY	APPEARANCE (hair, eyes, ...)	CLOTHES	WHAT HE/SHE DOES/LIKES
...	...	...	...	...	...	...

b) Work with students who picked the other characters and complete the table for the three main characters. Ask questions to get the information.

c) Copy this chart for one character (Cindy, Tim or Cal) and put an X on the lines in the right place. Then talk about your character.

Character's name: _____

	not at all	not very	quite	very	extremely
kind					
brave					
honest					
adventurous					
funny					
hard-working					
reliable					

d) Write a characterization of Cindy, Tim or Cal. Say what you think they are like and give reasons.

e) Then swap your text with other students and compare. ▶ Skills file 6.7, p. 169

More challenge 4 | p. 127

4 Cindy's diary

You're Cindy. Write a short diary entry for each of these times:
- after your day at school
- after you've arrived at the motel
- after you've met the other people who work at the motel
- after your trip to the Hall of Mirrors
- after the hurricane

▶ Workbook 18–20, p. 41

65

3 SPEAKING COURSE (3) Doing well in job interviews
▶ DFF 3.8 ▶ INKL p. 56–57

1 VIEWING Interview stress

a) What do you need to think about when you're preparing for a job interview? Make a network.

Preparing for job interviews

b) Watch part 1 of the film. Do you think Mike has prepared well for the interview?
Can you add more ideas to your network in a)? Discuss.

c) Watch part 1 of the film again. Make a list of the mistakes that Mike makes.

d) Watch part 2 of the film. What things does Mike do better this time? ▶ Skills file 7.3, p. 171

e) What questions does the interviewer ask Mike? Watch part 2 again and write them down.

More help p. 127

2 NOW YOU Answering interview questions

a) Choose typical interview questions and prepare answers to them.

More help p. 128

b) Practise your questions and answers.

c) Take turns to perform your answers.
The others should give feedback on *what* you say and *how* you say it.

> I think your answer was very good / interesting / …
> You could also talk about …

> I think you were very polite / enthusiastic / …
> I think you spoke confidently / too quietly / …
> Your body language was good / OK / not great / …

! Be as positive as you can when you're giving **feedback**.
- First pick out one good thing in the **performance** – more if you can.
- Then pick out one important thing that they could do better.

▶ Wordbank 5, p. 145

66

▶ KV 25   ▶ DFF 3.9   ▶ INKL p. 56–57

3

3 YOUR TASK   Who will get the job?
You're going to take part in an interview for a part-time job.

Step 1: Look at the advert
Think about these questions:
1. What skills are needed?
2. Why are you a good candidate?
3. Why do you want the job?
4. What questions can you ask?

| More help | p. 128 |

Restaurant team member
in busy fast-food restaurant

Improve your service and teamwork skills in our restaurant. We're looking for very hard-working, enthusiastic *individuals*. Part-time or full-time work. Experience not *necessary*.
The ideal *candidate* has to:
- be able to work as part of a team
- speak clearly and listen carefully to guests and staff members
- have a professional, energetic and enthusiastic *approach*

If you like the sound of us, please send your CV by email.

Step 2: Perform the interviews
👥 Work in groups of at least three. Each member of the group will be interviewed for the job. The others will take turns to be the interviewer(s) or the assessor(s).

❗ Read the instructions below together.
Everybody must know what to do.
Then perform and assess the interviews.

The interviewers should talk like this:

Greet the candidate:	Hello, *pleased* to meet you. My name is …
Ask at least three questions:	Can you describe yourself? What are your strengths and weaknesses? Why do you want the job?
You can also ask follow-up questions:	Can you give me an example? What exactly do you do?
At the end say:	Do you have any questions? Thank you for coming. We'll *contact* you soon.

The assessors need a copy of this form. They should make notes.

	very good	OK	needs work
1 How did the candidates present themselves? (e.g. handshake, body language, eye contact, smile, clear speech?)			
2 How good were their answers?			
3 Did they ask good questions?			

Step 3: Decide who should get the job
The assessors should use their notes to give feedback to the candidates.
👥 The group should decide who performed best in the interview. Then tell the class who got the job and why.

| More help | p. 129 |

STOP! CHECK! GO!
▶ KV 26 ▶ DFF 3.7 ▶ INKL p. 58–61

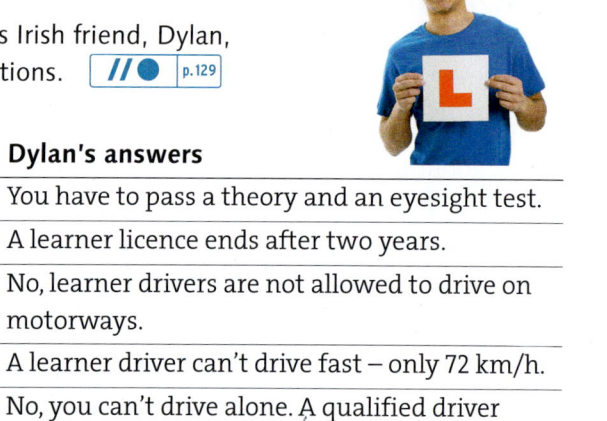

1 REVISION Driving in Ireland

a) Michael (17) from Germany is asking his Irish friend, Dylan, about his learner licence. Write Michael's questions. p. 129

	Michael's questions	Dylan's answers
1	have / you / to / pass / tests? / Do / any	You have to pass a theory and an eyesight test.
2	does / licence / learner / When / end? / a	A learner licence ends after two years.
3	motorways? / Are / drivers / allowed / on / learner / to / drive	No, learner drivers are not allowed to drive on motorways.
4	fast / a / driver / drive? / can / How / learner	A learner driver can't drive fast – only 72 km/h.
5	alone? / you / Can / drive	No, you can't drive alone. A qualified driver must be in the car with you.
6	is / qualified / Who / a / driver?	A qualified driver is someone who has had a full licence for two years.

b) Michael and Dylan speak on the phone after Dylan's driving test. Complete Michael's questions.

	Michael's questions	Dylan's answers
1	Do you …?	No, I don't have good news.
2	Was …?	No, the theory test was easy. But the driving test ended really badly.
3	Did …?	Yes, I had a bad accident.
4	Were you …?	No, I wasn't driving too fast. I wasn't moving.
5	Where did …?	It happened in the city centre. A lorry crashed into our car.
6	Was the lorry driver …?	No, the lorry driver wasn't talking on his phone. He was writing a text message.
7	Was anybody …?	Only the lorry driver was hurt. An ambulance took him to hospital.
8	What … … driving teacher …?	My driving teacher called the ambulance.
9	When are you …?	I am going to take the test again next week.

More challenge 5 p. 130

▶ KV 26   ▶ DFF 3.5   ▶ INKL p. 58–61

2 Writing a CV

Nele wants to do three weeks' work experience with a travel agency where she can use her English. Read the advert and Nele's biography and then write Nele's CV in English.

Work experience

At F&S TRAVEL we offer students work experience in our travel agency.

- You must be friendly and reliable and enjoy working in a team.
- You should be interested in travelling and should speak English well because we have a lot of international customers.
- Our opening hours are: Mon – Sat, 8 am – 9 pm

To apply, please send us your CV in English.

Biography:
Nele was born in Stade on 12 Dec 2002. She went to Grundschule Eickum (2008–2012). When her family moved to Hamburg, she went to Otto-Hahn-Gesamtschule there. Now she is in year ten. At school she likes languages best. She is also very good at geography, politics and computer science, and she likes learning new things.
Nele thinks she is a reliable and well-organized person. She likes talking to people, doing group work and has lots of friends. In her free-time Nele plays volleyball and likes reading. She is very interested in other countries. Nele often skypes with her English friends. Last year she did three weeks' work experience in a hotel. For references please contact Nele's class teacher, Mrs Kurz, or the manager of Hotel Nordsee, Mr Rüttgers.

3 Completing a cover letter

a) Complete and *improve* Nele's cover letter using words and phrases from the box.

Stankeweg 3
22457 Hamburg

The Manager
F&S TRAVEL
Tomeustraße 54
22438 Hamburg

… (1)

Dear … (2)
I would like to … (3) for work experience with your company. I am in my last … (4) at Otto-Hahn-Gesamtschule and I will leave school with Fachhochschulreife in June. My favourite … (5) are English, German and French and I am also … (6) in geography and computer science. I speak good English.
I'm (7) a friendly, hard-working and reliable person and I like working with other people. I *don't* (8) mind working *Sats* (9) and in the evenings. Last year I did work experience at a hotel for *3* (10) weeks, where I welcomed people from all over the world. I really enjoyed helping and advising people.
Here's (11) my CV. *Write back soon* (12).

Yours *sincerely* (13)

Sir / Madam • interested • year • 20th March 20… • apply • subjects • *faithfully* • *I am* • on Saturdays • I am looking forward to hearing from you • I enclose • three • do not

b) Write your own CV and cover letter to F&S TRAVEL.

▶ Skills files 8.5–8.6, pp. 176–177

STOP! CHECK! GO!
▶ KV 26 ▶ DFF 3.1 ▶ DFF 3.3 ▶ INKL p. 58–61

4 READING Catherine Cook: A teenage millionaire

Catherine Cook is a young entrepreneur who started her own business in 2005 while she was still a sophomore at Montgomery High School in New Jersey. At the age of 15, she and her 16-year-old brother David were both new to their school. They wanted to get to know their new classmates and make friends, so they looked at the school yearbook. But they didn't find it very helpful, so they created a free interactive online version and called it MyYearbook. MyYearbook is a social networking website where members can sign virtual yearbooks, swap photos and share information. It's made for people who live in the same region, are a similar age, or like to play the same games. Catherine and David's older brother Geoff thought this was a great idea and supported them financially to get the project started. After just a few weeks MyYearbook had about 400 users, and after only six years 25 million users across the USA.

Catherine's parents were important in her success. They always wanted her to find her own way and to do things for herself. And Geoff, who is 11 years older than Catherine, was more than just an investor. His experience was extremely helpful. Geoff is the person Catherine looks up to most. He started a successful company while he was still a student at Harvard University, and when Catherine saw this she wanted to be an entrepreneur too.

Catherine's advice for anyone who wants to start something new: "Use all the resources that are available to you and never be scared of asking for advice. If you can't find the answer to a problem, get a friend to help you out."

After high school Catherine went to college. Sometimes she found it very difficult to run a business and to study at the same time, but she never gave up. Catherine is now a multimillionaire, and people compare her to Facebook founder Mark Zuckerberg. But she says that she is just a normal girl who works really hard.

a) Complete these sentences with phrases from the text. Use four to six words.
1 Catherine was still a student when she …
2 She and her brother David went to …
3 They got the idea for a digital way of meeting teens after they …

b) Are these statements true, false or not in the text?
1 The aim of the website is to help people to meet people and make new friends.
2 Catherine and David's older brother Geoff went to the same school.
3 Geoff invested money in the project.
4 It took them many years to be successful.

c) Geoff has been a good example to Catherine. Give two reasons (lines 30–37).

d) Complete each sentence with a phrase from the text (no more than seven words).
1 In Catherine's opinion you shouldn't be afraid of …
2 Catherine says that if you can't find a solution, you should …

5 WRITING Who is important in your life?
Say who is important in your life and give reasons for your choice. Write an article. [More help p. 130]

▶ Skills file 8.1, pp. 172–173

▶ DFF 3.8 ▶ DFF 3.9 ▶ INKL p. 58–61

3

6 LISTENING   Phoning about a job

River Tours, a river cruise company, needs someone to help international customers on their boats. Sarah Richter, a sixteen-year-old German teenager, is phoning about the job.

a) 🎧 Listen to the dialogue and complete these phrases.
2.05
1 Can I … a message?   2 I saw a … on the internet.   3 I'll … again at 1:30.   4 … welcome.

b) Partner B: Go to page 97.
2.06
Partner A: Listen to the dialogue between Sarah and Mr Thomson. Fill in the gaps. Talk to B to find out if your answers are correct.

S I'm very interested in the part-time job as a cruise assistant.
T Do you have any … (1) experience?
S I've done two work placements so far.
T That sounds … (2). We need somebody to work at the weekends from … (3) or from 4 pm to 10 pm.
S Working at the weekends is perfect for me.
T We can talk about more details in an interview. Can you come on … (4)?
S Yes, that's fine. What do I need to bring?
T Can you bring … (5), please?
S I'm looking forward to meeting you on Saturday.

c) Read your role card and act out a dialogue with your partner.

> **Role card**
>
> **Partner A**
> You are the manager of a coffee shop in an international holiday park. You need some motivated part-time workers for your young team. Your mobile is ringing …
> 1 (*Melde dich höflich.*) Frage den Anrufer, was du für ihn tun kannst.
> 3 (*Drücke Freude über sein Interesse aus.*) Frage, ob Arbeitserfahrung vorhanden ist.
> 5 (*Zeige dich erfreut.*) Deine Firma braucht jemanden, der freitagabends und samstags arbeiten kann.
> 7 Schlage ein Vorstellungsgespräch für nächsten Freitag, 16 Uhr vor.
> 9 Es soll ein Lebenslauf mitgebracht werden.
> 11 Verabschiede dich (*höflich*).

7 SPEAKING   Talking about jobs

a) Say what you can see in the pictures and talk about the two jobs:
- What do you have to do in the job?
- What personal qualities and skills do you need to do the job?
- What's good / bad about the job?

b) Would you like to do one of these jobs? Say why (not). Talk about your plans for the future.

> Keep the conversation going for at least three minutes.
> - Always react to your partner's opinion.
> - Ask your partner questions.
> - **Answer more than just *yes* or *no*.**

MORE CHALLENGE 3

Creative writing

! Den Wortschatz von diesen Seiten findest du im Vocabulary auf S. 234.

1 WRITING   Looking to the future

a) Pick one of the tasks below (A–D).

A
About me: Ten years from now

Look into the future and write about yourself and your life – ten years from now. Start like this:

I'm a very different person now than when I was a teenager ten years ago. …

- You're writing about the future, but use the present tense – it's more exciting.
- Use your °imagination. Add lots of interesting details about what you look like, your personality, your job, your family, your °relationships, your feelings.

B
A story: The change

Continue this story:

When Andrew started his first job at the ice cream shop last Saturday, he had no idea that his life was going to change – °forever! …

- Your story can be as long or as short as you like. But keep it simple.
- Write about only one setting.
- Use only one main character, but you can have °minor characters.
- Only one plot – one thing should happen.

C
A scene: The new °flatmate

Finish this scene:

Emma and Julia are in their first flat. They're very excited about it. But now they need a third person to share the flat, so they're interviewing Justin.

Emma	Hi Justin, I'm Emma.
Julia	And I'm Julia.
Justin	… Er … hi …
Emma	And this is our flat …
Julia	It's nice, isn't it?
Justin	Yeah, but it looks very dark.

…

- Justin doesn't sound very enthusiastic, does he?
- But the girls really need a new flatmate, so make them sound really enthusiastic.
- You decide. Does Justin get the room?

D
A poem: You're nearly an adult

Read this poem from a parent to a teenager. Then write a °response from a teenager to a parent. It can be a poem.

You aren't a kid any more, are you?
You don't need your mummy, do you?
You can think for yourself, can't you?
You don't want my advice, do you?
You can stand on your own two feet, can't you?
You're nearly an adult, aren't you?
But you still expect pocket money, don't you?

- This isn't a °serious poem, so your response can be funny too.
- Think of the °typical things a teenager says to parents.
- If you write a poem, it doesn't have to °rhyme.

b) Swap your texts. Give each other feedback. Then read or perform some of the texts for the class.

2 LANGUAGE Question tags

a) Compare these two speech bubbles. What's the difference? Which sentence is better for conversations, 1 or 2? Does 2 expect the other person to agree or to disagree?

1 It's a fantastic flat!

2 It's a fantastic flat, isn't it?

b) Complete the FOCUS box.

FOCUS

"You can think for yourself, can't you?" "You aren't a kid any more, are you?"

1 You can use a **question tag** (*Frageanhängsel*) when you want the other person to …
2 A **question tag** is negative when the **main verb** is …
3 A **question tag** is positive when the **main verb** is …

▶ *Language file 31, p. 203*

c) Here are some more sentences. Pick the correct question tag for each one.
1 Colleges in the US can be very expensive, …
2 You don't have to go to college to be successful, …
3 Steve Jobs was the head of *Apple*, …
4 Steve Jobs went to college, …
5 *Apple* is a very successful company, …
6 *Pixar* made some great films, …

can't they? • didn't he? • didn't they? • do you? • isn't it? • wasn't he?

d) Listen to the short conversations and check your answers in c).

e) Use question tags and make these sentences more suitable for a conversation.
1 The weather is great today.
2 The history test was difficult.
3 We don't have any homework.
4 The new Bond film looks exciting.
5 Manchester United didn't play well.
6 You can swim well.

f) Write a good conversation for the people in this picture. Use a few question tags.
Example:

Girl	Hi. You're new here, aren't you?
Boy	Yeah, we just moved here.
Girl	The weather is terrible, isn't it?
Boy	Yeah, it is. Stand under my umbrella.
Girl	Thanks. So, how do you like our town?
	It's nice, … …

Unit 4

Generation *like*

▶ KV 27   ▶ DFF 4.1   ▶ INKL p.62–63

1 What's cool and what's not?

a) **Think:** Pick five images that you like and five images that you dislike.

b) **Pair:** Explain your reactions.

c) **Share:** Which images got the most *likes* and the most *dislikes* in the class?

2 LISTENING   Teens react

a) Copy this table. Listen to four teens talking and note down which five images (A–R) the teens are talking about.

b) Listen again. Note down if the teens think the things are cool (✓) or not (✗).

	1	2	3	4	5
Which picture?	B	G	F	H	E
Amelia	✗	✓	✗	✗	✓
Scarlett	✓	✗	✓	✓	✗
Mohammed	✓	✓	✓	✗	✓
Thomas	✗	✗	✓	✗	✗

74

▶ KV 28   ▶ INKL p. 62–63

3 YOUR TASK   A survey in your class

Step 1: Collect pictures of things you think people in your class will find cool (films, music groups, styles, gadgets, etc.). 👥 Together choose the six coolest pictures. Label them 1–6.

Step 2: 👥 Do a survey in your class. Find out which of your six pictures people think are cool (or not), and why. Before you start, design a table so you can note down the reactions and reasons. Then talk to as many people as you can.

More help | p. 130

Step 3: 👥 Analyse your results. Which were the most and least popular pictures? Discuss why you think some pictures were or weren't popular with everybody.

Step 4: Present the results of your survey to the class.

More help | p. 130

▶ Workbook 1, p. 47

4 THEME 1

▶ KV 29   ▶ INKL p. 64–65

Screenagers

1 Before you read

a) What do you think a screenager is? Discuss and make notes.

b) Read the text and find out if you were right.

Being a screenager

Today's teenagers were born into the digital world, a world where screens are everywhere – TV screens, smartphone screens, tablet screens, laptop screens ... The average American teen spends 8.5 hours per day in front of a screen! In Britain it's a little less, about 7 hours per day. These screenagers don't look at only one screen – they usually multitask. They video-chat on their smartphone, play a game on their tablet and watch a programme on TV, all at the same time.

Not every teen is like this of course, and many have hobbies and interests away from their screens. But digital technology is part of every teen's world and the attraction of TV, video games and social media is strong. Most teens feel the pressure to do as their friends do. About 60% of teenagers today watch at least 20 hours of TV per week. About 94% of teenagers have social media accounts. So what are the pros and cons of being a screenager?

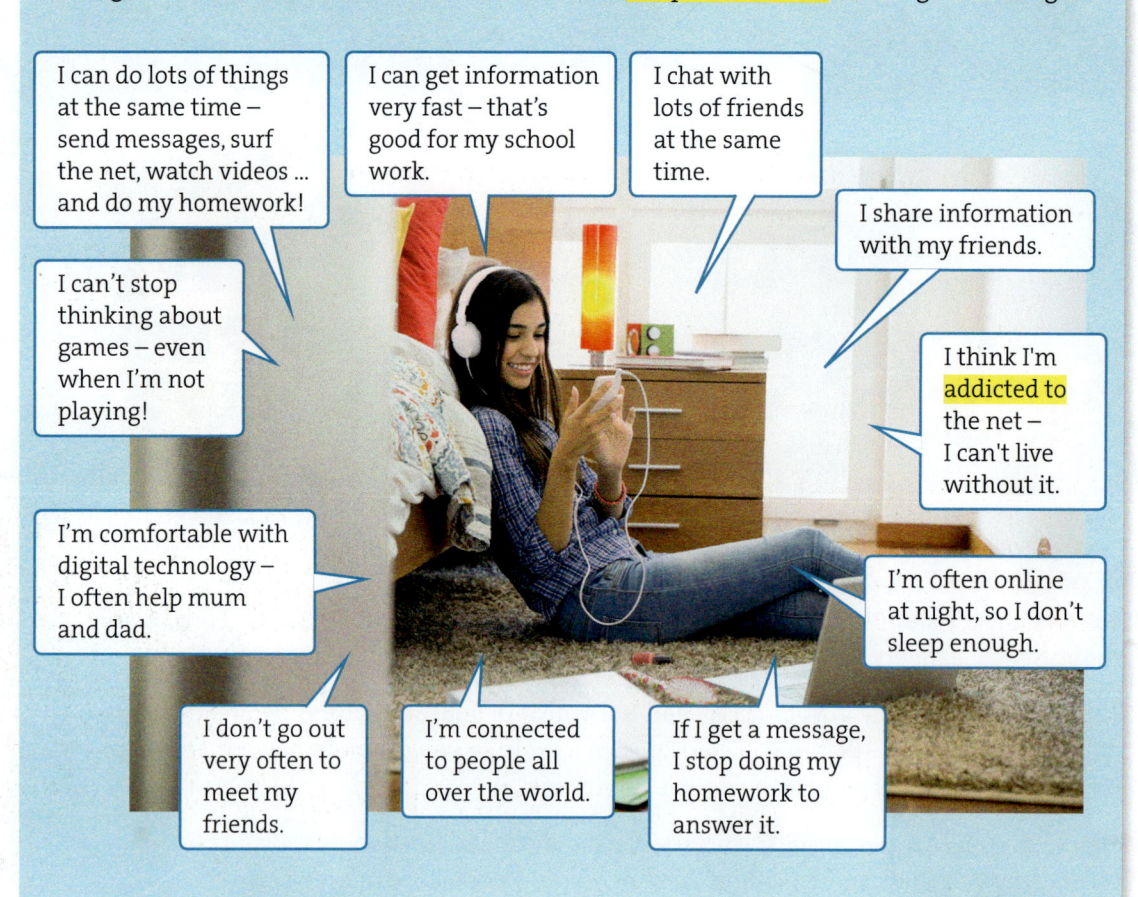

- I can do lots of things at the same time – send messages, surf the net, watch videos ... and do my homework!
- I can get information very fast – that's good for my school work.
- I chat with lots of friends at the same time.
- I share information with my friends.
- I can't stop thinking about games – even when I'm not playing!
- I think I'm addicted to the net – I can't live without it.
- I'm comfortable with digital technology – I often help mum and dad.
- I'm often online at night, so I don't sleep enough.
- I don't go out very often to meet my friends.
- I'm connected to people all over the world.
- If I get a message, I stop doing my homework to answer it.

▶ KV 29   ▶ DFF 4.2   ▶ DFF 4.3   ▶ INKL p. 64–65

2 READING — Working with the text

a) Copy this table and take notes from the text on p. 76.

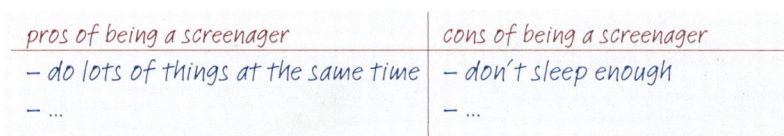

pros of being a screenager	cons of being a screenager
– do lots of things at the same time	– don't sleep enough
– ...	– ...

▶ Skills file 6.6, p. 169

b) Finish this sentence:
A screenager is someone who ...

c) Are you a screenager? Why (not)?

d) ⬤ Write about your digital world. You can find ideas on p. 76. Put your text in your DOSSIER.

3 LISTENING — Digital habits

3.02

a) O Some people are talking about digital habits. First read the tasks. Then listen and pick the correct endings.

1. Kumar can't focus on his school work because of Ⓐ video games. Ⓑ videos. Ⓒ messages.
2. Oscar wants to Ⓐ stop playing games. Ⓑ find new games. Ⓒ do more homework and sport.
3. Devon isn't allowed to use her phone Ⓐ at breakfast. Ⓑ at school. Ⓒ in bed.
4. Devon's mother complains that Devon Ⓐ doesn't talk to her. Ⓑ doesn't do her homework. Ⓒ doesn't sleep enough.
5. Mr Davis says that kids need to Ⓐ learn more. Ⓑ give their brains a rest. Ⓒ do more homework.

▶ Skills file 5, p. 166

b) Now read these sentences. Then listen again and complete them.

1. Kumar says he's a *drifter* because he ...
2. Someone who plays a lot of games is a ...
3. Devon is a social *butterfly* because she ...
4. Devon's mother misses ...
5. Mr Davis says most young people use computers for ...

More challenge 1 | p. 131

4 SPEAKING — Young people together

Partner B: Go to page 97.
Partner A:

a) Look at the photo and think about these questions:
- What's happening? What are they doing?
- Do they know each other? Are they friends?

b) Describe your photo to your partner. Then listen to her / him. Compare your photos.

▶ Skills file 9, p. 179

c) ⬤ Talk about these questions:
- How do you communicate with your friends?
- What kind of things do you and your friends do together?

▶ Text file 4, pp. 154–155   ▶ Workbook 2–4, p. 48

4 THEME 2

Perfect profiles

1 Profile pictures

a) Look at the article below. Which kind of profile picture do you like best? Can you think of any other kinds of profile pictures? Compare ideas with a partner.

More practice 1 — p. 132

Your kind of profile picture?

If you use social media, then you probably have a profile picture. So which kind of picture do you prefer?

1 The standard profile picture
Many people just use a basic profile photo. But you could be more imaginative.

2 The group picture
Usually a group photo is taken somewhere cool and everyone in the photo looks extremely happy.

3 The action picture
Some people spend hours trying to take the perfect action photo.

4 The pet photo
Pets are cute. Who doesn't love a picture of a puppy or a kitten?

5 The avatar profile picture
If you don't want to show your real face on your page, then this is perfect.

6 The °arty picture
Some people love to be creative and do something different.

7 The 'here's some stuff that I like' picture
This could be anything at all: a place, your favourite food, a pair of shoes …

There's one more thing. Before you put up a picture, think about this. If someone searches the internet for your name and this picture comes up, are you happy for them to see it? If the answer is yes, go ahead. If the answer is no, don't!

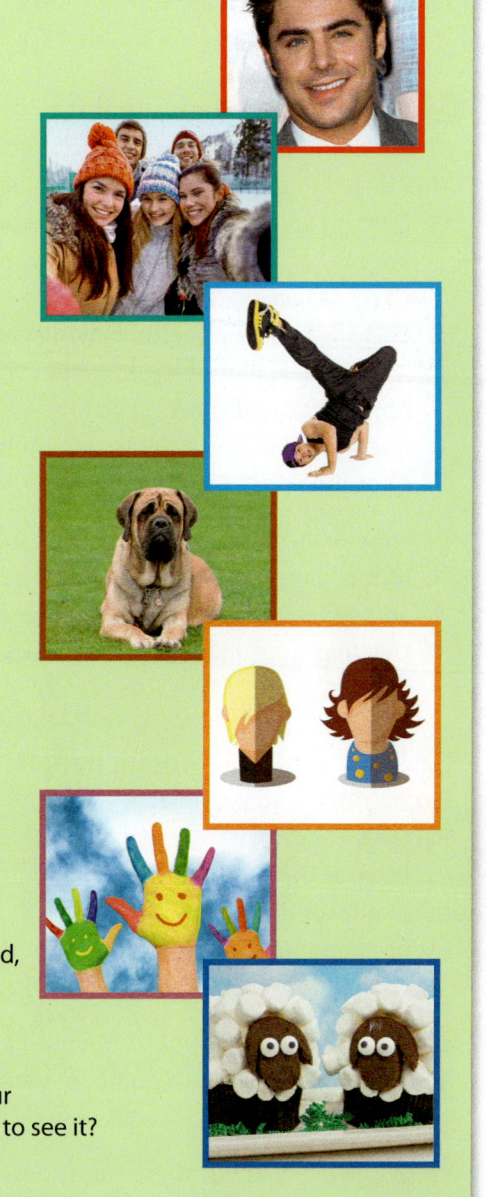

---

b) Find a profile picture that you like, e.g. of a celebrity. Prepare a talk about it. (1–2 mins.) First describe the picture. Then say why you like it and what it tells you about that person.

More help — p. 132

▶ Workbook 5, p. 49

▶ KV 30 ▶ KV 31 ▶ KV 32 ▶ DFF 4.4 ▶ INKL p. 66–67

2 Selfies

a) Which of these pictures would you call a selfie? Explain.

A   B   C

b) Put the paragraphs (A–D) into a logical order. What words or phrases helped you decide?

A
Why do some people hate selfies? Firstly, they say that the people who take them are *vain*. For example, people often use special apps to improve their photos and make themselves look good. Secondly, *critics* say that selfies can *actually* make you feel bad. For example, if you *post* your selfie on social media and nobody likes it, it can be *depressing*.

B
Selfies are the photos that people take of themselves with their phones or tablets. Today everybody takes selfies – teenagers, adults, celebrities, presidents and *astronauts*. We post them on social media to show other people what we are like and what we're doing.

C
To sum up, I think it's normal to take selfies. I definitely don't hate them. Like lots of famous people, I take them because they're fun!

D
On the other hand, maybe the critics are too negative about selfies. Lots of *artists* have painted *self-portraits* over the years. They usually wanted to look good, and they definitely wanted people to look at their picture. *In other words*, selfies are °*modern-day* self-portraits.

c) ● You could add these sentences to the text. Where do they fit best? Compare ideas.

So they feel that selfies are a bad idea.

Although the word selfie is new, self-portraits aren't.

In my opinion, the critics can relax.

People started taking them in about 2002 with the first camera phones.

More practice 2 | p. 132

3 WRITING   For and against tattoos

a) Collect ideas for a written discussion on this topic: "Tattoos – are they a good idea or not?" Make a plan, then write your text.

More help | p. 133

b) Reading circle: Put your texts on the wall. Read other people's texts. Write positive comments on the texts you like best. Read out the most popular essays.

! A typical **written discussion** looks like this:

Paragraph 1 introduction – describe the general topic
Paragraph 2 *arguments* for (or against)
Paragraph 3 arguments against (or for)
Paragraph 4 *conclusion* – give your personal opinion

▶ Skills file 8.7, p. 178

Box: Voc., p. 227

Box: Voc., p. 228

▶ Workbook 6–7, p. 49

THEME 3

▶ INKL p. 68–69

Targeting teens

1 You and ads

a) 👥 Talk about these questions.
- Where do you see ads?
- How many ads do you think you see in one day?
- What kind of ads do you look at? Why?

b) Read the article for more information on ads. Does anything surprise you?

Are you ad-savvy?

A **Do you know** why ads target teens? Firstly there are lots of teens, about 33 million in the USA. Teens have money. Teens want to be cool. Teens want to fit in. A teen can see up to 3000 ads in one day – on °billboards, in shop windows, on buses and trains, on TV and in magazines, and of course on the internet.

B **Do you know** that one in three teens who drink alcohol are influenced by ads? And most of the fast food ads target young people. So if we understand how ads work, we can reduce the dangers for teens.

C **Do you know** that advertisers understand that teens like to be cool? But what is cool? This changes all the time. So to find out what cool means, advertisers use '°coolhunters'. These are people who go out and meet teens. They look for new trends, different and interesting styles. Then the companies use this information to design the next products and make the next ads.

D **Do you know** that there are lots of tricks in ads? Here are some examples:
> Products often look amazing in ads but not so good in real life.
> Ads repeat a product name many times so that you remember it.
> They show beautiful people who are happy. And you want to be happy too.
> Ads use stars from films, music and sport. If they like the product, it must be good!
> They suggest that if you use the product you'll be 'cool' and have 'good times'.
> They often use music – a jingle. And when you hear the jingle again you think of the product.
> They hide the truth. For example, they don't tell you that there's lots of sugar in cola.

E **Do you know** that teen vloggers do advertising too? They tell the world what they like on the internet. The big ad companies watch this and if a vlogger has lots of followers, the ad companies get interested. They send free °samples to the vlogger – things like shoes, clothes, make-up, etc. Then the vloggers talk about these products in their vlogs – that's advertising. So let's get ad-savvy!

▶ DFF 4.5   ▶ INKL p. 68–69

2 Headings

O Pick a heading for each paragraph (A–E).
Note – there's one extra heading.   p. 133

	Heading	Paragraph
1	Advertising strategies	
2	Teens influence teens	
3	Ads can be bad for teens	
4	Looking for cool people	
5	Stop ads for teens today!	
6	Teens are good customers	

3 WORDS

Find words and phrases that mean:
1. be like other people (paragraph A)
2. big ads that you see in the street (A)
3. make less or smaller (B)
4. fashion (2 possible answers) (C)
5. things that you buy (D)
6. say something again (D)
7. advertising music (D)
8. someone who does a video blog (E)
9. understand how ads work (E)

4 MEDIATION   The ad industry

Jemand interessiert sich für den Artikel auf Seite 80. Erzähle – auf Deutsch:
1. … warum Jugendliche besser über Werbung Bescheid wissen sollten.
2. … warum viel Werbung auf Jugendliche zielt.
3. … welche Strategien in der Werbung verwendet werden (mindestens drei).
4. … wie die Werbeindustrie herausfindet, was Jugendliche mögen.
5. … welche Jugendlichen besonders interessant für die Werbeindustrie sind und warum.

▶ Skills file 10, pp. 180–181   More practice 3+4   p. 134

5 ACTIVITY   Get ad-savvy!

Pick one of these activities.

Your ad diary

a) Keep an ad diary for a day. Note down:
- How many ads do you see?
- Where do you see them?
- How do they target teens?
- Which ads do you find interesting?
- Do any ads make you want to buy something?
- Do any ads irritate you? Why?

b) Report about your ad diary to the class.

Ad report

a) First, collect ads. Cut them out of newspapers and magazines. You can take photos of billboards and posters. And you can take screenshots of internet ads too.

b) Next, find examples of the tricks in paragraph D on p. 80.

c) Do a poster presentation for the class. Talk about the tricks you've found.

More practice 5 p. 134   More challenge 2 p. 134

4 FOCUS ON LANGUAGE

▶ INKL p. 73

1 Social media: what can go wrong

a) Read the text and find the answers to these questions:
1. What was the problem at the party?
2. How had Leah invited her friends?
3. What were Mr Smith's two mistakes?
4. Who phoned the police?

Hundreds of teenagers gatecrash party

On Friday evening police were called to an address in north London. When they arrived, they found over 200 young people at the house. The owner of the house,
5 Don Smith, wasn't there, and his 15-year-old daughter, Leah, couldn't control the situation.

Leah's father knew about the party. He had agreed that she could have a party for her 16th birthday with about 30 guests. Leah sent out an invitation on social media.
10 That was the first mistake. She found out later that lots of people saw the invitation and decided to join the fun and gatecrash the party.

Then came the second mistake. Because everything seemed calm, Leah's father decided to go out for a while. After he
15 left, the gatecrashers started to arrive, and Leah wasn't able to reach him on his phone. He had left it at home – another mistake. Leah said, "It was very scary. I didn't know the people. I didn't want them to come in, but they just pushed the door and walked in."

20 There was no damage in the house, but the party-goers left a lot of rubbish, and a few things were stolen, including Don Smith's smartphone. The next day Don and Leah had to do a big clean-up. Mr Smith wasn't cross with his daughter. "Poor Leah, it wasn't her fault. I should have stayed at home.
25 But we've all learned a lesson about using social media. You have to be careful. We were lucky. If the neighbours hadn't phoned the police, things would have been different," he said.

b) Leah made several mistakes.
What would you have done?
I would have …
I wouldn't have …

c) If you had been Leah's dad, what would you have done?
I would have …
I wouldn't have …

> used social media.
> sent the invitations by email.
> asked my dad to take his phone.
> let my dad leave.
> …

> helped Leah organize the party.
> left Leah alone in the house.
> checked that I had my phone.
> …

▶ DFF 4.6   ▶ INKL p.73

d) How could things have been different? Match the parts.
1. If Leah had sent emails, only thirty people would have come …
2. If Leah's dad had stayed, he would have …
3. If Leah's dad had taken his phone, Leah would have …
4. If Leah had phoned her dad, he would have …

A come home straight away.
B phoned him.
C to the party.
D stopped the gatecrashers.

2 If I had … (Conditional sentences type 3)
Look at what Leah says. Then answer the questions in the FOCUS box.

After the party

If I had been more careful, everything would have been OK.

FOCUS
1. First think about the meaning of what Leah says: Was she careful? Was everything OK?
2. What verb form goes with 'If' here?
   (a) simple present (b) simple past (c) past perfect
3. The other verb form has three parts. What are they?
   ? + ? + past participle

▶ Language file 24, p. 197

3 What would you have done? p.135
a) Read the sentences. Then choose A or B.
1. **Ben** Leah didn't invite me to her party, but I went. What would you have done?
   You A I would have gone to the party.
   B I wouldn't have gone to the party.
2. **Ben** For my birthday my parents said I could have a party or I could go to a theme park. I chose the party.
   You A I would have done the same.
   B I would have chosen the theme park.
3. **Ben** My friend and I wanted to go to the cinema. I waited at the cinema but he didn't come, so I went home.
   You A I would have phoned my friend.
   B I would have gone in without him.
4. **Ben** I was angry because my friend bought the same shirt as me.
   You A I would have been angry too.
   B I would have been happy.

4 Oh dear, what a shame! p.135
Complete the sentences with the correct form of the verb in brackets.
1. I was in trouble because I was late.
   If I *had got up* (get up) earlier, I wouldn't have been late.
2. My test results weren't great. If I had worked harder, I … (get) better marks.
3. I chatted with friends after class and missed my bus. If I … (not chat) for so long, I wouldn't have missed it.
4. I couldn't do my homework because I forgot my book. If I had remembered my book, I … (do) my homework.
5. I didn't tell my friend that I was going out. If I had known that she wanted to come, I … (phone) her.
6. I don't have any money for a phone. If I … (work) in the holidays, I would have earned some.

More challenge 3 p.135

▶ Workbook 10, p. 52

4 TEXT

▶ KV 33   ▶ DFF 4.7   ▶ INKL p. 70–72

1 Before you read

a) Discuss these questions:
1. What do you think the story below is about? (Look at the pictures, headings and slogans.)
2. Do you play computer games? If so, what kind of games?
3. Do you think there are any risks with computer games?

b) Now read *Gamer*. You can read an easier version on pp. 136–138.

Gamer (adapted from the novel by Chris Bradford)

Part 1   Bread

I can't stop watching the fighters – *Thunderbolt*, the kickboxer and *Destroy*, the °heavyweight boxer. *Destroy* puts his head
5 down and runs at *Thunderbolt* … everybody shouts. *Destroy* wins, the game is over for *Thunderbolt*.

Then a big red and black logo comes onto the 3D screen: **VK**.
10 A voice says,

"**Virtual Kombat**, so real that it hurts."

After that an ad comes on for *Synapse Drinks* – the company that sponsors Virtual Kombat. I try not to look. Adverts just make me want
15 what I can't have.

Now the fight is over, the street kids °turn away. They move into the lanes with the other rubbish that fills this city. Unwanted. Ignored. Forgotten. I'm one of them. I lost my parents to
20 the killer virus of 2030. It killed millions.

The strange thing was that kids didn't get the virus. The doctors said that the kids were °spreading it. Some parents even dumped their own kids on the streets. Now there are
25 thousands of us.

The whole world went crazy. Then the °army °took over. After that, people stopped going outside. The adults were still scared they might catch something. Most people escaped into life
30 on the net. That's when **VK** first started:

"**Virtual Kombat – the most realistic fighting game ever!**"

That's what the ads say. Virtual Kombat is *the* number 1 game show in the world. Everyone
35 watches or plays it. Huge street screens are everywhere in the city. On the screen in front of me there's a huge 3D picture of a *Zing* °energy bar. I turn away – it's °torture. Then I hear the **VK** jingle, and we see the highlights of today's
40 fights. They show every horrible detail of the fights.

"**Virtual Kombat. So real that it hurts!**"

The only thing that hurts me at the moment is my stomach. I haven't eaten in days. **VK** helps
45 me to forget that I'm hungry. When the show is on, you don't think about it. But when it's over, you feel hungry again.

▶ KV 33 ▶ INKL p. 70–72

I go up a narrow backstreet. There are big bins here, behind the restaurants where the rich
50 people eat. They still go out – to the huge shopping malls in their big cars. If I'm lucky, I might find some food in the bins.
Then I hear a voice. "Give it to me!"

In the lane I see two °lads standing over a little
55 girl and boy. The girl is holding a bag. The taller lad hits her in the face and pulls the bag from her. The girl doesn't cry. Street kids are tough.
"Leave my sis alone," shouts the boy as he °steps
60 between them.
"Give that back. It's ours!"
"Finders keepers, losers weepers," the other lad says. He's short, with dark red hair. He pushes the boy to the ground and laughs as the kid
65 hits his head on the street.
"You won't believe this, Juice," says the taller lad. "They have bread!"

Part 2   Street fighter

"Give me a bit, Stick," Juice says.
70 "No way." Stick holds the bag away.
"Ah, come on," Juice says. "The others won't know if I eat some."
While they're arguing, I creep up and take the bread.
75 "Oi," Stick shouts, as he turns around.
"That's ours!" he says.
"Finders keepers, losers weepers," I say. I'm not afraid. You can't be afraid in this city. Stick and Juice are just bullies who °pick on smaller kids.
80 But it's two against one.
"Now °zap off," I say.
Stick has a °weapon. He tries to hit me. I drop the bread and move forward to stop him. I catch his arm and he drops his weapon. Juice
85 jumps on me, but I hit him in the stomach and I throw him over my shoulder onto the ground.

"Wait till Shark hears about this," Stick says.
"He'll get you!" I say nothing as they walk away. But inside I'm shouting at myself, "IDIOT!"
90 Shark is bad news.
The little boy and girl stare at me. It's clear they're twins – blond hair, blue eyes. They look afraid and it breaks my heart.
"What are your names?" I ask.
95 "Tommy – and my °sis is Tammy," the boy says. As hungry as I am, I give the little girl the bag of bread. She says nothing, but she takes it.
"Who are you?" whispers Tommy.
"Scott," I say.
100 "Where did you learn to fight like that?" Tommy asks.
"*Street fighter 7*."
Before the virus I lived with my parents in a

85

house on the south side of the city. I had some
105 great video games and my dad and I were
addicted to *Street Fighter*. We trained every
day.

Tammy opens the bag. Then she looks around
the lane like a °frightened mouse.
110 "She doesn't say much, your sis," I say to
Tommy. Tommy °shakes his head. Tammy
takes out a big piece of bread, gives half of it to
Tommy and passes the bag to me. I look in the
bag. She has left me more than half. I eat it
115 hungrily.
"This bread is fresh," I say with my mouth full.
"The cook always makes a little extra for us,"
Tommy says.
I eat the bread quickly. "That was great."
120 Tammy smiles for the first time. But suddenly
her smile is gone.
"THERE HE IS!"
I turn around. Stick and Juice are at the end of
the lane. This time they have the Shark gang
125 with them. Shark himself is in front. He's
wearing a black °leather jacket. He grins at me,
and I see his broken teeth. °No need to guess
how he got his name. Shark takes out a knife.
It's time to fight or run. I run.

Part 3   Roof escape
130 They run after me as I run down a narrow side
street. I know this area of the city °like the back
of my hand and I take a °short cut onto Main
Street. I run between the cars, across the road
and into a lane on the other side. But I can't
135 lose Shark's gang. They're °closing on me fast.
I can hear Shark's voice. I have to escape over
the roofs. As I run around a corner, I see what

I need. I jump onto a big bin and then onto a
140 fire escape ladder. I climb and climb until I get
to the roof – 12 floors up. Below me I see the
city, the lights, the big screens, ... And I see
Shark and the gang – they're following me.

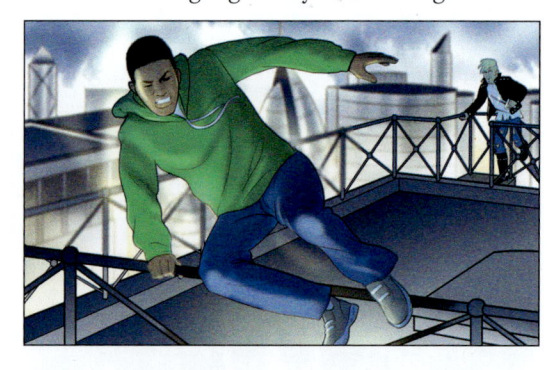

I jump from one roof to another one – a big
145 jump. I turn around and watch. Shark jumps
too. He runs – he's fast ... then I can't see him.
Suddenly he's in front of me. My only escape is
a building to the right, but the roof is a long
way down. Shark grins from ear to ear as he
150 takes out his knife. I have no °choice, I have to
jump. I throw myself into the air. For a few
seconds I seem to fall and fall. Then I crash
onto the roof of the other building. I hurt my
leg. Then something flies through the air ...
155 and Shark lands next to me. I can't run ...
I see the °flash of Shark's knife.

At that moment we hear the **VK** jingle.
We both °freeze. We know what that means.
"I'll get you later," Shark says and he
160 disappears.

Part 4   The **VK** truck
As I get to the square I see a lot of street kids
around a big white truck with the **VK** logo on
the side.

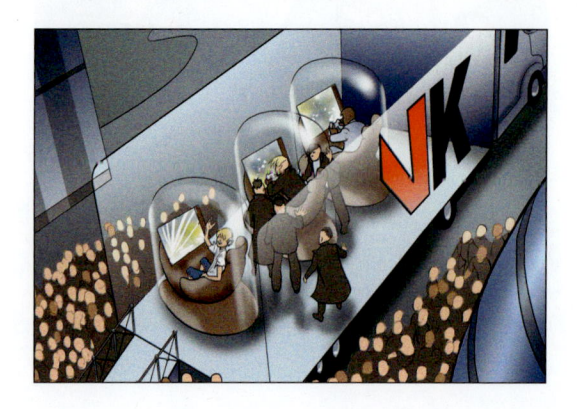

▶ KV 33   ▶ KV 34   ▶ INKL p. 70–72

165 The **VK** truck is the only way to get off these streets. It's a mobile **VK** game station. If you're good enough, you can become a **VK** games tester. That means food every day, a bed, school – a chance of a normal life.
170 Even if they don't pick you, you get free food. But I'm too late. All the food is gone, all the seats are full. Then I see Shark. He has a seat and his gang is near him. As I move away, I hear my name.

175 I see Tommy. He has a seat too and he's waving at me to come over.
"Take my place," he says.
"Are you crazy?" I say.   Box: Voc., p. 230
"I can't leave my sis, can I?" he says.
180 He gets off his seat.
"I was holding it for you," he says.
"Everybody ready to play?" a loud voice says.
The game begins.

2 Which part …
- shows us what kind of person Scott is?
- gives information about street kids?
- gives some hope for Scott's future?
- describes an exciting race through the city?

3 Information in the text
Complete the following sentences with information from the text.
1 In this story there are lots of street kids because … (part 1, lines 18–25)
2 Not everybody is poor and hungry, for example … (part 1, lines 49–51)
3 Scott can fight well because … (part 2, lines 102–107)
4 Tammy and Tommy know that Scott is hungry, so … (part 2, lines 111–114)
5 Scott is happy when he sees a fire escape ladder, because … (part 3, lines 137–141)
6 If Scott becomes a games tester, he … (part 4, lines 167–170)

4 Characters in the story
a) Make notes about two or more characters in the story under these headings:
NAME, AGE, PERSONALITY, APPEARANCE, WHAT YOU THINK OF HIM/HER   ▶ Skills file 6.7, p. 169

b) **Walk around:** Compare your notes with other students.   More practice 6 p. 139

5 WRITING   An email to the author
Write an email (100–120 words) to the author of *Gamer*, Chris Bradford.   ▶ Skills file 8.3, p. 174
Say what you think of …
- the story and why you think that
- the main characters and why
- the setting and why
- the mood of the story and how it makes you feel
- gaming and why it can be bad   More challenge 4 p. 139

▶ Workbook 15–17, p. 55

4 SKILLS TRAINING Speaking course (4)
▶ INKL p. 74–75

Taking part in discussions

1 VIEWING Box: Voc., p. 231 **Shocking** news!

a) First look at these scenes from the film. Then talk about these questions:
- Where is the teenager? - What is he / she doing? - Why? - What is he / she thinking?

① Amy
②
③ Marek
④

b) Now watch the film and find a caption for each of the four scenes above.

c) Here are some phrases from the film. Can you guess the missing words? More help p. 139
1 How can they do that? That's … news!
2 Well, maybe it's … that teenagers do too much '**vamping**'.
3 Well actually, I don't think that's such a … idea.
4 Sorry, I just can't agree … that.
5 Yes, that's a … point.
6 In my opinion, … has to be done.
7 Another … is 'sleepy texting'.
8 It's true to … that we can decide things ourselves.
9 I see … you mean.
10 You're right … that.

d) Now watch the film again and check your answers to c). Note down more good phrases for discussions. More practice 7 p. 140

2 Expressing your opinion

a) Make six groups. Each group gets a statement from the box. Write it on a poster. Discuss your statement. Then write a short comment on it and put it on the wall.

b) Gallery walk: Move to other statements with your group. Discuss them and add your comments.

c) Return to your own statement and discuss all the comments.

1 Social media is dangerous – you have to be careful.
2 Digital technology is the best **invention** ever.
3 Phones shouldn't be allowed in teenagers' bedrooms at night.
4 Phones should be allowed in schools.
5 Gaming is great, it trains you for life.
6 Gaming is a waste of time, you don't learn anything.

▶ INKL p.74–75

3 NOW YOU Listen and speak
You're going to take part in a class discussion on this statement:
"Video games are good for you."

Step 1: Prepare your arguments
a) Each group prepares a list of arguments. You will either be <u>for</u> video games, or <u>against</u> them, or <u>not sure</u>. [More help p.140]

b) Choose at least three of your arguments. Think of examples and reasons to support them. Make notes. [More help p.140]

Step 2: Take part in a discussion
a) Arrange the classroom like this. At least one person from each group should take part. The **observers** will watch and make notes on a feedback sheet. [More help p.140]

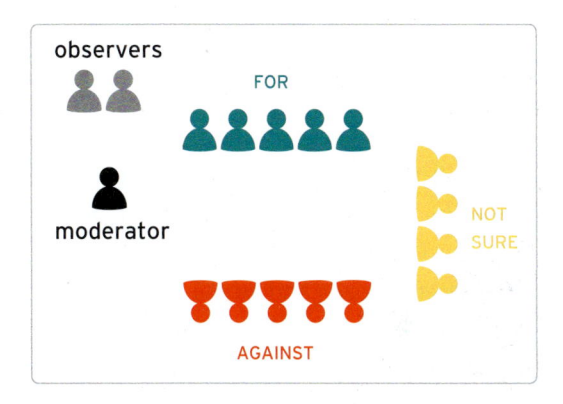

b) The **moderator** will lead the discussion. If you want to speak, put up your hand. Everybody should speak at least once in the discussion.

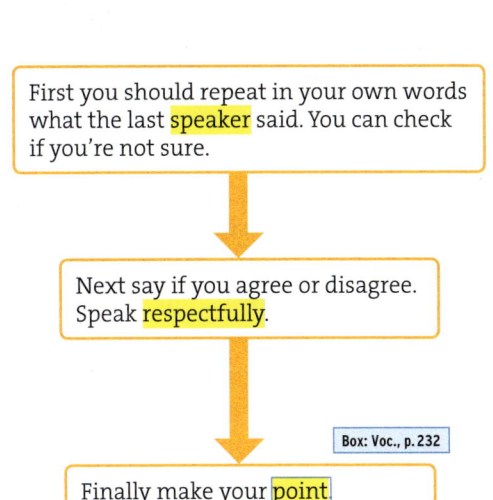

> First you should repeat in your own words what the last **speaker** said. You can check if you're not sure.

> You said that … / So you think that …
> Is that right?

> Next say if you agree or disagree. Speak **respectfully**.

> I agree. / That's a good point / true.
> I see what you mean but …
> I don't think you can say that.
> Sorry, I don't agree with you because …

[Box: Voc., p.232]

> Finally make your **point**. Give reasons and examples.

> In my opinion, / I think / I feel / …
> That's why … / For example, …
> Don't forget that … /

c) During the discussion: If different speakers persuade you with their arguments, you can change sides in the classroom.

> ❗ Don't change sides when someone is speaking. Wait until they have finished.
> Observers shouldn't move. They just watch.

Step 3: Think about the discussion
Go back to your groups.
If you took part in the discussion:
- What do you think you did well?
- What didn't you do so well?

If you watched the discussion:
- Give feedback to your group member(s).
- Use the feedback sheet. ▶ Skills file 7.4, p. 172

▶ Workbook 18–21, pp. 57–58

STOP! CHECK! GO!
▸ KV 35 ▸ DFF 4.6 ▸ DFF 4.7 ▸ INKL p. 76–77

1 WORDS   Media buddies
Read the text. For the underlined words, choose a word with a similar meaning from 1–8.
1. **A** arrive in **B** influence **C** accept
2. **A** details **B** mistakes **C** dangers
3. **A** book **B** newspaper **C** paper
4. **A** education **B** school **C** subject
5. **A** habits **B** tips **C** news
6. **A** arguments **B** advantages **C** descriptions
7. **A** difficult **B** realistic **C** illegal
8. **A** support **B** stay away from **C** post

Computers, smartphones and tablets <u>affect</u> (1) students' lives in many ways. But some young people are not aware of the <u>risks</u> (2). That's why some schools train media buddies. These students take part in a training course to improve their digital media skills. They get a <u>certificate</u> (3) that confirms they are experts in internet safety, computer security or computer games. Communication skills <u>training</u> (4) is part of the course. This helps them later to teach and advise other students. And students find it easier to accept <u>advice</u> (5) from their peers, than from their parents or teachers.

Some teachers don't think media buddies are a good idea. Here are some of their <u>reasons</u> (6): They argue that the training takes too much time after school or at the weekend. In addition, media buddies in schools can't really deal with <u>criminal</u> (7) internet activities – only the police can do that.

However, I think working with media buddies has many advantages. They can help people to <u>avoid</u> (8) serious problems.

2 LANGUAGE   If I had known …
a) Match sentences 1–4 with sentences A–D.
1. I got a virus after downloading a game from the internet.
2. A media buddy told me to change the settings of the app so that only some people can see my posts.
3. I found a website with lots of cool songs, but then my problems started.
4. I'm a fool! I bought a new gadget last week because of a cool ad.

A. If I had spoken to a media buddy first, I wouldn't have got into trouble for using an illegal music site.
B. If I hadn't done that, my parents could have seen all my conversations with my friends.
C. If I had spoken to the media buddies, I would have got something much better for the same price.
D. If the media buddies hadn't helped me to get rid of it, my dad would have been very angry.

b) 🔵 A media buddy is talking with another student. Complete his sentences with the correct verb form.
1. If you … (tell) your parents about the cyberbullying at once, they … (do) something very quickly.
2. If you … (send) me a screenshot, I … (see) the problem at once.
3. I … (show) you a more interesting computer game, if I … (know) what you like best.
4. Your PC … (crash), if you … (install) an antivirus programme.

▶ KV 35 ▶ DFF 4.2 ▶ INKL p. 76–77

3 READING Reviews

a) 🔍 Scan the teens' comments (1–5). What are they talking about – a book, a film or a game? Copy and fill in the table.

	Finn	Owen	Tess	Jamie	Aliyah
a book					
a film					
a game					

1 **Finn** "You have to think about money, fitness and lots of other things. It's not just about your players winning a game."

2 **Owen** "The best part is playing against other players who like the same tracks as you. It's a bit like dancing – but you use your fingers, not your feet."

3 **Tess** "It's a good mix of scary and funny. And the music is cool too. I love the eighties soundtrack."

4 **Jamie** "This is funny and serious at the same time. It's a great story and I loved the main character. I just couldn't stop reading it!"

5 **Aliyah** "English footballer, Wayne Rooney, is a big fan of this. I read that he has got over 4.5 million points. He must have run a long way and escaped from a lot of monsters to get that far."

b) Now read texts A–G and match them with the comments above.
(Careful: You can only match five texts.)

▶ Skills file 6.2, p. 167

A
Trillium: The twentieth and thirty-eighth centuries meet in a time-travel romance. Two totally different characters fall in love, but there are thousands of years and millions of miles between them. In the year 3797 Nika lives on a science station and does research on aliens to save the earth. In 1921, the English adventurer William goes on an expedition into the jungles of Peru to find a lost Inca temple. How do these two characters get together? Read and find out.

B
The absolutely true diary of a part-time Indian: This tells the story of Arnold, a poor boy with no hope and no future, who lives on a reservation. He decides to go to a new school where he is the only Indian. The author's writing is great! You feel you really know Arnold and you can identify with him. In the end Arnold learns that it's important to follow your dreams.

C
Top eleven: It's an entertaining game for your smartphone or tablet which allows you to live your dream as a top manager of your own football team. You create your own club and manage its finances. You buy and sell players, choose strategies and train your team. Your goal is to be the best in your league.

D
Tap tap revenge: With this app you touch your screen to the beat of music from many different bands. The aim of the game is to tap each of the coloured balls when they reach a line at the bottom of the screen. If you hit the ball on the beat, you get points. There are also "shakes", which means you have to move your gadget. There are hundreds of songs you can choose from to tap along to the beat.

E
The lost boys: It's an American teen film from the eighties, but it's still very popular. It's a bit unusual because it is a horror film and a comedy. Two brothers, Michael and Sam, move to a small town in California and they discover that there is a gang of teenage vampires in the area. Will they fight the vampires and win?

F
Temple run: Download the app on your smartphone and start running through the temple as fast as you can. At the same time, you must stay away from the scary things that look like apes. Depending on how far you run, you get points. You can play on your own, or against other players.

G
Dirty dancing: This romantic drama produced in the eighties is about a relationship between a teenage girl, Baby, and her dancing teacher. She meets him during her family's summer holiday. As Johnny teaches Baby to dance, a romance begins. The soundtrack has won many awards.

STOP! CHECK! GO!
▶ KV 35 ▶ DFF 4.1 ▶ DFF 4.4 ▶ INKL p. 76–79

4 LISTENING I can't live without my …
3.05

You are going to listen to part of a radio programme. You will hear it twice. While you are listening, first complete tasks a) and b). Then listen again and complete tasks c) and d).

a) Listen and match the people (1–4) to their favourite gadgets (A–F).

1 Blake   2 Michelle   3 Jacob   4 Dana

A game console
B tablet
C TV
D smartphone
E camera
F laptop

b) Lynn's guests mention lots of things that they do with their smartphones. Name at least six of them.

c) Listen again and complete these sentences.
1 Blake says he usually texts his friends because it's easy and …
2 Michelle likes her laptop more than her smartphone because she prefers …
3 Jacob isn't a couch potato because he plays … and he …
4 If Dana takes photos, she doesn't need a camera. She …

d) Which sentence ending is correct?
Lynn McCarthy's radio show is about …
A a new survey on digital habits.
B social networking.
C teenagers' favourite digital gadgets.

5 WRITING One week without technology

For a reality show, *PQR Radio* is inviting 35 teenagers from all over the world to one week in a camp on a beautiful island. But the camp will be 100% technology-free (no internet and no mobile gadgets).

Write an email to *PQR Radio*. Say why you would like to take part in the camp. Write 150–200 words.

! - Start your email politely.
- Introduce yourself: name, age, where you are from, …
- Talk about how important digital gadgets are for you: Which gadgets do you use most? Why are they important? What do you usually use them for?
- Say why you would like to take part in the camp.
- Talk about what you can probably learn from a week without gadgets.
- Write about the activities that you would like to do with the other young people in the camp.
- End your email politely.   ▶ Skills file 8.3, p. 174

▶ DFF 4.3 ▶ DFF 4.5 ▶ INKL p. 76–79

6 SPEAKING   Talking about a photo

Talk with your partner about the photo for 3–5 minutes. Ask your partner for his/her opinion. React, e.g. ask follow-up questions. These questions can help you.
1. What are the people doing?
2. What do they think about the situation?
3. What do you think about the situation?
4. Can you think of another situation when people shouldn't use mobiles? Give reasons.

7 MEDIATION   Generations Y and Z

Bei der Online-Recherche für eine Präsentation zum Thema *Die Generationen Y und Z* hast du den unten stehenden englischen Text gefunden. Nenne 7 Bereiche, in denen Y und Z verglichen werden und notiere die Aussagen des Textes dazu (auf Deutsch).   ▶ *Skills file 10, pp. 180–181*   More help p. 141

	Generation Y	Generation Z
1 Umgang mit Geld		
2 …		
3 …		
4 …		
5 …		
6 …		
7 …		

Contrasting Generations Y and Z

Generation Y are the kids who were born in the 1980s and grew up with desktop computers. After them comes Generation Z: They were born in the late 1990s and have grown up with touchscreens. The following statements summarize the results of new studies contrasting these two generations.

1. While Generation Y enjoyed spending money straight away, 57 per cent of Generation Z prefers saving money to spending it.
2. Generation Y spent loads of time in shopping malls, but Generation Z prefers shopping online for almost everything.
3. Generation Y grew up at a time when the economy was strong, but the economy was weak when Generation Z was growing up in times of terrorism and violence.
4. While Generation Y watched videos on YouTube, Hulu and Netflix, the kids of Generation Z create and share their own videos.
5. Generation Y loved sports and adventure, but Generation Z sees sports as something that is important for health, not for play. Their games are played inside.
6. While Generation Y used text messages, Generation Z prefers communicating through images, icons and symbols.
7. Generation Y worried about their social status and their *likes* on social media, but Generation Z worries about the economy and world ecology.

More challenge 5   p. 141

MORE CHALLENGE 4
▶ DFF 4.8

Street art

> Den Wortschatz von diesen Seiten findest du im Vocabulary auf S. 234.

1 LISTENING An outdoor art gallery

3.06

a) Look at the pictures on this page. They are all examples of street art. How are they different from the kind of art that you'd find in a museum?

b) A girl is talking to her class about some street art she saw when she was visiting London.
Listen, then answer these questions:
1 What is special about the picture and the place where she saw it?
2 What does she think the artist wanted to say with the picture?
3 Do you agree with her °analysis? Explain.

Listen again if you need to.

2 SPEAKING Talking about street art
Make notes about one of these pictures. Give a short talk about it. Speak from your notes.
- First describe it, its °location, and the materials the artist used.
- Then talk about what the artist might be trying to say.
- Finally, give your personal reaction to it.

▶ *Skills files 7.1, p. 170; 9, p. 179*

▶ KV 36

3 READING and WRITING — A Banksy film

a) Read this review of a film about the famous British street artist, Banksy. Does it make you want to watch the film? Why (not)?

°Exit through the gift shop
by Michael A., Jr.

Some films about art are boring, but this one isn't. It's basically a documentary about street art, and you find out a lot about the street artists and how they work. But there's more to it than that.

First of all we meet the film-maker, a crazy French guy living in Los Angeles. He's not a professional camera man. He just loves making films and he loves street art. So he follows the artists everywhere, and even climbs up to very dangerous places to film them as they quickly make their pictures before the police arrive. This part of the film is very °lively and interesting.

Then the French guy °gets lucky. He meets the British street artist Banksy, who is probably the most famous street artist of all. Some of his art has °sold for millions, but his identity is a secret. In the film we never see his face and his voice has been changed.

At that point the film changes. The French guy becomes a street artist himself, and the film is now all about him. °Incredibly, he becomes very successful, °even though he isn't really an artist. His art starts selling for huge °sums and things seem to go crazy.

Maybe that's the message of the film. Money is a bad influence on art. The title gives us a °hint. Art galleries and museums make people exit through their gift shops so that they spend money.

Personally I thought this film was brilliant. It was very interesting, but it was also very funny.

I think that Banksy's art is amazing. He is definitely a true artist, though I'm not so sure about the French guy. °In fact I'm not even sure if he's real. Maybe he's just a °made-up character. Nobody seems to be sure about that. But it doesn't matter. It's still a very °entertaining film.

b) Plan and write a review about a film that you've seen recently.

> ! Before you write your review, **make notes** about the film.
> - What kind of film is it?
> - Where was it made?
> - Who made it?
> - Who is in it?
> - What °aspects of the film are especially important (story, acting, music, setting, costumes, special effects)?
>
> Also think about these questions:
> - Does the film have a message?
> - Did you enjoy the film? Why (not)?
> - Would you recommend it?

▶ *Skills file 8.1, pp. 172–173*

PARTNER B

Unit 1 — Stop! Check! Go!

4 SPEAKING Talking about a picture ▶ *Unit 1, p. 26*

Partner B:

a) Describe to your partner what you can see in your picture. These questions can help you: Who? What? Where? When? Why?
▶ *Skills file 9, p. 179*

b) Listen to your partner.

c) Together find out what the pictures have in common and what is different.

Unit 2 — Stop! Check! Go!

7 SPEAKING Role-play ▶ *Unit 2, p. 49*

Partner B: Read your role card and prepare a role-play with your partner.
Start your conversation very politely. Don't forget to introduce yourselves to each other.
You have 7 minutes to prepare.

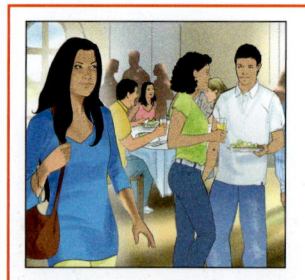

> You're a student at Green Valley High School and you're at a welcome party for exchange students from Germany. The party is great: excellent food, cool music, some people are dancing. You're standing next to the buffet when you notice an interesting looking person coming over to get a drink. Start a conversation to find out more about him / her. Keep the conversation going for at least three minutes.

Unit 3   Stop! Check! Go!

6 LISTENING   Phoning about a job   ▶ Unit 3, p. 71

b) **Partner B:** Listen to the dialogue between Sarah and Mr Thomson. Fill in the gaps. Talk to partner A to find out if your answers are correct.

S   I'm very interested in the ... (A) as a cruise assistant.
T   Do you have any work experience?
S   I've done ... (B) work placements so far.
T   That sounds really good. We need somebody to work at weekends from
    10 am to 4 pm or from 4 pm to 10 pm.
S   Working at the weekends is ... (C) for me.
T   We can talk about more details in an interview. Can you come on Saturday at 10 am?
S   Of course. What do I ... (E) to bring?
T   Bring your CV, please.
S   I'm ... (F) on Saturday.

c) Read your role card and act out a dialogue with your partner.

> **Role card**
>
> **Partner B**
> You need some extra money to buy a cool bike. An international holiday park has just opened nearby and they are offering seasonal part-time jobs in their coffee shop. You're phoning about the job ad that you saw in the coffee shop window yesterday.
> 2 Stell dich (*höflich*) vor. Sage, dass du wegen des Stellenangebots als Kellner/in anrufst.
> 4 Letzten Sommer hast du ein Betriebspraktikum in einem griechischen Restaurant gemacht.
> 6 Sage, dass das perfekt ist und du gern freitagabends und samstags arbeiten kannst.
> 8 Nimm das Angebot (*erfreut*) an. Frage, was du zum Bewerbungsgespräch mitbringen sollst.
> 10 Bestätige, dass du die Unterlagen mitbringen wirst. Bedanke und verabschiede dich (*höflich*).

Unit 4

4 SPEAKING   Young people together   ▶ Unit 4, p. 77
Partner B:

a) Look at the photo and think about these questions:
- What's happening? Where are the people?
- Do they know each other?
- Are they friends? What are they doing?

b) Describe your photo to your partner. Then listen to her / him. Compare the two photos.
   ▶ Skills file 9, p. 179

1 DIFF BANK

Unit 1

More help | **2b** VIEWING | An Australian road trip ▶ Unit 1, p. 9

Pick words from the two boxes and make phrases.

activities	
swimming	cycling
surfing	washing
running	dancing
walking	skateboarding
diving	cooking
jumping	riding
climbing	camping

places	
in a river	near a reef
on a boat	beside a road
in a wood	in the outback
in the sea	in the city
on a rock	through a desert
on a beach	in a town
on a track	at a campsite

More practice 1 | More about the film ▶ Unit 1, p. 9

- Watch the film again and make notes about these questions.
- Then compare your notes.

1. What kind of music was used in the film? Did you like it?
2. The film-maker uses °time lapse in the film – that means that these parts of the film are very fast.
- Why do you think time lapse is used?
- How does it make you feel?
- Do you like the effect of time lapse?

More challenge 1 | Your road trip film ▶ Unit 1, p. 9

a) What would you include in a two-minute film about a road trip in Germany?
First think about these questions. Then talk to a partner.

- Where would you make your film?
- What things would you show?
- What music would you use?
- When would you use time lapse (make a part of the film very fast)?

b) Write a plan for your film.

More practice 2 | An Aussie network ▶ Unit 1, p. 11

Make an Australia vocabulary network. Find words and phrases in the articles on pages 10 and 11 to add to it.

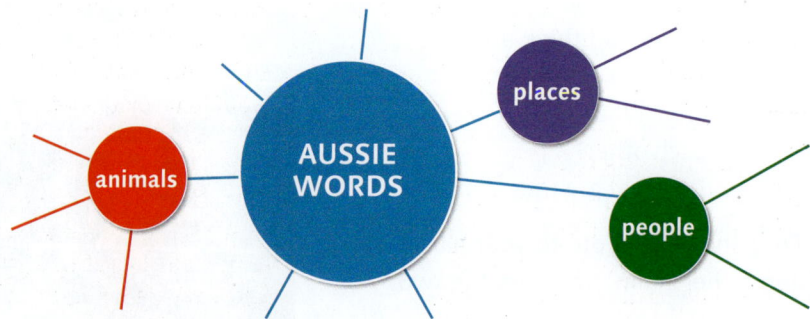

- AUSSIE WORDS
  - animals
  - places
  - people

98

More practice 3 **What have you learned about Oz?** ▶ Unit 1, p. 11

Complete these sentences. Use information from the texts on pages 10 and 11.

1. The most popular places for tourists are ...
2. Some people decide not to climb Uluru because ...
3. 25% of the Australian population today are ...
4. Many people in Australia live ...
5. Australian teenagers who want to fight fires join ...
6. It's important to stop bush fires because ...
7. Examples of Australian native animals are ...
8. Camels are a problem because ...
9. When people think of dangerous Australian animals, they first think of ...
10. But the most dangerous animals in Australia are ...

More challenge 2 **Another point of view** ▶ Unit 1, p. 11

Write a story from the perspective of one of these people:

- You're a tourist at Uluru. Do you decide to climb it or not?
- You're a new Australian. How do you spend the day after you °take the pledge and become an Australian citizen?
- You're a teenage °firefighter. You get a call to go into action. How do you feel?
- You're on a lonely road in central Australia. You see a big herd of camels on the road in front of you. What do you do?
- You're swimming in the sea at a beach in Sydney. You see a shark. How do you feel? What do you do?

More practice 4 **What's the problem?** ▶ Unit 1, p. 12

What are the problems of the four people below? Match the people and their problems.

a) ... got lost in the outback.
b) ... drank too much water.
c) ... was bitten by a snake.
d) ... didn't have a mobile phone.
e) ... suffered from heat stress.
f) ...'s car broke down.
g) ... didn't get to a doctor.

Erin: I was hiking in the outback and I was very hot and tired. So I found some shade under a tree, and I sat down on some rocks. Then I felt a terrible pain in my hand. The doctor at the hospital gave me an anti-venom, so I was OK ...

Danny: We left the main road. It was getting dark and we wanted somewhere to camp. We drove along a track. Then there was a terrible noise and the car stopped. Something was wrong. We didn't know what to do, and it was still hot ...

Rob: I love the sun ... and I never have any problems when it's hot, really. Well, I was sitting in the garden, reading ... and I guess I fell asleep. When I woke up, I felt quite funny ... a bit sick ... I didn't know what was wrong ...

Laura: We were walking through the outback. One track went left and another went right. I looked at the map and decided to go right. But after a little time I didn't know where we were ... and there were no other people °around ...

DIFF BANK
▶ KV 4B

Unit 1

3b Emergencies on the beach ▶ Unit 1, p. 13

Complete these sentences with the missing verbs. Then listen again and check your answers.

1. "G'day. I don't ... you ... swim here. It's dangerous."
2. "If I were you, I'd ... between the flags – it's safer over there."
3. "G'day. Can you ... us? My mate has ... his foot."
4. "It isn't bleeding, but I ... some redness. Does it ... now?"
5. "I ... a bit sick and I ... a headache."
6. "... me ... your temperature. It's quite high and you ... a bit red."

More practice 5 At the doctor's ▶ Unit 1, p. 13

a) **Silent dialogue:** Decide who's partner A and who's partner B.

Partner A: Look at the picture. You are at the doctor's. You feel sick and have a headache. Try to tell the doctor about your problem. Write the first line of your dialogue on a piece of paper. Then give it to B. Don't speak. Continue.

Partner B: You're a doctor. You're talking to a young person with a problem. Try to help. Read what A wrote and write your answer. Give it to A. Don't speak. Continue.

b) When you've finished the silent dialogue, practise saying it with your partner.

c) Act your dialogue for the class.

More practice 6 Understanding Aboriginal people ▶ Unit 1, p. 15

Read the text on p. 15 again and pick the correct answer.

1. Indigenous people came to Australia ...
   - A after the Europeans.
   - B just before the Europeans.
   - C at the same time as the Europeans.
   - D a long time before the Europeans.

2. °Farming has been popular in Australia for about ...
   - A 300 years.
   - B 50,000 years.
   - C 1700 years.
   - D 500,000 years.

3. The outback is a ... place to live.
   - A good
   - B easy
   - C difficult
   - D hot

4. ... Aboriginal people have big problems today.
   - A No
   - B Many
   - C Some
   - D All

5. In Aboriginal paintings you see lots of ...
   - A kangaroos.
   - B dots.
   - C people.
   - D boomerangs.

6. According to the text, Indigenous Australians ...
   - A have lost their culture.
   - B have their own special culture.
   - C now have a European culture.
   - D don't care about culture.

100

More challenge 3 — **Aboriginal culture in the song** ▶ *Unit 1, p. 15*

a) Look again at the two verses of 'Eyes Wide Open' on p. 14.
Which lines in the song tell us these things?
1 Lots of things have changed for Aboriginal people.
2 Aboriginal people feel positive about the future.
3 Aboriginal people should be proud of their culture.
4 Don't always think about the difficult past.
5 We should be proud of where we come from.

b) Write a text about the song. You can start like this:
I understand the song 'Eyes wide open' better now, for example the line about …

4 It was my 18th birthday ▶ *Unit 1, p. 17*
Complete the sentences with the correct form of the *simple past* or the *past progressive*.
1 It *was* (be) my 18th birthday and I *was travelling* (travel) with my mate Simon in the outback.
2 One day we … (come) to a river. Two tourists … (wait) there.
3 We … (not try) to cross because the water … (move) very quickly. But we … (not panic).
4 So we … (decide) to make camp for the night.
5 When we … (get up) the next morning, it … (rain) hard. The river … (be) even higher than the night before.
6 We … (start) to panic when we saw that the water … (get) closer and closer to our tent.

Role card ▶ *Unit 2, p. 35*

BLUE PEOPLE

Ask this question:

If you moved to a desert island, what three things would you take with you?

Tips:
- You like the blue people best. So talk to other blue people first.
- The orange people aren't so important. You can answer their question if you like, but don't ask your question.
- The green people aren't very interesting. You can talk to one or two if you like.
- Forget the red people. Don't even look at them when they talk to you. Just walk away.
- You aren't very polite.

1 DIFF BANK

Unit 1

More help | **5a** | **NOW YOU** — A window on your life ▸ *Unit 1, p. 17*

1) Do you need more **ideas for your story**?

> Ask yourself questions like this:
> Do you like the place where you live? Why (not)? (Think of Aaron in Text A.)
> What are you really interested in – a hobby, a sport, ...? (Think of Ella in Text B.)
> Do you want to write about a day in your life? (Think of Ava in Text C.)
> Did something happen to you recently that changed your life? (Think of Ethan in Text D.)

2) Do you know how to **structure your text**?

> Look again at the texts for ideas and look at ▸ *Skills file 8.1, pp. 172–173*.

3) Do you need **a good first sentence**?

> Aaron, Ethan and Ella used good first sentences:
> Friday September 21st is the night that changed my life.
> It was the day before my 16th birthday.
> This is probably the most (remote / beautiful / interesting) place that you can live in ...

4) Do you need **a good last sentence**?

> Aaron and Ava used good last sentences:
> Life here is sometimes hard, but I don't want to live anywhere else.
> Where I live is a really special place.

Role card ▸ *Unit 2, p. 35*

ORANGE PEOPLE

Ask this question:

If you could eat only one thing for lunch every day, what would that be?

Tips:
- The blue people are the most important. Try to talk to all of them.
- The green people are interesting. Talk to two or three of them.
- The red people aren't interesting. Don't answer their question and don't ask them any questions. Tell them you're too busy.
- Be polite to everybody (except the red people).

TEXT – Easier version

1 Before you read

Skim the pictures and headings and find out:
1 What are the names of the three main characters in the story?
2 How many kilometres did they plan to drive?
3 Where did the trip start and finish? ▶ *Skills file 6.1, p. 167*

Swerve
(adapted from the novel by Phillip Gwynne)

1 Sydney School

An old guy with a ponytail was at the school gate one afternoon.
"Hugh," he said as I walked past. "I want to talk
5 to you. You're my grandson."
"No, I'm not!"
Stranger danger, I thought. My mum's real father is dead.
"You were born on the seventeenth of
10 February," he said.
He knew lots of stuff about me and my mum. And he looked like us, the same nose and chin. That night I told mum that her father had come to the
15 school.
"My father is dead!" she said. "He's dead to me!"
Every day he
20 came to the school. At first I ignored him. But the third day I stopped and talked to him. Looking at him was like looking in a funny mirror.
25 He was my grandfather – my 'Poppy'!
One day Poppy phoned me at school. He said he wanted to go to the Big Rock – Uluru.

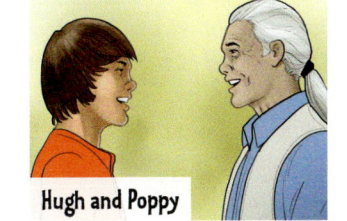

2 Plans

I visited Poppy at his apartment. He had a map
30 of Australia open on the table. "We're here," he said, pointing at Sydney.
"And Uluru is here," he said, pointing at the centre of Australia.
"Two thousand, eight hundred ks[1] away."

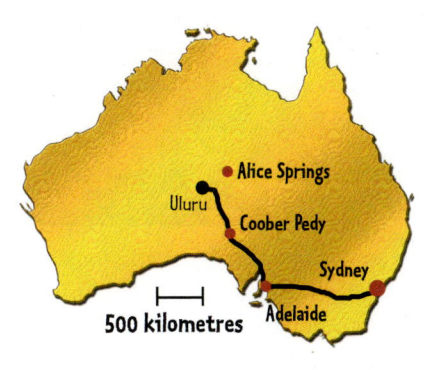

35 He looked at me. "Let's drive there together."
"But why?" I asked.
"Because I always wanted to go there, and now is the time to do it."
"And you want me to drive you there?" I asked.
40 "Well, I can't," he said. "I'd like to show you something."

I followed him to an old garage behind the building. Box: Voc., p. 211
There was a car in the garage – but it wasn't
45 just any car. It was a muscle car, a Holden Monaro – a fantastic muscle car with a big engine. It looked amazing. I love cars, especially muscle cars.
"So are you up for it?" he asked. Box: Voc., p. 212
50 "Whose is it?" I asked. It was his.
I thought about my school, my music exam next week, my parents, my future …
Then I thought about 2800 ks to Uluru in a Holden.
60 "I'm up for it," I said.

3 The Million Star Motel

We were on the highway going west. In the mirror Sydney got smaller and smaller and I got more and more excited.
65 I looked over at Poppy and smiled. He smiled back at me.
It was getting dark, so we left the highway and drove on a track.

---

[1] k (Abkürzung, *infml*) Kilometer

1 DIFF BANK

Poppy had some advice: "If you see a roo² on
70 the road, don't swerve. It's better to hit the roo than risk your life," he said.
We stopped the car at a clearing beside a river – the Darling.

At the Million Star Motel

Poppy had cooking equipment, camping chairs
75 and two swags³ – our beds. He made a fire and some tea. Poppy pointed to the sky.
"They call this the Million Star Motel," he said.

4 South Australia

A road train

We were driving through the desert. It was
80 1700ks to the Big Rock.
There were lots of huge trucks on the highway – road trains. And there were lots of animals too – horses, sheep, kangaroos, emus and goats. I saw a hitchhiker on the road and I stopped.
85 He was small and thin and he was wearing a hoodie. He said he was Jimmy from Broken Hill. After about half an hour a big black car went past us very fast. It was a Typhoon – another muscle car.
90 We stopped at a roadhouse⁴ for fuel and for something to eat, but the hitchhiker stayed in the car.

5 In the roadhouse

I ordered a sandwich while Poppy went to
95 the toilet. A man and a woman came in. The man was short, but big – like a bodybuilder.

The woman was kind of glamorous.
"We're looking for our daughter," the woman
100 said, taking out a photo of a girl about my age.
Back in the car I looked at the
105 hitchhiker and saw

Bella

pink nail polish on his fingernails.
"Hey, your parents are looking for you," I said.
"They aren't my parents," she answered.
"Please don't say anything. Those people are
110 really dangerous," she said.
Then the bodybuilder and the woman came out and they left the roadhouse car park in their black Typhoon – very fast.
"They're gone now," I said.
115 She sat up and pulled her hood back. Short messy hair. Big eyes. Nose stud …
She said her name was Bella and she was seventeen.

6 At Yulara, near Uluru

120 *Hugh, Poppy and Bella drive to Coober Pedy together. Hugh really likes Bella, and he thinks that she likes him. But at Coober Pedy Bella meets another guy. She decides to travel to Uluru with him. Hugh is disappointed. Hugh*
125 *and Poppy go on without Bella, and they arrive at a campground in Yulara, a small town near the Big Rock – Uluru.*

I heard my phone. It was Bella.
"Hello," I said. But there was no answer, only
130 the sound of a big car engine and voices.
Then I heard Bella.
"Help! We just passed *The Brain*. Please help!"
Then the phone went dead.
I knew that the bodybuilder and the woman
135 had found Bella.
"Bella's in trouble," I said to Poppy, getting into the car.
"I'm coming," he said, jumping out of his swag.
"Where's *The Brain*?" I asked Poppy.
140 "It's at this end of the Big Rock," he said.
We drove fast along the road to Uluru …

---

² roo (infml) [ruː] Känguru   ³ swag (AustE [swæg], infml) Bettrolle (Gepäckrolle, die man auf der Schulter trägt)
⁴ roadhouse [ˈrəʊdhaʊs] Raststätte

104

▶ KV 5

2 True, false or not in the text?
1. Poppy was Hugh's grandfather. (part 1)
2. Hugh thought Poppy's car was terrible. (2)
3. Hugh saw a kangaroo and swerved. (3)
4. They stopped for a hitchhiker near Uluru. (4)
5. Poppy ate a sandwich in the roadhouse. (5)
6. Hugh was worried about Bella. (6)

3 Retell the story
a) Use the ideas in the boxes.

1. One day Hugh's grandfather came to …
Poppy said he wanted to go to …

2. Hugh visited Poppy at his …
Then Poppy showed Hugh a …
Hugh decided to go to …

3. Hugh and Poppy camped beside a …
They made a fire and some …
In the sky they saw lots of …

4. Hugh and Poppy saw a hitchhiker and they …
He was wearing a …
They stopped at a roadhouse for …

5. In the roadhouse a man and a woman were looking for their …
The hitchhiker said they were … / they weren't …

6. Bella phoned Hugh because she was …
Hugh and Poppy drove …
They wanted to …

b) Compare your texts.

4 At the Million Star Motel
Look at the picture in part 3 of the story. Then do task a) or task b).
a) Write a message from Hugh to his mum.
b) Write a dialogue between Poppy and Hugh.

5 The end of the story
1.07
What do you think happens next? Tell a partner. Then listen to the end of the story and find out.

6 A character network
Make a character network for the people in the text.
More help p. 106

Unit 1

More practice 7 Work with the text ▶ Unit 1, p. 21
a) Look at **1 Sydney School**. Pick the right words and finish the sentences.
1. When Hugh first saw Poppy, he was Ⓐ excited Ⓑ careful Ⓒ scared.
2. Hugh's mum is Poppy's Ⓐ daughter Ⓑ sister Ⓒ mother.
3. The police Ⓐ arrested Poppy Ⓑ came to the school Ⓒ did nothing.
4. Hugh thought Poppy Ⓐ didn't look like him Ⓑ looked like him Ⓒ looked funny.
5. Hugh Ⓐ can't drive Ⓑ doesn't like driving Ⓒ is learning to drive.

1 DIFF BANK

b) Look at **2 Plans**.
Put the sentence parts together.
1. Poppy lived — to go to Uluru.
2. It's a long way from — a muscle car.
3. Poppy always wanted — in an apartment.
4. A Holden Monaro is — to drive Poppy.
5. Hugh agreed — Sydney to Uluru.

c) Look at **3 The Million Star Motel**.
What do you think? Finish these sentences.
1. Hugh felt excited when …
2. Poppy looked happy because …
3. Poppy told Hugh not to …
4. At the Darling River Hugh and Poppy …
5. The 'Million Star Motel' means …

d) Look at **4 South Australia**.
Fill in the gaps with words from the text.
1. Poppy didn't want Hugh to drive …
2. Hugh stopped the car to let a … pass.
3. Another danger on the highway were the …
4. Hugh couldn't see Jimmy's face because …
5. A Typhoon is a …

e) Look at **5 In the roadhouse**.
Find and correct a mistake in each sentence.
1. Hugh ate a brown bread sandwich.
2. Hugh helped the people to find Bella.
3. When Hugh went back to the car, Jimmy was gone.
4. The people in the black car were nice.
5. The hitchhiker was a teen boy.

f) Look at **6 At Yulara, near Uluru**.
Answer these questions.
1. How did Hugh know that Bella was in trouble?
2. Do you think that Hugh was a good friend? Why (not)?

More help **6** **A character network** ▶ Unit 1, p. 21

a) Copy and complete this character network for the story.
- You can make notes about how the characters are connected (e.g. boyfriend / girlfriend; father / daughter; etc.).

- You can write notes about how the characters feel about each other (e.g. likes / doesn't like / hates / loves / is afraid of / trusts / doesn't trust / thinks … is cool; etc.).

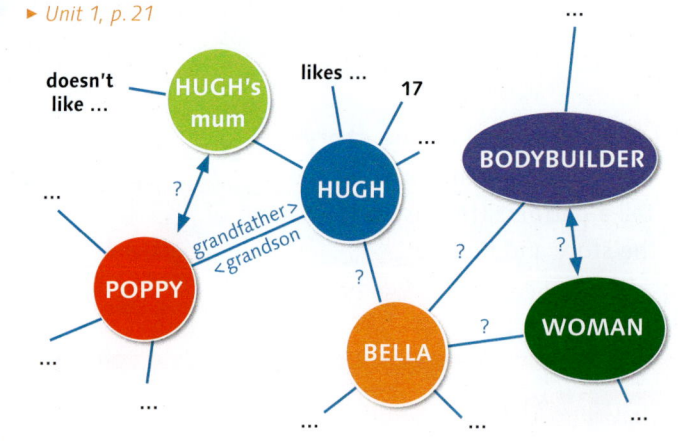

Character network diagram with nodes: HUGH's mum (doesn't like …), HUGH (likes …, 17), BODYBUILDER, POPPY (grandfather > / < grandson with HUGH), BELLA, WOMAN.

b) Pick words from this box and put them in your character network. If you don't know some words, check in a dictionary.

> big eyes • brave • °cowardly • °dishonest • friendly • glamorous • grey hair • helpful • honest • loving • messy hair • nice • old • ponytail • short • strange • stupid • terrible • thin • unfriendly • violent • young • …

▶ KV 6

More practice 8 **An interesting character** ▶ Unit 1, p. 21

a) Pick one of the characters in the story and write a description. Write about:
- what he/she looks like
- what he/she is like (his/her °personality)
- what the other characters think of him/her
- if you like him/her and why (not)

Give reasons for your ideas – from the story.

b) 👥 Swap your description with other students. Do you agree with each other? What do you agree about? What do you disagree about?

More challenge 4 **Hugh and Poppy** ▶ Unit 1, p. 21
Describe the relationship between Hugh and Poppy. How did it change in the story?
At the beginning Hugh …   Then Poppy and Hugh …   In the end they …

More help **Step 4: Give your presentation / Prepare your feedback** ▶ Unit 1, p. 23
While listening, prepare your feedback with a feedback sheet.

a) Copy this table:

important things for a presentation	very good	good	OK	needs work	notes
1					
2					
3					
4					
5					

▶ Skills file 7.1, p. 170

b) For the first column (important things for a presentation) choose a maximum of five things from this list:

- Your presentation was interesting.
- You used your own words.
- Your notes were short.
- Your presentation had a clear structure.
- You used good phrases.
- Your visuals were clear and interesting.
- The audience could read your visuals.
- You didn't read from your notes.
- You talked slowly and clearly.
- You looked at the audience and smiled.
- You asked for questions at the end.

❗ When you choose from the list, think especially of the things you all agreed on in task 2 on p. 22. Everybody should use copies of the same feedback sheet.

1 DIFF BANK

c) When you're listening, make notes on your feedback sheet like this:

important things for a presentation	very good	good	OK	needs work	notes
1 a clear structure		✓			intro – very clear middle – less clear
2 short notes			✓		a bit long
3 an interesting presentation	✓				very interesting!
4 speaking slowly and clearly			✓		clear, but a little too fast
5 using good phrases				✓	use more good phrases, e.g. for intro: "Now I'm going to talk about ..."

Unit 1 — Stop! Check! Go!

2 LANGUAGE Rani's Oz Travel Blog ▸ Unit 1, p. 24
Complete the sentences with the correct verb forms.

> Use the *simple present*, *simple past*, *past progressive*, *going to-future* or *infinitive*.

July 1st: We're still at the airport. When we ... (1 arrive), the pilots ... just ... (2 begin) to strike. But we're lucky and in about an hour our plane for Australia ... (3 be) ready for take-off.

July 3rd: We ... (4 get to) our hostel in Darwin early in the morning and ... (5 meet) our tour guide, Tony, who ... (6 wait) for us. Tomorrow we ... (7 see) Aboriginal rock paintings in Kakadu National Park. It's 10 pm now and we ... (8 need) some sleep.

July 4th: It was amazing to see the ancient rock paintings. You can still ... (9 find) traditional Aboriginal art all over Oz. While I ... (10 enjoy) the art, Sophie ... (11 chat) with the tour guide ;-))

July 6th: Yesterday we ... (12 spend) a lazy day. Tonight we ... (13 visit) Mindil Beach Sunset Market. The market ... (14 start) at 5 pm every Thursday. It's famous for live music.

July 7th: When we ... (15 have breafast) breakfast and making plans for the day, Tony arrived and ... (16 invite) us to Crocosaurus Cove. There we ... (17 swim) with crocodiles – well, we were in a cage and the crocodiles were swimming all around us. It was an awesome experience – the highlight of an amazing first week in Oz.

▸ Language file 10, p. 187

More challenge 5 Our trip to Oz ▶ Unit 1, p. 24

After their trip to Australia, Sophie and Rani write an article about Oz for their school magazine. Think about their plans, their internet research and their blog, and write the article (about 150 words) from their perspective.

More challenge 6 What do you think? ▶ Unit 1, p. 25

a) In your opinion, which of these four sports is the most dangerous: horse racing, surfing, car racing or Australian Rules Football? Give reasons.

b) You win a competiton and your prize is a ticket to go and watch one of the four sports in a). Which one would you choose? Give reasons.

More help **5b** WRITING Slip, slop, slap, seek and slide ▶ Unit 1, p. 26

Some ideas for your comment:
- People like to lie in the sun when they're on holiday.
- People think that a suntan looks beautiful / healthy / ...
- People don't understand the dangers of too much sun (e.g. skin cancer).
- Skin must get used to the sun slowly.
- More and more people like spending their holidays in hot countries.
- Skin cancer is the most common cancer among young people.
- Sun makes your skin look old at an early age.

Unit 2

More help **3a** I thought we were friends ... (part 2) ▶ Unit 2, p. 31
- Will the cyberbullying continue?
- Can the teacher help Patrick? If so, how?
- Who should Patrick talk to next?
- What will Robert, Shaz and Simone do?
- Should the other kids °say sorry?
- What will Patrick's dad do?
- Do you think Patrick will talk to the police?
- What would Patrick need to feel happy again?

More help **3c** I thought we were friends ... (part 2) ▶ Unit 2, p. 31

3 ⬤ What is the main message of the film?

A It was only a bit of fun!
B Bullying is bad – it has to stop.
C Good friends always stay together.
D °Messaging can be dangerous.
E If you see (cyber-)bullying, °do something about it. Don't do nothing.

DIFF BANK

Unit 2

More challenge 1 — **Write about your experience** ▸ Unit 2, p. 31

Imagine you're Patrick. Write to a student magazine about your experience.

- Ask to °remain °anonymous. Don't give your real name or the name of your school, etc.
- Write about the text messages.
- Say how you felt.
- What did you do? Did you talk to friends?
- Who did you talk to? What did they say?
- Did anybody else notice your problem?
- Did he / she do anything about it?
- Were the bullies sorry?
- Do you think that you'll be friends again?
- What advice would you like to give other kids who are victims of cyberbullying?

More help **3** **WRITING Now you:** "Peer pressure is a big problem …" ▸ Unit 2, p. 33

Do you agree? Write a comment (about 100 words). Give reasons and examples.

Step 1: Think of situations when you (or other teenagers) feel peer pressure. Is it a problem? Make notes like this. 👥 Compare your ideas with a partner.

Situation	Problem or not?
My friends wanted to train for a 5 km run / join a club / …	Not a problem
Sometimes people want other teens to smoke / drink / shoplift.	Problem because …
My best friend did a good presentation. I wanted to do the same.	Not a problem
Some people in class want to get a piercing / a tattoo	…

Step 2: Start writing your comment. Choose one of these first sentences. Or write your own.
- Teenagers often feel peer pressure, and it is a big problem for them.
- Peer pressure is sometimes a big problem for teenagers, but not always.
- It's true that teenagers feel peer pressure, but I don't think that it is a big problem for them.

Step 3: Choose two examples of peer pressure from your notes and write about them.
Describe the situation. ➔ Say if it's a problem or not, and why.

Describe the situation.	Say if it's a problem or not, and why.
For example, some of my friends decided to do a 5 km run, and they wanted me to do it too. I decided to join them and I got fitter.	So this wasn't a problem. °In fact it was very good for me.
But sometimes people want you to do something that you don't feel comfortable with. For example …	So this is a problem because it's hard to say no.

Step 4: Write a conclusion. You could start like this:

So to sum up,	I think I definitely think in my opinion,	peer pressure	is isn't can be	a problem for …

More challenge 2 A °tricky problem   ▶ Unit 2, p. 34

👥 Read the situation below. Write a dialogue between the two friends. Perform it for the class.

> There's a party on Friday night and everybody is going. You and your friend would like to go. Plus, if you don't go, everybody will say that you're losers.
> But there's a problem.
> **Partner A:** You're worried because you have a swimming competition on Saturday, and the trainer doesn't want swimmers to °have a late night.
> **Partner B:** You're worried because you don't want to go to the party °on your own.
>
> Talk together and try to find a solution, so that you can both go to the party.

More practice 1 About the article   ▶ Unit 2, p. 35

a) Look at the article again. Who said these things?
1 "She called me a racist name."
2 "I'm sorry."
3 "I'll never use racist names again."
4 "I don't blame the girl."
5 "She's only 13 years old, and she's still so innocent."

b) What do you think the slogan **Racism: It stops with me** means? Pick the best meaning.
1 Don't talk about racism.   2 I'm not racist.   3 I say no to racism.

---

1 ACTIVITY Badges – a group experiment   ▶ Unit 2, p. 35

> **Role card**
> ### RED PEOPLE
> Ask this question:
> **If you could visit any country, where would you go?**
> **Tips:**
> - The blue people are the most important. Try to talk to all of them.
> - The green people are nice and funny. Talk to two or three of them.
> - The orange people aren't so important. So don't worry if you don't have time for them. Maybe just talk to one.
> - Be polite to everybody.

DIFF BANK

Unit 2

More help **3e** SONG "What you say matters" by Brothablack ▶ Unit 2, p. 36

Discuss in groups: What is the message of the video? Does the video work for you? Give reasons. Make sentences with these notes:

This video is about	discrimination against prejudice against	black / white / Asian ... people. all kinds of people.
	racism. bullying. all kinds of discrimination.	

It tells us to	say no to face fight	racism. discrimination. prejudice.

I think the video	is great works well doesn't work	because it has / doesn't have a really good message. because the actors are / aren't great. because the music / song is powerful / not great ... because my experience is very similar / different to ...

More challenge 3 Your review ▶ Unit 2, p. 36

Write a review of the video "What you say matters". Write about:
- who sings the song
- the °style of music
- the important lines / slogans of the song
- the message of the video
- what you like / don't like about the video (and why)
- the different scenes in the video

More help **4** Project A Scenes of discrimination ▶ Unit 2, p. 37

You can write a dialogue like this for the first scene:

We're in a classroom. The students are about 16 and they're sitting down. The teacher starts to give the students their tests and their results.
Teacher   Here are your maths tests from last week. You have 79 Tom – that's good. And you have 61 – that's OK. Kat – only 55! You can do better. Jane – 98 – great work.
Jane smiles and takes her paper. Kat is sitting behind her. She doesn't look happy. She looks at Jane and whispers:
Kat   You think you're so good! Of course you're the teacher's favourite. ...
Jane looks ... Will she say something or ...? Then she gets up and walks ... She talks to ... She says ...
Jane   ...

More help | **4** | **Project B** | **Immigrants' stories** ▸ Unit 2, p. 37

If you can, ask these questions in English. (Or you can ask them in German or in your own language.)
- What country does your family come from?
- When did they come here?
- Do you visit your family's country?
- Can you speak the language?
- Do you like it there? What's special?
- What's different to Germany?
- Would you recommend it for holidays? Where should people go?

You can write texts like this:

> Alex's family comes from ... They came to Germany ... ago.
> The family left ... because they wanted a better life / because of the war ...
> Alex and his family go back to ... every summer.
> They can't go back to ... at the moment because it's too dangerous / ...
> Alex can / can't speak some ...
> It's very different to Germany – it's ...
> Alex loves it there. He likes ...
> Is it a good place for holidays? Yes, it is – you should visit ... / No, it isn't a good place right now.
> Here's a map and some of Alex's photos:

3 **What were their exact words?** ▸ Unit 2, p. 39

Complete the speech bubbles.
1. The girl told Kai's brother that her name was Emily.
2. He said that his name was Dan.
3. Dan told Emily that he often came to the club.
4. She told him that she didn't come very often.
5. She explained that she played soccer, and practice was usually on the same night.
6. He suggested that she should come to the talent show on Saturday night if she was free.
7. She thought that was a great idea.

1 ... name ... Emily.
4 I ... ... very often.
5 ... ... soccer, and practice ... usually on the same night.
7 ... ... a great idea.

2 ... name ... Dan.
3 ... often ... to the club.
6 ... should come to the talent show on Saturday night if ... ... free.

DIFF BANK

Unit 2

More challenge 4 — **More about indirect speech** ▶ Unit 2, p. 40

a) Jessie wants to copy Tim's homework. But at their school, you get into big trouble if you copy. He's telling his mum about it. What did Tim and Jessie say exactly (1–7)?

> ! Remember that the tenses often change in indirect speech.
> "I <u>have</u> a problem." → She said she <u>had</u> a problem.
>   **simple present** → **simple past**

A girl at school talked to me yesterday. She told me that she <u>had</u> a problem. She asked me if <u>I had done</u> (1) my maths homework. I said <u>I had finished</u> (2) it the day before. She said that <u>she hadn't started</u> (3) hers. Then she asked me if <u>she could copy</u> (4) my homework.
I said that <u>wasn't</u> (5) a good idea. I also said that our teacher <u>would notice</u> (6) and we <u>would</u> both <u>get</u> (7) into big trouble.

I <u>have</u> a problem. … (1) <u>you done</u> your maths homework?

Yes, I … (2) it yesterday.

Oh dear, I …n't (3) started mine. … (4) I copy your homework?

That …n't (5) a good idea. Mrs Brown … (6) notice. We … (7) both get into big trouble.

b) How do the verbs change in indirect speech? Complete this table.
Then check in ▶ Language file 20, p. 194.

direct speech	→	indirect speech
simple present	→	simple past
simple past	→	…
present perfect	→	
will	→	
can		

c) Here Tim is reporting what he and Jessie said when they met again later. Complete his report.

Jessie	Do you have that homework for me?
Tim	Ah no, Jessie, I can't do that.
Jessie	Are you crazy? I copied from Julia last time and there wasn't a problem.
Tim	Well, I have thought about it, and I really don't feel comfortable with it.
Jessie	You're a pain.
Tim	I'll explain the homework if you like.
Jessie	I don't have time for that.

Jessie asked me if …
I told her that …
Jessie asked me if …
She said that she … and there …
I said that I …
and I really …
She told me …
I told her that …
But she said that …

114

TEXT – Shorter version

▶ KV 16

1 While you read

a) Think about these questions while you read your side of the story.
Then talk about them with other students who have read the same side. Compare answers.

1. Who is the hero of the story?
2. Where does he or she live?
3. Who does he or she live with?
4. What is he or she interested in?
5. What does he or she think about the neighbour from across the road?

b) Find a partner who has read the other side. Compare your answers to the five questions.

Matt's side of the story ...

(adapted from the novel *Watching you, watching me* by Chloe Rayban)

1 Number twenty-five was empty. I checked the address again. I opened the gate and walked to
5 the back door. There were lots of °tools in the back garden.

When dad told me that we had to move to London for his job I was quite happy.
10 Dad found a school in London – West Thames °College. There were girls and no uniforms. I started to imagine a school like you see in American college movies, where everyone sits on the grass and drives around in big old cars.
15 So that's why I came up to London alone – to start at my new school.

Mum and dad had warned me that the °building work on the house wasn't finished. "I can °keep an eye on the °builders," I said to
20 them. So they agreed that I could come to London alone.

London – it's a special place – it's full of life! You can feel that in the streets. You can see it in the faces of the people. You can hear it in
25 the traffic noise. And when the lights come on at night the city is °magic, man!

I went through the house – the hallway was full of boxes. I switched the light on but nothing happened.
30 The building work wasn't finished downstairs ... up the stairs ... oops, one step missing! ... The bathroom was old. The two bedrooms on the first floor were big, but there were holes in the floors.

35 Up more stairs ... the top floor ... this was what I was waiting for – my floor! Two big attic rooms ... the back room was for my music.

I went into the front room, opened the window and looked out. The view! I looked down
40 Frenshaw Avenue. I could see the tops of the trees ... cars ... and the city of London. I could hear it too. I looked back into our street. Hey ... look at that! A girl ... she looked nice. She crossed the road and disappeared. I hoped
45 she wasn't just visiting ...

I went to the bathroom to have a °shower. There was no hot water, so it was a very cold shower. Oh no – I had forgotten to bring the towel ... That's when some crazy guy started
50 to hammer on the front door.

"OK, OK, OK!" I shouted down.
I took a candle and went down the stairs ... oh! – I forgot the missing step.
"What do you want?" I shouted through the door.
55 " I saw your light. You can't do this!"
"What?"
"You can't just move into this house like this."
"Look. I have every right to be here." I was really cold now.

2 DIFF BANK
▶ KV 16

"Well, I'm giving you a warning …"
I was really cold and I just wanted him to go away.
"Yeah right! °Go on, piss off!"

70 I went back upstairs and I sat in the window and looked out at the city again. Then I saw the window of the attic room in the house on the other side of the street. The curtains moved … it was that girl again. She was
75 opening the window … and then she was closing the curtains. Oh no, please don't go … but the curtains closed.

60 "I'll call the police."
This old busybody thought that I was a tramp or a squatter or something … destroying his nice life in this nice neighbourhood …
"Look, you old busybody! Why don't you °get
65 lost?"

2 Paragraph headings
Match these headings (A–F) to the six paragraphs of Matt's story.
A I love London
B The girl across the street
C Going through the house
D My horrible neighbour
E A new home, a new school
F Number 25 – an empty old house

3 Talking about the text
a) Answer the questions and finish the sentences about the story.
1 The **characters**: Who is the story about?
   - The main character in this story is …   He's …   It's also about his neighbours, …

2 The setting: Where does the story happen?
   - The story happens in a street in …   We're in Matt's …   He's moving into a house in …

3 The plot: Say what happens in the story – in a few sentences.
   - First Matt arrives …   When he goes into the house, …   He wants to have a shower, but …
     Then someone comes to the door – it's …

4 The mood: How do you feel when you read this story? Why?
   - I think that it's interesting when …   It's funny when …   It's exciting when …   It's …

▶ Skills file 6.7, p. 169

b) 👥 Now find a partner who has read Natasha's side of the story. Compare your notes.

4 A book recommendation?
👥 Discuss in class: Did you like Matt's story? What did you like? What didn't you like? Would you like to read the book? Vote in class.

> Role card ▸ Unit 2, p. 35

> ## GREEN PEOPLE
>
> Ask this question:
> **If you were an animal, which animal would you like to be?**
> **Tips:**
> - The blue people are the most important. Try to talk to all of them.
> - The orange people aren't so important. So don't worry if you don't have time for them. Maybe just talk to one.
> - The red people are a bit stupid. Their question is stupid, too. Don't answer it and don't ask them any questions.
> - Be polite to everybody (except the red people).

More practice 2 **Matt and Natasha** ▸ Unit 2, p. 43

● Imagine …
Pick a) or b):
a) Imagine that Matt and Natasha meet in the street. Write a dialogue between the two.
b) Imagine that you're the writer – Chloe Rayban. Write the next chapter of this story.

More help **4b** **A review of the story** ▸ Unit 2, p. 43

Write a review of the story. Write about the plot, the setting, your favourite characters and the mood of the story. Say if you would like to read the book and why (not).

Here are some ideas:

First say something about the story in a few sentences. Use your ideas from 3.
Example: *Who is the story about? Do you have a favourite character? Where does the story happen? What happens? How do you feel when you read the story?*

You could °comment on the structure of the book – the girl's story and the boy's story.
Example: *The book is °unusual because you can read the boy's story or the girl's story. I think that's interesting / not so interesting / boring / fun / … because …*

So would you like to read the book? Why (not)? Who do you think might enjoy the book?
Example: *Personally I'd like to read the book because it's funny / interesting / I really want to know what happens next / …*
I wouldn't like to read this book because I don't like this kind of story / I'm not interested in the characters / …
I think that this book will be popular with girls / boys / anybody who likes a mystery / …

2 DIFF BANK

Unit 2

More challenge 5 **Different points of view** ▶ Unit 2, p. 43

Pick a) or b):

a) If you've read Natasha's story, describe what happened (from line 18 to line 49) from Jamie's point of view.

b) If you've read Matt's story, describe what happened (from line 46 to line 69) from the neighbour's point of view.

More practice 3 **Do it again!** ▶ Unit 2, p. 45

👥 Pick another situation from page 45. Make another dialogue and practise it together. Then swap roles.

Unit 2 Stop! Check! Go!

1c LANGUAGE How to talk to your parents ▶ Unit 2, p. 46

What did Jay tell her friends about this discussion with her parents? Complete the sentences.

Jay	Mum and dad, can I talk to you about the concert? I really want to go.	I asked my parents if I *could talk to them about the concert* (1). I told them I really … (2).
Dad	Do you have any homework to do?	Dad asked if I … (3).
Jay	No, I don't. It's all finished.	I … (4).
Mum	How much do the tickets cost?	Mum wanted to know how much the tickets … (5).
Jay	They are expensive, but I have the money from my birthday.	I told them that they … (6) but I … (7).
Dad	What time does the concert end?	Dad asked … (8).
Jay	Ten o'clock.	I said ten o'clock.
Dad	It's a bit late for a school night.	Dad said it … (9).
Mum	Yes, I don't want you to be tired at school.	And mum agreed with him. She … (10).
Jay	It's just one night. But OK, I respect your opinion.	I said it … (11), but I … (12).
Mum	I really like your attitude, Jay.	Mum said … (13).
Dad	I agree. You can go to the concert, Jay.	Dad said that … (14)! Wow! Great advice, guys!

More challenge 6 **The morning after the concert** ▶ Unit 2, p. 46

The next morning Jay was chatting online with her cousin. Write what she said to him.

Max	I will always remember this concert.	1	Max said …
Meg	It was the best concert I have ever been to.	2	Meg said …
Tia	I've never been to a concert before.	3	Tia said …
Tia	Can one of you take a photo of me beside the poster?	4	Tia asked if one of us …
Elli	I've forgotten my phone!	5	Elli said …
Tia	Don't worry. I'll take some photos of you.	6	Tia told Elli … She said she …
Max	I started to record the concert on it but after about 30 minutes my phone died.	7	Max said that …

2a LANGUAGE **Volunteering** ▶ Unit 2, p. 47

Find words / phrases that mean:
1 very good (A)
2 team of people who work together (A)
3 things you need to rescue someone (A)
4 kids who have disabilities (B)
5 feel unhappy because something you hoped for doesn't happen (B)
6 organizing your own time (C)
7 able to deal with a difficult situation without getting fed up (C)
8 be polite and kind to others (C)

More challenge 7 **An article** ▶ Unit 2, p. 47

Choose A or B and write a short article for your school website.

A
Do you volunteer in your free time? Write an article about your volunteering activities like Lily and Mike did.

B
Do you agree or disagree with Lily? Give your opinion about volunteering. If you agree that volunteering is a good idea, find more °arguments and write about the advantages of volunteering. If you don't agree say what you think and give reasons.

2-3 DIFF BANK

Unit 2 — Stop! Check! Go!

More help 5 WRITING Schools against racism ▶ Unit 2, p. 48

Look in the text in Task 4 on page 48 for ideas for your project. Here are some more ideas:

- a carnival of cultures at our school (music / flags / fashion / … of all the different countries that our students come from)
- a photo or art show
- visiting a museum
- interviewing people from different cultures
- inviting a speaker to the school
- competitions and quizzes
- sports events against racism
- music against racism (e.g., analysing songs and / or writing songs against racism)
- putting up posters against racism in our city

Unit 3

More practice 1 Talking about jobs ▶ Unit 3, p. 57

a) Finish these sentences.

1. Someone who paints houses is a …
2. Someone who helps with animals is …
3. Someone who flies planes is …
4. Bar staff are people who …
5. A camp assistant is someone who …
6. A hotel worker …
7. A cleaner …
8. A receptionist …
9. A cook …
10. A waiter …

b) Think of five other jobs. Write questions about them.
Example: What do you call someone who …

> … works in a …? • … helps …? • … looks after …? • … cuts …? •
> … sells …? • … writes …? • … drives …? • … makes …?

Then read your questions to a partner. Can he / she guess what the job is? Even in German?

More practice 2 MEDIATION Tell a friend ▶ Unit 3, p. 57

a) Read this advert for film and °TV extras and make notes in English under these headings:
- Job title   - Type of show   - Skills needed   - Experience   - Where   - When   - Pay

Komparsen gesucht

Tätigkeit: Raum Berlin
Drehtage: 1. bis 5. Dezember (6 Tage; 2 – 3 Stunden täglich)
Vergütung: 40 Euro pro Drehtag
Für eine Reality-Sendung: Eine amerikanische Familie zieht von New York City nach Berlin um. Es geht um Freundschaften, aber auch um Mobbing und Auseinandersetzungen. Die Darsteller/innen sprechen Englisch und Deutsch.
Voraussetzungen: Du bist zwischen 14 und 19 Jahre alt, wohnst in Berlin oder Umgebung, da weder Fahrt- noch Übernachtungskosten übernommen werden. Du sprichst fließend Deutsch und gutes Englisch. Dreherfahrungen sind von Vorteil.
Bewerbung: Per E-Mail, bitte auf Englisch (da amerikanisches Drehteam), an: americanlife@casting100.com
Einsatzort: Berlin

> ! If you can't guess what some important words in the advert are in English, use a dictionary.

b) Now tell your partner about it. Would you like the job? Why (not)?

▶ Skills file 10, pp. 180–181

More help 5 Your ideal job ▸ Unit 3, p. 57

You can use this checklist to help you to make notes for your text about an ideal job:

Do you need …	experience? / special skills? / a driving licence? / qualifications?
Do you have to …	work with other people? / go to school or college? / work shifts? / do special training? / work indoors/outdoors? / work shifts? / use English?
Can you …	train on the job? / learn new skills?
What …	is the job title? / hours do you work? / is the pay like? / duties do you have? / training do you need? / kind of work do you have to do? / holidays do you get?

More challenge 1 Different countries – different CVs ▸ Unit 3, p. 58

Compare your CV in German to Paul Schulz's CV in English. Think about these questions:
- What's the same?   - What's different?   - What do you like especially in an English CV?

More practice 3 A cover letter ▸ Unit 3, p. 59

Apply for this job. Write a cover letter and try to 'sell yourself'.

> ### Schloss Granstein
> Are you looking for an exciting and °challenging summer job?
> Do you speak some English and good German?
> Would you like to live in a castle for the summer?
> We are offering a summer job in the °souvenir shop in the famous Granstein castle. Come and help us with our many visitors from all over the world.
> It's a great chance to improve your English.
>
> Apply (in English) to: The Manager, Schloss Granstein

More help 1b Questions for Emma ▸ Unit 3, p. 60

First complete these questions with words from the box.

> friends • go • good • move • name • next • played • since • was • work

Then match each question (1–10) with one of the points in the article.

1 How old was Emma when she first … Hermione?
2 When did Emma finish … on the last Harry Potter film?
3 Is Emma … with Harry and Ron in real life?
4 Where … Emma born?
5 When did Emma … to England?
6 What was the … of her first school?
7 What has Emma done … the end of the Harry Potter films?
8 Where did she … to university?
9 Why is she a … role model?
10 What will Emma do …?

3 DIFF BANK

Unit 3

3b REVISION — Word order in questions ▶ Unit 3, p. 61
Read the statements and ask follow-up questions to find out more.
1. My role model is my teacher, Mrs Smith. – Why *is she your role model?*
2. My friend Kadir wasn't born in Germany. – Where …?
3. Last year I was on work experience. – How long …?
4. I'm worried about my next work experience. – Why …?
5. I want a weekend job. I've sent out lots of CVs. – How many …?

More practice 4 — Questions for pop stars ▶ Unit 3, p. 61
These are the notes that a music reporter made before she interviewed a new pop band. What questions did she ask? Write them down.

Topics for interview

1. where they went to school
2. which schools they went to
3. if they enjoyed school
4. what their favourite subjects were
5. where they met
6. how long they have known each other
7. if they write their own songs
8. when their next album will be ready

More practice 5 — Find someone who ▶ Unit 3, p. 61
Talk to people in your class and find at least one person in the class who …
1. has been to France.
2. doesn't like tomato soup.
3. is wearing interesting socks.
4. was doing something fun at 8 o'clock yesterday evening.
5. is going to watch a football match this evening.
6. did something exciting last weekend.
7. has never seen any of the Harry Potter films.
8. has an unusual role model.

> **!** Don't forget to ask follow-up questions to find out more.
> **Examples:** When did you go? (1)
> What soup do you like? (2)
> Who bought you those sockets? (3)
> …

Answers for 2 REVISION — Questions words ▶ Unit 3, p. 60

1. **Who** played Harry in the Harry Potter films?
   Harry was played by Daniel Radcliffe.
2. **What**'s the name of the school that Harry, Hermione and Ron went to?
   Its full name is Hogwarts School of Witchcraft and Wizardry. (Hogwarts Schule für Hexerei und Zauberei)
3. **Why** didn't Harry Potter live with his parents?
   Harry didn't live with his parents because they were killed by Lord Voldemort when Harry was a baby.
4. **How many** Harry Potter books are there?
   There are seven Harry Potter books.
5. **How many** Harry Potter films are there?
   There are eight Harry Potter films.
6. **Why** are there more films than books?
   Because the last book was filmed in two parts.
7. **Who** wrote the Harry Potter books?
   They were written by Joanne K. Rowling.

TEXT – Easier version

Seashell Motel (adapted from a short story by Lois Metzger)

1   Cindy Fisher, age sixteen, lied to get her summer job.
Mrs. Karpinsky, a teacher at Cindy's high school in New York City, told her class that a summer job was a good idea. She talked about jobs in restaurants, offices and city parks. Then she talked about a job in the Seashell Motel in Atlantic City, New Jersey. Cindy put up her hand and said, "I'll take that one."
"Sorry Cindy, you have to be nineteen," Mrs. Karpinsky said.
"I can do it," Cindy said.
When Cindy was younger, she had gone there every summer with her family for two weeks. She remembered the beautiful boardwalk along the ocean. She loved eating candy and hearing the ocean.
In Atlantic City, she thought, the ocean was everywhere.
"I'll give the application form to my older sister," she said. "She's nineteen." 
"How can your baby sister be nineteen?" said Charlotte, a friend. Cindy smiled.
When she got home, Cindy told her parents that there was a new summer program at school and that lots of sixteen-year-old girls could work in hotels on the east coast. Her parents looked impressed. So Cindy filled out the application form and wrote down her age as '19', not '16'. How easy, she thought. You just turn a six upside down!

2   Cindy read the Seashell Motel brochure on the bus to Atlantic City. 'Ocean view' it said, but when she got to Atlantic City the motel was far from the sea. And when she got to the motel, it wasn't very nice and it had no ocean view!
At the front desk there was a young man with short brown hair, a blue jacket and a tie – about twenty-two years old.
"Welcome," he said and smiled.
"My name is Cynthia Fisher," Cindy said. Cynthia sounded older, she thought.
"You look a bit young," he said.
It's my clothes and my hair, Cindy thought.
I have to look older.
"I'm nineteen," she lied.
"Fine," he said. "I'm Tim Chamberlain. I'm studying hotel management in Louisiana."
"Are you in college too?" he asked.
"High school ... I mean I finished high school last year ... now I'm at Queens College," she lied.
I'll have to tell lies all summer, Cindy thought.

3   Cindy stood behind the front desk, her hair pulled back, in a white blouse, a dark blue skirt. She wore make-up and lipstick. It felt funny.
Munny was the manager. He was a tall, cheerful guy with curly brown hair.
And there was Cal. He filled the drinks machine. He had long dark hair, green eyes and he always wore a neon T-shirt.

123

He was sixteen and a half and lived in Atlantic City. Cindy liked him.
And there were the guests. Cindy gave them their rooms, took their credit cards, and sometimes made wake-up calls.
One night Tim told her that a guest wanted a wake-up call at 5 am.
"Good morning," Cindy said on the phone.
"Are you crazy?" the man said. It was Tim's joke.
"Munny will fire me!" Cindy said to Tim.
"No, he won't," Tim answered, "Munny likes a joke."

4 One afternoon Cal gave Cindy three cans of Orange and said, "Want to go to the boardwalk tonight? We can just walk around."
"Yes, sure, that sounds like fun," she answered.
"I'll pick you up later," Cal promised.
Later, when they were on the boardwalk, Cal asked Cindy, "Want to go to the Hall of Mirrors?" Cindy saw Cal and herself in the mirrors. Cal took Cindy's hands and he wanted to kiss her, but she pulled back.
"I see," he said, "I'm too young. Hey, it's OK, Cynthia."
Cindy felt terrible. This summer in Atlantic City was a bad idea.
She felt trapped – trapped in her lies ...

5 The next week a hurricane hit Atlantic City. Cindy lay in her bed listening to it. The phone rang – it was Cal.

"I'm downstairs," he said. "Do you want to go for a walk?"
"A walk in the hurricane?" she asked.
"You'll see, it's so beautiful," he said.
Down in the lobby Cal took Cindy's hand. Outside the wind was very loud. They walked towards the boardwalk and they got very wet. The streets were flooded.
It was dangerous, but Cindy felt calm and safe with Cal. At the boardwalk the sky and the sea were the same dark grey. You couldn't see where the sea ended and the sky began.
"What do you think, Cynthia?" Cal said.
"I told you the truth, didn't I? It's so beautiful, isn't it?"

6 "Cal," Cindy suddenly said. "I haven't told you the truth. I'm not who you think I am."
"You're not?" Cal said.
"I'm only sixteen years old. So the way I dress, the way I act, the way I feel ... it's just one big lie!"
Cindy could see that Cal was trying to understand this. Finally he smiled at her.
"You're so brave. I'm sixteen and I've never been away from home – not even for a night," he said.
"I don't feel brave, I just feel trapped. I told lies to the motel, I told lies to my parents and I told lies to you."
Cindy knew that she had to tell the truth to everybody. But not yet. The hurricane was getting louder.

"Let's go back," Cal said.
Back at the motel the sea water was coming into the motel.
The brochure wasn't lying, Cindy thought. Seashell Motel does have an ocean view.

▶ KV 24

2 Questions for you

a) 👥 Answer these questions about part 1 (lines 1 to 36).
1. Why do you think Cindy wanted the job at Seashell Motel?
2. Cindy lied to her teacher. What did she lie about?
3. Cindy lied to her parents. What did she lie about to them?

b) 👥 Pick one part of the story (parts 2 – 6) and read it.
Then make two or three questions for your part, and agree on the answers.

c) 👥 Make groups of 5 students – with one student for each part (2 – 6). Ask and answer your questions.

3 The characters in the story

a) Copy this table and make notes about one of the characters in the story (Cindy / Tim / Cal). Use words and phrases from the story – and your own ideas.

NAME	FROM	AGE	PERSONALITY	APPEARANCE (hair, eyes, …)	CLOTHES	WHAT HE/SHE DOES/LIKES
…	…	…	…	…	…	…

b) 👥 Work with students who picked the other characters and complete a table for the three main characters.
Ask questions to get the information.

> Where's he / she from?
> How old is he / she? What kind of a person is he / she?
> What does he / she look like? What about his / her hair / eyes /…?
> What kind of clothes does he / she wear?
> What does he / she do / like / …?

c) Now put some of these adjectives into your table for all the characters:

> kind • brave • easy-going • honest • adventurous • funny • hard-working • reliable

d) Write a characterization of Cindy, Tim or Cal. Say what you think they are like and give reasons.

e) 👥 Then swap your text with other students and compare.

▶ *Skills file 6.7, p. 169*

DIFF BANK

Unit 3

More challenge 2 — **Who saw it? What did you see?** ▶ Unit 3, p. 61

Your friend is telling you what he did yesterday, but you can't quite hear what he is saying.
Ask questions about the underlined parts.

1. I saw <u>a great film</u> on TV last night. – Sorry, what …
2. <u>The story</u> really disturbed me. – Sorry, what …
3. It described <u>the life of a singer</u>. – Sorry, what …
4. <u>A new band</u> wrote the music for the film. – Sorry, who …
5. <u>Lots of people I know</u> watched the film. – Sorry, who …
6. <u>Our TV</u> wasn't working, so we °went round to our friends' house to watch it. – Sorry, what …
7. <u>My mum</u> watched it with me. – Sorry, who …
8. She thought <u>it was brilliant</u>. – Sorry, what … think?

> **Subject and object questions**
> You can ask questions about the **subject** (e.g. **Who** saw it? – **I** did.)
> or about the **object** of a sentence (e.g. **What** did you see? – **A film**.).
>
> If you ask about the subject, you <u>don't</u> use ~~do~~, ~~does~~ or ~~did~~.
> ▶ Language file 13, p. 189

More challenge 3 — **What are you laughing at?** ▶ Unit 3, p. 61

Make the follow-up questions.

1. The kids are waving to somebody. – Who *are they waving to?*
2. The teacher is cross with somebody. – Who is she …
3. I'm looking forward to the weekend. – What …
4. That girl is smiling at someone. – Who …
5. My friend Tim is afraid of lots of things. – What exactly …

> **Questions with prepositions**
> In English a preposition (*at, to,* etc.) which is closely °linked to a question word usually comes at the end of a question.
>
> This is different to German:
> *What are you laughing at?* –
> *Worüber lachst du?*
> ▶ Language file 15, p. 190

More practice 6 — **Summaries** ▶ Unit 3, p. 65

a) Read these two summaries (A and B) of the first part of the story.
Which one do you think is the best summary? Look at the tips on p. 127 and say why.

A Before the summer Mrs. Karpinsky, a teacher at Cindy's high school in New York City, told all the tenth graders that a summer job was a good idea. She mentioned the Seashell Motel in Atlantic City. They were looking for a front desk clerk. Mrs. Karpinsky walked over to Cindy and handed her the application form. Then she said to Cindy, "Sorry, you have to be nineteen."

B This is a story about Cindy, a teenager from New York City. It's early summer and Cindy is looking for a summer job. Her teacher gives Cindy an application form for a job at a motel in Atlantic City. Cindy really wants this job, but she's too young. So she lies about her age and she writes that she's nineteen on the application form.

b) Now pick one of the other parts of the story on pp. 63–65. Write a short summary.

c) Sit with students who have picked the same part and compare your summaries. Check and correct your summaries.

d) Now sit in groups of students who have written summaries on different parts. Read your summary to them.

> **Tips for summaries**
> - Use the simple present.
> - Don't use direct speech.
> - Keep it short (about 20% of the text).
> - Use your own words.
> - Answer the *wh*-questions.
> - Write the main points only.
>
> ▶ *Skills file 8.4, p. 175*

More challenge 4 **A trailer** ▶ *Unit 3, p. 65*

Imagine you plan to make a film of this story. But first you have to make a two-minute trailer to advertise it.

Step 1: The °**voice-over**
Write a short voice-over text about the story and make it interesting and exciting. Just tell some details of the story – don't tell the whole story.
Here are some example sentences:
 This is a film about Cindy – a sixteen-year-old girl from …
 Cindy wants a summer job at …
 But there's a problem because …
 Cindy's answer to the problem is simple …
 But things get complicated for Cindy when …
 This film is exciting, …,

Step 2: A scene from the film
Pick your favourite scene in the story. Write a short dialogue for it. Then get some actors to play the scene and give them their lines.
Practise the scene with your actors. You're the °**director**.

Step 3: Making the trailer
Perform your trailer for the class (remember, you have only 2 minutes). Read your voice-over. Use a °**dramatic** voice. Use music too, if you like. Your actors should act their scene. Tell the audience why they should watch the film.

More help **1e** **VIEWING** **Interview stress** ▶ *Unit 3, p. 66*

What questions does the interviewer ask Mike? Match the question parts.

Can you tell me something …	team player?
What are your strengths …	about the job?
Are you a good …	and weaknesses?
Why do you want …	a job with us?
Do you have any questions for me …	about yourself?

127

3 DIFF BANK

Unit 3

More help **2a** NOW YOU Answering interview questions ▶ Unit 3, p. 66

Here are some typical interview questions and some ideas on how to answer them:

How would you describe yourself?	Think of adjectives that you could use about yourself, e.g.: confident, hard-working, energetic, calm, responsible, friendly …

What are your strengths?	Think of skills that °employers look for:
	I can work carefully.
	I'm good at - reacting to criticism.
	               - organizing myself / other people.
	I like - working with people.
	               - finding solutions to problems.
	I have - a good head for heights.
	               - good communication skills.

What are your weaknesses?	When you talk about a weakness, make sure you say what you are doing to improve. Example: I don't have much work experience, that's why I'm applying for this job.
Are you a good team player? Give an example.	Examples could be: a team you play for, a project you worked on at school, something you organized in your youth group

More help **3** YOUR TASK Who will get the job? ▶ Unit 3, p. 67

Step 1: Look at the advert

Before you answer the questions, take a closer look at the advert.

Restaurant team member
in busy fast-food restaurant

Improve your service and teamwork skills in our restaurant. We're looking for very hard-working, enthusiastic individuals. Part-time or full-time work. Experience not necessary.

The ideal candidate has to:
- be able to work as part of a team
- speak clearly and listen carefully to guests and staff members
- have a professional, energetic and enthusiastic approach

If you like the sound of us, please send your CV by email.

> Teamwork is mentioned a lot in the advert – so be well prepared for a question on teamwork. Show that you like it.

> They expect you to be very hard-working and energetic. So tell them you have lots of °energy.

> How you speak and listen to others is important. In the interview you need to show how good your communication skills are.

> Don't forget to think of at least one question about the job.

Step 3: Decide who should get the job
Use the notes on the assessors' forms and your own impressions to help your discussion.

1. How did the candidates present themselves?
   Were their handshakes good?
   Did they have eye contact?
   Did they smile?
   Was their body language positive?
   Did they speak clearly?

   > **You could say things like this:**
   > They all had good handshakes.
   > Timo didn't have great eye contact.
   > They all smiled a lot.
   > Their body language was quite good. Nina was very good, very positive.
   > They all spoke clearly. Timo spoke °rather quietly, and Monique spoke rather fast.

2. How good were their answers?
   Did they say enough?

   > **You could say things like this:**
   > They all gave quite good answers, but Timo was very good because he sounded like he really wanted the job and said things that are in the advert.
   > Sometimes the answers were a bit short.

3. Did they ask questions?

   > **You could say things like this:**
   > They all asked questions.
   > Monique asked very good questions.

At the end you have to decide who should get the job.

> **Talk like this:**
> I think … should get the job because …
> I agree. / I don't agree. I think … was better because …
> That's true. Let's choose …

Unit 3 — **Stop! Check! Go!**

1a REVISION Driving in Ireland ▶ Unit 3, p. 68

Michael (17) from Germany is asking his Irish friend, Dylan, about his learner licence. Write Michael's questions.

	Michael's questions	Dylan's answers
1	Do you … any tests?	You have to pass a theory and an eyesight test.
2	When …?	A learner licence ends after two years.
3	Are …?	No, learner drivers are not allowed to drive on motorways.
4	How …?	A learner driver can't drive fast – only 72 km/h.
5	Can …?	No, you can't drive alone. A qualified driver must be in the car with you.
6	Who …?	A qualified driver is someone who has had a full licence for two years.

3-4 DIFF BANK

Unit 3 — Stop! Check! Go!

More challenge 5 **An accident** ▶ Unit 3, p. 68

Imagine that you are a police officer and you are writing a report about Dylan's accident.

a) Write down the three most important questions to ask the car driver (Dylan) and the lorry driver.

b) Write a short report. Use indirect speech.

More help 5 WRITING Who is important in your life? ▶ Unit 3, p. 70

You need to think of a person who is important in your life. It could be someone who:
- is always there when you need help
- gave you advice in a difficult situation
  (What advice? Give examples.)
- is a good example to you (Why?)
- did something special
- has the same interests or hobbies as you
- spends a lot of time with you

Unit 4

More help 3 YOUR TASK A survey in your class ▶ Unit 4, p. 75

Step 2: You can use a table like this for your survey. Use symbols (cool ✓ not cool ✗).

name	1	2	3	4	5	6
Emily	✗ too old-fashioned	✓ very cute	✓ clever and funny	...	...	...
Mehmet						

(Prepare at least 10 lines.)

Step 4: You can talk about your pictures like this. Show the images when you talk about them.

Start with the picture that most people liked.
> This is our most popular picture.
> Lots of people thought this picture was really cool.
> They said it was fun (clever / funny).
> Two people said they'd like to wear (watch / listen to) this.

Then talk about pictures that not everybody liked.
> This picture wasn't (very) popular.
> Only one person thought this picture was cool.
> Most people thought it was too old-fashioned (silly / stupid).

Say what surprised you (or didn't surprise you).
> That didn't surprise us because we think the same.
> That surprised us because we think this is really cool.

More challenge 1   *-ing*-form (gerund) or *to*-infinitive after verbs   ▶ Unit 4, p. 77

FOCUS

1) *I enjoy playing games.* ⟷ *I want to buy a new game.*
After some verbs you **only** use an ***-ing*-form** (a **gerund**), e.g. *dislike, enjoy, finish, imagine, miss, practise.*
After others you **only** use *to* + an **infinitive**, e.g. *would like to …, want to …, need to …, hope to …*

2) *I like playing games.* ⟷ *I like to play games.* ⇨ *same meaning*
After some verbs you can use an ***-ing*-form** (a **gerund**) or *to* + an **infinitive** and **the meaning is the same**, e.g. *start, begin, continue, like, love, prefer, hate.*

3) *I stopped using my phone.* ⟷ *I stopped to use my phone.* ⇨ *different meaning*
After some verbs you can use an ***-ing*-form** (a **gerund**) or *to* + an **infinitive**, but **the meaning is different**.

stop doing something (aufhören, etwas zu tun) ⟷ *stop to do something* (stoppen / anhalten, um etwas anderes zu tun)

forget doing something (vergessen, dass man früher etwas getan hat) ⟷ *forget to do something* (vergessen, später etwas zu tun)

remember doing something (sich daran erinnern, dass man etwas getan hat) ⟷ *remember to do something* (daran denken, etwas zu tun)

▶ Language file 29, p. 201

a) Complete the sentences with an ***-ing*-form** (a **gerund**) or *to* + an **infinitive**.

1 I remember … (switch off) my phone last night. I don't understand why it's still on. ⟷ I must remember … (switch off) my phone tonight. If I don't, Mum will be cross.

2 I've stopped … (send) my friend texts late at night. I need to go to sleep earlier. ⟷ I was doing my homework. But I got a text from my friend and I stopped … (text) her back.

3 I'll never forget … (play) Angry Birds for the first time. I thought it was brilliant. ⟷ I forgot … (do) my homework because I was playing a brilliant computer game.

b) Complete the text with ***-ing*-form** (**gerunds**) or ***to*-infinitives**. Sometimes you can use both.

I think I'm a typical screenager. I really enjoy … (1 use) social media and I like … (2 video chat) with my friends. My parents want me … (3 spend) less time in front of a screen. They get very angry when I don't stop … (4 read) a text when I'm eating with them. I also love … (5 play) video games. Sometimes I get into trouble because I don't stop … (6 play) until really late. I also forget … (7 do) my homework quite often. I'm trying … (8 be) less chaotic. But hey! I'm a teenager. I don't always remember … (9 do) things. It's normal!

DIFF BANK 4

Unit 4

More practice 1 — Talk about profile pictures ▶ Unit 4, p. 78

👥 What do you think profile pictures tell us about a person? Give examples.

I'm not sure if / I think that	profile pictures tell us a lot about a person.

Perhaps a profile picture can tell us that a person	would like to be … / is …

artistic • boring • careful • clever • cool • crazy • different • easy-going • energetic • exciting • friendly • fun • independent • interesting • likeable • normal • old-fashioned • popular • romantic • shy • silly • sporty • strange

---

More help — **1b** Profile pictures ▶ Unit 4, p. 78

First describe the profile picture:
- This is a picture of …
- He / She is wearing …
- He / She is with …
- He / She / It looks …
- In the background you can see …

Then say why you like this profile picture:
- I like this picture because …
- I think this picture tells us that this person is …
- Perhaps he / she wants to look …
- …

More practice 2 — More on the text ▶ Unit 4, p. 79

a) Choose the most likely title for the written discussion on page 79. Explain your choice.
1. What are selfies?
2. Selfies: Do you love them or hate them?
3. Why have selfies become popular recently?

b) Do you agree with the writer's conclusion about selfies? Why (not)? Talk like this:

The writer likes selfies,	and I do too. / but I don't.

Now say why. Use your own ideas or choose from this list. You can choose more than one.

I think	it's fun to take selfies. everybody takes selfies. It's normal. a selfie is a nice way to remember a time when you felt good. selfies are boring – who wants to see pictures of other people? people only take selfies because they want to look good or cool.

More help 3a WRITING — For and against tattoos ▶ Unit 4, p. 79

Collect ideas:
Which of the arguments below are <u>for</u> tattoos and which are <u>against</u>? Make two lists.
Add your own ideas.

- My parents don't like the idea.
- Lots of celebrities have them.
- They're very trendy.
- They are very expensive.
- All my friends have them.
- Once you have one, it's hard to get rid of it.
- You can get an infection.
- They are artistic.
- You might not like it in a few years' time.
- Maybe it will be difficult to get a job. Employers might not like it.

Make a plan:

Paragraph 1 introduction – describe the general topic

> Today tattoos are becoming more popular.
> I don't have any tattoos, but …
> None (Some) of my friends have tattoos.
> Lots of footballers have tattoos. For example …
> So is this a good idea or not?

Paragraph 2 arguments for (or against)
Are you're <u>against</u> tattoos? Then start with arguments <u>for</u> in this paragraph.
Are you're <u>for</u> tattoos? Then start with arguments <u>against</u>.

> Firstly / Secondly …
> For example,
> On the one hand – on the other hand …
> In other words …
> Maybe …
> Don't forget that …
> Lots of people say that …
> I'm not so sure about that.

Paragraph 3 arguments against (or for)

Paragraph 4 conclusion – give your personal opinion

> I (definitely) think …
> In my opinion, …
> To sum up …
> … tattoos are / aren't a good idea.

2 Headings ▶ Unit 4, p. 81

Find a good heading for each paragraph of the text on p. 80.

4 DIFF BANK

Unit 4

More practice 3 — **Working with the text** ▶ Unit 4, p. 81

Finish these sentences with ideas from the text.
1. If teenagers become ad-savvy, ...
2. The advertising industry is interested in teens because ... (Give 2 reasons.)
3. Ads use special strategies, for example by showing perfect, beautiful people, or ... (Give 3 more examples.)
4. The advertising industry is interested in finding out about ...
5. Popular vloggers are interesting for the ad companies because ...

More practice 4 — **TV fun** ▶ Unit 4, p. 81

a) Sit down with your family or friends – or both. Watch some German TV ads and comment on them.
Try to spot the tricks, e.g. the jingles, the slogans, the cool people, etc.
Who can spot the most tricks?

b) Tell the class about what you found – in English, of course.
What was the best trick that you spotted? Why?

More practice 5 — **Your own advert** ▶ Unit 4, p. 81

If you want to understand how adverts work, you need to make one.
Work in pairs.
Invent a product (make-up, food, drink, clothes … anything you like).
Think of a good name for your product.
Think of a slogan for your advert.
Find or make a good jingle.
Then perform the advert for the class.
Ask the class which of your tricks they can spot.

More challenge 2 — **WRITING   Your opinion** ▶ Unit 4, p. 81

"Teenagers are influenced by all kinds of ads."
Do you agree or disagree with this statement?
Explain your opinion and give examples.

> Write about things like this:
> - ads that you and your friends like (and why)
> - where you see these ads
> - the products that you and your friends buy
> - if you are influenced by ads (and how)

3 What would you have done? ▶ Unit 4, p. 83

Read the sentences. Then decide what you would have done.

1. **Ben** Leah didn't invite me to her party, but I went. What would you have done?
   You *I would / wouldn't have gone to the party.*
2. **Ben** For my birthday my parents said I could have a party or I could go to a theme park. I chose the party.
   You …
3. **Ben** My friend and I wanted to go to the cinema. I waited at the cinema but he didn't come, so I went home.
   You …
4. **Ben** I was angry because my friend bought the same shirt as me.
   You …

4 Oh dear, what a shame! ▶ Unit 4, p. 83

Complete the sentences with the correct form of the verbs in brackets.

1. I was in trouble because I was late. If I *had got up* (get up) earlier, I … (not be) late.
2. My test results weren't great. If I … (work) harder, I … (get) better marks.
3. I chatted with friends after class and missed my bus. If I … (not chat) for so long, I … (not miss) it.
4. I couldn't do my homework because I forgot my book. If I … (remember) my book, I … (do) my homework.
5. I didn't tell my friend that I was going out. If I … (know) that she wanted to come, I … (phone) her.
6. I don't have any money for a phone. If I … (work) in the holidays, I … (earn) some.

More challenge 3 Poor me! ▶ Unit 4, p. 83

What is the person thinking? Use conditional 3.

- If I … got up late, I wouldn't have missed …
- If I … caught …, I … taken my bike.
- If the car driver … suddenly opened the door, …
- If I … °crashed, …
- … if I hadn't hurt myself.
- …

4 DIFF BANK
TEXT – Easier version
▶ KV 33

Gamer (adapted from the novel by Chris Bradford)

Part 1   Bread

On the big 3D screen in the street two fighters are fighting. When the fight is over, a big red and black logo comes onto the screen. It says: *VK*.
5   A voice says,
"*Virtual Kombat. So real that it hurts.*"
Now the street kids go into the lanes and backstreets.
Unwanted. Ignored. Forgotten. I'm one of them.
10   I lost my parents to the killer virus of 2030. It killed millions.
The strange thing was that kids didn't get the virus.
Now there are thousands of us in the streets.
15   After that people stopped going outside. The adults were still scared they might catch something. Most people started to play games on the net.
That's when *VK* first started.

20   "*Virtual Kombat – the most realistic fighting game ever!*"
That's what the ads say. Virtual Kombat is the number 1 game show in the world. Everyone watches or plays it.
25   Huge street screens are everywhere in the city.

I haven't eaten in days. When the show is on, you don't think about being hungry. But when it's over, you feel hungry again.
I go up a narrow backstreet. There are big bins
30   here, behind the restaurants where rich people eat. If I'm lucky, I might find some food in the bins.

Then I hear a voice. "Give it to me!"
I see two teens standing over a little girl and boy. The girl is holding a bag. The taller teen pulls the
35   bag from her. The girl doesn't cry. Street kids are tough.
"Leave my sis alone," the boy shouts. "Give that back. It's ours!"
"Finders keepers, losers weepers," the other
40   teen says.
He's short, with dark red hair. He pushes the boy to the ground and laughs.
"You won't believe this, Juice," says the taller teen. "They have bread!"

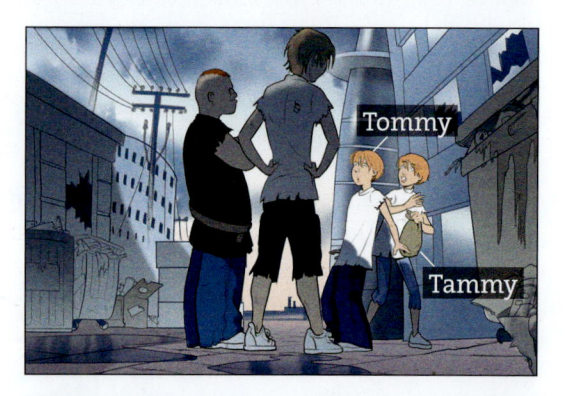

▶ KV 33

Part 2 Street fighter

I creep up and take the bread from the teenagers.
"Oi," Stick shouts, as he turns around. "That's ours!"
"Finders keepers, losers weepers," I say.
Suddenly Stick has a long piece of metal in his
50 hands and tries to hit me. I drop the bread and move forward to stop him.
Juice jumps on me, but I throw him over my shoulder onto the ground.
"Wait till Shark hears about this," Stick says.
55 "He'll get you!"
I say nothing as they walk away. But inside I'm shouting at myself, "IDIOT!" Shark is bad news.

The little boy and girl stare at me. It's clear they're twins – blond hair, blue eyes.
60 "What are your names?" I ask.
"Tommy – and my sis is Tammy," the boy says.
I give the little girl the bag of bread. She says nothing, but she takes the bag.
"Who are you?" whispers Tommy.
65 "Scott," I say.
"Where did you learn to fight like that?" Tommy asks.
"*Street fighter 7*."
Before the virus I trained with my dad every day.
Tammy takes out a big piece of bread, gives half
70 of it to Tommy and gives some bread to me. I eat it hungrily.
"That was great."
Tammy smiles for the first time. But suddenly her smile is gone.
75 "THERE HE IS!"
I turn around. Stick and Juice are at the end of the lane. This time they have the Shark gang with them. Shark himself is there too. He grins at me, and I see his broken teeth. Shark takes out a knife.
80 It's time to fight or run. I run.

Part 3 Roof escape

They run after me. I run across the road and into a lane on the other side. I jump onto a big bin and then onto a fire escape ladder. I climb and climb
85 until I get to the roof – 12 floors up. Below me I see the city, the lights, the big screens, ... And I see Shark and the gang – they're following me. I jump from one roof to another. At first I can't see Shark. But then suddenly he's in front of me. Shark grins
90 from ear to ear as he takes out his knife.
At that moment we hear the *VK* music. We both stop.
"I'll get you later," Shark says and he disappears.

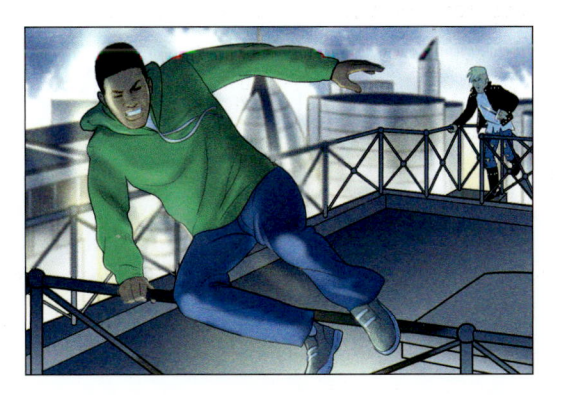

4 DIFF BANK
▶ KV 33

Part 4 The *VK* truck

As I get to the square I see a lot of street kids
95 around a big white truck with the **VK** logo on the side.
The **VK** truck is the only way to get off these streets. It's a mobile **VK** game station. If you're good enough, you can become a **VK** games tester.
100 That means food every day, a bed, school – a chance of a normal life. But I'm too late. All the seats are full. Then I see Shark. He has a seat and his gang are near him. As I move away, I hear my name. I see Tommy. He has a seat too and he's
105 waving at me to come over.
"Take my place," he says.
"Are you crazy?" I say.

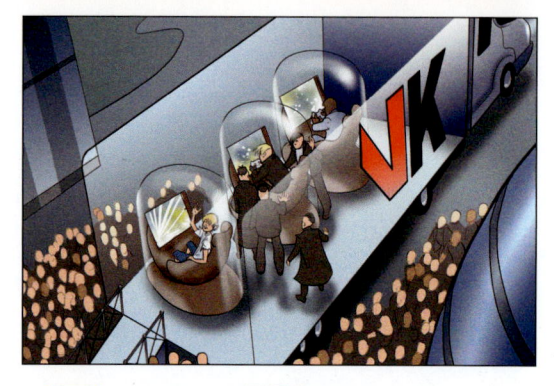

"I can't leave my sis, can I?" He gets off his seat.
"I was keeping it for you," he says.
110 "Everybody ready to play?" a loud voice says.
The game begins.

Box: Voc., p. 230

2 Which part …

Which part (1 – 4) …
- shows us what kind of person Scott is?
- gives information about street kids?
- gives some hope for Scott's future?
- describes an exciting race through the city?

3 ◯ Information in the text

Complete the following sentences with information from the text.
1 In this story there are lots of street kids because lots of adults have died from … (line 10)
2 Not everybody is poor and hungry, for example the … people eat in restaurants. (line 30)
3 Scott can fight well because he practised with his … (line 69)
4 Tammy and Tommy know that Scott is hungry, so they give him … (line 71)
5 Scott is happy when he sees a fire escape ladder, because he can climb up to … (line 86)
6 If Scott becomes a games tester, he'll have … (lines 101–102)

4 Characters in the story

a) Make notes about one character in the story under these headings:
NAME, AGE, PERSONALITY, APPEARANCE, WHAT YOU THINK OF HIM/HER

▶ Skills file 6.7, p. 169

b) **Walk around:** Compare your notes with other students.

5 WRITING An email to the author

Complete this email to the author of *Gamer*, Chris Bradford. You can write more, if you like.

> Dear Mr Bradford,
>
> I read your book Gamer, and I thought it was …   The main character is Scott and I think he's …   I really liked it when he …   The setting for this story is very interesting because …   I think the story is sad when …   It's exciting and a bit scary when …   Gaming can be bad for you if …

▶ Skills file 8.3, p. 174

Unit 4

More practice 6 — **An email to Scott** ▶ Unit 4, p. 87

Fill in suitable words from the box on the right.

Hi Scott

I was very interested to read … (1) your adventures in 2030. I love stories about the future, but I think that your world is … (2), and I'm very … (3) that I don't live in it. I was very sad when I read that your parents had … (4) of a killer virus. I really liked the … (5), Tammy and Tommy – they're so sweet! But I thought that Shark and his … (6) were horrible. You were … (7) when you helped Tammy and Tommy. And it was nice when the twins gave you some … (8). I thought that it was very exciting when you … (9) over the roofs of the city. I really hope that you … (10) the Virtual Kombat game and find a better life. But I think that your story shows that people can be addicted to … (11), and that's bad.

Best wishes … (12) a big fan

Kirsty

(1) over / about / on / to
(2) scary / fun / comfortable / cold
(3) sad / °hopeful / angry / happy
(4) lived / had / died / saw
(5) boys / girls / teens / twins
(6) teens / gang / kids / family
(7) brave / frightened / stupid / quiet
(8) money / drink / meat / bread
(9) drove / rode / escaped / flew
(10) get / win / lose / play
(11) fighting / food / games / fun
(12) to / for / at / from

More challenge 4 — **WRITING** **A blurb** ▶ Unit 4, p. 87

Write a blurb for *Gamer*. Include information about:
- the author
- the setting and time of the story
- the main characters
- what happens
- why it's a good story

! Look at the blurb in task 1 on page 62 in Unit 3.

More help **1c** **VIEWING** **Shocking news!** ▶ Unit 4, p. 88

Here are some phrases from the film.
Find the missing words in the box.

about • bad • good • point • say • shocking • something • true • what • with

1 How can they do that? That's … news!
2 Well, maybe it's … that teenagers do too much vamping.
3 Well actually, I don't think that's such a … idea.
4 Sorry, I just can't agree … that.
5 Yes, that's a … point.
6 In my opinion, … has to be done.
7 Another … is 'sleepy texting'.
8 It's true to … that we can decide things ourselves.
9 I see … you mean.
10 You're right … that.

4 DIFF BANK

Unit 4

More practice 7 — **Banning social media at night** ▶ Unit 4, p. 88

What do Marek, Tim, Amy and Grace think about this idea?
Who agrees? Who disagrees?
Who isn't sure?

More help **3 NOW YOU** Listen and speak

Step 1 ▶ Unit 4, p. 89

a) Each group prepares a list of arguments. You will either be <u>for</u> video games, or <u>against</u> them, or <u>not sure</u>. Choose from this list or use your own ideas:

- If you play video games, your reactions are very fast.
- Playing video games is unhealthy because you sit for so long.
- Video games are often violent. / aren't always violent.
- Playing video games is a good way to get rid of stress.
- When people start playing games, they can't stop.
- Gamers can / can't tell the difference between the game and the real world.
- When you play video games, time °goes by° very quickly.

b) Think of examples and reasons to support your arguments like this:

- People often play alone and this is a bad thing because … (Give a reason.)
- It's true that people sometimes play alone, but on the other hand they also play with other people. (Give an example.)
- Video games are often violent. / aren't always violent. For example, … (List games that you know that are or aren't violent.) In my opinion, … (Say why you think games are violent or not violent.)

Step 2 ▶ Unit 4, p. 89

The observer(s) need a copy of this form. They should make notes.

	very good	OK	needs work
Repeat what the last speaker said.			
Say if you agree or disagree.			
Make your point cleary.			
Give reasons and examples.			
Speak respectfully.			

Unit 4 — Stop! Check! Go!

More help **7** **MEDIATION** Generations Y and Z ▶ Unit 4, p. 93

	Generation Y	Generation Z
1 Umgang mit Geld		
2 Kaufverhalten		
3 Lebensbedingungen		
4 Art des Filmkonsums		
5 Sport		
6 Online-Kommunikation		
7 Sorgen		

More challenge 5 **MEDIATION** A German article ▶ Unit 4, p. 93

Hilf deinem amerikanischen Freund, der nur etwas Deutsch kann, diesen Zeitungsartikel zu verstehen. Sage ihm, worum es generell geht, wer zur Generation Z gehört, was ihre besonderen Merkmale sind, wie sie kommuniziert, wie sie lernt, was für sie im Leben wichtig ist.

Generation Z heißt der neue Trend

Als Generation Z wird die Generation bezeichnet, welche in den späten 90ern auf die Welt kam. Typisch für sie ist vor allem, dass es die erste Generation ist, die vollkommen in einer digitalen Welt aufgewachsen ist. Mit vielfältigen Folgen. Nicht umsonst heißen die Menschen der Generation Z im Englischen *digital natives*.

Die Welt der Generation Z ist noch digitaler als die ihrer Vorgänger, der Generation Y. Mit Freunden wird über Facebook und Co. kommuniziert, aber man trifft sich nicht unbedingt in Vereinen oder mit Freunden. Alles wird gepostet, *geliked*, kommentiert, aber nur digital.

Generation Z hat nicht mehr nur ein Leben, sondern viele: auf Instagram, Tumblr, Snapchat, Viner …

Außerdem hat man mit 5000 bis 10000 *Followern* auf Twitter einen riesigen Freundeskreis. Die Art, wie Lernen stattfindet, ist eine völlig andere: Wissen ist jederzeit und überall verfügbar, und jeder *user* muss in der Lage sein, aus der Informationslawine das zu filtern, was in der jeweiligen Situation gerade wichtig ist.

Generation Z besteht auf einer klaren Trennung zwischen Beruflichem und Privatem. Freizeit und Familie sind wichtiger als Arbeit. Sie ist – anders als die Generation vor ihr – nicht mehr teamorientiert, denn die meisten Menschen der Generation Z haben kein direktes Interesse an ihren unmittelbaren Mitmenschen. Wichtige Themen sind vor allem Umwelt und Fairness.

WORDBANK

Wordbank 1: At the doctor's ▸ Unit 1, p. 13

What the doctor says / asks

What's the problem?

Where does it hurt?

What are your symptoms?

How long have you been feeling like this?

What have you eaten today?

Are you on any sort of medication?
Nehmen Sie Medikamente?

Do you have any allergies?
Haben Sie Allergien?

Are you diabetic? / Do you have diabetes?
Sind Sie Diabetiker/in?

Let me take your blood pressure / temperature / pulse.
Lassen Sie mich Ihren Blutdruck / Ihre Temperatur / Ihren Puls messen.

Could you roll up your sleeve?
Könnten Sie den Ärmel hochkrempeln?

Your blood pressure is low / normal / high.
Ihr Blutdruck ist hoch / normal / niedrig.

Open your mouth, please.
Öffnen Sie bitte den Mund.

Show me your tongue, please.
Zeigen Sie mir bitte Ihre Zunge.

Cough, please.
Bitte husten.

You're going to need a few stitches.
Sie müssen genäht werden.

I'll desinfect and dress the wound.
Ich werde die Wunde desinfizieren und verbinden.

I'm going to give you an injection.
Ich werde Ihnen eine Spritze geben.

I'm going to prescribe you some antibiotics.
Ich werde Ihnen ein Antibiotikum verschreiben.

Take two of these pills three times a day.
Nehmen Sie zwei von diesen Tabletten dreimal täglich.

You need an X-ray.
Ich möchte Sie zum Röntgen schicken.

You need to be vaccinated against tetanus.
Sie brauchen eine Tetanusimpfung.

What you say

I've got a cold / cough / temperature.
Ich habe eine Erkältung / Husten / Fieber.

I've got a sore throat.
Ich habe Halsschmerzen.

I've got a headache / stomach ache.
Ich habe Kopfschmerzen / Magenschmerzen.

My arm / back / hand / knee / leg / neck / shoulder hurts. I can't move it.
Ich habe Schmerzen im Arm / Rücken / an der Hand / am Knie / am Fuß / im Nacken / an der Schulter. Ich kann ihn / es / sie nicht bewegen.

I feel sick.   Mir ist schlecht.

I feel dizzy.   Mir ist schwindlig.

My joints are aching.   Ich habe Gliederschmerzen.

I've got diarrhea.   Ich habe Durchfall.

I'm constipated.   Ich habe Verstopfung.

I've hurt my foot / wrist / arm / …
Ich habe mich am Fuß / Handgelenk / Arm / … verletzt.

I've got a swollen foot / arm …
Mein Fuß / Arm / … ist geschwollen.

I've sprained my ankle.
Ich habe mir den Knöchel verstaucht.

I'm in a lot of pain.
Ich habe starke Schmerzen.

I think I've pulled a muscle.
Ich glaube, ich habe eine Muskelzerrung.

I can't breathe (properly).
Ich kann nicht (richtig) atmen.

I'm allergic to some antibiotics.
Ich bin allergisch gegen Antibiotika.

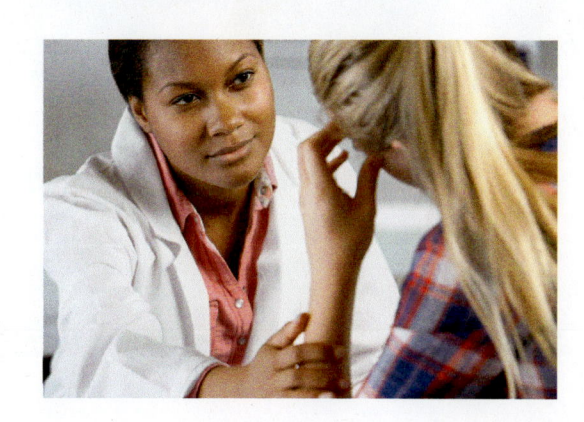

▶ INKL p. 104

Wordbank 2: Strengths and weaknesses ▶ Unit 3, p. 55

Strengths

caring	warmherzig, liebevoll	independent	unabhängig
confident	selbstbewusst	motivated	motiviert
commited	engagiert	organized	organisiert, strukturiert
creative	kreativ	patient	geduldig
disciplined	diszipliniert	practical	geschickt
easy-going	gelassen	polite	höflich
energetic	aktiv	punctual	pünktlich
flexible	flexibel	quiet	ruhig
friendly	freundlich	reliable	verlässlich
hard-working	fleißig, tüchtig	responsible	verantwortungsbewusst
helpful	hilfsbereit	sporty	sportlich
honest	ehrlich, integer	tidy	ordentlich

Weaknesses

aggressive	aggressiv	messy	unordentlich
dishonest	unehrlich	selfish	egoistisch
disorganized	unstrukturiert	shy	schüchtern
impolite	unhöflich	(very) slow	(sehr) langsam
impatient	ungeduldig	stubborn	stur
insecure	unsicher	undisciplined	undiszipliniert
lazy	faul	unfriendly	unfreundlich

I'm good at / I'm not so good at

- giving and taking advice
- managing my time well
- solving problems
- organizing things
- working with my hands
- making decisions
- working with computers
- reacting to criticism
- looking after people
- dealing with children
- communicating
- working in a team
- languages
- dealing with stress

WORDBANK
▶ INKL p. 105

Wordbank 3: Jobs and job titles ▶ Unit 3, p. 57

Management/Commerce   Verwaltung/Handel
administrative assistant   Verwaltungsangestellte/r
assistant tax inspector   Steuerfachangestelle/r
assistant bank manager   Bankkaufmann/-frau
sales representative   Industriekaufmann/-frau
insurance sales representative   Versicherungskaufmann/-frau
legal assistant   Rechtsanwaltsfachangestellte/r
assistant logistics manager   Speditionskaufmann/-frau
sales representative in wholesale and foreign trade   Kaufmann/-frau im Groß- und Außenhandel
office management assistant   Bürokaufmann/-frau
retail assistant manager   Kaufmann/-frau im Einzelhandel
sales assistant   Verkäufer/in
travel agent   Reiseverkehrskaufmann/-frau

Health and care   Gesundheit und Pflege
animal keeper   Tierpfleger/in
dentist's assistant   Zahnarzthelfer/in
doctor's assistant   Arzthelfer/in
geriatric assistant/care worker   Altenpfleger/in
nursery teacher   Erzieher/in
midwife   Hebamme / Entbindungspfleger
nutritionist   Ernährungsberater/in
optical technician   Feinoptiker/in
orthopaedic technician   Orthopädietechniker/in
paramedic   Sanitäter/in
physiotherapist   Physiotherapeut/in, Krankengymnast/in
nurse   Krankenpfleger/-schwester

Craft   Handwerk
baker   Bäcker/in
bricklayer   Maurer/in
carpenter   Zimmerer/Zimmerin
electrician   Elektriker/in
florist   Florist/in
joiner   Schreiner/in
mechanic   Mechaniker/in
metalworker   Schlosser/in
painter   Maler/in

Service   Dienstleistung
beautician   Kosmetiker/in
cook   Koch / Köchin
assistant hotel manager   Hotelkaufmann/-frau
lorry driver   LKW-Fahrer/in
postman/-woman   Briefträger/in
waiter/waitress   Kellner/in

Technology   Technik
automotive engineer   Fahrzeugtechnik-Ingenieur/in
chemical engineer   Chemieingenieur/in
design engineer   Konstrukteur/in
electrical engineer   Elektroingenieur/in
mechanical engineer   Maschinenbauingenieur/in
mechatronics technician   Mechatroniker/in
motor vehicle technician   Kfz-Mechaniker/in
telecom(munication)s engineer   Fernmeldeingenieur/in

IT and Media   IT und Medien
digital web analyst   Webanalyst/in
IT technician   IT-Techniker/in
media designer   Mediendesigner/in
media technician   Medientechniker/in
programmer   Programmierer/in
software engineer   Software-Entwickler/in

▶ INKL p. 106

Wordbank 4: Describing jobs ▶ Unit 3, p. 57

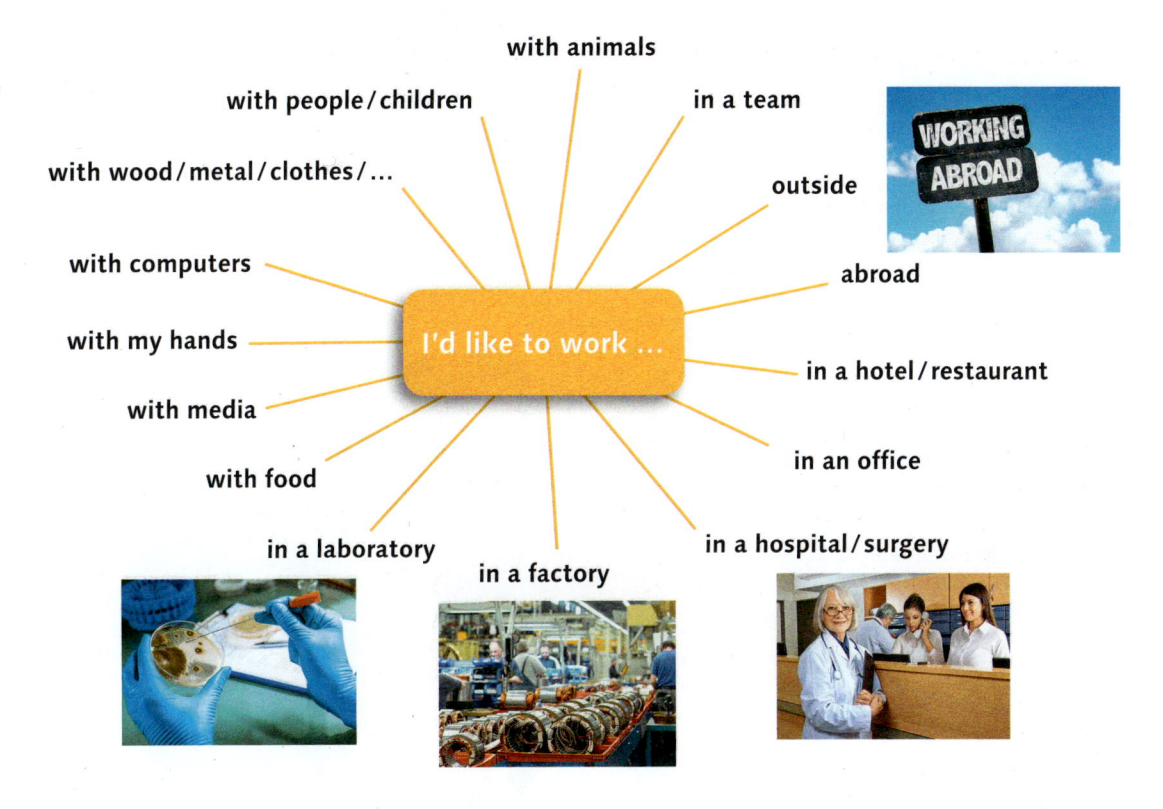

I'd like to work …

- with animals
- with people / children
- with wood / metal / clothes / …
- with computers
- with my hands
- with media
- with food
- in a laboratory
- in a factory
- in a team
- outside
- abroad
- in a hotel / restaurant
- in an office
- in a hospital / surgery

Wordbank 5: In a job interview ▶ Unit 3, p. 66

Why you want the job

I am really interested in this job because I want to gain experience in this area.	Ich bin sehr interessiert an dieser Stelle, weil ich in diesem Bereich Erfahrung sammeln möchte.
I have always wanted to work in this field.	Ich wollte schon immer in diesem Gebiet arbeiten.
I'm interested in …	Ich interessiere mich für …
I would like to develop my … skills.	Ich würde gerne meine …fähigkeiten weiterentwickeln.
I really enjoy working in a team.	Ich arbeite sehr gerne im Team.
I think this is a job I could do well, because …	Ich glaube, ich wäre gut in diesem Beruf, weil …

Experience

I have some experience of office work.	Ich habe etwas Erfahrung mit Büroarbeit.
I have already worked at / in …	Ich habe schon in … gearbeitet.
I have helped out in …	Ich habe in … ausgeholfen.
I have done work experience in …	Ich habe ein Praktikum in … gemacht.
I can use standard software.	Ich kann mit Standardsoftware umgehen.

145

TEXT FILE
▶ INKL p. 78–81

TF 1 Oz: Facts for visitors
Australia – an infographic

CURRENCY
Australian dollar (AUD)

THE AUSTRALIAN NATIONAL FLAG
The British flag in the top left-hand corner represents Britain's role in the history of Australia. The Southern Cross, on the right, is a group of stars that Australians can see 'down under', but which can't be seen in Europe.

NICKNAMES
Australia is called 'Oz' or 'Aus', or the land 'down under', because it is 'under' the equator[1].

SIZE
7,700,000 km^2
▶ Australia is 21 times bigger than Germany (357,000 km^2).

POPULATION
23,600,000
▶ Germany has 3.4 times more people (81,000,000).

GOVERNMENT
Federal parliamentary constitutional monarchy

CLIMATE
The northern third of the country is tropical[2], with two seasons: a hot wet summer and a warm dry winter. Most of Australia is warm or hot all year, but the coldest winter temperatures are in the south and the warmest winter temperatures are in the north. Most of the country gets only 100 to 500 mm of rain per year and 40 % of Australia is desert.

CAPITAL CITY
Sydney and Melbourne both applied to be the capital, but in the end Canberra was chosen.

LANGUAGE
English

WHERE PEOPLE LIVE
89 % of the population lives in towns or cities. The five largest cities are: Sydney, Melbourne, Brisbane, Perth and Adelaide.
More than 85 % of the population lives near the coast.

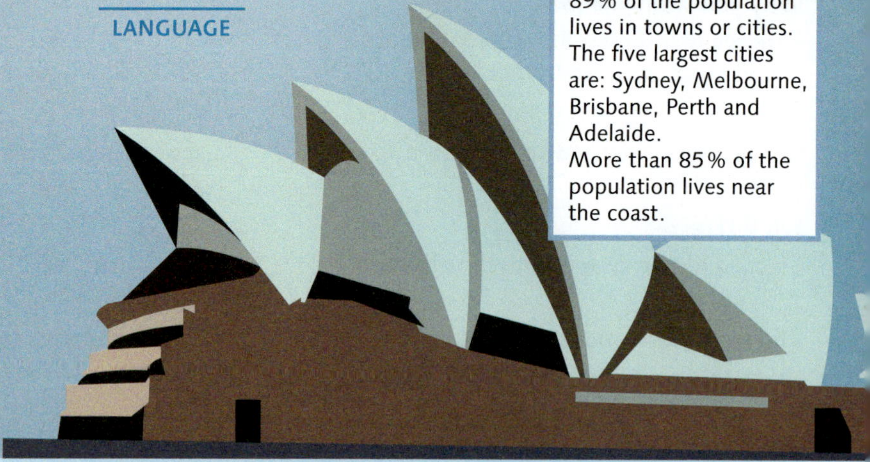

WHEN TO TRAVEL
Most visitors arrive in summer (December to February), when the weather is sunny and warm in places like Sydney, Melbourne and Brisbane. But at that time it's hot and wet in the north, so it's best to visit this area in winter (June to August).

1 Find some more facts about Australia (e.g. online).
   Take notes and present them to a partner.
   Example: Did you know that ... Australia has over 10,000 beaches / you drive on the left in Oz / the seasons in Oz are opposite to those of the northern hemisphere[3] (e.g. Europe) / ...?

---
[1] equator [ɪˈkweɪtə] *Äquator*   [2] tropical [ˈtrɒpɪkl] *tropisch*   [3] hemisphere [ˈhemɪsfɪə] *Halbkugel*

146

▶ INKL p. 78–81

Oz highlights for visitors

1. **The outback:** The huge deserts in the centre and the west are full of special places, including the big rock Uluru. It's a great place to learn about Aboriginal culture.
2. **Sydney:** Must-sees are Sydney Harbour and Bondi Beach.
3. **Cairns:** From here you can visit the Great Barrier Reef and the tropical rainforests of the north.
4. **Tasmania:** This island is famous for wild landscapes, beautiful waterfalls and clean air.
5. **Australian wildlife:** See animals, birds and plants that aren't found anywhere else in the world, like the platypus[4], the wombat, the koala and the kookaburra[5].

2 Match the pictures A – E to the texts 1 – 5.

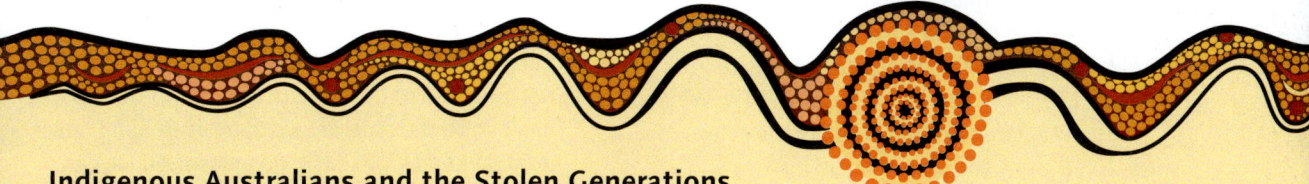

Indigenous Australians and the Stolen Generations

There are two groups of Indigenous Australians: the Torres Strait Islanders from the islands to the north of Queensland, and Aboriginal people from mainland Australia and Tasmania.

No one's land[6]?

When the British arrived at the end of the 18th century, they saw that people were already living there, but they also saw that there were no fences. They said that the land was *terra nullius*, 'no one's land', and they took it for themselves. Indigenous people didn't get their land rights[7] back until 1992, when it was decided that the idea of *terra nullius* was wrong and they were the traditional owners of Australia.

The Stolen Generations

From 1910 to 1970 at least 100,000 children were forcibly[8] taken from their Aboriginal mothers to be brought up[9] by white foster[10] families or in institutions. They weren't allowed to see their families or speak their own languages. These children are called the Stolen Generations. The film *Rabbit-proof fence* is based on the true story of some girls who were 'stolen' in this way.

The Founding of Australia, 1788

Sorry

Finally, in 2008, the Australian government officially said 'sorry' to Indigenous Australians. Many of them were very emotional[11] when Prime Minister Kevin Rudd made his speech because they had waited for so long to hear the word 'sorry'.

3 Explain the terms 'terra nullius' and 'Stolen Generations' in German.

Audience at Kevin Rudd's 'Sorry Speech', 13th February 2008

---

[4] platypus ['plætɪpəs] *Schnabeltier*   [5] kookaburra ['kʊkəbʌrə] *Kookaburra, Lachender Hans (= spezieller australischer Vogel)*
[6] no one's land ['nəʊwʌnz lænd] *Niemandsland*   [7] land rights [lænd raɪts] *Bodenrecht*   [8] forcibly ['fɔːsəbli] *gewaltsam*
[9] bring up [brɪŋ 'ʌp] *großziehen*   [10] foster ['fɒstə] *Pflege-*   [11] emotional [ɪ'məʊʃənl] *bewegt, gerührt*

147

TEXT FILE

▶ KV 37   ▶ INKL p. 82–85

TF 2 Waiting for something to happen (from the story *Riot* by David Fermer)

3.07

In the summer of 2011, North London became the scene of street protests and violence after the controversial police shooting of a man in Tottenham. Riot is the story of Danny, a teenage boy from Tottenham, who gets caught up in events.

Read the beginning of the story and do the tasks at the end of each part.

Saturday 4 pm

So this is it? This is my life? Hanging out with my mates on a Saturday afternoon with nothing to do but watch people walking up
5 and down Tottenham High Road? They're all out shopping, buying nice things for themselves and their family. All I have in my pocket is £1.50. That's not even enough to buy a Mars bar and a Coke. I can't even afford[1] a
10 kebab. Is this what I came into the world for?
"Hey, lads, see that bird over there?" says Kyle. Kyle is the oldest in our gang. He calls all girls 'birds', like they've got wings and can fly. We're not really a gang. Not like The Smalley Boys or
15 the BWF gang, the guys who do business around here, the ones who deal the drugs. We're just friends who hang out together. We all live on the Broadwater Farm Estate up the road. We've known each other forever.
20 Kyle points at this Muslim girl who's walking past us. She's done up all nice and pretty, with big long eyelashes[2] and lots of make-up. She's wearing a blue headscarf[3] which sparkles[4] in the afternoon sun.
25 "I bet she's hot under there," Kyle says with a grin, and we all know he's not talking about her body temperature.

"Hey there, beautiful!" he calls out, jumping down from the wall and going over to the girl
30 with a big smile on his face. "How about a little kiss for Uncle Kyle?"
The girl takes one look at him and walks off, as if Kyle has got some horrible disease. Kyle just laughs. "What's the problem, love? Aren't
35 I good-looking enough for you?"
Kyle can be a real idiot sometimes.
That's what we've been doing all afternoon. Watching people. Talking about people. Laughing at people. That's all. There is
40 nothing else to do. We can't go shopping, we can't go to the cinema, we can't even hang out at McDonald's. No cash, no splash. All we can do is just sit here on this wall, watching people.
"Look at that old man over there. He walks
45 like he just did it in his trousers." Or: "Check out the bird at the cash machine. How much do you think she's taking out? 100? 200? Maybe we should just take her money?"
We don't, of course. We might look like scum[5]
50 to some people, but we're not. We don't steal. We don't do drugs. We don't mess with the law. Drugs are too expensive anyway. No cash, no hash either. Besides, if you get into drugs around here, you're in serious trouble. The best
55 thing that can happen to you is to end up in prison and get clean. It's downhill[6] all the way.
Kyle likes to think he's a real bad guy. Mr Dangerous. Like he's some Mafia boss or something. But he's not. It's just a role he likes
60 to play. I can understand him in a way. It's all he's got. His fantasies, his role-play. He hasn't got anything else. He's seventeen and unemployed. At least Todd and Reeko are on a job programme. They're both sixteen, a year
65 older than me. They've finished school. None of them have got any qualifications. Zee too. He's seventeen as well. He works in his dad's shop. His parents are from Pakistan, but that's OK. I'm the only one who's still at school.

---

[1] afford [əˈfɔːd] *sich etwas leisten (können)*   [2] eyelash [ˈaɪlæʃ] *Wimper*   [3] headscarf [ˈhedskɑːf] *Kopftuch*
[4] sparkle (v) [ˈspɑːkl] *funkeln, glitzern*   [5] scum [skʌm] (Schimpfwort) *Abschaum, Dreck*   [6] downhill [ˌdaʊnˈhɪl] *bergab*

148

Everyone calls me 'The Professor'. They say they'll kill me if I don't get a GCSE[7]. Hang me naked[8] from Big Ben if I fail[9]. It's just a joke, of course. I'm not making any promises. You never know what's going to happen around here next.

> **a)** How do Danny and his friends spend their afternoons?
>
> **b)** Explain from Danny's point of view why they do what they do.

Saturday 5.30 pm

Time goes slowly when you don't have anything to do. It's a waiting game. Killing time. Waiting for something to happen. Waiting for the next laugh.
Zee has a cool sense of humour[10]. I get along with him really well, but he's not around much these days. Busy, he says. When he's around, we always have a laugh together.
I get along with Reeko too. Most of the time. Todd's not the sharpest knife in the drawer, if you know what I mean. He and Reeko always do whatever Kyle says. They think Kyle is God. Kyle thinks so too. He's always talking about money. How much things cost, how much people earn, how the banks are corrupt, how one day he's going to make a million. If you heard him talk, you'd think he already owned half of North London. He thinks he's the smartest person in the world.
We're just about to go home when we see this crowd coming down the street. About a hundred people walking towards us really slowly. It looks kind of beautiful, like a funeral procession or some ritual, like the ones you see on TV from India. Some of the people are carrying[11] banners, others are holding cardboard[12] signs. They're waving their banners and shouting. As they get closer I can read the slogans:
JUSTICE[13] FOR MARK DUGGAN.
WE WANT THE TRUTH.
WHO SHOT MARK DUGGAN?

I didn't know Mark Duggan personally, but I knew of him. He grew up on the Broadwater Farm Estate too. He used to be in the Star Gang, but he quit[14] a while back. So people say. But you can't really quit a gang, can you? Once you're in, you're in for life. You can't just leave. It's not like working at the Post Office. "Sorry, sir, I've found another job. I'd like to hand in my notice if that's OK. Can you give me a reference, please?" It doesn't work like that. Anyway, the police killed Mark Duggan on Thursday. They shot him dead. They were following him in connection with a killing at a nightclub. Duggan's best friend got stabbed[15]. The police thought Duggan was going to take revenge. That's why they were following him. To prevent[16] more bloodshed[17]. Or so they say. They stopped Duggan in his car. They said he was carrying a gun and that he shot first. That's why they killed him. No one really knows the truth. Mark's family and friends say Mark would never have been carrying a gun. He wasn't a criminal. Not any more.
As the protesters pass by, Kyle jumps down from the wall. "Come on, lads. Let's join them," he says.
Todd looks at him like he has no idea what he is talking about. "What for?" he asks.

---

[7] GCSE [ˌdʒiː siː es ˈiː] = General Certificate of Secondary Education *Schulabschluss im britischen Schulsystem* [8] naked [ˈneɪkɪd] *nackt* [9] fail [feɪl] *scheitern; hier: durch die Prüfung fallen* [10] sense (of humour) [sens] *Sinn (für Humor)* [11] carry [ˈkæri] *tragen* [12] cardboard [ˈkɑːdbɔːd] *Karton, Pappe* [13] justice [ˈdʒʌstɪs] *Gerechtigkeit* [14] quit [kwɪt] *verlassen, kündigen* [15] stab [stæb] *niederstechen, erstechen* [16] prevent [prɪˈvent] *verhindern* [17] bloodshed [ˈblʌdʃed] *Blutvergießen* [18] grit (one's teeth) [grɪt] *die Zähne zusammenbeißen* [19] punch [pʌntʃ] *mit der Faust schlagen*

"You know … because …" At first Kyle can't think of a good reason, then he has a moment of inspiration. "Because the pigs killed our
140 bro'," he says, gritting his teeth[18].
That's a good enough explanation to get Reeko down from the wall. He punches[19] the air and says, "Yo. We want answers, man."
"That's right," says Kyle, waving a fist. "Or we'll
145 teach them a lesson they won't forget!"

> c) What does Danny criticize about Kyle?
>
> d) Describe who Mark Duggan is and what happened to him.
>
> e) Explain why the people are protesting.

Saturday 5.45 pm

The protesters stop in front of the police station. Kyle tells his friends to wait and see what happens next. Danny doesn't like the idea.
150 *He would prefer to go home and work on his geography project. But then he sees a girl from his school, Riya, in the crowd.*

Saturday 8.20 pm

I stay at the demo longer than I planned. I just
155 can't leave. Not because of the protest. And not because of Kyle, who's going on about police incompetence and institutional racism[1]. I stay because of Riya. I can't take my eyes off her. I keep looking at her from the side, but she
160 doesn't see me. Every time I look at her, I feel a warm glow[2] in my stomach, a tingling[3] like the bubbles[4] of a fizzy drink[5]. The tingling goes right through my body, to every fingertip and down to my toes. My feet almost lift off
165 the ground.
I feel like I'm floating[6].
I've just decided to go home when a group of people at the front of the crowd starts shouting. A girl throws a leaflet[7] at one of the
170 policemen at the main entrance[8]. She can't be much older than me. All of a sudden three or four police officers spring into action. They pull out their batons[9] and jump on the girl. They beat her to the ground. The crowd
175 surges[10] forward to protect her. People push and shove[11] me in the back. There's no way out. Even if I wanted to leave, I couldn't. I'm pushed forward as if the ground under my feet is moving.
180 Everyone is shouting and waving their fists and telling the police to leave the girl alone. Then all hell breaks loose[12].
Someone picks up a stone. They hurl[13] it through the air and it hits one of the
185 policemen in the face. Blood explodes from his eyebrow[14] and he goes straight to the ground. The coppers[15] around him look really shocked. They freeze[16] and stare at him like they've never seen blood before. They wake up after a
190 second and help the man to his feet. The girl is still lying on the ground, knees tucked up[17] under her chin like an unborn baby. The police retreat[18] up the steps, carrying their wounded[19] colleague, regrouping. They look scared.
195 They should be.

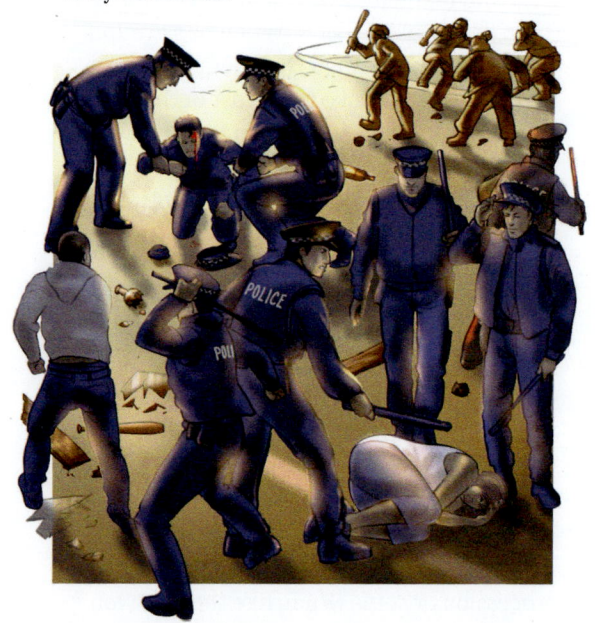

A couple of people start kicking down an old wall in front of the station. They loosen a couple of bricks[20] and throw them at the police officers. All of a sudden dozens[21]
200 of objects start showering down on the men in uniform. They escape into the building. I look back over my shoulder. About ten or twelve guys are running down the High Road

---

[1] institutional racism [ˌɪnstɪˈtjuːʃənl ˈreɪsɪzəm] *institutioneller Rassismus*   [2] glow [gləʊ] *Strahlen, Glühen*   [3] tingling [ˈtɪŋglɪŋ] *Kribbeln*   [4] bubble [ˈbʌbl] *Blase, Bläschen*   [5] fizzy drink [ˈfɪzi] *Erfrischungsgetränk*   [6] float [fləʊt] *schweben*   [7] leaflet [ˈliːflət] *Flugblatt, Broschüre*   [8] entrance [ˈentrəns] *Eingang*   [9] baton [ˈbætɒn] *Schlagstock*   [10] surge [sɜːdʒ] *drängen*   [11] shove [ʃʌv] *schieben*   [12] (all) hell (breaks loose) [hel] *die Hölle (ist los)*   [13] hurl [hɜːl] *schleudern, werfen*   [14] eyebrow [ˈaɪbraʊ] *Augenbraue*   [15] copper (infml) [ˈkɒpə] *Bulle*

▶ KV 37   ▶ INKL p. 82–85

with petrol cans and rags[22] in their hands.
205 Their hoods are up, scarves over their faces. They look like they mean business. I look for Riya, but I can't see her anywhere. The police come out of the building again, more of them this time, armed[23] with riot shields[24] and
210 batons. They look like they mean business too. Some people in the crowd move away from the station. Others start to move forward, ready to fight. Next to me Kyle is throwing stones at the police shouting, "Pigs
215 die! Pigs die!" I look again for Riya, but she's nowhere to be seen.
"Let's get out of here," I say to Kyle, grabbing him by the arm and stopping him from throwing the next stone.
220 "What for?" Kyle says. He breaks free of my grasp[25] and hurls his stone at the police. "Die, pigs!"
"This is bad, Kyle. Really bad."
"The pigs are bad."
225 "Yeah, I know, but this is worse." I can feel my heart beating in my throat.
"You wuss[26]," says Kyle.
Typical. Sometimes it's scary how predictable[27] Kyle is. Next to him Todd is
230 going crazy. He's throwing stones like a human howitzer[28]. His face is a deep shade of red. The spit[29] is dripping from his mouth. Reeko has run out of ammunition[30]. It's not as if the streets of London are filled with stones.

235 We're not in Gaza here. Reeko looks around, but he can't find any more stones, so he just pulls off one of his shoes and throws it at the police.
"Scum!"
240 I see Zee pushing his way through the crowds towards us. His T-shirt is torn and soaked in sweat. His eyes are shining.
"You all right, lads?" he asks us.
"Couldn't be better," says Kyle with a smile.
245 "I'm going to go home and get changed into something more comfortable," Zee explains, pointing at his torn T-shirt. "I don't want to ruin these jeans as well."
Kyle looks puzzled for a moment, then he nods.
250 "Whatever."
"You'll be here when I get back?" Zee asks, talking to me.
I shrug my shoulders[31]. All of a sudden my geography project doesn't feel like the most
255 important thing in the world.
I nod.

> **f)** Why does Danny stay longer at the demo?
>
> **g)** Describe what happens after the police beat a protester.
>
> **h)** Compare Danny's reaction and his friends' reactions to the violence.

More challenge 1 — The main characters
Collect adjectives to describe Danny and Kyle. Then write a paragraph about each of them.

More challenge 2 — The plot
Tell the story so far in a few sentences. You can start like this: *Danny hangs out with his friends Kyle, Todd, Reeko and Zee in the street. They are watching people because …*

More challenge 3 — What happens next?
Read lines 253–256 again.
What do you think Danny is thinking and feeling at this point? Write the next part of the story.

> You can read the full story about Danny in the Cornelsen reader *Riot*.

---

[16] freeze [friːz] *erstarren, gefrieren*   [17] tuck: knees tucked up under the chin [tʌk] *(die Knie bis unters Kinn) angezogen*
[18] retreat (v) [rɪˈtriːt] *zurückweichen*   [19] wounded [ˈwuːndɪd] *verletzt, verwundet*   [20] brick [brɪk] *Ziegelstein*   [21] dozens (of) [ˈdʌzn] *Dutzende (von)*   [22] rag [ræg] *Stofffetzen, Lumpen*   [23] armed [ɑːmd] *bewaffnet*   [24] riot shield [ˈraɪət ʃiːld] *Schutzschild*
[25] grasp (n) [ɡrɑːsp] *Griff*   [26] wuss (sl) [wʊs] *(Schimpfwort) Waschlappen*   [27] predictable [prɪˈdɪktəbl] *voraussagbar, berechenbar*
[28] howitzer [ˈhaʊɪtsə] *Haubitze*   [29] spit (infml) [spɪt] *Spucke, Speichel*   [30] ammunition [ˌæmjuˈnɪʃn] *Munition*   [31] shrug (one's shoulders) [ʃrʌɡ] *mit den Achseln zucken*

TEXT FILE
Bilingual module GEOGRAPHY ▶ INKL p. 86–89

TF 3 Job description: Cleaner of the world's oceans

1 A teenager with a vision

a) If you saw rubbish in the ocean or on a beach, how would you react? Tell a partner and give reasons. Then read the text.

Boyan Slat was 16 when he went diving in Greece on a summer holiday. He was shocked. "I saw more plastic than fish," he says. It opened the Dutch teenager's eyes to the
5 problem of plastic pollution in the sea. He began to take interest in the problem. Millions of tonnes[1] of plastic rubbish – bags, bottles, old fishing nets, etc. – are floating[2] around the world's oceans. Seabirds, dolphins
10 and other sea life eat the plastic or get caught in it. Many of them suffer and die. Chemicals[3] in the plastic enter the food chain through the fish we eat, so it's a danger for humans[4] too. Cleaning up plastic pollution is a huge
15 challenge with no easy solutions.
Boyan Slat was interested in how the plastic rubbish is carried[5] by the oceans' currents. These currents move in huge gyres that circle the oceans. The plastic
20 collects in large "patches" inside the gyres.

The movement of the plastic gave Slat an idea: a system of swimming barriers that stay in place could catch the plastic. The plastic could then be collected and
25 recycled. Slat worked on his idea in high school and in his first year at Delft University of Technology. Then he decided to go a step further: he left university and started an organization
30 called *The Ocean Cleanup*. Using the internet, he gathered[6] support and money to research and test his idea. Slat and his volunteer team of researchers[7] now plan to have their ocean cleaning system ready by 2020.
35

Key terms
barrier [ˈbæriə] *Barriere; Schwelle*
current [ˈkʌrənt] *Strömung*
food chain [ˈfuːd tʃeɪn] *Nahrungskette*
garbage patch [ˈgɑːbɪdʒ pætʃ] *Müllstrudel, Müllhalde*
gyre [ˈdʒaɪə] *Drehung, Strudel*
particle [ˈpɑːtɪkl] *Stückchen, Teilchen*
pollution [pəˈluːʃn] *Umweltverschmutzung*

b) Answer these questions.
1 Why is the plastic in the oceans a big problem?
2 What role do the ocean currents play?
3 What is Boyan Slat's idea?
4 What has Slat done with his idea so far?

---
[1] ton, *pl* tons / tonnes [tʌn, /tʌnz] *Tonne/n (Maßeinheit: 1000kg)* [2] float [fləʊt] *treiben, schwimmen* [3] chemical [ˈkemɪkl] *Chemikalie* [4] humans [ˈhjuːmənz] *Mensch/en* [5] carry [ˈkæri] *tragen, transportieren* [6] gather (support) [ˈgæðə səˈpɔːt] *(Unterstützung) sammeln, gewinnen* [7] research / researcher [rɪˈsɜːtʃ] / [rɪˈsɜːtʃə] *forschen / Forscher/in*

▶ INKL p. 86–89

2 Slat's ocean cleaning system

a) Look at the photo and the diagrams.
👥 Talk about how the system works. You can use the words and phrases in the box.

Activate your English
- The currents move / carry / push / pass …
- The rubbish moves / floats / is carried / collects …
- The barriers stop / catch / collect …
- They are fixed / attached[8] to the ocean floor …
- Sea life can pass under …

b) 👥 Some experts see problems with Slat's ocean cleaning system. What possible problems could you imagine? Discuss.

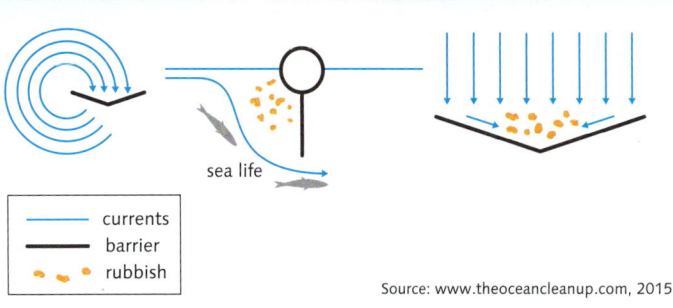

sea life
— currents
— barrier
• • rubbish

Source: www.theoceancleanup.com, 2015

3 A complex problem

Boyan Slat's project deals with one part of a much bigger problem. Most of the millions of tonnes of plastic in the sea have been there for a long time (see the infographic). The sun and the movement of the water have broken the plastic down into small particles of less than 5 millimetres. These particles absorb[9] other toxic[10] chemicals, becoming even more dangerous for animals and humans. The plastic particles never break down completely. So they are everywhere, and there is no effective way to get rid of them.

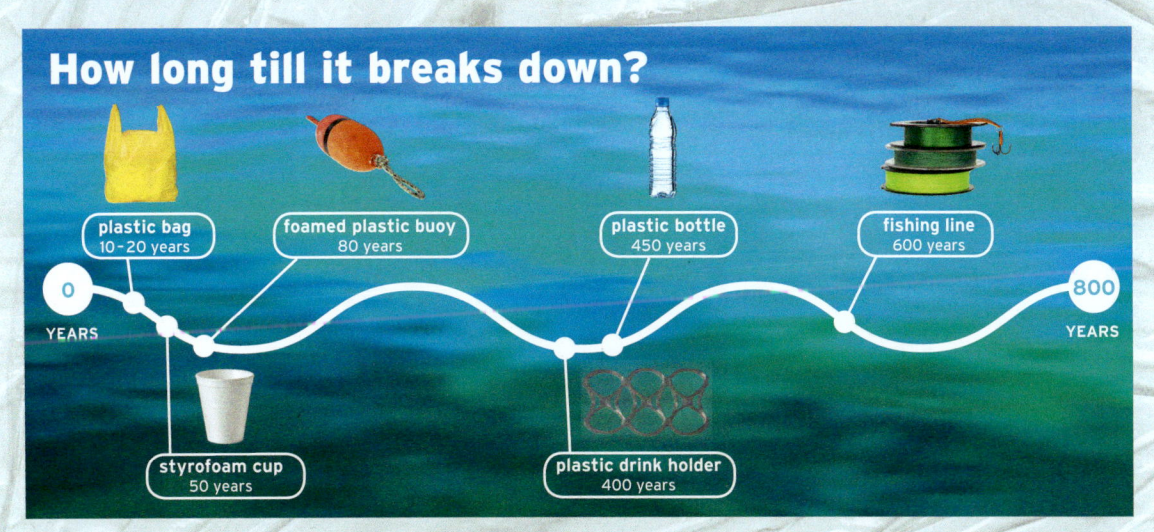

a) 👥 Describe and explain what the infographic shows.

How long till it breaks down?

- plastic bag — 10–20 years
- foamed plastic buoy — 80 years
- styrofoam cup — 50 years
- plastic drink holder — 400 years
- plastic bottle — 450 years
- fishing line — 600 years

0 YEARS — 800 YEARS

b) 👥 Discuss how young people can help to deal with plastic pollution. Present your ideas to the class.

---

[8] attach [əˈtætʃ] *befestigen* [9] absorb [əbˈzɔːb] *aufnehmen, absorbieren* [10] toxic [ˈtɒksɪk] *giftig*

153

TEXT FILE
▸ KV 38 ▸ INKL p. 90–93

TF 4 Music in your life

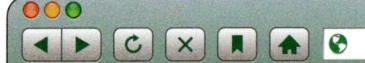

Bibi's blog

About me
Hi! I'm Bibi. I'm 16 years old. I love technology, photography and fashion. I started this blog ten months ago when my family moved from England to New Zealand. I wanted something to help me to remember this special time in my life. It's also a place for my family and friends back in the UK to read about my adventures on the other side of the world. I really had no idea what I was getting into when I started blogging! I'm pleased and proud to say that people from 45 different countries have liked my blog.
A whole new world has opened up for me and I have learned about cultures from all over the world. Welcome everybody!

Posted by Bibi, 17th March
Your favourite song (Yes, you have to choose just one!)
Choosing a favourite is tough, isn't it? But my absolute favourite song of all time is *Wake Me Up* by Avicii. I like Electronic Dance Music because it gives you energy and makes you feel good. To me this song says wake up, look around you and do something different today. The video is great because it reminds you that you shouldn't waste[1] your time. You should try to enjoy every day. I think the message of the video is: don't be a part of gangs, fighting and hating. Wake up, find out who you really are and just be you. Don't be someone you're not. – So what's your favourite song???

Cara from Wellington, NZ, says:
I find this task too stressful! It's impossible to choose just one song! So here is my favourite song 'this week'. Next week it might change! The song is *What a Wonderful World* by Louis Armstrong. It's a really old song, but I just love it! I am a very positive, happy kind of person. It doesn't matter what is happening around me or how difficult things are, I always think that the world is a wonderful place. That's just how I am, so this song really suits me :-)

---
[1] waste (v) [weɪst] verschwenden

▶ KV 38 ▶ INKL p. 90–93

Alex from Texas, USA, writes:
Just one song? Just one? It's so hard to choose! I love rock music by bands like Queen, The Beatles and AC/DC. To me this is real music. I think my favourite song is *Black Dog* by Led Zeppelin. I like other music genres – you can find pop, EDM[2], and hip hop on my music player too – but this is a song I could not live without. I first heard it when I was 12. That was when I decided that I wanted to learn to play the guitar. I'm part of a band now and I know how complicated this song is to play. Led Zeppelin are excellent musicians and Robert Plant's voice is amazing. I always sing when I listen to this, but it's not really a song that you can dance to.

Billie in Scotland writes:
All of the stars by Ed Sheeran. I love all of Ed Sheeran's music, but this song reminds me of my grandmother. We were really close[3] and she died five years ago. We used to look at the stars together. She said I was "the brightest[4] star in her sky". Now she is gone, I think she is the brightest star in mine. It reminds me of all the times we sat together watching the stars and talking about the world.

1 Your kind of music – or not?

a) Go online and listen to the songs the blog is about. Which song do you like best? Which song do you like least? Why?

b) Work alone. If you had to choose your own favourite song, what would it be?

c) **Walk around:** Talk to different people about their own favourite song. Ask them to explain their choice.

d) Report the results to the class. What are the most popular songs in your class?

2 Music and me

a) ○ Write a short text about music and you (80–100 words). Think about:
- How important is music to you? Why?
- What kind of music do you listen to?
- How often do you listen to music?
- Where and when do you listen to music?
- Who do you listen to music with?
- What's your favourite song? Why?

OR

b) ● Think of at least one important event in your life (e.g. first day at school, a special family trip, a family event, winning first place in a competition, a concert, …). Match a song to the event(s). Write a text and explain your choice(s).

---

[2] EDM = Electronic Dance Music   [3] (be) close (to sb.) [kləʊs] *(jmd.) nahestehen*   [4] bright [braɪt] *hell, leuchtend*

EXAM FILE 1

▶ KV 39 A/B ▶ INKL p. 94–95

> Students who are getting ready for exams at the end of year 9 (level A2/A2+) will find extra practice here. ▶ Skills file 3, p. 164

1 READING   Signs

a) Where can you see these signs?

1. **A** in a park
   B at a pool
   C at the beach

2. **A** in a hospital
   B by a road
   C in a playground

3. **A** at a post office
   B on a letter box
   C on a computer

b) What information do these signs give? Choose **A**, **B**, **C** or **D**.

1. **A** You can only go to the beach on Sundays between 9.00 and 1.00.
   B Dogs are allowed on the beach.
   C If you want to surf, you should always do it between the flags.
   D There will be lifeguards at the beach on Sunday morning.

2. **A** Let people get on the train before you try to get off.
   B Nobody is allowed to get off the train.
   C Let people get off the train first.
   D People who want to exit the train must use this door.

3. **A** You aren't allowed to bring a mobile into the library.
   B You can take calls in the library.
   C It's not OK to bring your phone into the library even if it's off.
   D You can have your phone in the library, but put it on silent.

156

▶ KV 39 A/B   ▶ INKL p. 94–95

2 LISTENING   A strange story

Listen twice to the story about a boy and a kangaroo. Are the sentences true or false?
1 A boy was visiting an Australian national park with his family.
2 They were worried about the boy because there were salt water crocodiles in the park.
3 The boy was missing all night.
4 The boy said that a kangaroo looked after him.
5 Everybody believed the boy's story about the kangaroo.

3 LANGUAGE   Sam, the koala

Complete the text with the correct words in the brackets.

Firefighter gives koala a drink

Sam, a two-year-old koala, became an internet star after a forest fire in Victoria, Australia. Volunteer firefighter David Tree … (1 found / finds / find) her and … (2 gave / give / will give) her some water from a bottle. Another firefighter filmed her with Tree, and the film … (3 was seen / is seen / saw) by thousands of Australians on the internet. Koalas are often hurt in fires … (4 but / because / so) they usually spend all … (5 his / her / their) time up in trees and they move slowly on the ground. The fires spread so quickly that the koalas can't move … (6 fast / slow / slowly) enough to escape.

Many koalas are hurt every year in forest fires

4 WRITING   An email to a host family

You're planning a trip to Australia and looking for a host family. Read this website and write to the family (60–80 words). Give information about yourself and ask them questions.

We're an average Australian family – mum, dad and three kids. We love meeting new people, and foreign students come and stay with us every year.
We'd like to find out something about you before you come, so tell us:
- your name, age and hobbies,
- why you'd like to come to Australia,
- what you'd like to see while you're here.
Feel free to ask us anything you like about us, our family, our house, our town, etc.

The Hanson family

EXAM FILE 2
▶ KV 40 A/B   ▶ INKL p. 96–97

1 SPEAKING   Tourist talk

a) Talk to a partner about these questions.
1. What's happening in this picture?
2. What do you think the people are saying?
3. Talk about a holiday that you've had.
4. Describe your dream holiday.

b) ROLE-PLAY   At a bus stop in Dublin

PARTNER A
You're at a bus stop and you speak to a tourist.

- help you?
- number 16 to city centre
- tickets on bus
- €2.55 / where from?
- like Dublin?
- how long staying?
- visited Dublin before?
- 'hop-on-hop-off' bus tour
- my bus coming / bye

PARTNER B
You're a tourist in Dublin and you're a little lost.

- bus to city centre?
- where buy bus ticket?
- how much to centre?
- Germany
- Dublin fun / friendly people
- a week / staying in a hostel
- first visit / any good tips?
- good suggestion
- bye / thanks for help …

2 MEDIATION   Say it in English

a) Du bist in London Heathrow gelandet und brauchst nun ein U-Bahn Ticket nach Covent Garden. Kaufe es am Schalter und frage höflich, wie lange die Fahrt dauert und wie du zum richtigen Gleis kommst.

Clerk	Can I help you?	You	…
Clerk	That's £4.80, please.	You	…
Clerk	It's about 50 minutes.	You	…
Clerk	Follow the signs to the Piccadilly Line.	You	…

b) Die U-Bahn ist recht voll, doch du siehst einen wahrscheinlich freien Platz. Frage höflich, ob du dich dort hinsetzen darfst.

You	…	Man	Yes, of course. I'll move my bag.
You	…	Man	You're welcome.

▶ KV 40 A/B   ▶ INKL p. 96–97

3 READING   16 – too young to love?

a) Read the following opinions about teen love.

Mandy It's ridiculous to fall in love when you're 16. You should spend your time with lots of friends – boys <u>and</u> girls! There'll be time for more serious relationships later.
5 I say stay free!

Dwight Of course I believe in teenage love. I have a steady girlfriend – we've known each other for more than a year. We spend all our free time together, sit together in
10 school, have lunch together … we're head over heels in love!

Charlie Some of my friends say that they're in love, but I think that they watch too many soaps on TV. I guess they're just acting
15 because they think you have to have a girlfriend or boyfriend to be cool. I don't think like that. Maybe one day I'll meet the right girl … but I'm not in a hurry!

Anna Some kids really want to fall in love …
20 Sure – it's romantic. When I was a teen, I just wanted romance too. I read the books, saw the films, dreamed the dreams. With my friends, that was all we talked about. I thought I was in love lots of times, but
25 I don't think it really was love. As a teenager I liked the idea of being in love, just like all the other kids.

Said For me falling in love means getting married, having kids, a home, a job … and
30 all that kind of thing. Sure, I want to do that some day, but not now when I'm 16. I have a girlfriend, and she's great! But love … I don't know …

Sofia I totally believe in teen love! I met
35 someone on holidays and we just clicked. It was love at first sight. I never want us to part. We're mad about each other!

b) The following words have various meanings in German. Pick the right one for this text.

	A	B	C
free (line 5)	frei	kostenlos	freilassen
steady (l. 7)	ruhig	sicher	fest
acting (l. 14)	sich verhalten	spielen	so tun als ob

c) Now find the German meaning of these words as used in the text.
fall in love (l. 19)   mean (l. 28)   click (l. 35)   mad (l. 37)

d) Who says what? Find at least one name for every question.

Who …
- is in love now?
- thinks that falling in love is silly when you're 16?
- says that teens are influenced by television?
- isn't a teenager?

4 WRITING   Someone you respect

We all have heroes – people we really respect. They can be sports stars, family, friends, etc. Who do you respect a lot? Write about him / her (60–80 words). Use these questions to help you:

- Who is it? Why is he / she special?
- What is he / she like?
- Have you ever met him / her?
- Would you like to meet him / her?
- What would you say to him / her?

EXAM FILE 3

▶ KV 41 A/B   ▶ INKL p. 98–99

1 READING   My first real job (adapted from 'Climbing the Golden Arches' by Marissa Nuñez)

a) Read the text.

❶ Two years ago, while my cousin Susie and I were doing our Christmas shopping on Fourteenth Street, we decided to have lunch at a fast food place.
"Look at the job ad," Susie said. "They're hiring. Let's give it a try." I looked at her and said, "Are you serious?" She gave me this look that made it clear that she was.

❷ When Susie and I got home from school one day about a month later, my mother told us that the fast food place had called. They wanted to interview us both. We walked straight over there. They asked us why we wanted to work there and how we felt about tasks like cleaning the bathroom. Then they told us to wait for a while. Finally the manager came out and said we had the job.

❸ Susie worked for only three months, but I stayed on. I liked having a job because I was learning how to be a responsible person. I was meeting all kinds of people. I started making friends with my co-workers and getting to know many customers. And I was in charge of my own money for the first time. I didn't have to go asking Mom for money when I needed something. I could just go and buy it.

❹ Working at a fast food place does have its downsides. The worst thing about the job is that the customers can be real jerks sometimes. They just don't seem to understand the pressure we're under. At times they try to make you look stupid. Or they blame you for a mistake they made. If you don't watch and listen carefully, some of them try to short-change you for some money.

❺ Working here has taught me a lot. The most important thing I've learned is that you have to start at the bottom and work your way up. You need to know how to do all the jobs. I also have more patience and have learned to control my emotions. I've learned how to get along with all different kinds of people. I'd like to have my own business some day, and working at this fast food place has shown me I could do that.

b) Match the headings (A–F) with the paragraphs (1–5).
There is one more heading than you need.
A "You have the job!"
B The disadvantages of the job
C Let's apply for the job!
D I've learned a lot.
E Training for a month
F The advantages of the job

c) Complete the notes with three details per box.

The advantages of the job	What some customers do	What the writer learned
…	…	…

d) Complete these sentences with words from the text.
1 The writer saw an advert for a job in a …
2 After a month, she and her cousin went to …
3 With the new job the writer was more independent because …
4 At a fast food place the workers are under a lot of …
5 The writer has plans for the future – she wants to …

▶ KV 41 A/B   ▶ INKL p.98–99

2 MEDIATION
Read the job advert. Write down what you have to do and what skills you need – in German.

The Sandwich Bar, 14th St, New York
IMMEDIATE OPENINGS
Hours: 11 a.m. to 7 p.m. / 1 p.m. to 9 p.m.
Pay: To be discussed
Duties: Preparing and cooking food, serving customers, working at the cash register, helping to keep the restaurant safe and clean

We're looking for hard working, friendly and enthusiastic people who can deliver excellent customer service with a smile.
You must be able to work quickly and be a team player.

APPLY HERE

3 LISTENING   Looking for work experience
a) You will hear a telephone conversation about work experience twice. Pick **A**, **B** or **C**.
1. Sanjay wants to work at   **A** a cafe.   **B** a school.   **C** a supermarket.
2. The name of the manager is   **A** Robert.   **B** Ms Walker.   **C** Mr Rath.
3. Sanjay can work   **A** for one week.   **B** for two weeks.   **C** for three weeks.
4. Sanjay has to work   **A** seven days a week.   **B** six days a week.   **C** five days a week.
5. In July Sanjay has to send   **A** a CV.   **B** an email.   **C** a letter.

b) You will hear a conversation between Sanjay and Asha twice. Complete the table.

	Where they worked	Duties (at least 2)	Hours	What it was like
Sanjay	...	...	...	...
Asha	...	...	...	...

4 WRITING   Jobs and work experience
Pick a) or b).

a) You want to apply for the job at *The Sandwich Bar*. Write a letter of application (at least 80 words).
Say:
- who you are
- if you have relevant experience
- why you'd be good at this job
- when you could start

b) Write a short text (80–100 words) about your work experience.
Write about:
- where you worked
- what jobs you had to do
- what hours you worked
- what you liked / didn't like
- what you learned

SKILLS FILE

Inhalt

STUDY AND LANGUAGE SKILLS — page
- **SF 1** Dealing with unknown words — 162
- **SF 2** Using a dictionary — 163
- **SF 3** Exam skills: How to do better in tests — 164
- **SF 4** Doing research — 165

LISTENING AND READING SKILLS
- **SF 5** Listening — 166
- **SF 6** READING COURSE
    - Skimming — 167
    - Scanning — 167
    - Finding the main point of a text — 167
    - Reading for details — 168
    - Reading between the lines — 168
    - Marking up and note-taking — 169
    - Working with fictional texts — 169

SPEAKING AND WRITING SKILLS — page
- **SF 7** SPEAKING COURSE
    - Giving a presentation — 170
    - Successful conversations — 170
    - Doing well in job interviews — 171
    - Taking part in discussions — 172
- **SF 8** WRITING COURSE
    - The steps of text writing — 172
    - Writing a comment — 174
    - Writing an email / a letter — 174
    - Summarizing texts — 175
    - Writing a CV — 176
    - Writing a cover letter — 177
    - A written discussion — 178
- **SF 9** Describing photos and pictures — 179
- **SF 10** MEDIATION SKILLS — 180

STUDY AND LANGUAGE SKILLS

SF 1 Dealing with unknown words

Du kannst englische Texte verstehen, auch ohne alle Wörter zu kennen. Nicht immer ist Nachschlagen nötig.

- Schau genau auf Titel und (Zwischen-)Überschriften sowie den Zusammenhang (Kontext), in dem das unbekannte Wort steht.

- Achte auf Abbildungen und Bildunterschriften. Was könnte bedeuten "… the Typhoon muscle car that had rocketed past us earlier …"?

- Viele Wörter sind im Deutschen und in anderen Sprachen dem Englischen ähnlich, z.B. *democracy, humour, loyal, religion, souvenir*.

- Wie ist das Wort aufgebaut? Unbekannte Wörter enthalten oft bekannte Teile.

    - in **Zusammensetzungen** (Komposita, *compounds*), z.B.
      one-way street – *a street where vehicles are allowed to move in one direction only* (Einbahnstraße)
      baby car seat – *a car seat for a baby* (Kindersitz)

    - in **Ableitungen** mit Vor- und Nachsilben (*prefixes and suffixes*), z.B. <u>anti</u>social, <u>dis</u>appear, <u>multi</u>lingual, <u>over</u>sleep, <u>re</u>appear; wash<u>able</u>, nation<u>al</u>, use<u>ful</u>, child<u>ish</u>, attract<u>ive</u>, care<u>less</u>, percent<u>age</u>, perform<u>ance</u>, found<u>ation</u>, open<u>er</u>, rac<u>ism</u>, move<u>ment</u>, happi<u>ness</u>, leader<u>ship</u>, press<u>ure</u>

- Kennst du das Wort evtl. <u>schon</u> in einer anderen Wortart? Z.B. kennst du *campaign* als Nomen. In *We've successfully <u>campaigned</u> against cyberbullying at our school* ist es ein Verb und bedeutet …?

- Aber: Nicht alle englischen Wörter, die im Deutschen ähnlich sind, haben in beiden Sprachen dieselbe Bedeutung. Achte auf so genannte *false friends*: z.B. heißt *become* „werden" (nicht „bekommen").

- Oft hilft dir der Textzusammenhang (Kontext), also die umstehenden Wörter und Sätze: *In case of a snake bite try to identify the snake, so the doctors can find an <u>anti-venom</u> more quickly.*

Two muscle cars

A Typhoon

A Holden Monaro

> **Typical prefixes and their meanings:**
> *again / back*
>   re- (*rebuild, remarry*)
> *after*
>   post- (*post-war, postmodern*)
> *before*
>   pre- (*premature, preschool*)
> *do / be more than / too much*
>   out- (*outrun*)
>   over- (*overeat, overcrowded*)
> *not / against / opposite*
>   anti- (*anti-war*)
>   dis- (*disloyal, disorder*)
>   in- (*incorrect, incredible*)
>   mis- (*mislead, misuse*)
>   non- (*non-smoker*)
> *put in(to)*
>   en- (*endanger, encircle*)

SF 2 Using a dictionary ▶ More challenge 1, p. 29; ▶ Unit 2, p. 36

Wenn du ein Wort nicht erschließen kannst, helfen das *Dictionary* (*English-German* pp. 235 – 263) oder ein Wörterbuch für das Englische (entweder in Buchform oder im Internet).

1 Wörterbucheinträge sind immer alphabetisch

- *U* kommt vor *V*
- *val*ue kommt vor *veg*etables
- *vampin*g kommt vor *vampir*e

2 Zusammengesetzte Ausdrücke und *idioms*

Der Haupteintrag (z.B. *ear*) steht farbig oder fett am Anfang. Daneben oder darunter findest du oft zusammengesetzte Wörter oder Redewendungen und Idiome, z.B. **(be) all ears**.

3 Wortarten und Wortbedeutungen

- Oft ist das gleiche Wort ein Nomen (Substantiv), ein Adjektiv oder ein Verb, mit je unterschiedlichen Bedeutungen. Überlege zuerst, zu welcher Wortart das gesuchte Wort gehört und suche den passenden Eintrag. Diesen liest du dann genauer.

- Die Ziffern 1, 2 usw. bei einem Eintrag zeigen, dass ein Wort mehrere Bedeutungen hat. Lies immer alle Einträge bei der passenden Wortart und entscheide dann, welche Bedeutung in deinem Satz passt. Zusätzlich findest du Verweise auf den Gebrauch im *American* oder *British English* (AE bzw. BE).

  Welche Bedeutungen hat *fall* hier?

  The number of unemployed people has fallen since last fall.
  Is September a summer or a fall month?
  I fell asleep very fast yesterday because I was so tired.

- Besonders wenn du ein Wort in einem deutsch-englischen Wörterbuch suchst, achte genau darauf, welche Bedeutung in deinem englischen Satz passt.

4 Weitere Informationen im Wörterbuch

- Die Lautschrift zeigt dir, wie ein Wort ausgesprochen wird.
- Unregelmäßige Verbformen, Pluralformen, Steigerungsformen usw. stehen in Klammern hinter dem Haupteintrag.

5 Online-Wörterbücher

- Wenn du ein Online-Wörterbuch verwenden möchtest, erkundige dich vorher bei deiner Lehrperson, welche zu empfehlen sind.
- Achte auf dieselben Dinge wie bei gedruckten Wörterbüchern.
- Vorteil online: Du kannst dir meist die Aussprache per Audiodatei anhören.

---

usually [ˈjuːʒuəli] meistens, normalerweise I

V

vacation [vəˈkeɪʃn], [veɪˈkeɪʃn] (AE) Ferien, Urlaub IV
vacuum cleaner [ˈvækjuəm kliːnə] Staubsauger V 3 (52)
vain [veɪn] eitel V 4 (79)
valley [ˈvæli] Tal IV
value [ˈvæljuː] Wert I **It's good value.** Es ist sein Geld wert. I
vamping [ˈvæmpɪŋ] spät in der Nacht noch aktiv sein V 4 (88)

---

ear [ɪə] *Substantiv*
1 Ohr **2** Gehör **3** Ähre
IDM **(be) all ears** ganz Ohr sein
(be) up to one's ears in sth. bis zum Hals in etwas stecken
go in one ear and out the other (umgs) zum einen Ohr rein- und zum anderen rausgehen

---

fall [fɔːl] *Verb, Substantiv*
Verb (fell, fallen)
1 fallen, stürzen **The book fell off the table.** Das Buch fiel vom Tisch.
2 (Zahlen) fallen, sinken, zurückgehen **Their profits have fallen by 30%.** Ihr Gewinn ist um 30% zurückgegangen.
3 in einen Zustand geraten **fall asleep** einschlafen, **fall ill** krank werden, **fall in love (with)** sich verlieben (in)

Substantiv **1** Fall, Sturz
2 falls (Plural, bes. in Namen) (Wasser)fall **the Niagara Falls** die Niagarafälle
3 (AE) Herbst
4 (Zahlen) Rückgang

---

child [tʃaɪld] (**children** [tʃɪldrən])

SKILLS FILE

SF 3 Exam skills: How to do better in tests ▶ *Exam file, pp. 156–161*

VOR DEM TEST

Eine Klassenarbeit oder ein Test in Englisch ist angekündigt? Keine Panik. **Frage** am Tag der Ankündigung deine Lehrperson und **notiere** dir, worum es gehen wird und was du besonders wiederholen solltest.

Nimm dir Zeit zur **Vorbereitung**. Beginne **10 Tage** vor dem Termin. Mach dir einen **Plan**, den du wirklich Tag für Tag abarbeitest. Plane auch einen vorbereitungsfreien Tag ein.

Schätze dich selbst ein
- Bitte deine Lehrperson um einen Selbsteinschätzungsbogen.
- Stell fest, welche Bereiche du noch üben musst. Wenn du unsicher bist, sprich mit deiner Lehrperson.
- Steh am Tag des Tests früh genug auf. Frühstücke etwas Gutes.

WÄHREND DES TESTS

Sei ruhig und optimistisch
- Du bist gut vorbereitet. Konzentriere dich, alles Andere ist jetzt unwichtig.

Lies zuerst alle Arbeitsanweisungen sehr <u>genau</u>.

Vom Einfachen zum Schwereren
- Löse zuerst die einfachen Aufgaben.
- Hake erledigte Aufgaben ab.

Achte auf die Zeit
- Schau beim Arbeiten ab und zu auf die Uhr, damit du weißt, wie viel Zeit dir noch bleibt.
- Nutze die letzten fünf Minuten dazu, alles nochmal durchzulesen und Fehler zu korrigieren.

NACH DEM TEST

Lerne aus deinen Fehlern
- Lies genau durch, was deine Lehrperson korrigiert hat. Gibt es Tipps und Hinweise für dich? Merke sie dir, beachte sie beim nächsten Mal.
- Gibt es ein Kompetenzraster? Lies dir genau durch, wo deine Schwächen und Stärken liegen.
- Berichtige deine Fehler sorgfältig. Frage bei Unsicherheiten deine Lehrperson.
- Führe deine persönliche **Fehlerliste**, in der du Fehler, die du immer wieder machst, sammelst (z.B. in einem kleinen Heft, auf Karteikarten oder als Notizensammlung im Smartphone – Hauptsache, du kannst immer schnell darauf zugreifen).

VOR DEM TEST

Bereite dich wieder sorgfältig vor
- Geh noch einmal deine typischen Fehler der letzten Tests und die Berichtigungen durch.
- Schau dir das Kompetenzraster und eventuelle Tipps der Lehrperson nochmal an.
- Du bist gut vorbereitet. Konzentriere dich ruhig und optimistisch.
- Erstelle und bearbeite wieder deinen Vorbereitungsplan.

SF 4 Doing research ▶ Unit 1, p. 23

1 Nutze unterschiedliche Quellen für deine Recherche

Bei der Informationssuche für ein Referat, eine Präsentation o.Ä. benutze mehrere unterschiedliche Quellen und Medien. Beachte auch die Hinweise zum Skimming und Scanning ▶ *Skills files 6.1, 6.2, p. 167*. Gleiche die gefundenen Informationen miteinander ab.

für alle Wissensgebiete	• Lexika (gedruckt und online, ggf. englischsprachig)
	• Schulbücher und Begleitmaterialien
für aktuelle Informationen	• Zeitungen, Zeitschriften (gedruckt und online, ggf. englischsprachig)
für geographische und politische Informationen	• Karten und Atlanten (gedruckt und online)

2 Tipps zur Internetrecherche

Puhh, fast 60.000.000 Ergebnisse für Koala! Was mache ich damit?!

So wird deine Internetrecherche leichter und bringt bessere Ergebnisse:

Wie suche ich, um weniger und bessere Ergebnisse (*hits*) zu bekommen?	• Überlege dir gute Stichwörter für dein Thema. Bereitest du z.B. eine Präsentation zu *Koalas in Australia* vor, wären *koala bear* und *Australia* ein Anfang. Weitere Ideen: *life of koalas, enemies of koalas*,…
	• Gib die Stichwörter in eine Suchmaschine ein und setze die Einstellungen auf englischsprachige Websites.
Welche Websites sind zuverlässig?	• Offizielle und zuverlässige Websites im englischsprachigen Internet haben *domain names*, die auf *.gov* oder *.edu* enden.
	• Weniger vertrauenswürdig sind Websites von Firmen (*.com*), persönliche Blogs, Fanseiten oder Websites von Interessengruppen. Auch hier kannst du Interessantes finden, solltest aber kritisch bei der Verwendung von Inhalten sein.
Wie verschaffe ich mir einen Überblick?	• Du kannst mit dem Skimming eines Artikels in einem online-Lexikon beginnen, z.B. der englischsprachigen Wikipedia (https://en.wikipedia.org).
	• Häufig finden sich im Artikel bzw. am Ende weitere Links zum Thema.
	• So findest du auch genauere Stichwörter für deine weitere Recherche.
Wie finde ich Websites wieder?	• Leg dir besonders interessante Websites in die Favoriten deines Webbrowsers. Strukturiere sie in eigenen Ordnern, die du innerhalb der Favoriten anlegen kannst.
Was kommt nach dem Suchen?	• Setz dir ein Zeitlimit für deine Recherche. Danach ordne dein Material. Prüfe, was evtl. fehlt und suche dann gezielt nur danach.
Was tun mit den gefundenen Informationen?	• Mach dir Notizen in weitgehend <u>eigenen</u> Worten ▶ *Skills file 6.6, p. 169*. *Copy and paste*, also bloßes Zusammenkopieren, ist nicht sinnvoll.
	• Zu jeder Notiz vermerke die Quelle (die Webadresse sowie das Zugriffsdatum).
Was tun mit unbekannten Wörtern und Wendungen?	• Unbekannter Wortschatz begegnet dir immer wieder in fremdsprachigen Texten. Für den ersten Überblick musst du nicht jedes Wort genau verstehen – erschließe die Bedeutung ▶ *Skills file 1, p. 162*.
	• Wichtige Wörter schlage im (Online-)Wörterbuch nach, v.a. wenn du sie selbst in deiner Präsentation verwenden willst. Vergiss die Aussprache nicht! Hör dir das neue Wort online an und übe es.

SKILLS FILE

LISTENING AND READING SKILLS

SF 5 Listening
▶ Unit 1, p. 13 ▶ Unit 2, p. 34
▶ Unit 3, p. 55 ▶ Unit 4, p. 77

1 Vor dem Hören: bereite dich vor

- Lies sorgfältig die Aufgabenstellung. Die Aufgaben sagen oft, worum es in dem Text geht oder enthalten Schlüsselwörter.
- Stell dir die Situation oder die Geschichte vor: Worum wird es im Text gehen? Wer wird sprechen? Versuche vorauszuschauen.
- Überlege, was du selbst zum Thema schon weißt und welche englischen Begriffe vorkommen könnten.
- Wenn du dem Hörtext Abbildungen zuordnen sollst, schau sie dir vor dem Hören genau an.
- Konzentriere dich, denn du kannst den Text meist nur bis zu zweimal hören.

> Versuche zu erkennen, **was für eine Art Text** du hören wirst:
> Nachrichten, Werbung, ein Gespräch, ein Interview, eine öffentliche Ansage oder eine *story*?

2 Beim Hören

- Beantworte schon beim ersten Hören möglichst viele Aufgaben (mach dir kurze Notizen, verwende Symbole und Abkürzungen).
- Die Informationen könnten in einer anderen Reihenfolge auftauchen.
- Im Hörtext können andere Wörter benutzt werden als in der Aufgabe, doch die Bedeutung ist ähnlich.
- Gib nicht auf, wenn du etwas nicht verstehst. Bleib ruhig und hör weiter zu. Vielleicht verstehst du beim zweiten Hören mehr.
- Achte auf Signalwörter, die dir das Verstehen erleichtern, z.B.:
  - Reihenfolge (*before, after, then, next, later, first, …*)
  - Gegensätze (*however, but, …*)
  - Gründe, Folgen (*because, so, …*)
  - Vergleiche (*larger/older than …, more, most, as … as*)
- Beachte auch, wie etwas gesagt wird: zum Beispiel verärgert oder besorgt, überrascht, freudig? Das kann ein Hinweis auf die Lösung sein.

> Höraufgaben können unterschiedliche **Arten des Zuhörens** von dir verlangen:
> - **detailliertes Hören** Hier musst du genau zuhören, um wichtige Einzelheiten zu erfassen (z.B. bei einer Ansage am Bahnhof die Abfahrtszeit des Zuges).
> - **globales Hören** Hier sollst du verstehen, worum es generell geht, z.B. den Hauptgedanken eines Textes erfassen. Du musst dafür nicht jedes einzelne Wort verstehen.
> - **schlussfolgerndes Hören** Hier werden deine Vorüberlegungen und Vermutungen wichtig. Achte auf die Zusammenhänge. Wird etwas evtl. nur angedeutet, aber nicht vollständig ausgesprochen? Wie klingt die Stimme der Sprecher?

3 Nach dem Hören

- Vervollständige deine Notizen sofort.
- Konzentriere dich beim nächsten Hören auf eventuelle Lücken.
- Manchmal hilft auch Kombinieren (es ist in jedem Fall besser als gar nichts zu schreiben).

> **Tausche** dich mit Mitschülern und -schülerinnen **aus**. Haben sie gute **Tipps und Tricks**, z.B. für kurze Notizen und Symbole?
> Ihr könnt, wenn das erlaubt ist, auch eure Notizen und Lösungen vergleichen.

SF 6 Reading course

1 Skimming ▸ Unit 1, pp. 15, 18, 25, 103
▸ Unit 2, p. 32

Wofür? Mit dieser Technik verschaffst du dir einen **Überblick**, z.B. über eine Website oder eine Zeitungsseite.

Wie? Du musst nicht jede Einzelheit verstehen, also auch **nicht jedes Wort** lesen und verstehen. Achte vor allem auf Überschriften, Abbildungen und Bildunterschriften, hervorgehobene Wörter und den ersten Satz.

Beispiel: Du möchtest mehr über Australien wissen. Ist dies dafür eine geeignete Website?

Für wen ist sie vor allem gedacht?

☐ Sportler ☐ Touristen ☐ Geschäftsleute

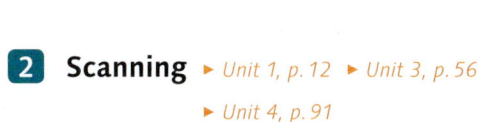

2 Scanning ▸ Unit 1, p. 12 ▸ Unit 3, p. 56
▸ Unit 4, p. 91

Wofür? Mit dieser Technik kannst du einen Text schnell nach **bestimmten Informationen** durchsuchen.

Wie? Du suchst nur bestimmte Informationen, die du über geeignete **Schlüsselwörter** findest. Lies nur dort genauer, wo sie stehen.

Beispiel: Du möchtest mehr darüber erfahren, was du bei einer Reise nach Australien beachten musst. Welchen Reiter musst du bei der obrigen Website anklicken?

3 Finding the main point of a text
▸ Unit 2, pp. 33, 47

Wofür? Um herauszufinden, was die **Hauptaussage** eines Textes ist und wie sie sich aus seinen Hauptgedanken formt.

Wie? Für deinen **Überblick**, worum es in dem Text generell geht, benutzt du das Skimming (siehe **1**).

Die **Hauptaussage** eines Textes findest du oft in seinem **ersten Absatz**, und dort oft im **ersten** oder **letzten Satz**.

Jeder **Absatz** eines Textes beinhaltet einen **Hauptgedanken**, der zur Hauptaussage beiträgt. Du findest den Hauptgedanken meist im **ersten** oder **letzten Satz** des Absatzes.

Beispiel: Lies Text **(A)** auf S. 10 noch einmal. Schau dir dann rechts oben die blaue Markierung an. Welcher Satz beinhaltet die Hauptaussage des Texts?

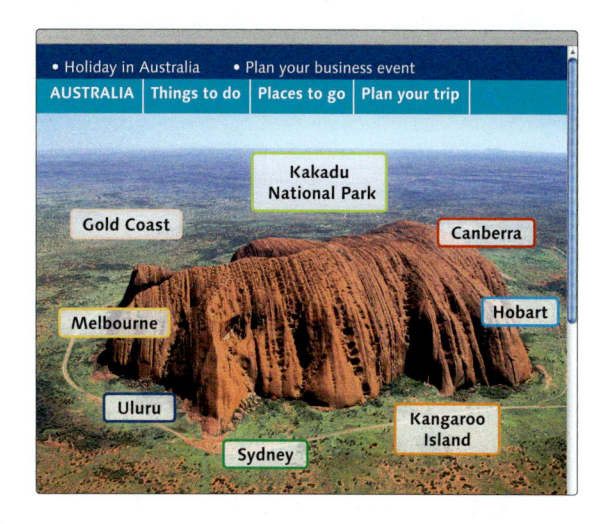

Ban on climbing Uluru comes nearer

Together with Sydney Harbour Bridge and the Great Barrier Reef, Uluru is probably the best-known tourist sight in Australia. 200,000 visitors travel there every year, and at the moment they are allowed to climb the rock. But for how long?

But Uluru is more than a tourist sight. For the local Anangu people Uluru is sacred, and they don't climb it. According to their law, only a few people are allowed to go up the rock at special times. That's why they politely ask visitors not to climb the rock.
In the past most visitors went up on the rock. Today more and more people decide not to

SKILLS FILE

4 Reading for details ▶ Unit 2, p. 33
▶ More challenge 1, p. 50

Wofür? Manchmal musst du in einem Text **jedes Detail** im Zusammenhang genau verstehen, z.B. bei Gedichten, Rezepten, Gebrauchsanweisungen und Aufgabenstellungen. In längeren Informationstexten oder Tabellen und Diagrammen ist es oft nur ein bestimmter Bereich, den du detailliert liest, weil du eine Information suchst. Welcher Bereich das ist, findest du mithilfe des Scanning heraus (siehe **2**).

Wie? Lies **jedes Wort** und **jede Zahl** sehr **genau**. Achte auch auf Maßeinheiten. Benutze ein Wörterbuch für unbekannte Wörter.

Beispiel: Wie viele Ziffern musst du hier eingeben, damit der Safe schließt?
Wann sollst du den Safe offen hinterlassen?

> **OPERATING INSTRUCTIONS**
> You can operate this safe with your own 4-digit personal code.
> **TO LOCK:** Close the door and enter your own 4-digit code.
> Press # (LOCK). The safe will lock automatically and the word CLOSED will be displayed.
> **TO OPEN:** Enter the 4-digit code that was used to lock the safe. It will unlock automatically and the word OPEN will be displayed.
> **IMPORTANT:** Always leave the safe open at checkout.

5 Reading between the lines ▶ Unit 2, pp. 33, 47
▶ More challenge 1, p. 50

Wofür? Wenn du Fragen zu einem Text beantworten sollst, ist es möglich, dass du die Antworten nicht eins zu eins im Text findest. Hier hilft es dir, **Schlussfolgerungen** aus dem Gelesenen zu ziehen. Wichtig ist diese Technik z.B. bei Kommentaren, persönlichen Texten (wie Tagebucheinträgen) und literarischen Texten.

Wie? Einfaches Schlussfolgern bedeutet, dass du Informationen aus **unterschiedlichen Textstellen** zusammenführst.

Beispiel: Sieh dir den Text auf S. 63–64, Parts 3 und 4 an und beantworte Frage 1 rechts.

Manchmal werden im Text **andere Wörter** benutzt als in der Aufgabe, doch die Bedeutung ist ähnlich oder gleich.

Beispiel: Schau im selben Text auf S. 63, in Part 2 die Zeilen 72 – 74 an und beantworte Frage 2 rechts.

Es gibt auch Fragen, auf die du im Text gar keine direkte Antwort findest. Und doch ist sie im Text enthalten, man könnte sagen, sie steht „**zwischen den Zeilen**". Du musst sie schlussfolgern, also z.B. dein eigenes Wissen, aber auch begründete Vermutungen beim Lesen einbringen.

Beispiel: Lies auf S. 62, in Part 1 die Zeilen 40 – 43 und beantworte Frage 3 rechts.
Die Antwort für Frage 4 findest du auf S. 64, in Part 4, Zeilen 149 – 150 und in Part 5, Zeilen 164 – 176.

(1) How do you know that Cindy has fallen in love with Cal?
(lines 116–121; 149–150)

(2) What does *mature* mean here?
Cynthia sounded much more mature, she thought.
a) showing great understanding and skill ☐
b) fully grown and developed ☐
c) behaving in a responsible way, like an adult ☐
d) no longer young ☐

(3) Does Charlotte believe what her friend says?
(4) What's the difference between Cindy's two names? How are they used in the story?

6 Marking up and note-taking ▶ Unit 4, p. 77

Wofür?
Du hast einen längeren Text mit vielen Fakten vor dir und sollst ihn später zusammenfassen oder inhaltliche Fragen beantworten. Wähle die für diese Aufgabe wichtigen Informationen aus und markiere sie.

Wie?
Du kannst die Stellen mit den für dich wichtigen Informationen z.B.:

- mit **Textmarker** hervorheben
- umkreisen
- unterstreichen

All das geht nur in elektronischen Texten oder auf Fotokopien bzw. Ausdrucken, aber nicht in geliehenen Büchern.

Wenn du dir zu den markierten Stellen **Notizen** machst (*note-taking*), kannst du diese später leichter weiterverarbeiten, z.B. für eine Präsentation ▶ *Skills file 7.1, p. 170*, einen Bericht oder eine Zusammenfassung ▶ *Skills file 8.4, p. 175*.

Being a screenager

Today's teenagers were born into the digital world, a world where screens are everywhere – TV screens, smartphone screens, tablet screens, laptop screens ... The average American teen spends 8.5 hours per day in front of a screen! In Britain it's a little less, about 7 hours per day. These screenagers don't look at only one screen – they usually multitask. They videochat on their smartphone, play a game on their tablet and watch a programme on TV, all at the same time.
Not every teen is like this of course, and many have hobbies and interests away from their screens. But digital technology is part of every teen's world and the attraction of TV, video games and social media is strong. Most teens feel the pressure to do as their friends do. About 60% of teenagers today watch at least 20 hours of TV per week. About 94% of teenagers have social media accounts.

❗ Schreibe nur Schlüsselwörter auf, nutze Ziffern (statt Zahlwörter: **7** statt **sieben**) und Symbole (?, !, ✓, ≠, +, =, ~). Zum Beispiel:

screenagers:
- born into digital world (= world of screens)
- ~ 8 hrs daily screen time (multitasking)
- strong attraction + peer pressure
- ...

---

7 Working with fictional texts ▶ Unit 2, p. 43
▶ Unit 3, p. 65 ▶ Unit 4, p. 87

Literarische oder fiktionale Texte, z.B. **Romane** *(novels)* oder **Kurzgeschichten** *(short stories)* handeln von einer erdachten Welt. Der Autor oder die Autorin entwickelt Figuren *(characters)* und erzählt, was sie tun und fühlen sowie häufig auch, warum sie sich so verhalten.

Beim Erschließen des Texts achte auf diese Elemente:

- *characters:* Wer sind die wichtigen Figuren? Wie werden sie beschrieben? In einer Figurencharakterisierung *(characterization)* nenne Namen und Alter. Sage etwas über ihr Verhalten, ihr Aussehen und ihre Persönlichkeit. Wie sprechen sie? Inwiefern verändern sie sich im Lauf der Handlung?
- *plot:* Der Grundaufbau der Handlung. Fasse knapp zusammen, worum es in der Geschichte geht, was passiert und warum.
- *setting:* Gib an, zu welcher Zeit und an welchem Ort bzw. welchen Orten sich die Handlung abspielt.
- *mood:* Welche Stimmung oder Atmosphäre prägt die Geschichte? Ist sie z.B. fröhlich oder spannend, traurig oder gruselig? Verändert sich die Grundstimmung im Verlauf der Handlung? Achte darauf, <u>wie</u> eine Situation beschrieben wird (Adjektive, Vergleiche, Sprachbilder, usw.).

❗ **USEFUL PHRASES**
for talking and writing about fictional texts:

The **main character(s)** in this story is / are ...
  - He / She is ... years old and lives in ...
  - He / She is a tall / small / ... person with ...
  - He / She likes / hates ... / typically ...
  - He / She is a strong / weak / brave / reliable / an easy-going ... person.

Plot: The text tells the story of ...
  - The story is about ...
  - First ... / Then ... (because of ...) / In the end ...
  - The story is **set** in ... at the beginning of the ... century / just before World War II / ...

The story starts in a very sad **mood**. However, that changes when ...

Reading this story was very exciting. Its mood is scary / threatening / ... because phrases like ... are used.

SKILLS FILE

SPEAKING AND WRITING SKILLS

SF 7 Speaking course

1 Giving a presentation ▶ *Unit 1, pp. 22, 23, 107*

▶ *More challenge 4, p. 94*

Beachte diese Schritte, damit deine Präsentation erfolgreich wird.

a) PLANNING YOUR PRESENTATION

- **Recherchiere** dein Thema ▶ *Skills file 4, p. 165* und fertige dir Notizen an (am besten gleich in Englisch ▶ *Skills file 6.6, p. 169*).
- **Strukturiere** die Informationen, z.B. in einer Mindmap oder einer Gliederung (*outline*). Prüfe nochmal, ob alle Informationen zum Thema passen.
- Wähle die **Form deiner Präsentation** aus: z.B. Vortrag, Folienpräsentation am Computer, Poster.
- Überlege, wie du dein Thema **anschaulich** und **interessant** gestaltest (Beispiele, und Visualisierungen, z.B. Abbildungen, Karten, Diagramme, evtl. Filmausschnitte). Überlege dir einen guten Einstieg.
- Bereite deine **Notizen** für die Präsentation (nur Stichwörter). Notiere kurze Erklärungen zu schwierigeren Begriffen, die deine Zuhörer/innen evtl. nicht verstehen.
- Bereite deine **Materialien** sorgfältig vor (Computerfolien, Fotos usw.): Achte auf Lesbarkeit und Übersichtlichkeit.
- **Übe** deine Präsentation zu Hause und / oder mit Freunden. Achte auf die Zeit. Nummeriere deine Notizzettel bzw. Karteikärtchen. Überprüfe die technischen Hilfsmittel, die du verwenden willst (Laptop, Beamer usw.).

b) GIVING YOUR PRESENTATION

- **Schau** die Zuhörenden **an**. Warte bis es ruhig ist. **Erkläre**, worüber du sprechen wirst und wie deine Präsentation aufgebaut ist.
- **Sprich langsam**, deutlich und möglichst **frei** (d.h. lies nicht nur ab).
- **Schau** die Zuhörenden **an**, **lächle**. Zeige, dass du deinen Vortrag gern hältst.
- Sprich in **kurzen**, **verständlichen Sätzen**. Vermeide zu viele unbekannte oder schwierige Wörter. Erkläre sie bei Bedarf.
- **Verweise** auf deine **Abbildungen** oder Fotos. Erkläre sie bei Bedarf.
- **Beende** deine Präsentation mit einer kurzen **Zusammenfassung** der wichtigsten Punkte, evtl. auch mit einer abschließenden Schlussfolgerung.
- **Bedanke** dich fürs Zuhören und frage, ob jemand **Fragen** hat oder sich äußern möchte.

> **OUTLINE**
> **Topic: The outback**
> 1) Introduction:
>   Today I'm going to talk about Australia's most exciting …
> 2) Main body:
>   First: how big
>   Second: weather
>   Third: animals
>   Fourth: people
> 3) Summary / Conclusion:
>   To sum up, I'd love to spend …

Klar strukturierte Folien:
- nur 7 Zeilen pro Folie
- nur 7 Wörter pro Zeile
- lesbare Schriftgröße (ca. 16 Punkt)
- nur eine Abbildung pro Folie

- My presentation is about …
- First I'd like to talk about …
- Now let's have a look at the screen.
- The photo shows …
- Here's a new word. It's … in German.
- Finally, I'd like to point out …
- That's the end of my presentation. Thank you for listening. Do you have any questions?

2 Successful conversations ▶ *Unit 2, p. 45*

Unterhaltungen mit Menschen aus anderen Ländern gelingen gut, wenn du diese Hinweise beachtest. Sei höflich und aufgeschlossen! Verwende häufig *please*, *thank you* und *sorry*.

a) STARTING OFF

- **Eröffne** das Gespräch mit einer freundlichen Anrede oder Frage, möglichst mit etwas **Verbindendem**, z.B. über den Ort, die Situation usw. Mit jemandem, den du zum ersten Mal triffst, sprichst du etwas förmlicher als mit jemandem, den du schon kennst.
- Wenn es angebracht ist, stell dich vor.

> **USEFUL PHRASES**
> Excuse me, please.
> Do you know …? / Can I sit here?
> Hello, how are you?
> My name is … Nice to meet you.
>
> Hi there, are you from Sydney?
> Hi, how is it going?
> Hi, have you been here before?

b) KEEP THE CONVERSATION GOING

- Zeige dein **Interesse**, indem du Fragen stellst, z.B. auch Nachfragen.
- Antworte nicht nur mit wenigen Worten, das kann unfreundlich wirken.
- Erzähle auch etwas **von dir**, möglichst auf eine **positive** Art (vermeide es, zu jammern oder zu nörgeln).
- Wenn du etwas nicht verstehst, frage höflich nach.
- Wenn du etwas nicht sagen kannst, umschreibe das Wort.

> **USEFUL PHRASES**
> Fine, thanks. / Yeah, sure.
> Yes, I am. / No, not really.
>
> What about you? Do you like …? / I'm new here in … / I really like these … What do you think …?
>
> Could you say that again, please?
> I don't know the English word. It's something that … / like …

c) A GOOD ENDING

- **Beende** das Gespräch so freundlich, wie du es begonnen hast.
- **Bedanke** dich, wenn du um Hilfe gebeten oder z.B. Tipps bekommen hast.
- **Verabschiede** dich höflich.

> ❗ Mache dir vor dem Gespräch möglichst klar, mit wem du sprichst. So wirst du z.B. mit Gleichaltrigen informeller umgehen als mit Älteren.
>
> Denke auch an eventuelle kulturelle Unterschiede, z.B. beim Begrüßen und Verabschieden.

3 Doing well in job interviews ▶ Unit 3, p. 66

a) PREPARE YOURSELF

- **Bereite dich sorgfältig** auf das Vorstellungsgespräch **vor**. Übe deine **Gesprächsanteile**, z.B. vor einem Spiegel oder mit Freunden. Achte besonders auf eine freundliche, aber angemessen formelle **Körpersprache**.
- Wo liegen deine **Stärken** und **Schwächen**? ▶ Wordbank 2, p. 143 Was sind deine besonderen **Interessen**?
- **Warum** bewirbst du dich um diese Tätigkeit?
- Welche **Arbeitserfahrungen** hast du? ▶ Wordbank 5, p. 145
- **Informiere dich vorab** über das Unternehmen bzw. den Betrieb und bereite auch einige **Fragen** an die Interviewer vor.

> **USEFUL PHRASES**
> Good morning, Ms / Mr …
> My name is … and I'm really interested in this job because I like working with …
>
> I think this is a job I could do well because I already have some experience with …
> I'm quite good at … / I'm not very good at …
>
> I'd like to know if I'll be working in a team or on my own.
> Do I have to work at the weekends?

b) IN THE INTERVIEW

- Plane **genügend Zeit** für die Anfahrt und das Finden des genauen Interviewortes ein. Schalte dein **Smartphone stumm**, bevor du dort ankommst.
- **Begrüße** dein Gegenüber freundlich, stell dich nochmal vor.
- Bleib **ruhig**, sei **freundlich** und **positiv**.
- Hör gut zu, sprich **deutlich** und nicht zu schnell. Sieh dein Gegenüber beim Gespräch an.
- Kontrolliere immer mal wieder deine **Köperhaltung**.
- Bleibe **ehrlich**, übertreibe nicht.
- Am Ende des Gesprächs **bedanke** dich und **verabschiede** dich freundlich.

SKILLS FILE

4 Taking part in discussions ▶ Unit 4, p. 89

In einer (Klassen-)Diskussion tauschst du dich über Ideen und Meinungen aus. Dabei sollst du auf die Äußerungen deiner Gesprächspartner/innen eingehen und gleichzeitig deinen eigenen Standpunkt darstellen und begründen.

a) PREPARING A DISCUSSION

- Eine **inhaltliche Vorbereitung** auf das Thema der Diskussion ist sinnvoll, damit du nützliche **Wörter** und **Wendungen** parat hast. Notiere sie dir.
- Mache dich mit **unterschiedlichen Standpunkten** zum Thema vertraut und denke darüber nach, was deine Position ist.
- Notiere dir **Argumente**, die deinen bzw. andere Standpunkte unterstützen. (Beispielsweise in einem Rollenspiel kann deine Aufgabe sein, einen anderen Standpunkt als den eigenen zu vertreten.)
- Bereite deine **erste Äußerung**, mit der du in die Diskussion eintrittst, besonders gut vor.

> **STATING YOUR OPINION**
> In my opinion, / view, …
> Well, I'd say …
> (Personally,) I think / feel / believe …
> If you ask me, …
> First of all, …
> To start with, I'd like to point out that …

b) HAVING THE DISCUSSION

- Wenn du die Diskussion **eröffnest**, beginne mit deinem vorbereiteten **Einstieg**.
- Häufiger wirst du dich auf deine **Vorredner/innen** beziehen. Du kannst ihrem Standpunkt **zustimmen** oder **nicht zustimmen** und dann deine vorbereitete Äußerung und passende **Argumente** vorbringen.
- In jedem Fall **höre** den Argumenten der anderen **genau zu** und beziehe dich in deiner Äußerung darauf.
- Bleibe stets **höflich** und lass andere ausreden.
- Manchmal wirst du **nachfragen** müssen, wenn dir etwas unklar oder unverständlich ist.

> **AGREEING**
> I quite agree. (+)
> You're quite right. (+)
> I think so too. (+)
> You've got a (good) point there. (+)
> That's true / right. / That's just it. (++)
> I agree completely. (++)
> I couldn't agree with you more. (+++)

> **DISAGREEING**
> I'm afraid I don't (quite) agree (there). (-)
> I'm not so sure, really. (-)
> Well, that's one way of looking at it, but … (-)
> It's not as simple as that (I'm afraid). (-)
> I don't believe that at all. (--)
> I don't agree with you at all. (--)
> (Sorry,) I definitely disagree. (--)
> (Sorry,) I think you're wrong. (--)

> **ASKING FOR CLARIFICATION**
> Sorry, I didn't get that. / Are you saying that … ?
> Does your last statement mean that … ?
> Could you please give an example of … ?

SF 8 Writing course

1 The steps of text writing ▶ Unit 1, pp. 13, 17 ▶ Unit 2, p. 33 ▶ Unit 3, p. 70

a) PLANNING YOUR TEXT

- Über welches Thema willst / sollst du genau schreiben?
- Was für einen Text sollst du schreiben: z.B. eine E-Mail, das Ende einer Geschichte oder einen Sachtext (Beschreibung – *Describe* …; Erläuterung – *Explain* …; Erörterung – *Discuss* …; Zusammenfassung – *Summarize* …)?
- Sammle Ideen und / oder Argumente – z.B. in einem Mindmap oder in einer Liste.
- Recherchiere die für dein Thema notwendigen Informationen
  ▶ *Skills file 4, p. 165*.
- Strukturiere dein Material: Schreibe deine geplante Gliederung (*outline*) auf.

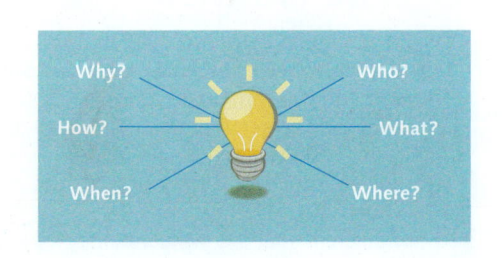

Du brauchst
- eine **Einleitung** (*beginning / introduction*): Hier steht, worum es im Text insgesamt geht.
- einen **Hauptteil** (*middle / main body*): Dieser Teil ist in mehrere **Absätze** (*paragraphs*) gegliedert, die Details (Fakten, Beispiele usw.) und Argumente enthalten.
- einen **Schluss** (*ending / summary / conclusion*): Hier gibst du dem Text ein passendes, einprägsames Ende.

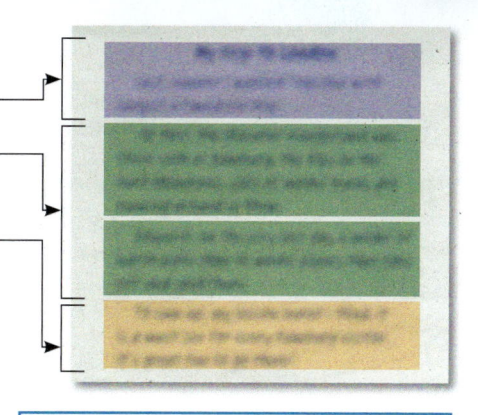

b) WRITING YOUR TEXT

- Nun schreibe den **ersten Textentwurf**. Halte dich an deine Gliederung.
- Beginne für jeden neuen Gedanken einen **neuen Absatz**.
- Jeder Absatz sollte mit einem **Einleitungssatz** (*topic sentence*) beginnen. Er drückt aus, worum es in diesem Absatz gehen wird.
- **Verbinde** deine Sätze mit passenden *linking* und *time phrases*.
- Verwende passende, **ausdrucksstarke** Wörter und Wendungen, z.B.:
  - **Adjektive** (zum näheren Beschreiben von Personen, Dingen, Orten usw.): *a peaceful voice*
  - **Adverbien** zum näheren Beschreiben von Handlungen, Vorgängen und Zuständen:
    It was raining terribly.
    oder zum Verstärken von Adjektiven: *an extremely sad story*;
    He was deeply disappointed.

c) CHECKING AND REWRITING YOUR TEXT

- Wenn dein erster Textentwurf geschrieben ist, hast du viel geschafft, bist aber noch nicht fertig. Jetzt solltest du deinen Text **jemand anderem** zu lesen geben und um **Feedback** bitten.
- **Lies** selbst deinen Text **mehrmals** durch, je mit einem anderen Schwerpunkt:
  - Stimmt der **logische Aufbau**, die Struktur (Einleitung – Hauptteil – Schluss)? Sind die Absätze in sich logisch aufgebaut?
  - Sind die Sätze gut verbunden, liest sich der Text **flüssig** (*linking* and *time phrases*)?
  - Prüfe, ob du alle **typischen Fehlerquellen** vermieden hast (wenn du eine persönlich Fehlerliste führst, schau dort nochmal nach).
  - Schau dir ein eventuelles **Feedback** genau an und überlege, was du davon übernehmen willst.
- Schreibe nun deinen Text in der **endgültigen Version**. Lass dir etwas Zeit, dann lies auch diese Version nochmal kritisch durch und verbessere, wo das noch nötig ist.

🔗 USEFUL LINKING PHRASES

Konjunktionen (*conjunctions*):
but, *and*, *because*, *so*, *on the one hand – on the other hand* (einerseits – andererseits), *although*, *however*

Demonstrativpronomen (*demonstrative pronouns*): *This is exactly …. That's the point.*

Relativsätze (*relative clauses*):
The platypus is an animal that I've never seen in real life.

⌛⌛⌛ USEFUL TIME PHRASES

Adverbiale Bestimmungen der Zeit (*time markers*): *at first*, *next*, *finally* (Reihenfolge)
for half an hour (Dauer)
immediately, *faster than …* Geschwindigkeit)
during our holiday, *as he arrived*, *while …* (zeitgleiches Geschehen)
two years ago, *last spring* (Zeitpunkt)

❗ Typische Fehlerquellen

- Groß- und Kleinschreibung
- Wörter die ähnlich klingen, aber unterschiedlich geschrieben werden: *your / you're; than – then; quiet – quite*
- unregelmäßige Pluralformen: *woman – women, child – children*
- Wörter mit „stummen" Buchstaben: *know, talk, listen*
- *word order* in Aussagen, Fragen
  ▶ Language files 11, 12, pp. 188–189
- unregelmäßige Verben und unregelmäßige Schreibungen: *try → tries, tried*
- Präpositionen: *on the internet, in the photo, go by bus, be good at …*
- Typische Wendungen, z.B.: „Was gibt's zum Abendbrot?" – *What's for dinner?* „Alles Gute!" – *All the best!*

SKILLS FILE

2 Writing a comment   ▸ Unit 1, pp. 11, 26   ▸ Unit 2, p. 33

Auch beim Verfassen eines Kommentars bzw. einer Stellungnahme beachte die *Steps of text writing*. ▸ p. 173
In einem *comment* vermittelst du deine persönliche Meinung, begründest und argumentierst.

a) PLANNING YOUR COMMENT

- Lies die Aufgabe und den evtl. dazugehörigen Text genau. Notiere dir z. B. Stichwörter, fertige ein Mindmap an.
- Wenn du für oder gegen etwas Stellung nehmen sollst, sortiere deine Ideen schon in Pro und Contra-Argumente.

Denke bei der Gliederung (*outline*) an:
- **beginning / introduction** (Einleitung): Hier teilst du deinen Lesern mit, worauf du dich beziehst und was deine Meinung ist.
- **middle / main body** (Mittelteil): Hier begründest du deine Meinung mit (Pro-)Argumenten und Beispielen. Berücksichtige auch Gegenargumente (Contra).
- **end / conclusion** (Schluss): Hier ziehst du deine Schlussfolgerung aus den Argumenten des Mittelteils. Greife deine Meinung vom Anfang wieder auf.

smartphones in class?	
PRO	CONTRA
- looking up words easily	- noisy - unconcentrated

USEFUL PHRASES FOR COMMENTS

- In my opinion, / experience, …
- I (definitely / really) think / don't think (that) …
- I agree / don't agree / disagree with …

- First of all, / first(ly), second(ly), …
- On the one hand – on the other hand / Additionally, …

- To sum up, …
- I'd like to finish by saying / underlining …

b) WRITING YOUR COMMENT

- Einige nützliche Wendungen (*useful phrases for comments*):
  – for the **beginning / introduction** of your comment
  – for the **middle / main body** of your comment
  – for the **end / conclusion** of your comment

c) CHECK AND CORRECT YOUR COMMENT

- Auch bei *comments* plane mindestens einen Textentwurf und eine gründliche Überarbeitung ein.

3 Writing an email / a letter   ▸ Unit 3, p. 59   ▸ Unit 4, pp. 87, 92

- **(E-Mail-)Adresse und Betreff:** Schreibe die korrekte Adresse sowie kurz und deutlich das Thema (*subject*) deiner E-Mail in die entsprechenden Felder. (Das Datum fügt das Programm automatisch ein.)

- **Persönliche Anrede:** E-Mails an **Organisationen** beginnst du mit *Dear Mr …* / *Dear Mrs …* / *Dear Ms …* Kennst du den Namen nicht, schreibst du *Dear Sir or Madam*.
  An Zeitungen, Online-Magazine oder Sender kannst du auch *Dear Editor* (Herausgeber/in bzw. Redakteur/in) schreiben.

  An **Freunde** schreibst du z. B. *Dear Lily* oder *Hi Max*.

- **Beginn:** Bedanke dich, wenn das angebracht ist. Sage dann, warum du schreibst und worauf du dich beziehst.

  Thank you for your article …
  I'd like to add my view on …

- **Mittelteil:** Hier teilst du dem Empfänger Wichtiges mit, nimmst Stellung oder kommentierst.

  I (completely) agree with the first part of your …
  However, the second …

- **Schluss:** Schließe mit eventuellen Wünschen und freundlichen Worten:

  An **Organisationen**: *Yours sincerely* (AE: nur *Sincerely*) / *Best wishes* / *regards* (+ dein Name), wenn du oben in der Anrede einen Namen geschrieben hast.
  Yours faithfully (+ dein Name), wenn die Anrede keinen Namen enthält.

  An **Freunde**: *Lots of love* / *All the best* / *Best wishes* (+ dein Name)

4 Summarizing texts ▸ Unit 3, p. 127

Wenn du einen Text (mündlich oder schriftlich) zusammenfasst, gibst du die wichtigsten Informationen oder Ereignisse in kurzer Form wieder.

a) PLANNING YOUR SUMMARY

- Lies den Text: Für den ersten Überblick beginne mit dem Skimming und lies danach genauer, aber noch ohne etwas zu markieren oder dir Notizen zu machen.
- Bestimme die **Textsorte**, denn einen erzählenden Text fasst du etwas anders zusammen als einen Sachtext.
- Beim Finden der **wichtigen Informationen** helfen dir die **5 Wh-questions**. Markiere die wichtigsten Informationen im Text (auf einer Kopie) und fertige dann kurze Notizen an. Mit diesen schreibst du dann deine Zusammenfassung.

ERZÄHLENDE TEXTE (Geschichten, Romane, Romanauszüge usw.):	SACHTEXTE (Zeitungs- oder Magazinartikel usw.):
Thema, Ort, Zeit, grobe Handlungszüge	Thema, Fakten, Argumente (und ggf. wichtige Ereignisse)

WHO	WHAT
is the text about?	
WHAT happens	WHAT are the **main points** or **arguments**
in the text?	
WHERE / WHEN / WHY does it happen?	WHERE / WHEN / WHY is it important?

b) WRITING YOUR SUMMARY

- *beginning / introduction*: Hier nennst du das Thema, Titel und Autor/in des Originaltexts. Bei Zeitungsartikeln solltest du hier auch die Quelle nennen.
- Im **Hauptteil** fasst du die wichtigsten Fakten (eines Sachtexts) bzw. Handlungsschritte (eines erzählenden Textes) zusammen.
  - Fasse dich **kurz** (Der Umfang einer Zusammenfassung ist maximal **20%** des Originaltexts).
  - Fasse jeden Abschnitt in einem kurzen Satz zusammen.
  - Verwende deine eigenen Worte, schreibe den Text nicht ab.
  - Verwende keine direkte Rede.
  - Verzichte auf Einzelheiten und Beispiele.
  - Schreibe im *simple present*, auch wenn der Originaltext eine oder mehrere andere Zeitformen verwendet.
  - Verbinde die Sätze und Textteile, so dass sich deine Zusammenfassung gut und flüssig liest. ▸ p. 173

USEFUL PHRASES
- the text / story is about ...
- ... is a story about ...
- the article shows ... / deals with ...

c) CHECK AND CORRECT YOUR SUMMARY

- Auch bei *summaries* plane mindestens einen Textentwurf und eine gründliche Überarbeitung ein.
  - Enthält deine Zusammenfassung das Thema und die wesentlichen Fakten bzw. Handlungsschritte?
  - Hast du unwichtige Einzelheiten weggelassen?
  - Korrigiere Rechtschreib- und Grammatikfehler. ▸ p. 173
  - Ist dein Text logisch aufgebaut und gut zu verstehen?

Falls möglich, überprüft eure Zusammenfassungen im *partner check*.

SKILLS FILE

5 Writing a CV ▶ Unit 3, p. 58

Die Abkürzung CV kommt aus dem Lateinischen (*curriculum vitae*) und bedeutet „Lebenslauf". Es handelt sich dabei um die Zusammenfassung deiner bisherigen Ausbildung, deiner Fähigkeiten und deiner Interessen. Du benötigst einen CV häufig bei Bewerbungen. Im Amerikanischen wird anstelle von CV meist der Begriff *résumé* verwendet.

Adriane Wibbing
Rüterweg 122, 48032 Bielefeld, Germany
Telephone: +49(0)521-549765 Mobile: +4917126282054
Email: ari.wib@mail-bi.de

Personal statement
I am a confident and polite person with good communication and computer skills. I am looking forward to getting more practical work experience in the workplace.

Key Skills
- friendly and well-organized   - good at foreign languages
- strong team member   - good at organizing things

Education
2012 to present: Olof-Palme-Gesamtschule, Bielefeld
2008 – 2012:   Regenbogen Grundschule, Herford

Work experience
Travel agency: research on hotels and flights (online and in print catalogues)
Kindergarten: working with small children

Hobbies and interests
My hobbies include travelling, reading books about foreign countries, taking photos and creating photo shows. At school my favourite subjects are foreign languages and geography. I am a member of the school drama club.

References
Mrs Sprengel (class teacher), OPG, Nordhofstraße 75, …
Mrs Diel (manager), Reisebüro Globus-Reisen, Ringstraße 9, …

- In GB und den USA ist **kein Bewerberfoto** in einem CV üblich.
- **Geburtsdatum und -ort** werden in CV in GB und den USA meist **nicht** genannt.
- Beginne mit einem **personal statement**. In einem Absatz beschreibst du dich kurz.
- **Fettgedruckte Überschriften** und eine klare **Gliederung** erleichtern das Lesen.
- Du beginnst die Aufzählung deiner Schulen, Praktika usw. **chronologisch rückwärts**.
- Schreibe zum Schluss einen kurzen **Absatz** zu deinen Hobbys und Interessen.
- Nenne zwei **persönliche Fürsprecher/innen** (Referenzengeber/innen) mit Adresse.

Check and correct your CV:
- Hast du ein weißes Blatt A4-Papier benutzt, das ordentlich und sauber ist?
- Ist dein computergeschriebener CV gut gegliedert und übersichtlich?
- Ist dein CV frei von Rechtschreib- und Grammatikfehlern?
- Denke daran, dass du im CV keine Kurzformen verwendest (*I'm* -> *I am* usw).

- Informiere deine Fürsprecher/innen, dass sich eventuell eine britische oder US-amerikanische Institution bzw. Firma bei ihnen melden wird.

6 Writing a cover letter ▶ Unit 3, p. 59

Ein *cover letter* (auch: *covering letter, letter of application*) ist ein Begleitschreiben zu einer Bewerbung und ist nicht länger als eine Seite. Du musst dabei auf bestimmte Regeln achten.

Lessingstraße 3
46562 Voerde
Germany

> Schreibe **deine Anschrift** und das **Datum** in die rechte obere Ecke.

Peter Tiger
Peter's Pet shop
Adalbertstraße 10
40545 Düsseldorf

> Die **Anschrift des Adressaten** steht links.

30 May 20…

Dear Mr Tiger

> Wenn du den Adressaten **nicht kennst**, beginne mit *Dear Sir / Madam*. Wenn du den Adressaten **kennst**, beginne mit *Dear Mr … / Mrs … / Ms …*

I am writing to you about the advertisement for a pet shop assistant on your website that I saw yesterday. I would like to apply for this job.

> Schreibe, **worauf** du dich **beziehst** und um welche **Position** du dich bewirbst.

I am a student, and I really like pets. Our family has a cat, a dog and two budgies. I take care of them. I am reliable and hard-working and I love working with animals. I am good at English, so I can also take care of your English-speaking customers.

In my last summer holidays I volunteered at the Berlin Zoo. Please find the reference enclosed.

> Nenne **Erfahrungen** und Fähigkeiten, die dich für die Stelle qualifizieren. Erwähne ggf. **Referenzen**.

I also enclose my CV and I am looking forward to your answer.

Yours sincerely
Jonathan Held
Jonathan Held

> Wenn du den Adressaten nicht kennst (und oben mit *Dear Sir or Madam* beginnst), beende mit **Yours faithfully**. Wenn du den Adressaten kennst (und oben mit *Dear Mr … / Mrs … / Ms …* beginnst), beende mit **Yours sincerely**.

> Ende mit einem **freundlichen Ausblick** oder mit **Dank** vorab.

Check and correct your cover letter:

- Hast du ein weißes Blatt A4-Papier benutzt, das ordentlich und sauber ist?
- Ist dein computergeschriebener *cover letter* gut gegliedert und übersichtlich?
- Ist dein *cover letter* frei von Rechtschreib- und Grammatikfehlern?
- Denke daran, dass du im *Cover letter* keine Kurzformen verwendest (~~I'm~~ -> *I am*; ~~ad~~ -> *advertisement*; ~~paper~~ -> *newspaper* usw).

> Dein Bewerbungsschreiben sollte **kurz** sein, aber das **Wesentliche** enthalten: was genau dich für diese Stelle qualifiziert. Bleib bei der Wahrheit und übertreibe nicht.

SKILLS FILE

7 A written discussion ▶ Unit 4, p. 79

Oft sollst du zu strittigen Fragen schriftlich Stellung nehmen und deine Sichtweise überzeugend darlegen. Zeige dabei, dass du dich gründlich mit dem Thema beschäftigt und die Pro-/ Contra-Argumente abgewogen hast.

a) PREPARING YOUR TEXT

- **Sammle** zuerst alle **Argumente** (z.B. in einem kurzen Brainstorming). Evtl. musst du vorher weiter recherchieren
  ▶ *Skills file 4, p. 165*
- Ordne deine Argumente gleich beim Sammeln in zwei Listen: *pro* und *contra*.
- Schau dir die Argumentlisten an und bereite so die Gliederung *(outline)* deines Texts vor:
  – Was sind die **besten drei Argumente contra** und die **besten drei pro**? Diese verwendest du, jeweils beginnend mit dem stärksten Argument.
  – **Nummeriere** die Argumente entsprechend dem Schema rechts.
- Notiere deine **Gliederung *(outline)*** gemäß dem Schema rechts.
  – Beginne mit den Argumenten, die **gegen *(contra)*** deine Sichtweise sprechen und stell **danach** die Argumente vor, die deine Meinung **unterstützen *(pro)***. (Auf diese Weise lassen sich die Contra-Argumente wirkungsvoller entkräften. Prinzipiell kannst du aber auch mit den Pro-Argumenten beginnen.)
  – Notiere jeweils **Beispiele** zu den Argumenten.
  – Überlege und notiere, in welche Richtung deine **Schlussfolgerung *(conclusion)*** gehen soll.

> **OUTLINE FOR A WRITTEN DISCUSSION**
> **Topic: Should computer games be a school subject?**
> 1) Introduction: …
> 2) Arguments contra / against
>   2.1) First argument: …
>   2.2) Second argument: …
>   2.3) Third argument: …
> 3) Arguments pro / for / supporting
>   2.1) First argument: …
>   2.2) Second argument: …
>   2.3) Third argument: …
> 4) Conclusion: …

b) WRITING YOUR TEXT

- Nun formuliere mithilfe deiner *outline* die *written discussion* **ausführlich**.
- In der **Einleitung *(introduction)*** stellst du das Thema vor und beschreibst, worum es geht. Geh dabei von einem allgemein bekannten Problem oder einer persönlichen Erfahrung aus.
- Im **Hauptteil *(main body)*** präsentiere die Argumente *contra* und *pro*.
  – Nenne jeweils das Argument.
  – Erläutere es näher und begründe deine Meinung.
  – Unterstütze deine Meinung durch Fakten und Beispiele (aus deiner Recherche bzw. aus eigener Erfahrung).
  – Formuliere logisch und flüssig, verbinde deine Argumente.
    ▶ *p. 173*
- Am Textende steht deine persönliche **Schlussfolgerung *(conclusion)***. Achtung: Hier keine neuen Argumente und auch keine Argument-Wiederholungen aus dem Hauptteil!

> **USEFUL PHRASES**
> **… for your introduction:**
> A lot of people think …
> You often hear people say that …,
> … so the questions is: should … or not?
>
> **… for the main body of your text:**
> Firstly, …; Secondly, …;
> Another argument for / against … is …
> For example, …
> People think that because …
> However, a lot of people feel …
> On the one hand, …
> On the other hand, we should not forget …
> So …; That is why …; Finally, …
>
> **… for your conclusion:**
> To sum up, I think / I would say …
> After looking at all the arguments I think / I come to the conclusion that …

c) CHECK AND CORRECT YOUR TEXT

- Auch bei *written discussions* plane mindestens einen Textentwurf und eine gründliche Überarbeitung ein. ▶ *p. 173*

SF 9 Describing photos and pictures ▶ Unit 1, pp. 26, 96   ▶ Unit 4, pp. 77, 97

Wenn du ein Foto oder ein Bild beschreibst, beachte Folgendes:

1 Beginne allgemein

Sage zunächst, **was** du **allgemein** auf dem Foto oder Bild siehst. Welcher Ort, welche Gegenstände und welche Menschen siehst du? Was tun sie?

> In the photo we can see a little girl and a young man.
> They're sitting inside a big room, but not together.

2 Beachte eine Reihenfolge

Wen oder **was** siehst du; **wo** befinden sich die Personen oder Gegenstände im Foto?
Du kannst z.B. mit dem beginnen, was im Vordergrund bzw. im Hintergrund des Bildes zu sehen ist.
Benutze **Ortsangaben** wie
> in the middle / on the left / on the right
> at the top / bottom …

Ordne die Personen und Dinge einander zu, indem du **Präpositionen** benutzt, z.B.
> at / behind / between / in front of / near / next to / on …

> The (little) girl is in the foreground on the left sitting at a table.
> The young man is in the background sitting on the floor.
> In the background you can see windows and some trees outside.

3 Beschreibe Personen und Handlungen

Wie sehen die Personen aus (z.B. Alter, Kleidung, Gesichtsausdruck)? Um zu beschreiben, was sie gerade tun, benutze das *present progressive*.

> The man is using a laptop.
> The girl is smiling.
> The girl might be playing with dominoes or she might be building something with them.

4 Formuliere Vermutungen

In welchem **Verhältnis** stehen die Personen wahrscheinlich **zueinander**? Versetze dich in sie hinein und beschreibe, was sie gerade **fühlen** oder **denken** (könnten). Nützliche Wendungen dafür sind z.B.
> I think / I'm sure / perhaps / probably / would / could …

> The man might be working or surfing or writing an email. He looks busy. He might be her father.
> The girl is probably having fun or is happy that her father is at home.

5 Was denkst du persönlich?

Am Ende der Beschreibung sollst du häufig deine Meinung zur Situation und zum Verhalten der Personen formulieren.

Dabei hilft es, an deine eigenen Erfahrungen in ähnlichen Situationen zu denken. Du könntest auch Fragen stellen, die dir zu dieser Situation einfallen. Nützliche Wendungen sind hier z.B.:

> I think / I guess / In my opinion / For me it's absolutely (not) okay / it's alright / it's wrong
> If I was (the man / woman … in the photo), I'd / I wouldn't … because …
> I remember a similar situation / story …

> Maybe they're going to have a video-call with grandma.

> It's also possible that the man is just checking the rules of the domino game online.

SKILLS FILE

SF 10 MEDIATION SKILLS ▸ Unit 1, p. 27 ▸ Unit 2, p. 48 ▸ Unit 3, p. 59
▸ Unit 4, pp. 81, 93

Mediation (auch: Sprachmittlung) bedeutet, zwischen Sprecher/innen unterschiedlicher Sprachen zu vermitteln und Informationen in der jeweiligen Sprache wiederzugeben.

1 Worum geht es?

- Du gibst englische Informationen mündlich **auf Deutsch** wieder, wie im Beispiel rechts.

- Oder du vermittelst deutsche Informationen **auf Englisch**, z.B. wenn bei dir an der Schule ein Austauschschüler zu Gast ist. Das kann mündlich geschehen (im Gespräch mit Anderen) oder auch schriftlich, wenn du dem Gastschüler z.B. eine Nachricht schreibst.

- Die unterschiedlichen Möglichkeiten von *mediation* (Deutsch ⇄ Englisch, mündlich / schriftlich) fasst dieses Schema zusammen:

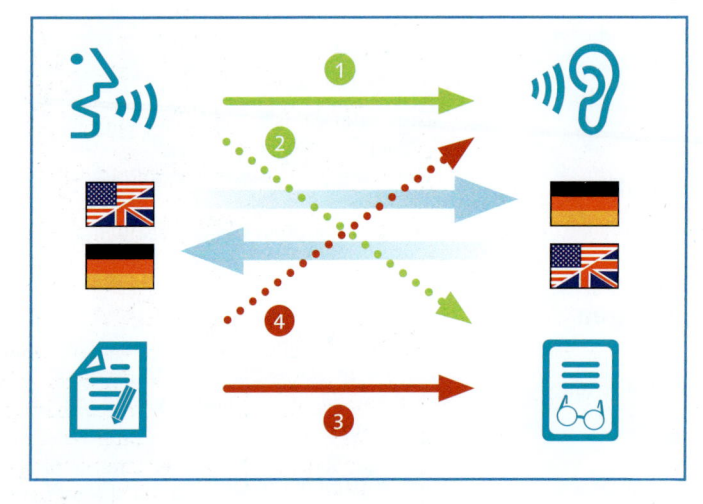

Freund: Können wir hier parken? Was sollen wir machen?

Du: Ja. Wir sollen einen Parkschein lösen und ihn sichtbar ins Auto legen.

Beispiele:

① Einem englischsprachigen Reisenden in Deutschland sagst du, was eben in der Bahnhofsdurchsage Wichtiges zu hören war.

② Bei einem Telefonat mit einem englischen Jobanbieter machst du Notizen, die du einem Freund mailst.

③ Du mailst einer künftigen Gastschülerin die wichtigsten Inhalte eurer Schulordnung auf Englisch.

④ Du erklärst eine schriftliche Information mündlich in der anderen Sprache, vgl. das Beispiel im Foto oben.

2 Worauf musst du achten?

- *Mediation* ist keine Übersetzung. Gib also nur das **Wesentliche** sinngemäß wieder, lasse unwichtige Informationen weg.

- Verwende kurze und einfache Sätze.

- Wenn du **schriftliche Informationen** sprachmitteln sollst:
  - **Scanne** den Text gezielt nach den notwendigen Informationen. ▸ *Skills file 6.2, p. 167*
  - Ist der Text länger und du brauchst viele Informationen daraus, **markiere** die wichtigsten Textstellen und mach dir ggf. **Notizen** in deinen eigenen Worten.
    ▸ *Skills file 6.6, p. 169*

- Wenn du **mündliche Informationen** sprachmitteln sollst:
  - **Höre zielgerichtet** auf die notwendigen Informationen.
    ▸ *Skills file 5, p. 166*

- Bei längeren Hörtexten und umfangreichen Informationen mach dir **kurze Notizen** während des Hörens. Überlege anschließend, wie du sie am besten in der anderen Sprache wiedergeben kannst.

> Wenn du schriftlich sprachmittelst, achte darauf, dass dein Text in der anderen Sprache nicht länger als ca. 40% des Originaltexts ist.

3 Paraphrasieren (Umschreiben unbekannter Wörter)

Manchmal fällt es schwer, Inhalte auf Englisch wiederzugeben, z.B. wenn dein Wortschatz nicht ausreicht oder dir manche Wörter im Stress nicht gleich einfallen. Dann nutze das Umschreiben *(paraphrasing)*. Die folgenden **Strategien** helfen dir.

- Umschreibe mit Wörtern, die eine ähnliche oder die **gleiche Bedeutung** haben (Synonyme) oder mit Vergleichen:
  It's the same as … / It's (very) similar to … / It works like …

- Umschreibe mit **gegensätzlichen** Wörtern (Antonymen):
  It's the opposite of …
  Seine Eltern leben getrennt.   – *His parents don't live together.*
  Der See ist künstlich angelegt. – *The lake is not a natural one.*

- Umschreibe mit dem **Oberbegriff** statt der einzelnen Unterbegriffe (das hilft dir auch, dich kurz zu fassen):
  Wir müssen noch ein paar Tulpen und Osterglocken kaufen.
     – *We need (to buy) some flowers.*
  Oh nein, Fahrradventil und Schlauch sind kaputt!
     – *She's angry because she can't ride her bike.*

- Umschreibe mit **Unterbegriffen**, wenn du den Oberbegriff nicht kennst:
  Haben wir ausreichend Geschirr für die Party heute Abend?
     – *Are there enough plates and glasses, etc. for the party?*

- Umschreibe mit einer näheren Erläuterung, z.B. in **Relativsätzen**. ▶ Language file 25, p. 198
  It's somebody / a person who is known for …
  It's something that you use for …
  It's a place that … / where …

- Oft hilft das Prinzip **Keep it simple**. Fällt dir eine einfache Erklärung des gesuchten Begriffs ein? Diese kannst du dann leicht auf Englisch formulieren, z.B.
  Selbstbedienung – *no waiter / waitress*
  Vollsperrung der A20 bis 24 Uhr
     – *The A20 motorway will be (completely) closed till midnight.*
  Schienenersatzverkehr
     – *There is no train, so we have to take the bus instead.*

> Denk dran, wir haben das Ding für die englischen Steckdosen vergessen.
>
> Excuse me, where can I find the piece for connecting international electronic things to electricity here?
>
> Oh, sure. You mean adapters? – You'll find them …

4 Kulturelle und regionale Unterschiede

- Manche ‚typisch deutschen' Alltagsdinge oder Traditionen wird dein Gegenüber eventuell nicht kennen. Hierfür gibt es im Englischen meist gar keinen direkten Begriff. Du musst dann erklären, was du meinst. Typische Beispiele:

- **Rosenmontag** – *It's the last day of carnival and very special for people in the Rhine area. It's a holiday. People celebrate and wear costumes, and there are parades in the streets.*

- **Schultüte** – *It's a kind of special bag kids are given on their first day at school. There are sweets in it and little things you need at school, like pens and exercise books.*

- Natürlich wird es für dich auch Unbekanntes geben, wovon dein Gegenüber ganz selbstverständlich spricht. Dann frage höflich nach und bitte um eine Erklärung:
- *I'm sorry, I'm afraid I don't know this tradition / rule / habit / meal …*
  Could you please explain?
  I've never done / eaten … this before. Could you help me, please?

LANGUAGE FILE

Inhalt

TALKING ABOUT THE PRESENT	page
LF 1 The simple present	182
LF 2 The present progressive	183

TALKING ABOUT THE PAST	
LF 3 The simple past	183
LF 4 The past progressive	184
LF 5 The present perfect	185
LF 6 The present perfect progressive	186
LF 7 The past perfect	186

TALKING ABOUT THE FUTURE	
LF 8 The *going to*-future	187
LF 9 The *will*-future	187

LF 10 Using tenses	187
LF 11 Word order in statements	188
LF 12 Word order in questions	189
LF 13 Subject and object questions	189
LF 14 Questions with passive and modals	190
LF 15 Questions with prepositions	190

	page
LF 16 The comparison of adjectives	191
LF 17 Adverbs of manner	191
LF 18 Adverbs of frequency	192
LF 19 The comparison of adverbs	192
LF 20 Indirect speech	192
LF 21 Modal verbs and *be allowed to*, *have to*, *be able to*	195
LF 22 *If …* (Conditional sentences type 1)	196
LF 23 *If …* (Conditional sentences type 2)	197
LF 24 *If …* (Conditional sentences type 3)	197
LF 25 Relative clauses	198
LF 26 Contact clauses	199
LF 27 Participle clauses instead of subordinate clauses	199
LF 28 Reflexive pronouns	200
LF 29 The *-ing*-form (the gerund)	200
LF 30 The passive	202
LF 31 Question tags	203
Grammatical terms	204

TALKING ABOUT THE PRESENT

LF 1 The simple present (Die einfache Form der Gegenwart)

Mit dem **simple present** drückst du aus, was **wiederholt** oder **nie** geschieht. Es steht häufig mit: *always, sometimes, often, never* oder Zeitangaben wie *every day, in the morning, at the weekend, on Monday*.

Bejahte und verneinte Aussagen

| I/you/we/they | like | sport. |
| He/she/it | like**s** | |

| I/you/we/they | **don't** like | sport. |
| He/she/it | **doesn't** like | |

Bei **bejahten Aussagen** fügst du bei *he/she/it* ein **-s** an das Verb.

! – *he/she/it* go**es**, watch**es**, tr**ies**, hurr**ies**

! Das Verb nach **doesn't** (hier: *like*) steht immer in der Grundform. Das gilt auch für **does** in Fragen.

Ja-/Nein-Fragen und Kurzantworten

| **Do** you like | sport? | Yes, I **do**./No, I **don't**. |
| **Does** he like | | Yes, he **does**./No, he **doesn't**. |

Ja-/Nein-Fragen im **simple present** beginnst du mit *Do* oder *Does*.

Fragen mit Fragewort

| **Why do** Ben's friends love football? |

Wenn die Frage mit einem **Fragewort** anfängt, folgt direkt *do* bzw. *does*.

*Fragen mit *Who* ▶ *LF 13, p. 189*

Wenn das **Fragewort** *Who* nach dem **Objekt** fragt (*wen? wem?*), folgt *do* bzw. *does*.
 – *Who **does** Ben like?* **Wen** mag Ben? – *Who/What **does** Ben dislike?* **Wen/Was** mag Ben nicht?

Fragt *Who* nach dem **Subjekt** (*wer?*), folgt direkt das Verb – **nie** ~~do~~ oder ~~does~~.
 – *Who likes Ben?* **Wer** mag Ben? – *Who/What makes Ben angry?* **Wer/Was** macht Ben ärgerlich?

LF 2 The present progressive (Die Verlaufsform der Gegenwart)

Mit dem *present progressive* sagst du, dass etwas **gerade jetzt** geschieht oder dass jemand **gerade etwas tut**.
Das *present progressive* benutzt du auch, um Bilder zu beschreiben.
Häufige Zeitangaben in Sätzen im *present progressive* sind: *now, at the moment, just, still, today*.
Eine Verlaufsform gibt es im Deutschen nicht. Man sagt aber z.B.: „Ich bin gerade dabei, etwas zu tun."

Bejahte Aussagen
I'm/You're
He's/She's   waiting.
They're

Verneinte Aussagen
I'm not/You aren't
He/She isn't   waiting.
They aren't

Das *present progressive* bildest du mit einer Form von *be* + *verb* + *-ing*.

! Beachte beim Schreiben:
write → writing   make → making
plan → planning   stop → stopping

Ja-/Nein-Fragen und Kurzantworten
Am I
Are you
Is he/she   waiting?
Are they

Yes, I am./No, I'm not.
Yes, he/she is./No, ... isn't.
Yes, they are./No, they aren't.

Ja-/Nein-Fragen beginnst du mit *Am/Are/Is*:

Is Mia going to football practice?
- *Yes, she is./No, she isn't. She's waiting for Li.*

Fragen mit Fragewort
What's Mia doing today?
Where is she going first?

Wenn die Frage mit einem **Fragewort** anfängt, steht das Fragewort vor *am/are/is*:

What's Mia doing at the moment?
Where are Mia and her friend going?

Present progressive oder simple present?

Mia is playing football. (*present progressive*)
   Mia spielt Fußball. (= gerade, jetzt im Moment)

Mia plays football. (*simple present*)
   Mia spielt Fußball. (= regelmäßig, es ist ihr Sport)

Mia often plays football, but she isn't playing today because it's raining.
   Mia spielt oft Fußball, aber heute spielt sie nicht, weil es jetzt regnet.

Für den Satz „Mia spielt Fußball." kannst du entweder das *present progressive* oder das *simple present* benutzen, je nachdem, was du ausdrücken möchtest:

present progressive:	*simple present:*
just, at the moment, now, today	always, often, sometimes, never, every day/week, on Saturdays

TALKING ABOUT THE PAST

LF 3 The simple past (Die einfache Form der Vergangenheit)

Mit dem *simple past* sagst du, was **zu einer bestimmten Zeit** in der Vergangenheit geschah.
Du verwendest es oft mit Zeitangaben wie *yesterday, last week, in July, two years ago*.

! Freie Wahl: Perfekt oder Präteritum   ! *Simple past*

Mia fuhr gestern zu Li./Mia ist gestern zu Li gefahren.   →   Mia went to Li's yesterday.

LANGUAGE FILE

a) Regelmäßige Verben (*Regular verbs*)

Bejahte Aussagen	
I/He/We/…	laughed a lot.

Bei **regelmäßigen** Verben bildest du das **simple past** durch Anhängen von **-ed** an das Verb:
! Beachte beim Schreiben: *try* → *tried*, *plan* → *planned*, *hurry* → *hurried*

b) Unregelmäßige Verben (*Irregular verbs*)

Bejahte Aussagen	
I/He/We/…	bought a book.

Lerne die **simple past**-Formen **unregelmäßiger** Verben.
▶ *Irregular verbs, pp. 264–265*

Verneinte Aussagen	
I/He/We/…	didn't know all the people.

Wenn du sagen willst, was **nicht** geschah, setzt du *didn't* vor das Verb in der **Grundform**:
Mia didn't buy a comic yesterday.

Ja-/Nein-Fragen und Kurzantworten		
Did you/she/…	like it?	Yes, I did./No, I didn't. Yes, she did./No, she didn't.

! Das Verb *be* (*was/were*) verneinst du **ohne** ~~did~~.
The comics weren't new.

Fragen mit *be* (*was/were*) und Kurzantworten		
Was I/he/she/it **Were** we/you/they	happy?	Yes he was./No, he wasn't. Yes, we were./No, we weren't.

Ja-/Nein-Fragen im **simple past** beginnst du mit *Did*.

! Ja-/Nein-Fragen mit *Was/Were* bildest du **ohne** ~~did~~, ebenso die Kurzantworten.

Fragen mit Fragewort
What did Mia like best about the comic?

Did folgt direkt auf das **Fragewort**.
! Das Verb nach *did* (hier: *like*) steht immer in der Grundform. ▶ *LF 13, p. 189*

LF 4 The past progressive (Die Verlaufsform der Vergangenheit)

At 5 pm Ben was taking part in a bike race.
Um 17 Uhr **nahm** *Ben (gerade) an einem Radrennen* **teil**.

His team was racing down a hill when a boy fell.
Sein Team **raste** *gerade …, als … stürzte.*

Bejahte und verneinte Aussagen		
I/He/She/It You/We/They	was/wasn't were/weren't	racing.

Mit dem **past progressive** drückst du aus, dass eine Handlung in der Vergangenheit **gerade im Gange** war.
Oder du beschreibst, was gerade vor sich ging, als etwas anderes geschah.

Das **past progressive** bildest du mit **was/were** + verb + **-ing**.
! Beachte beim Schreiben: *verb* + **-ing**
▶ *LF 2, p. 183*

Ja-/Nein-Fragen und Kurzantworten	
Was/Were … taking …?	Yes, I/he was./ No, they weren't.

Fragen mit Fragewort
What was Ben doing at 5 pm?

LF 5 The present perfect (Das *present perfect*)

Mia and Li are shopping at the new mall. They've already been to three clothes shops.
"We haven't found a shirt for me yet, Mia."
"I know, but I'm hungry. I haven't eaten enough today."

Das *present perfect* drückt aus, dass etwas irgendwann geschehen ist. Der Zeitpunkt ist unwichtig. Es steht häufig mit: *just, already, always, ever, never, not … yet.*
Du bildest das *present perfect* mit

have/has + 3. Form des Verbs.
▶ *Irregular verbs, pp. 264–265*

! Das *present perfect* wird **immer** mit *have/has* gebildet, auch wenn im Deutschen eine Form von „sein" steht.

Bejahte Aussagen

| I /… 've | bought … |
| He /… has | |

Verneinte Aussagen

| I /… haven't | bought … |
| He /… hasn't | |

Ja-/Nein-Fragen

| Have you/we … | bought …? |
| Has she/he … | |

Kurzantworten

Yes, I / we … have. / No, I / we … haven't.
Yes, she / … has. / No, she /… hasn't.

Fragen mit Fragewort

Why have Mia and Li gone to the new mall?

Present perfect with *since* and *for*

! Auch wenn das Präsens im Deutschen steht, musst du mit *since* und *for* das *present perfect* benutzen:
I've lived next door to Mia **since** my family came to the US. Mia has been my friend **for** six years.
Ich bin Mias Nachbarin seit …

Das *present perfect* mit *since* oder *for* drückt aus, **seit wann** oder **wie lange** etwas schon andauert.
Since nennt einen Anfangs**zeit**punkt: *since 6 am, since 2016, since I was a baby, …*
For umfasst einen **Zeit**raum: *for two months / years / hours / for a long time.*

Present perfect or simple past?

! Das *present perfect* steht häufig in Sätzen mit Zeitangaben wie *just, already, often, always, never, ever, not … yet, before.*
- um zu sagen, dass etwas **irgendwann** geschehen ist, oft mit **Auswirkungen auf die Gegenwart**.
   Greg has just come back from Oz.
- in Fragen mit *ever …?*
   Have you ever been to Uluru before, Greg?
- in Sätzen mit *since* und *for*
   His uncle has lived in Oz since 2011.

! Das *simple past* muss stehen in Sätzen mit Zeitangaben wie *yesterday, last week, in July, two years ago, in 2015.*
- um zu sagen, dass etwas **zu einer bestimmten Zeit** geschehen ist, oft mit genauer Zeitangabe.
   In 2015 Greg's uncle started a bar in Sydney.
- in Berichten und Erzählungen
   Greg asked his mum. Finally she agreed.
- in Fragen mit **When** …?
   When did you go on a trip last time?

LANGUAGE FILE

LF 6 The present perfect progressive
(Die Verlaufsform des *present perfect*)

Mit dem **present perfect progressive** sagst du, dass etwas **in der Vergangenheit** begonnen hat und **bis jetzt andauert** bzw. **gerade vorbei** ist.

Bejahte und verneinte Aussagen

I/…'ve He/…'s	been waiting for two hours.

I … He …	haven't been hasn't been	waiting long.

Häufige Zeitangaben in Sätzen im **present perfect progressive** sind:
  since 7 am / 2000 / … / I came here
  (**Zeitpunkt**)
  for two hours / a long time, in recent years
  (**Zeitraum**)

Du bildest das **present perfect progressive** mit **have/has been** + verb + **-ing**.

Ja-/Nein-Fragen und Kurzantworten

Have you/… Has he/…	been waiting long?	Yes, …have/has. No, … haven't/hasn't.

Fragen mit Fragewort

How long have you been waiting?

! Im Deutschen verwendest du meist das Präsens:
How long have you been learning English?
Wie lange lernst du schon Englisch?

LF 7 The past perfect (Das *past perfect*)

When Li **arrived** at the party, Ben **had** already **gone** home. *(Erst ging Ben, dann kam Li.)*
Ben **thought** that Li **had forgotten** about the party.
Had he **told** her about it at all?

! Das **past perfect** wird **immer** mit **had** gebildet, auch wenn im Deutschen „war" steht.

Mit dem **past perfect** (Plusquamperfekt oder **Vor**vergangenheit) drückst du aus, dass etwas noch **vor** etwas anderem in der Vergangenheit stattgefunden hatte.

Du bildest das **past perfect** mit **had** + 3. Form des Verbs (**past participle**).
▶ Irregular verbs, pp. 264–265

Bejahte und verneinte Aussagen

I/… He/…	had/hadn't	forgotten.

Ja-/Nein-Fragen und Kurzantworten

Had I …/he …	forgotten?	Yes, … had. No, … hadn't.

*Simple past or past perfect?

Before Li **left** home, it **had started** to rain heavily.

So Li **took** an umbrella with her, but she **forgot** her phone.

Mit dem **past perfect** sagst du, was zeitlich vorangegangen war. Oft stehen dabei Zeitangaben wie *after, when, before, already*.

! Keine Vorvergangenheit (**past perfect**), wenn etwas zur gleichen Zeit geschieht.

TALKING ABOUT THE FUTURE

LF 8 The *going to*-future (Das Futur mit *going to*)

Mia's going to have a football match next Saturday.
    Mia wird nächsten Samstag … haben.
Her brother Ben isn't going to come to the match.
    Ihr Bruder hat nicht vor, es zu sehen.
What are we going to do on Sunday?
    Was wollen wir am Sonntag machen?
Is the weather going to be fine?
    Wird das Wetter gut?

! *Going to* hat hier nichts mit dem deutschen Wort *gehen* zu tun. Es heißt hier „werden / wollen / vorhaben / beabsichtigen".

Wenn du ausdrücken möchtest, was jemand in der Zukunft **plant** oder **vorhat** sowie für **Vorhersagen** benutzt du das Futur mit *going to*.

Es wird mit einer Form von *be* (*am* / *are* / *is*) gebildet, oft mit den Kurzformen:
'm / 're / 's + going to + verb

Verneinung:
Ben isn't going to be at Mia's match.
But she's not going to be angry with him.

Fragen und Kurzantworten:
Is it going to rain?
- (Look at the sky!) Yes, it is. / No, it isn't.

LF 9 The *will*-future (Das Futur mit *will*)

Bejahte und verneinte Aussagen

I / You / He / She / It We / You / They	will like the concert. won't like all the songs.

Ja- / Nein-Fragen und Kurzantworten

Will	I / you / he / …	like all the songs?	Yes, … will. No, … won't.

Fragen mit Fragewort

Who will win the match tomorrow?
When will we get home?

! Englisch *I will* heißt im Deutschen „ich werde" und nicht „ich will".

Mit dem *will*-future kannst du über die Zukunft sprechen, z.B. über **Vermutungen** und **Vorhersagen**.

Eine **Vermutung** beginnt oft mit *I think, I'm sure, Maybe*.
I think I'll enjoy the concert. – I'm sure you will.

Bei **Vorhersagen** geht es oft um Dinge, die man nicht direkt beeinflussen kann:
It'll be winter soon.

Das *will*-future wird mit **will + Verb** gebildet.
Die Kurzform von *will* heißt *'ll*.

! Die **Verneinung** *will not* wird in der Kurzform zu **won't**.

! Verwechsle nicht *won't* mit *wouldn't*, der Verneinung von *would* (würden).

Die Formen **will** und **won't** sind für alle Personen gleich.

NEW LF 10 Using tenses (Die Verwendung der Zeitformen) ▶ Unit 1, p. 17

Du kannst die **wichtigsten Zeitformen des Verbs** im Englischen bilden. Manchmal werden sie anders **gebraucht** als im Deutschen. Das ist wichtig, wenn du **eigene Texte** schreibst.

simple present ▶ LF 1, p. 182

Cycling is Ben's favourite sport. He practises hard. He often wins races. He doesn't like to lose them.

Mit dem **simple present** drückst du aus, was wiederholt oder nie geschieht. Du benutzt es, wenn du **Orte, Zustände, Gewohnheiten** und **Vorgänge / Abläufe** beschreibst und bei **Zusammenfassungen**.
▶ Skills file 8.4, p. 175.

187

LANGUAGE FILE

present progressive (▶ LF 2, p. 183)

In this photo Ben **is cyling** down a street. Two boys **are following** him. A car **is** just **coming** from the right.

Mit dem **present progressive** drückst du aus, was **gerade geschieht**. Du benutzt es auch bei **Bildbeschreibungen** ▶ Skills file 9, p. 179.

simple past (▶ LF 3, p. 183)

Mia **met** her friend Li in a cafe yesterday. They **didn't eat** a lot because it **was** a very hot day. But they **had** a big ice cream together.

Mit dem **simple past** sagst du, was **zu einer bestimmten Zeit** in der Vergangenheit geschah. Das **simple past** verwendest du in **Berichten** und beim **Erzählen**.

going to-future (▶ LF 8, p. 187)

What **are** Mia, Ben and Li **going to** do next Sunday?
They**'re going to** go to a concert. (They've already got the tickets.)

Was jemand **in der Zukunft plant** oder **vorhat**, drückst du mit dem **going to-future** aus.

will-future (▶ LF 9, p. 187)

Ben: "I'm afraid I **won't** have time to come to your match, Mia. But I promise I**'ll** be at your next match.

Mit dem **will-future** kannst du über die Zukunft sprechen, z.B. über **Vermutungen** und **Vorhersagen**.

NEW LF 11 Word order in statements
(Die Wortstellung in Aussagen) ▶ Unit 3, p. 61

Die Regel zur Wortstellung im englischen Satz ist **subject – verb – object**, kurz **S-V-(O)**.
Subjekt – Prädikat – (Objekt) (Ein Objekt gibt es nicht immer.)

! Anders als im Deutschen wird von **S-V-O** nicht abgewichen, z.B. bei Orts- oder Umstandsangaben (In englischen Sätzen **stellst du** nicht um.) bzw. Zeitangaben (Gestern **wusste ich** das noch.)

subject	verb	object	adverbial (Adverbialbestimmung)	
Mia	plays	football.		
She	can't play	an instrument.		
Ben and Mia	have bought	tickets.		
Ben and Mia	are interested in	music.		
They	didn't go		to concerts	last year.

Mia **usually** plays football. Ben **sometimes** phones Li.

Die **Adverbien der Häufigkeit** usually, always, often, sometimes, never stehen **zwischen Subjekt** und **Verb**.

Mia and Ben **have already bought** tickets. They **are planning** how to get to the concert. Have you **ever been** to a concert?

Die **Adverbien der Zeit**, wie already, ever, just, never stehen **vor** dem **present participle** (-ing-Form) bzw. dem **past participle** (dritte Form) **des Verbs**.

Luckily Ben and Mia still got cheap tickets.
  Ben und Mia bekamen glücklicherweise noch …

Die **Adverbien**, die sich auf den **gesamten Satz** beziehen, wie perhaps/maybe, suddenly, finally, of course, at first stehen meist am **Satzanfang**.

After the date with Li, Ben walked home **happily**.

Adverbien, die sich auf ein Verb bzw. eine Tätigkeit beziehen, stehen in der Regel **am Satzende**.

Ben had first met Li **at Mia's club two months ago**.

! Gibt es in einem Satz eine **Orts- und** eine **Zeitangabe**, gilt die Regel „**Ort vor Zeit**".

NEW LF 12 Word order in questions (Die Wortstellung in Fragen)

▸ Unit 3, p. 61

Du erkennst eine Frage daran, dass hier **vor** dem **Subjekt** eine gebeugte (konjugierte) **Verbform** steht.

Fragen mit *do / does* und *did*

Viele Fragen bildest du mit einer Form von *do*, einem Hilfsverb (*auxiliary*). Es „hilft" sozusagen dabei, dass die Wortstellung des zugrundeliegenden Aussagesatzes einfach erhalten bleiben kann. Vergleiche:

Aussagesatz (S-V-O) → Fragesatz (Hilfsverb-S-V-O)
Mia and Li play football.   Do Mia and Li play football? (*Ja-/Nein*-Frage)
                              When do Mia and Li play football? (Frage mit Fragewort)

Weitere Fragesätze:

question word	auxiliary do(es)/did	subject	(main) verb	
	Does	Ben	work	on Fridays?
	Did	he and Li	go	to the cinema?
What	does	Ben	watch	on TV?
Where	did	you	buy	that DVD?

Du beginnst die Frage mit (Fragewort +) *do/does/did*, dann folgt das Subjekt und dann das Hauptverb (*main verb*).

! Keine **Umstellungen** von **Verb** und **Subjekt** wie im Deutschen:
Arbeitet Ben? → Does Ben work?

! Das Hauptverb steht **immer** in der **Grundform** (Infinitiv). Gebeugt (konjugiert) wird das Hilfsverb.

Fragen mit Formen von *be* und *have*

Wenn der Fragesatz eine Form von *be* oder *have* enthält, steht diese **vor** dem **Subjekt**.

question word	verb (forms of be / have)	subject	
	Is	Mia	Ben's sister?
	Are	Mia and Li	good friends?
	Have	you	been to school?
Where	were	you	last weekend?
What	are	Mia and Li	planning for Friday?

Ein **Fragesatz** mit *be* oder *have* wird gebildet, indem du die entsprechende Form, z.B. *is, was, were; have, has* **vor** das **Subjekt** stellst.

Fragewörter – *who, what, when, where, why, how, how long* – stehen am **Satzanfang**.

NEW LF 13 Subject and object questions
(Fragen nach dem Subjekt oder dem Objekt) ▸ Unit 3, More challenge 2, p. 126

Ben likes Li.

Who **likes** Li? – Ben. | Who **does** Ben like? – Li.
Wer mag Li? | Wen mag Ben?

The noise disturbed Li.
What **disturbed** Li? – The noise.
Was störte Li? – Der Lärm.
Li shut the window.
What **did** Li shut? – The window.
Was schloss Li? – Das Fenster.

Mit den Fragewörtern *who/what/which* kannst du nach dem Subjekt oder nach dem Objekt fragen.

Wenn das **Fragewort** nach dem **Subjekt** (*wer?/was?*) fragt, **folgt direkt das Vollverb** – nie ~~do~~ oder ~~does~~ als Hilfsverb.

Wenn das **Fragewort** nach dem **Objekt** fragt (*wen?/wem?/was?*), folgt *do* bzw. *does*.

Nach dem Subjekt der Frage, z.B. *Ben*, steht dann gemäß der **S-V-(O)-Regel** das Hauptverb.

! Das Hauptverb steht in der Grundform (Infinitiv).

LANGUAGE FILE

NEW LF 14 Questions with passive and modals
(Fragen im Passiv und mit Modalverben) ▶ Unit 3, p. 61

Fragen im Passiv

question word	form of be	subject	past participle	
	Is	Ben	called	Benny by his fans?
	Was	he	invited	to a party?
When	were	you	born,	Ben?
Why	isn't	your team	supported	by sponsors?

Da du das Passiv mit **be + past participle** bildest, beginnst du Ja-/Nein-Fragen mit der Form von **be**, die hier Hilfsverb ist.

Bei Fragen mit **Fragewort** steht die Form von **be zwischen** Fragewort und Subjekt.

Fragen mit Modalverben

question word	modal verb	subject	(main) verb	
	Can	Ben	meet	Li on Friday?
	May	she	go	to a party then?
	Should	Li	ask	her parents?
When	will	Ben and Li	meet?	
What else	must	Ben	prepare	for the party?

Ja-/Nein-Fragen mit **modals** beginnen mit dem **Modalverb**.

Bei Fragen mit **Fragewort** steht das **modal zwischen** Fragewort und Subjekt.

NEW LF 15 Questions with prepositions
(Fragen mit Fragewörtern und Präpositionen) ▶ More challenge 3, p. 126

Ben *waved goodbye to* his team. Then he *walked with* Li to her house.

Ben and Li *spent* the afternoon *with* Li's family. They *laughed at* her mum's funny stories.

Now they *are looking forward to* next weekend. They're *waiting for* a visitor from Germany.

Präpositionen, z.B. *after, at, for, from, in, of, on, to* stehen **vor Nomen** oder **Pronomen**.

Es gibt auch viele typische **Wendungen** (Verb + Präposition), z.B. *look at, wait for, be afraid of, wave to, …* .

Who did Ben wave goodbye **to**?
  Wem winkte Ben zum Abschied **zu**?
Who did he walk **with**?
  Mit wem ging er spazieren?
Who did Ben and Li spend the afternoon **with**?
  Mit wem verbrachten sie den Nachmittag?
What did they laugh **at**?
  Worüber haben sie gelacht/lachten sie?
What are they looking forward **to**?
  Worauf freuen sie sich?
Who/What are they waiting **for**?
  Auf wen/Worauf warten sie?

Wenn du **Fragen mit Präpositionen** bildest, stehen die **Fragewörter** *Who/What* **am Anfang**, die **Präpositionen** stehen häufig **am Ende der Frage**.

! Im Deutschen stehen die Präpositionen meist vor dem Fragewort, z.B.
Mit wem spielst du gern? → **Who** do you like to play *with*?

Häufig gibt es im Deutschen besondere Fragewörter, z.B.
- *Womit* spielst du gern? → **What** do you like to play *with*?

LF 16 The comparison of adjectives (Die Steigerung der Adjektive)

The comparison with -er /-est and more/most
Wenn du Personen oder Dinge vergleichst, benutzt du Steigerungsformen.
Mit der 1. Steigerungsform + **than** („als") vergleichst du zwei **unterschiedliche** Personen oder Dinge.

Ben thinks English is hard, but maths is harder than English.
But today PE seems to be the hardest of all.

Bei **kurzen** (einsilbigen) Adjektiven und bei Adjektiven mit der Endung **-y** hängst du für die Steigerung **-er** und **-est** an das Adjektiv:
cheap   cheaper   (the) cheapest

! Beachte beim Schreiben:
nic**e**   nic**er**   (the) nic**est**
health**y**   health**ier**   (the) health**iest**
big   bi**gg**er   (the) bi**gg**est

Li prefers a big bowl of ice cream – the biggest she can get.
But she doesn't have enough money for the most expensive one.
Chocolate looks good, it's better than vanilla. It's the best – and it's cheap too.

Bei **längeren** (zwei- oder dreisilbigen) Adjektiven stellst du **more** und **most** vor das Adjektiv:
expensive   more expensive   (the) most expensive

! Merke dir die **unregelmäßig** gesteigerten Adjektive, z.B.:
good   better   (the) best
much/many   more   (the) most

The comparison with as ... as
Li doesn't think that ice cream is unhealthy.
It's as healthy as all the other things on the menu.

Mit dem Vergleich (**not**) **as** ... **as** ... kannst du ausdrücken, dass zwei Personen oder Dinge gleich (oder nicht gleich) sind.

LF 17 Adverbs of manner (Adverbien der Art und Weise)

Adjektive beschreiben **Nomen** näher.

Adverbien der Art und Weise beschreiben **Verben** näher.

Luis was a happy boy after the basketball match.
Luis walked home happily.

Adverbien der Art und Weise stehen nach dem Verb, oft am Satzende:

Li's morning was going terribly.
(**Wie** lief der Morgen für Li? – Schrecklich.)

She couldn't find her ticket and looked for it very carefully, but still couldn't find it.
She left the house angrily.

Then she ran to school fast.
She worked very hard in maths that day.
In the evening her team played well in the basketball match.

So Li walked home happily. She felt good in the end.

Du bildest ein Adverb der Art und Weise meist durch Anhängen von **-ly** an das Adjektiv:

! Merke dir **unregelmäßige** Adverbformen:

Adjektiv
Li is a **fast** runner.
She had a **hard** day at school.
But she was **good** at sport.

Adverb
Li ran **fast**.
She worked **hard** in class.
She played **well**.

! Nach den Verben *feel, look, sound, taste, smell* folgt **kein** Adverb, sondern ein Adjektiv.

LANGUAGE FILE

LF 18 Adverbs of frequency (Adverbien der Häufigkeit)

Diese drücken aus, wie häufig jemand etwas tut oder wie häufig etwas geschieht: *always, usually, often, sometimes, never*. (Zur Wortstellung im Satz ▶ LF 11, p. 188)

> Hi guys,
> How's it going? I sometimes miss home, but seeing the famous sights of Oz is always exciting! You never get bored. I don't often check my emails because I don't have a lot of time. We usually do lots of things together. …

Adverbien der Häufigkeit stehen:
- nach **be**:
  *Uluru **is** always interesting for tourists.*
- vor einem Vollverb:
  *I sometimes **miss** home.*
- bei zusammengesetzten Verbformen nach dem Hilfsverb (*don't, have, …*):
  *I **don't** often **check** my emails.*

LF 19 The comparison of adverbs (Die Steigerung der Adverbien)

Du kannst auch Adverbien steigern. Du bildest die zwei Steigerungsformen wie bei Adjektiven.

▶ LF 16, p. 191

Ben spoke more slowly to help the new exchange student understand.
Of all students, Ben was the most friendly to Moritz.
Everyone was fast, but Li was the fastest.

Adverbien, die auf **-ly** enden, steigerst du mit **more/most**, z.B.

| slowly | more slowly | (the) most slowly |

Einsilbige Adverbien werden mit **-er/-est** gesteigert:

| fast | faster | (the) fastest |

The race went well, much better than Li had expected.

❗ Beachte:

| well | better | (the) best |

LF 20 Indirect speech (Indirekte Rede)

Direct speech (Direkte Rede)
Emily says/said, "I like my new friend Kai."
  Emily sagt/sagte: „Ich mag meinen neuen Freund Kai."

Indirect speech (Indirekte Rede)
Emily says _ (that) she likes her new friend Kai.
  Emily sagt, dass sie ihren neuen Freund Kai mag.

Mit der **direkten Rede** gibst du **wörtlich** wieder, was jemand sagt, schreibt oder denkt (bzw. gesagt/geschrieben/gedacht hat). Direkte Rede steht meist in Anführungszeichen.

Mit der **indirekten Rede** berichtest du, was jemand sagt, schreibt oder denkt. Einleitende Verben sind z.B.: *say, tell sb., add, answer, think, explain*.

❗ Im Englischen steht vor der indirekten Rede **kein** Komma, und *that* („dass") wird oft weggelassen.

❗ Achte bei der **indirekten Rede** darauf, **wer** spricht bzw. schreibt. Personen und Pronomen sowie Verbformen ändern sich:
"I like my new friend Kai." → *… she likes her new friend Kai.*

NEW Indirect speech: backshift (Indirekte Rede: *backshift*) ▶ *Unit 2, p. 39*

Emily said_ (that) she liked Kai.
    Emily sagte, dass sie Kai mag/gut finden würde.

She told Kai her name was Emily and she hadn't been to this club before.
She was there for the first time.
    Sie sagte (zu) Kai, ihr Name sei/wäre Emily und sie wäre noch nie in diesem Club gewesen. Daher sei/wäre sie zum ersten Mal dort.

Steht das einleitende Verb im **simple past**, z.B. *said, told, added, answered, thought, explained*, verschiebt sich auch die Zeitform des Verbs der ursprünglichen Aussage meist ins **simple past** oder ins **past perfect** (letzteres häufiger in der Schriftsprache).
Dieses (Rück-)Verschieben in die Vergangenheit heißt auf Englisch **backshift** *(of tenses)*.

Wenn **mehrere Aussagen bzw. Sätze in indirekter Rede** wiedergegeben werden, benötigst du nicht jedes Mal einen neuen Einleitungssatz.

Emily: "I'm 16. I live in Braxton."
→ Kai to Dan: "Emily told me she's (*was*) 16. And she lives (*lived*) in Braxton."

In der **Umgangssprache** wendet man den **backshift of tenses** bei immer noch gültigen (oder allgemeinen) Tatsachen **nicht immer** an.

NEW Indirect speech: questions (Indirekte Rede: Fragen) ▶ *Unit 2, p. 40*

Kai asked Emily, "Where do you live?"
→ Kai asked Emily where she lived.
    Kai fragte Emily, wo sie wohnt/wohne/wohnte.

He also asked, "How did you get here?"
→ He also wanted to know how she had got there.
    Er wollte auch wissen, wie sie hergekommen war.

Bei der Wiedergabe von **Fragen in indirekter Rede** musst du die **gleichen Regeln** wie bei Aussagen beachten:
- **Personen** und **Pronomen ändern** sich je nachdem, wer spricht, denkt oder schreibt.
- Steht das **einleitende Verb** im *simple past* (z.B. *asked, wanted to know, wondered, thought*), verschiebt sich auch hier die Zeitform des Verbs, meist ins *simple past* oder *past perfect* (**backshift** *of tenses*).

Emily asked, "How often are you at this club?"
→ Emily asked how often he was at that club.
    Emily fragt, wie oft er in diesen Club sei/wäre/sein würde.

! Wie im Deutschen steht **am Ende** einer indirekten Frage **kein Fragezeichen**, sondern ein **Punkt**.

Dan asked Emily, "Do you like our music?"
→ Dan asked Emily_ if she liked their music.
    Dan fragte Emily, ob sie die Musik seiner Band mochte.

Fragewörter werden übernommen, jedoch entspricht die Wortstellung im Nebensatz jetzt Aussagesätzen, vgl. *... how often ~~do/does/did~~ he was ...* -> **subject – verb**: S-V-(O)
▶ *LF 11, p. 188*

He asked, "Are you a good singer?"
→ He wanted to know if she was a good singer.
    ..., ob sie eine gute Sängern sei/wäre/sein würde.

Bei **Ja-/Nein-Fragen** wird (wie im Deutschen „ob") im Englischen *if* (oder *whether*) eingefügt. Auch hier gilt die **Wortstellung** von **Aussagesätzen: S-V-(O)**. ▶ *LF 11, p. 188*

He asked, "Can you come to the talent show?"
→ He asked if she could come to ...
    ... ob sie kommen könnte.

! Verwechsle *if* = **ob** in indirekten Fragen **nicht** mit *if* = **(falls) wenn**, was du aus *if*-Sätzen kennst. ▶ *LF 22–24, pp. 196–198*

LANGUAGE FILE

NEW Indirect speech: commands, requests, advice
(Aufforderungen, Bitten, Ratschläge in indirekter Rede) ▶ Unit 2, p. 40

Dan told Kai, "Go and get us something to drink."
➡ Dan told Kai to go and get them something to drink.
    Dan forderte Kai auf, ihnen etwas zu trinken zu holen.

Aufforderungen, Befehle und **Ratschläge** werden in **indirekter Rede** meist eingeleitet mit: tell/told sb. **to** (do sth.)

And he added, "Don't hurry!"
➡ And he told him not to hurry.
    Und er fügte hinzu, dass er sich nicht zu beeilen brauche/bräuchte.

Bei **Verboten** und **Verneinungen** wird <u>vor</u> dem Infinitiv mit to das **not** eingeschoben:
    tell/told sb. **not to** (do sth.)
bzw.   ask/tasked sb. **not to** (do sth.)

Kai told Emily, "You shouldn't listen to Dan."
➡ Kai told Emily not to listen to Dan.
    Kai empfahl Emily, Dan nicht zuzuhören.

Kai said to Emily, "Please, don't believe my brother."
➡ Kai asked Emily not to believe his brother.
    Kai bat Emily, seinem Bruder nicht zu glauben.

Bitten werden in **indirekter Rede** meist eingeleitet mit: ask/asked sb. **to** (do sth.).

Kai asked her, "Can you give me your address, please?"
➡ Kai asked her to give him her address.
    Kai bat sie, ihm ihre Adresse zu geben.

NEW Indirect speech: More on backshift
(Indirekte Rede: Weiteres zum *backshift*) ▶ Unit 2, More challenge 4, p. 114

Den **backshift of tenses** – das Rückverschieben in eine andere Zeitstufe in der Vergangenheit – hast du in der **indirekten Rede** z.B. bei der Änderung von **simple present** in **simple past** kennen gelernt, wenn der **Einleitungssatz im *simple past*** steht, z.B.

    Emily says, "I like Dan." ➡   Later Emily told her best friend (that) she liked Dan.

Emily said, "Dan is a nice guy."
➡ Emily told her friend Dan was a nice guy.

She told her, "We met at a music club."
➡ She told her they had met at a music club.

She added, "I have never been there before."
➡ She added she had never been there before.

She thought, "Next Saturday I'll meet him again. …"
➡ She thought she would meet him again on Saturday.

"And maybe I can learn more about their songs."
➡ (And) Maybe she could learn more about their songs.

> **simple present** (is) wird **simple past** (was)
>
> **simple past** (met) wird **past perfect** (had met)
>
> **present perfect** (have been) wird <u>ebenfalls</u> **past perfect** (had been)
>
> > **will (future)** (will meet) wird **would** (would meet)
>
> > **can** (can learn) wird **could** (could learn)

LF 21 Modal verbs and *be allowed to*, *have to*, *be able to*
(Modalverben und Ersatzformen)

Modal verbs (modale Hilfsverben) sind z.B. *can, must, should* und ihre Verneinungen. Du benutzt sie, um auszudrücken, was jemand **kann**, **darf**, **muss**, **soll** oder **nicht kann** usw.

Ben's coach said, "You may leave earlier tonight." Ben was happy because he could go to the party and meet Li.
> Bens Trainer sagte: „Du darfst heute Abend früher …". Ben war …, weil er … konnte.

But then his coach added that Ben shouldn't forget the match next week. So Ben asked, "Well, should I stay until the end of practice, after all?"
> … ergänzte sein Trainer, dass er … nicht vergessen sollte. Also fragte Ben „Hhm, soll ich doch …?"

"Can / May I borrow your black dress for the party, please?" Li asked her mum.
 - "Yes, you can / may. / No, you can't / may not."
> „Darf ich mir bitte dein … borgen?" …
> - „Ja, du darfst. / Nein, du darfst nicht."

Li to Mia: "I'm sorry, I must go now. I have to pick up mum's black dress from the dry-cleaner's. I'm allowed to wear it to the party!"

"I wasn't able to do it yesterday because I had to prepare my presentation on *Native Australians* for tomorrow morning."

Modal verbs haben nur eine Form, z.B. *can*, *must* oder *may* für alle Personen, d.h. kein **-s** bei *he/she/it*.

Die **Verneinung** und die **Frage** werden **ohne** ~~do/does/did~~ gebildet.

Modal verbs dürfen nur in Kurzantworten allein stehen.

Modal verbs haben nur eine **simple present**-Form. Weitere Zeitformen bildest du **mit anderen Verben** mit ähnlicher Bedeutung:
müssen:	must	→ **have to**
dürfen:	can / may	→ **be allowed to**
können:	can	→ **be able to**

Verneinte Aussagen

You **mustn't** play in the street.
❗ Du darfst nicht …

You **don't have to** play in a team.
You **needn't** play in a team.
   Du musst / brauchst nicht …

Verneinte Aussagen

You can't	play in the street.
You aren't allowed to	play in a team.
Du darfst nicht …	

Verneinte Aussagen

The team can't	
The team isn't able to	win the game today.
The team is unable to	

Mit diesen Verben kannst du **alle Zeitformen** bilden, auch das *simple present*:

müssen
simple present: must oder have / has to (muss)
simple past: had to (musste)
future: will have to (wird … müssen)

dürfen
simple present: can / may
   oder   am / are / is allowed to (darf)
simple past: was / were allowed to (durfte)
future: will be allowed to (wird … dürfen)

können (fähig sein)
simple present: can oder am / are / is able to
                                          (kann)
simple past: could oder was / were able to
                                          (konnte)
future: will be able to (wird … können)

LANGUAGE FILE

Ja-/Nein-Fragen

| Can/May / Should / Must | I/he practise now? |

Must I go now?
– No, but you may go.

| Do/Did I/you/they / Does/Did he/she | have to practise hard? |
| *Muss/Müssen/Musste(n) …* | *hart üben/trainieren?* |

Did he have to go?
– No, he didn't have to go.

| Am/Are/Is … / Was/Were … / Will … be | allowed to …? / able to …? |

Was he allowed to go?
– Yes, he was.

LF 22 If … (Conditional sentences type 1) (Bedingungssätze Typ 1)

Mit *if*-Sätzen (Bedingungssätzen Typ 1) sagst du, was unter bestimmten Bedingungen geschieht oder geschehen wird: „**Was ist, wenn …**"

Nebensatz
If Mia's team plays well next time,
    Hauptsatz
    they'll win the summer contest.
 Wenn Mias Team nächstes Mal gut spielt, werden sie den Sommer-Wettbewerb gewinnen.

Their team will only finish in second place _ if they don't fight hard.
 Ihr Team wird nur Zweiter sein, wenn sie nicht kämpfen.

= If they don't fight hard, their team will only finish in second place.
 Wenn sie nicht kämpfen, wird ihr Team nur Zweiter sein.

"I'll ask the coach for her advice when I see her."
 … wenn ich sie sehe.
 (Es steht fest, dass Mia die Trainerin trifft. Dann fragt sie.)

"I'll ask the coach for her advice if I see her."
 … falls ich sie sehe. *(Es ist unsicher, ob sie sich treffen.)*

If you need advice, you **can/should** ask the coach.
 Wenn ihr Rat braucht, könnt ihr /solltet ihr die Trainerin fragen.

Please phone me if you want to talk to me.
 Bitte ruft mich an, wenn ihr … wollt.

Bedingungssätze bestehen aus zwei Teilsätzen:

Die **Bedingung** wird im *if*-Satz (Nebensatz) genannt. Das Verb steht im **simple present**:

 If they **play** …,

Die **Folge für die Zukunft** steht im **Hauptsatz**. Hier steht meist das **will-future**:

 … they **will** … ▶ LF 9, p. 187

Der *if*-Teil kann am Anfang oder am Ende stehen.

❗ Anders als im Deutschen setzt man **kein Komma**, wenn der *if*-Teil am **Ende** steht.

❗ Nicht verwechseln:
 – **when** bedeutet „sobald wie", „dann, wenn"
 – **if** bedeutet „wenn", „falls"

Im **Hauptsatz** können auch stehen:
 – *can, must, should* + Infinitiv ▶ LF 21, p. 195

 – oder eine Aufforderung bzw. Bitte
  (ein **Imperativ**).

LF 23 If ... (Conditional sentences type 2) (Bedingungssätze Typ 2)

Mit Bedingungssätzen Typ 2 sagst du, was unter unwahrscheinlichen oder unsicheren Bedingungen geschehen würde: „**Was wäre, wenn ...**"

Nebensatz
If Greg had enough money,
　　　　　　　　　Hauptsatz
　　　　　　　　he'd travel everywhere.
Wenn Greg genug Geld hätte, würde er ...

Hauptsatz
But his friend Tina wouldn't travel
　　　　　　　　Nebensatz
　　even if she won a trip around the world."
Aber seine Freundin Tina würde nicht reisen, selbst/sogar wenn sie ... gewinnen würde.

If you were travelling around world, you could forget about school.
　Wenn du auf ... wärst, könntest du ... vergessen.

Da die **Bedingung** im **if**-Satz unwahrscheinlich ist (hier: genug Geld), ist unsicher, ob die **Folge** im **Hauptsatz** (hier: das Reisen überall hin) Wirklichkeit wird.
Im Deutschen verwendet man hier oft **würde/wäre/hätte**.
Auch **if**-Sätze Typ 2 bestehen wie **if**-Sätze Typ 1 aus zwei Teilsätzen: ▶ LF 22, p. 196
Die (unwahrscheinliche) **Bedingung** steht im **if**-Satz. Das Verb steht im **simple past**, z.B. had, won.
Die (unsichere) **Folge** steht im **Hauptsatz**. Dort benutzt du would (Kurzform **'d**) bzw. für die Verneinung wouldn't + Infinitiv.
! Auch bei Typ 2 kein Komma vor dem **if**-Teil.
Im **Hauptsatz** kann auch could + Infinitiv stehen.

Forms of would

Bejahte und verneinte Aussagen

I/You/He/... We/...	'd/would/wouldn't	travel to Oz.

Greg would travel everywhere if he could, but Tina wouldn't come with him.

Ja-/Nein-Fragen mit Kurzantworten

Would	I/he/we/...	travel to Oz?	Yes, ... would. No, ... wouldn't.

Would you go on a trip around the world if you had the chance? – Yes, you would.

Fragen mit Fragewort

Where/How/... would	I/you/he/... ...?

Where would you travel first – to the US or to Oz? How would you get there?

NEW LF 24 If ... (Conditional sentences type 3)
(Bedingungssätze Typ 3) ▶ Unit 4, p. 83

Mit Bedingungssätzen Typ 3 **stellst du dir vor**, was **in der Vergangenheit** unter bestimmten Bedingungen hätte geschehen können: „**Was wäre gewesen, wenn ...**"

Nebensatz
If it had been warmer,
　　　　　Hauptsatz
　　Li would have gone to the beach.
Wenn es wärmer gewesen wäre, wäre Li zum Strand gegangen. *(Es war aber nicht wärmer, und Li war nicht am Strand.)*

Da die **Bedingung** im **if**-Satz **nicht erfüllt** ist, können über die **Folge** im **Hauptsatz** nur Vermutungen angestellt werden.
Im Deutschen verwendet man oft **wäre** gewesen/gegangen/... oder **hätte** gehabt/gegeben/...

LANGUAGE FILE

Hauptsatz
Li would have phoned Mia
 Nebensatz
 if she had had her new number.
Li hätte Mia (ja) angerufen, wenn sie deren neue Telefonnummer gehabt hätte. *(Aber sie kannte sie nicht oder hatte sie verlegt.)*

If Li had asked Mia's brother Ben, he could have helped her.   … hätte er ihr helfen können.

If she'd asked Ben, he'd have given her Mia's number.   … gefragt hätte, hätte er ihr … gegeben.

Die (nicht erfüllte) **Bedingung** steht im *if*-**Satz**. Das Verb steht im **past perfect** z.B. *had been, had had, had helped.*   ▶ LF 7, p. 186

Die (vermutete) **Folge** steht im **Hauptsatz**. Dort benutzt du **would/wouldn't** + **have past participle** (3. Form).

! Auch hier steht kein Komma vor dem *if*-Teil.

Im **Hauptsatz** kann auch **could** + **have past participle** stehen.

! Die **Kurzform** von **would** und von **would** ist **'d**:
he'd (= he would) have given.
she'd (= she had) asked.

LF 25 Relative clauses (Relativsätze)

Mit Relativsätzen sagst du genauer, **wen** oder **was** du meinst.

Is there something wrong with people who don't use social media?

Someone who uses social media often has several profile pictures.

Wenn du **Menschen** genauer beschreibst, benutzt du meistens **who**:

 *the man / woman / people / someone **who** …*
 der Mann, **der** …/ die Frau, **die** …/ Leute, **die**…/ …

I prefer a profile picture that is creative and different.

But many people use standard pictures that look boring.

Wenn du **Dinge** (oder Tiere) genauer beschreibst, benutzt du meistens **that**:

 *a picture / (the) food / animals / the things **that** …*
 ein Bild/das Essen, **das** …/ Tiere/die Sachen, **die** …

Do you really want people that search your name to see that profile picture?

Ben chose the photo that/which Li took last summer.

Vor allem umgangssprachlich kannst du **that** auch für Personen benutzen:

 *the boy / girl / kids / users **that** …*
 der Junge, **der** …/ das Mädchen, **das** …/ Kids, **die** …

Für Dinge oder Tiere wird auch **which** statt *that* verwendet.

> ! Die Wortstellung im englischen Relativsatz ist anders als im deutschen:
> Someone **who uses** social media …
>
> Jemand, **der** soziale Medien **nutzt**, …

Die meisten englischen Relativsätze werden **nicht** durch **Komma** vor *who/that/which* abgetrennt. Es sind so genannte *defining relative clauses* (bestimmende Relativsätze). Sie geben Informationen, die zum Verständnis des Satzes unverzichtbar sind.
Ben chose the photo wäre ohne den Relativsatz *that Li took last summer* unverständlich.

LF 26 Contact clauses (Relativsätze ohne Relativpronomen)

Vergleiche:

              Subjekt des Relativsatzes
That's the girl **who** chatted with me yesterday.
  Das ist das Mädchen, **das** gestern … hat.

                  Subjekt des Relativsatzes
These are the pictures **that** were shared the most.
  Das sind die Bilder, **die** am häufigsten … wurden.

           Objekt   **Subjekt** des Relativsatzes
That's the girl ~~who~~ **I** chatted with yesterday.
  Das ist das Mädchen, mit **dem ich** …

                 Objekt   **Subjekt** des Relativsatzes
These are the pictures ~~that~~ **our friends** shared the most.
  Das sind die Bilder, **die** unsere Freunde am häufigsten teilten.

> **!** **Mit oder ohne Relativpronomen (*who/that*)?**
>
> Wenn das Relativpronomen (*who/that*) **direkt vor dem Verb** im Relativsatz steht, darfst du es **nicht** weglassen (weil es hier das **Subjekt** des Relativsatzes ist).
>
> Wenn aber **nach** dem Relativpronomen (*who/that*) ein Pronomen oder Nomen folgt und **vor** dem Verb steht, darfst du *who/that* **weglassen**.
> (Hier ist das Relativpronomen **Objekt** des Relativsatzes und zum Verständnis nicht unbedingt notwendig.)
>
> Relativsätze **ohne** *who/that* heißen **contact clauses**.

NEW LF 27 Participle clauses instead of subordinate clauses

(Partizipialsätze anstelle von Nebensätzen) ▶ *More challenge 2, p. 51*

What are you **do**ing? (*present progressive*)
Reading is fun. (*gerund*)

(1) **Walking** down the street to the youth club, Ben suddenly noticed a broken shop window.
While he was walking down the street, Ben suddenly noticed a broken shop window.
Während er … entlang ging, bemerkte Ben plötzlich …

(2) **Seeing** two men near a van, he decided to watch them.
He saw two men near a van **and** decided to …
Er sah zwei Männer nahe bei … und beschloss, …

(3) Ben shouted loudly, **expecting** some sort of crime.
Ben shouted loudly **because** he expected some sort of crime.
Ben rief laut, weil er … Verbrechen erwartete.

(4) **Having noticed** Ben, the men laughed, "It's OK. We're here to put in a new window."
When they noticed Ben, the men laughed, "It's OK …
Als sie Ben bemerkten, lachten die Männer: „…

(5) The two men **working** at the window talked to Ben.
The two men **who were working** … talked to Ben.
Die zwei Männer, die gerade …, sprachen mit Ben.

Das **present participle** – die **-ing-Form** – kennst du schon als Teil des **present progressive** (▶ *LF 2, p. 183*) sowie als **gerund** (▶ *LF 29, p. 200*).

Partizipalsätze enthalten das **present participle** und dienen der **knappen Formulierung** des gesamten Satzes, indem sie einen vollständigen Nebensatz ersetzen. Im Deutschen muss stattdessen ein vollständiger Nebensatz gebildet werden.

Solche **Partizipialsätze** kommen im Englischen vor allem in **geschriebenen** Texten vor.

Partizipialsätze können **ersetzen**:

- **Nebensätze der Zeit**, die mit *while, when* beginnen. Damit wird oft Gleichzeitigkeit ausgedrückt (1)
- zwei **Hauptsätze**, die mit *and* verbunden wären (2)
- **begründende** Nebensätze, die mit *because, as* beginnen (3)
- **Nebensätze**, die etwas als Ergebnis **Folgendes** ausdrücken (4)
- **Relativsätze**, die beschreiben, was gerade vor sich geht (*present progressive*) oder ging (*past progressive*) (5).

LANGUAGE FILE

LF 28 Reflexive pronouns (Reflexivpronomen)

I ask myself how we can enjoy ourselves this evening.
> Ich frage mich, wie wir uns heute Abend amüsieren können.

I think your little sister is old enough to look after herself.
> Ich finde, deine ..., auf sich selbst aufzupassen.

Reflexivpronomen (**myself**, **yourself**, **ourselves**, ...) beziehen sich auf das Subjekt:
(I – **myself**, you – **yourself**, people – **themselves**):

Subjekt		Reflexivpronomen
I	asked	**myself** ...
We	can enjoy	**ourselves**.
Your sister	can look after	**herself**.

Reflexive pronouns

(I)	myself	(ich)	mir / mich
(you)	yourself	(du)	dir / dich
(he)	himself	(er)	sich
(she)	herself	(sie)	sich
(it)	itself	(er/sie/es)	sich

(we)	ourselves	(wir) uns
(you)	yourselves	(ihr) euch
(they)	themselves	(sie) sich

! Den Plural bildest du mit **-selves**.

! Es gibt Verben, die im Deutschen reflexiv sind, im Englischen jedoch nicht. Das „sich, mich, mir, dir" usw. wird nicht übersetzt, z.B.:

		Beispiele:	
(to) feel	sich fühlen	He doesn't *feel* well.	Er fühlt sich nicht gut.
(to) hide	sich verstecken	Let's *hide*!	Verstecken wir uns!
(to) imagine	sich etwas vorstellen	I can *imagine* that.	Das kann ich mir vorstellen.
(to) look forward to sth.	sich auf etwas freuen	I'm *looking forward to* it.	Ich freue mich darauf.
(to) meet	sich treffen	Let's *meet* at six!	Treffen wir uns um sechs!
(to) remember	sich an etwas erinnern	I don't *remember*.	Ich erinnere mich nicht.
(to) wonder	sich fragen	I *wonder* if ...	Ich frage mich, ob ...
(to) worry	sich Sorgen machen	Don't *worry*.	Mach dir keine Sorgen.

LF 29 The -ing-form (the gerund) (Die -ing-Form bzw. das Gerundium)

Du kannst von vielen Verben eine **-ing-Form** bilden, etwa für die Verlaufsform (*present progressive*), z.B. Li is driv*ing* to school in her own car today. ▶ LF 2, p. 183.

Driving a car is cool.
> (Das) **Autofahren** ist cool. / Ein Auto **zu fahren**, ist *cool*.

I love driving a car.
> Ich liebe das **Autofahren**. / Ich liebe es, **Auto zu fahren**.

Als **gerund** bezeichnet man die *-ing*-Form, wenn sie als **Nomen** verwendet wird, hier z.B. als **Subjekt** oder **Objekt**:

Sport is cool. ◄► *Driving is cool.* **(Subjekt des Satzes)**

I love sport. ◄► *I love driving.* **(Objekt des Satzes)**

Im Deutschen wird das **gerund** oft durch einen Infinitiv mit „zu" wiedergegeben.

I enjoy **helping** people. So I keep **working** with kids. I'd miss **teaching** them music.

Die **-ing-Form** (*gerund*) folgt oft auf bestimmte **Verben** als **Objekt**, z.B. *(dis-)like, enjoy, hate, miss, start, finish, …*

I prefer **learning** languages. (or: *I prefer* **to learn** *languages.*)
I'll start **learning** German next term.
(or: *I'll* start **to learn** *German …*)

❗ Nach *like/love/hate/prefer/start/begin* kann auch **to** + **Infinitiv** *folgen*:
love/like **to play**   *hate* **to learn**   *begin/start* **to sing**

❗ Nach allen übrigen Verben darf **nie** der **Infinitiv** stehen: *enjoy* ~~to help~~   *miss* ~~to learn~~   *keep* ~~to go~~

I'm good at **playing** basketball. Our team is looking forward to **playing** against Boston City. We've always dreamed of **winning** against them.

Die **-ing-Form** (*gerund*) folgt nach **Präpositionen**: *at, about, after, for, in, of, to.*

❗ Es gibt einige **Wendungen**, denen das *gerund* **folgen muss**, z.B.:
- *dream of/about* …*ing*
- *(be) good/bad at* …*ing*
- *(be) interested in* …*ing*
- *get used to* …*ing*
- *look forward to* …*ing*

NEW -*ing*-form (*gerund*) or *to*-infinitive? (Gerundium oder *to*-Infinitiv?)

▶ Unit 4, More challenge 1, p. 131

Ben: I enjoy **chatting** with people.

Das *gerund* (*-ing*-**Form**) folgt meist nach bestimmten **Verben** als **Objekt**, z.B. *(dis-)like, enjoy, hate, start, …*

I want **to tell** them everything.

Nach **bestimmten Verben** darfst du **nur** den **to-Infinitiv** verwenden, z.B. *want to, would like to, need to, hope to …*

Li prefers **meeting** people. She prefers **to meet** them in real life.

Nach bestimmten Verben kannst du das **gerund** oder den **to-Infinitiv** verwenden. Die **Bedeutung** ändert sich **nicht**, z.B. bei *like, love, hate prefer, start, begin*.

"Stop **chatting** all day long."
  Hör auf, … zu chatten.
At the door Ben stopped **to check** his emails.   … Ben stehen, **um** seine …

❗ **Unterschiedliche Bedeutungen** hat die Verwendung von *gerund* oder *to*-Infinitiv nach diesen Verben:

stop + *gerund* ◂ mit etwas aufhören (… es zu tun)
stop + *to* … ◂ aufhören/anhalten, um etwas anders zu tun

I'll never forget **skiing** for the first time.
  Ich werde nie vergessen, wie ich …

forget + *gerund* ◂ vergessen, was man (früher mal) getan hat

Oh, I won't forget **to send** you the photos.
  … werde nicht vergessen, dir die Fotos …

forget + *to* … ◂ vergessen, was später (noch) zu tun ist

Mum remembers **buying** her first mobile.
  … erinnert sich, dass/wie sie … hat.

remember + *gerund* ◂ sich erinnern, was man mal getan hat

Will dad remember **to give** me his headphones?   … daran denken, dass er …?

remember + *to* … ◂ daran denken, etwas (noch) zu tun

LANGUAGE FILE

LF 30 The passive (Das Passiv)

Advertising companies make all sorts of ads.
Werbefirmen machen alle Arten von Werbung.

Special ads are made to target teens only.
… Werbung wird gemacht, nur um auf Teens abzuzielen.

"I'm often asked how much money is spent on ads."
Ich werde oft gefragt, … ausgegeben wird.

Of course, ads aren't made for teens only.
Natürlich wird Werbung nicht nur … produziert.

Yesterday a new tablet was presented on TV.
Gestern wurde ein neues Tablet …präsentiert.

Years ago ads for cigarettes were shown everywhere.
Vor Jahren wurde noch Werbung … überall gezeigt.

Slogans are often repeated in ads.
Man wiederholt oft Slogans in der Werbung.

The song in this ad was first sung by the Beatles.
Das Lied in dieser Werbung wurde zuerst von … gesungen.

New game created by XYZ company

Mit einem **Aktivsatz** sagst du, wer oder was etwas tut. Das Subjekt des Aktivsatzes führt die Handlung aus.

Mit einem **Passivsatz** drückst du aus, mit wem oder was (= womit) **etwas geschieht** ohne zu sagen, wer der/die „Verursachende" ist. (Subjekt ist im Passivsatz der, die bzw. das, womit etwas geschieht.)

Du bildest das Passiv mit einer **Form von be** und der **3. Form des Verbs** (past participle).
▶ Irregular verbs, pp. 264–265

simple present: am/are/is + past participle:
　　　　　　　　I'm　asked …
　how much money is　spent on …

simple past: was/were + past participle:
　The street　　　was　used in …
　… houses that　　were　shown …

❗ In vielen Passivsätzen wird **be** im Deutschen mit **werden** ausgedrückt (werde, wird, wurdest, wurde, …).

❗ Im Deutschen gibt man englische Passivsätze häufig durch einen Aktivsatz mit „man" wieder:

❗ Will man in einem Passivsatz doch den/die „Verursachende" nennen, verwendet man die Präposition **by** (von/durch).

Das Passiv wird oft in Nachrichten verwendet. In Überschriften und Schlagzeilen entfallen zudem meist die Artikel, die Form von be sowie Satzzeichen:
~~A~~ new game ~~was~~ created by ~~the~~ XYZ company~~.~~

The passive: will-future and modals
(Das Passiv: will-future und Modalverben)

Passivsätze im **will-future** (will/won't) und mit **Modalverben** bildest du mit　**be + past participle**.

The meeting will be held next Friday.
Das Treffen wird … abgehalten/stattfinden.

The pictures can be seen online.
Die Bilder kann man online sehen.

Which problems should be fixed first?
Welche Probleme sollten zuerst gelöst werden?

The email couldn't be sent.
Die E-Mail konnte nicht versendet werden.

will/won't		served
can/can't		seen
could/couldn't		missed
should/shouldn't	**be**	booked
may/mustn't		bought
must/needn't		spotted
have to/has to		shown
may		taken

202

NEW LF 31 Question tags (Frageanhängsel) ▶ More challenge 3, p. 73

Question tags werden im Englischen **in Gesprächen** oft verwendet. Diese Frageanhängsel an Aussagesätze benutzt man, um **Zustimmung** beim Gesprächspartner zu erreichen.
Sie werden aber auch verwendet als „echte" **Nachfrage**, wenn man unsicher ist.
Im Deutschen kennen wir „…, nicht wahr?" oder „…, nicht?" bzw. auch „ne?/ gell?/ woll?/ ja?/ oder? /…?".

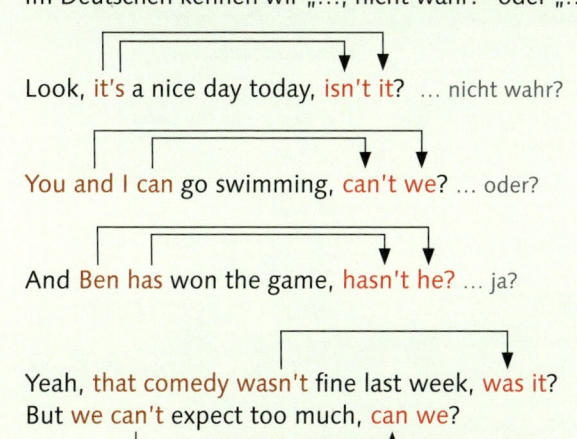

Look, it's a nice day today, isn't it? … nicht wahr?

You and I can go swimming, can't we? … oder?

And Ben has won the game, hasn't he? … ja?

Yeah, that comedy wasn't fine last week, was it?
But we can't expect too much, can we?

Im Englischen muss das Frageanhängsel aber jeweils unter **Rückbezug** auf das **(Modal-) Verb** und **die Person** des Aussagesatzes neu gebildet werden.

Wenn der **Aussagesatz bejaht** ist, wird das **Frageanhängsel verneint**.
Das Personalpronomen steht wie in einer Frage hinten.

Wenn der **Aussagesatz verneint** ist, wird das **Frageanhängsel bejaht**.

The bus to the beach leaves at 4 pm, doesn't it?
You didn't repair your bike, did you?
And you don't want to walk there, do you?

Vollverben werden im Frageanhängsel durch *do/does* im **simple present** bzw. *did* im **simple past** ersetzt.
▶ Vocabulary, p. 230

We have something in common, haven't we?

Grammatical terms (Grammatische Fachbegriffe)

active	[ˈæktɪv]	Aktiv	Li **went** to the party.
adjective	[ˈædʒɪktɪv]	Adjektiv	good, red, new, boring, …
adverb	[ˈædvɜːb]	Adverb	today, there, outside, very, …
adverb of frequency	[ˈfriːkwənsi]	Häufigkeitsadverb	always, often, never …
adverb of manner	[ædvɜːb əv ˈmænə]	Adverb der Art und Weise	slowly, happily, well, …
article	[ˈɑːtɪkl]	Artikel	the, a, an
auxiliary	[ɔːɡˈzɪliəri]	Hilfsverb (zur Bildung von Fragesätzen, Zeitformen usw.)	**Did** Ben go to the party?
backshift of tenses	[ˈbakʃɪft]	Rückverschiebung der Zeitformen	"I**'m** tired." She said (that) she **was** tired.
comparative	[kəmˈpærətɪv]	Komparativ (1. Steigerungsform)	older; more expensive
comparison	[kəmˈpærɪsn]	Steigerung	old – older – oldest
conditional sentence	[kənˈdɪʃnl ˈsentəns]	Bedingungssatz	If we win, we'll go to London.
contact clause	[ˈkɒntækt klɔːz]	Relativsatz ohne Relativpronomen	She's the girl **I love**.
defining relative clause	[dɪˈfaɪnɪŋ]	bestimmender Relativsatz	I like teachers **who laugh a lot**.
direct speech	[ˌdaɪrekt ˈspiːtʃ]	direkte Rede	"I love my dog."
future	[ˈfjuːtʃə]	Zukunft, Futur	
gerund	[ˈdʒerənd]	Gerundium, -ing-Form	I like **dancing**.
going to-future	[ˈɡəʊɪŋ tʊ fjuːtʃə]	Futur mit *going to*	I**'m going to stay** at home tonight.
if-clause	[ˈɪf klɔːz]	*if*-Satz, Nebensatz mit *if*	**If we meet**, we'll talk.
imperative	[ɪmˈperətɪv]	Imperativ (Befehlsform)	**Open** your books. **Don't** talk.
indirect speech	[ˌɪndərekt ˈspiːtʃ]	indirekte Rede	She said (that) **she loved her dog**.
infinitive	[ɪnˈfɪnətɪv]	Grundform des Verbs, Infinitiv	go, open, see, read
-*ing*-form		Gerundium, -ing-Form	I like **dancing**.
irregular verb	[ɪˈreɡjələ ˈvɜːb]	unregelmäßiges Verb	go – went – gone
main clause	[ˌmeɪn ˈklɔːz]	Hauptsatz	If we meet, **we'll talk**.
main verb	[meɪn vɜːb]	Hauptverb (trägt die Hauptbedeutung im Satz)	Did Ben **go** to the party?
modal verb	[ˌməʊdl ˈvɜːb]	Modalverb, modales Hilfsverb	can, must, should, may, …
negative statement	[ˈneɡətɪv]	verneinter Aussagesatz	I don't like oranges.
noun	[naʊn]	Nomen, Substantiv	Ben, girl, man, time, name, …
object	[ˈɒbdʒɪkt]	Objekt	Ben has **an idea**.
object question		Objektfrage, Frage nach dem Objekt	**Who did** Mrs Miller invite to tea?
participle clause	[ˌpɑːtɪsɪpl ˈklɔːz]	Partizipialsatz	Li shook her head, **laughing out loud**. The man **waiting at the bus stop** is my uncle.
passive	[ˈpæsɪv]	Passiv	Lots of films **are made** in LA.
past participle	[pɑːst ˈpɑːtɪsɪpl]	Partizip Perfekt, 3. Form des Verbs	happened, eaten, gone, …
past perfect	[ˌpɑːst ˈpɜːfɪkt]	*past perfect* (Vorvergangenheit, Plusquamperfekt)	I **had** already **gone** to bed when they arrived.
past progressive	[pɑːst prəˈɡresɪv]	Verlaufsform der Vergangenheit	He **was playing** a drum.
persononal pronoun	[pɜːsənl ˈprəʊnaʊn]	Personalpronomen	I, you, he, she, it, we, they, …
plural	[ˈplʊərəl]	Plural, Mehrzahl	sweets, carrots, sheep, …
positive statement	[ˈpɒzətɪv]	bejahter Aussagesatz	I like oranges.
possessive determiner	[pəˌzəsɪv dɪˈtɜːmɪnə]	Possessivbegleiter	my, your, his, her, its, our, their

possessive pronoun	[pəˌzəsɪv ˈprəʊnaʊn]	Possessivpronomen	mine, yours, his, hers, ours, theirs
preposition	[prepəsˈzɪʃn]	Präposition	after, at, in, next to, under, with, …
present participle	[ˌpreznt ˈpɑːtɪsɪpl]	Partizip Präsens	checking, phoning, trying, planning, going, …
present perfect	[preznt ˈpɜːfɪkt]	present perfect	He **has drunk** your water.
present progressive	[preznt prəˈgresɪv]	Verlaufsform der Gegenwart	They**'re having** lunch.
pronoun	[ˈprəʊnaʊn]	Pronomen, Fürwort	
question	[ˈkwestʃən]	Frage(satz)	What did you do yesterday?
question tag	[ˈkwestʃn tag]	Frageanhängsel	isn't he?, are you?, can't we?, …
question word	[ˈkwestʃən wɜːd]	Fragewort	what?, when?, where?, how?, …
reflexive pronoun	[rɪˌfleksɪv ˈprəʊnaʊn]	Reflexivpronomen	myself, yourself, himself, …
regular verb	[ˈregjələ ˈvɜːb]	regelmäßiges Verb	help – helped – helped
relative clause	[ˌrelətɪv klɔːz]	Relativsatz	This is the dog **that bit me**.
relative pronoun	[ˌrelətɪv ˈprəʊnaʊn]	Relativpronomen	who, that, which
short answer	[ʃɔːt ˈɑːnsə]	Kurzantwort	Yes, I am. / No, I don't. / …
simple past	[sɪmpl ˈpɑːst]	einfache Form der Vergangenheit	I **loved** the holidays.
simple present	[sɪmpl ˈpreznt]	einfache Form der Gegenwart	I always **go** to school by bike.
singular	[ˈsɪŋgjələ]	Singular, Einzahl	
statement	[ˈsteɪtmənt]	Aussage(satz)	
subject	[ˈsʌbdʒɪkt]	Subjekt	**My dad** is working.
subordinate clause (*also:* sub-clause)	[səˈbɔːdɪnət klɔːz] [ˈsʌbklɔːz]	Nebensatz	I like cycling **because I like the sport**.
superlative	[suˈpɜːlətɪv]	Superlativ	cheapest, most expensive, …
tense	[tens]	Zeitform des Verbs	
time word / time phrase	[ˈtaɪm wɜːd] [ˈtaɪm freɪz]	Zeitangabe	yesterday, this morning, after school,
verb	[vɜːb]	1. Verb 2. Prädikat	go, help, look, see, … Reading **can be** fun. **Did** Ben **go** to the party?
will-future	[ˈwɪl fjuːtʃə]	Futur mit *will*	I think our trip **will be** fun.
yes / no-question	[ˈjes ˈnəʊ kwestʃən]	Entscheidungsfrage / Frage ohne Fragewort / Ja- / Nein-Frage	Are you 15? Do you like films?
word order		Wortstellung (im Satz)	

VOCABULARY

Das **Vocabulary** (S. 206–234) enthält alle neuen Wörter und Wendungen des Buches, die du **lernen** musst. Sie stehen in der Reihenfolge, in der sie im Buch zum ersten Mal vorkommen.

Hier siehst du, wie das **Vocabulary** aufgebaut ist:

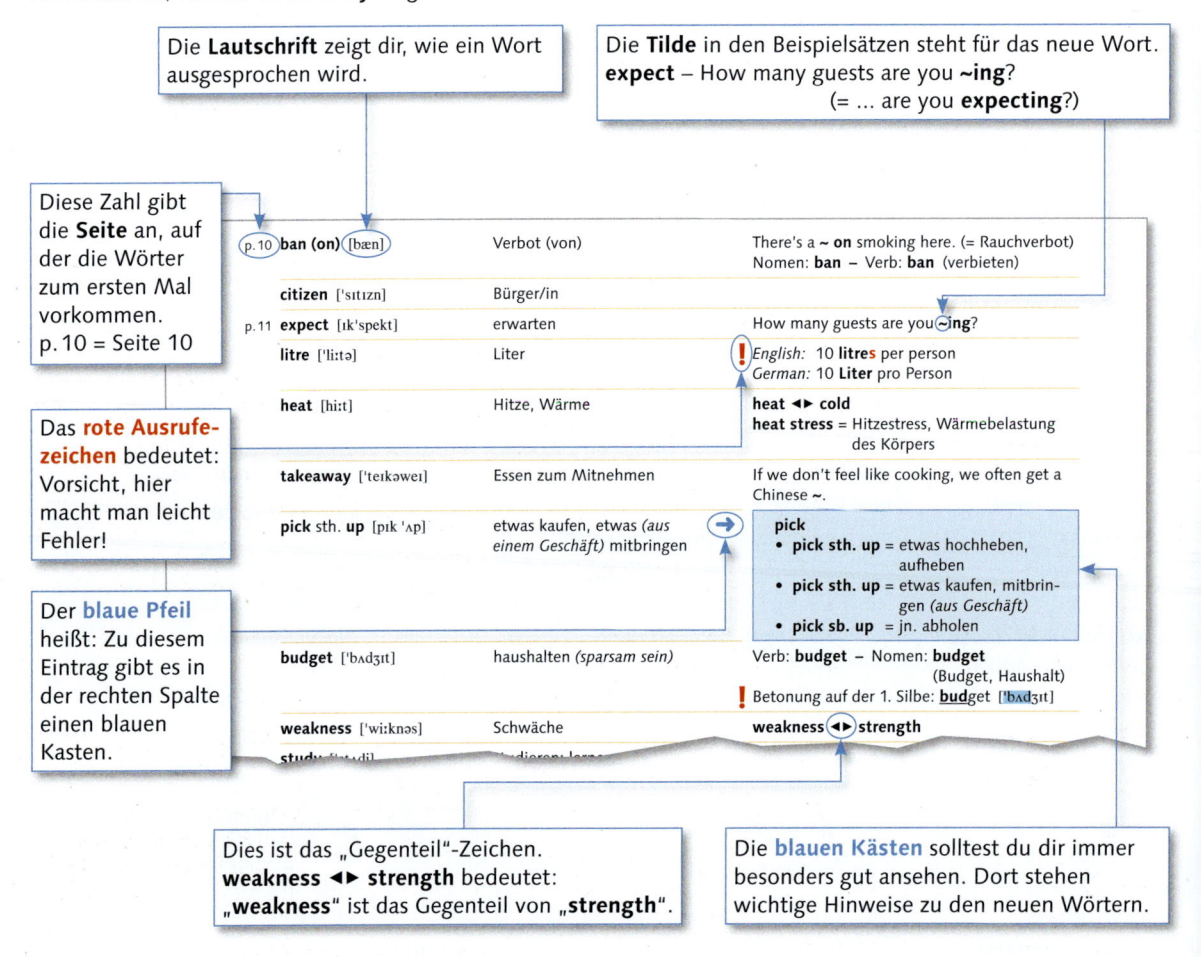

Die **Lautschrift** zeigt dir, wie ein Wort ausgesprochen wird.

Die **Tilde** in den Beispielsätzen steht für das neue Wort.
expect – How many guests are you **~ing**?
(= ... are you **expecting**?)

Diese Zahl gibt die **Seite** an, auf der die Wörter zum ersten Mal vorkommen.
p. 10 = Seite 10

Das **rote Ausrufezeichen** bedeutet: Vorsicht, hier macht man leicht Fehler!

Der **blaue Pfeil** heißt: Zu diesem Eintrag gibt es in der rechten Spalte einen blauen Kasten.

p.10	**ban (on)** [bæn]	Verbot (von)	There's a ~ **on** smoking here. (= Rauchverbot) Nomen: **ban** – Verb: **ban** (verbieten)
	citizen ['sɪtɪzn]	Bürger/in	
p.11	**expect** [ɪk'spekt]	erwarten	How many guests are you ~ing?
	litre ['liːtə]	Liter	! *English:* 10 **litres** per person *German:* 10 **Liter** pro Person
	heat [hiːt]	Hitze, Wärme	**heat** ◄► **cold** **heat stress** = Hitzestress, Wärmebelastung des Körpers
	takeaway ['teɪkəweɪ]	Essen zum Mitnehmen	If we don't feel like cooking, we often get a Chinese ~.
	pick sth. **up** [pɪk 'ʌp]	etwas kaufen, etwas (aus einem Geschäft) mitbringen	**pick** • **pick** sth. **up** = etwas hochheben, aufheben • **pick** sth. **up** = etwas kaufen, mitbringen *(aus einem Geschäft)* • **pick** sb. **up** = jn. abholen
	budget ['bʌdʒɪt]	haushalten *(sparsam sein)*	Verb: **budget** – Nomen: **budget** (Budget, Haushalt) ! Betonung auf der 1. Silbe: **bud**get ['bʌdʒɪt]
	weakness ['wiːknəs]	Schwäche	**weakness** ◄► **strength**
	study		

Dies ist das „Gegenteil"-Zeichen.
weakness ◄► **strength** bedeutet:
„**weakness**" ist das Gegenteil von „**strength**".

Die **blauen Kästen** solltest du dir immer besonders gut ansehen. Dort stehen wichtige Hinweise zu den neuen Wörtern.

Im **Vocabulary** werden folgende **Abkürzungen** verwendet:

p.	= *page* (Seite)		pl	= *plural* (Mehrzahl)
pp.	= *pages* (Seiten)		infml	= *informal* (umgangssprachlich)
sb.	= *somebody* (jemand)		AE	= *American English*
sth.	= *something* (etwas)		BE	= *British English*

Wenn du **nachschlagen** möchtest, was ein englisches Wort bedeutet oder wie man es ausspricht, dann solltest du das **Dictionary English – German** auf den Seiten 235–263 verwenden.

Unit 1: Life down under

p.8	**Aboriginal** [æbəˈrɪdʒənl]	Aborigine- *(die Ureinwohner/-innen Australiens betreffend)*	
	nickname [ˈnɪkneɪm]	Spitzname	His name is "Hundt". "Bello" is his ~.
	inland [ɪnˈlænd]	landeinwärts, im Landesinneren/ins Landesinnere	
	landscape [ˈlændskeɪp]	Landschaft	
	climate [ˈklaɪmət]	Klima	❗ Aussprache: **climate** [ˈklaɪmət]
p.9	**reef** [riːf]	Riff	rocks or a sandbank under the water

Theme 1

p.10	**ban (on)** [bæn]	Verbot (von)	There's a ~ **on** smoking here. (= Rauchverbot) Nomen: **ban** – Verb: **ban** (verbieten)
	best-known [best ˈnəʊn]	der/die/das bekannteste; am bekanntesten	**well-known – better-known – best-known**
	flat [flæt]	flach, eben	❗ **flat** = 1. Wohnung; 2. flach, eben
	central [ˈsentrəl]	zentral	**central** Sydney = Sydney Stadtmitte
	burn [bɜːn]	(ver)brennen	The candles on the table were still ~**ing**. Don't ~ the newspapers. Recycle them.
	citizen [ˈsɪtɪzn]	Bürger/in	
	continue [kənˈtɪnjuː]	weitergehen, weitermachen, (sich) fortsetzen	= go on
	be born [bɔːn]	geboren werden/sein	**be born** ◄► **die** (sterben)
	compare (with/to) [kəmˈpeə]	vergleichbar sein (mit), sich vergleichen lassen (mit), vergleichbar sein (mit)	❗ **compare** = 1. vergleichen – **Compare** the two texts. 2. vergleichbar sein – Nothing **compares with/to** my old bike!
	settle [ˈsetl]	sich niederlassen, sich ansiedeln	
	large [lɑːdʒ]	groß	❗ **large** und **big** sind oft austauschbar. Aber **large** wird in der Regel nicht benutzt, um Menschen zu beschreiben.
p.11	**exam** [ɪgˈzæm]	Prüfung	❗ *English:* **take/do** an exam *German:* **eine Prüfung machen** the **final (school) exam** = die (Schul-)Abschlussprüfung
	camel [ˈkæml]	Kamel	❗ Betonung auf der 1. Silbe. **camel** [ˈkæml]
	as [æz], [əz]	da, weil	I can't come to your party ~ I'll be on holiday next week. ❗ **as** = 1. da, weil; 2. als, während
	expert [ˈekspɜːt]	Experte, Expertin	❗ Betonung auf der 1. Silbe: **expert** [ˈekspɜːt]
	native animals/plants [ˈneɪtɪv]	(ein)heimische Tiere/Pflanzen	
	such as [ˈsʌtʃ əz]	wie zum Beispiel	My father likes rock bands ~ **as** AC/DC and Deep Purple.
	suffer (from) [ˈsʌfə]	leiden (an), erleiden	• I often ~ **from** headaches. (= leiden an) • He ~**ed** a heart attack. (= Er erlitt einen Herzinfarkt.)

1 VOCABULARY

deadly ['dedli]	tödlich	
spider ['spaɪdə]	Spinne	spiders
likely ['laɪkli]	wahrscheinlich	**!** **be likely to do sth.** = wahrscheinlich etwas tun (werden) Take a raincoat – it**'s likely to** rain, they said.
allergic (to) [ə'lɜːdʒɪk]	allergisch (gegen)	I can't eat that. I'm **~ to** nuts.
sting [stɪŋ]	(Insekten-)Stich	
sting [stɪŋ], stung [stʌŋ], stung	stechen (Insekt); brennen	Be careful – bees can ~. Your eyes ~ if there's a lot of smoke.
salt [sɔːlt]	Salz	
pepper ['pepə]	Pfeffer	
spot [spɒt]	Stelle, Ort; Fleck	**a tourist hot spot** = ein touristischer Anziehungspunkt

Theme 2

p.12 expect [ɪk'spekt]	erwarten	How many guests are you ~ing?
litre ['liːtə]	Liter	**!** *English:* 10 **litres** per person *German:* 10 **Liter** pro Person
break down	eine Panne haben, kaputtgehen *(Auto)*	Their car **broke** ~ on their way to the coast.
shade [ʃeɪd]	Schatten	shade shadow
shadow ['ʃædəʊ]	Schatten	
light [laɪt], lit [lɪt], lit	anzünden	**light a fire** = (ein) Feuer machen
heat [hiːt]	Hitze, Wärme	**heat ◄► cold** **heat stress** = Hitzestress, Wärmebelastung des Körpers
I'm/I feel sick. [sɪk]	Mir ist schlecht/übel.	**!** 1. **sick** = krank – her **sick** mother = ihre kranke Mutter 2. **I'm/I feel sick.** = Mir ist schlecht/übel.
cool down [kuːl 'daʊn]	sich abkühlen; sich beruhigen	
bite [baɪt]	Biss, (Insekten-)Stich	Verb: **bite, bit, bitten** – Nomen: **bite**
still [stɪl]	still, ruhig	**!** **still** = 1. (immer) noch; 2. still, ruhig
phone for an ambulance	einen Krankenwagen rufen	

p. 13	care [keə]	Sorgfalt, Vorsicht	Choose your words **with ~**. (vorsichtig, mit Bedacht)
	protect (from) [prəˈtekt]	(be)schützen (vor)	**Protect** your head **from** the sun. Wear a hat.
	over there [əʊvə ˈðeə]	da drüben, dort drüben	
	bleed [bliːd], bled [bled], bled	bluten	Verb: **bleed, bled, bled** – Nomen: **blood**
	redness [ˈrednəs]	Rötung, Röte	

> **-ness**
>
> Die Endung **-ness** wird verwendet, um Nomen aus Adjektiven zu bilden. Beispiele:
>
> | | | | | | |
> |---|---|---|---|---|---|
> | **cleverness** | Schlauheit | **friendliness** | Freundlichkeit | **redness** | Rötung, Röte |
> | **darkness** | Dunkelheit | **happiness** | Glück | **sadness** | Traurigkeit |
> | **fitness** | Fitness | **illness** | Krankheit | **weakness** | Schwäche |

	take sb.'s temperature	(bei jm.) Fieber messen	You feel very hot. I think we should **take** your **~**.

Theme 3

p. 14	**crew** [kruː]	Mannschaft, Team; Clique	
	body [ˈbɒdi]	Körper	
	paint [peɪnt]	lackieren, (be)malen, (mit Farbe) streichen	Verb: **paint** Nomen: **painting** (Gemälde, Bild; Malerei) **body painting** = Körperbemalung
	traditional [trəˈdɪʃənl]	traditionell	Nomen: **tradition** – Adjektiv: **traditional**
	wide [waɪd]	breit, weit	The river is too **~**. We can't get across. **wide ◀▶ narrow** (schmal)
p. 15	**almost** [ˈɔːlməʊst]	fast, nahezu, beinahe	= **nearly**
	indigenous (to) [ɪnˈdɪdʒənəs]	einheimisch (in)	• **indigenous people** = Einheimische, Ureinwohner/innen • **indigenous Australian** = australische(r) Ureinwohner/in
	simple [ˈsɪmpl]	einfach, simpel	
	disease [dɪˈziːz]	Krankheit	❗ • **disease** wird für ansteckende oder sehr ernsthafte Erkrankungen verwendet: She has a blood **disease**. Thousands of trees died from **disease**. • Das allgemeinere Wort für „Krankheit" ist **illness**: After a week of **illness**, she went back to school.
	continent [ˈkɒntɪnənt]	Kontinent	Europe and Asia are **~s**.
	way of life	Lebensweise	
	health [helθ]	Gesundheit	Nomen: **health** – Adjektiv: **healthy** Apples are **good for your ~**. = Äpfel sind **gesund**.
	dot [dɒt]	Punkt, Pünktchen	**dot painting** = Punktmalerei; Punktgemälde
	secret [ˈsiːkrət]	geheim; Geheimnis	The deal was **~**. Nobody knew about it. I can't tell you. It's a **~**.

1 VOCABULARY

• fantastic [fæn'tæstɪk]	fantastisch, wunderschön	

Focus on language

p.16	• enter ['entə]	sich anmelden (für), teilnehmen (an) (Wettbewerb)	Jay has **~ed** a marathon. He has only two more months to train!
	• personal ['pɜːsənl]	persönlich	
	cattle (pl) ['kætl]	Vieh, Rinder	**cattle station** (AustE) = Rinderfarm
	• the nearest …	der/die/das nächstgelegene …	**!** • nearest = nächstgelegen (räumlich): The **nearest** shop is just round the corner. • next = nächstfolgend (Reihenfolge): We have to get off at the **next** stop.
	horse [hɔːs]	Pferd	

horses   cattle

• repair [rɪ'peə]	reparieren	**repair** a bike = **fix** a bike (infml)
• worth [wɜːθ]	wert	**It was worth it.** = Das war es wert. **!** English: The film is **worth watching**. German: Es lohnt sich, den Film anzuschauen.
turn over [tɜːn 'əʊvə]	(sich) umdrehen; (Auto) sich überschlagen	**Turn** the burger **~** or it will burn! The car went off the road, **turned ~** and crashed into a tree.
• upside down [ˌʌpsaɪd 'daʊn]	verkehrt herum, auf dem/den Kopf	Can you read when the book is **~ down**?
tyre ['taɪə]	Reifen	
• waterproof ['wɔːtəpruːf]	wasserdicht, wasserfest, wasserundurchlässig	You'll need **~** clothes and a **~** watch if you want to go sailing.
• race [reɪs]	rasen, schnell fahren	Verb: **race** Nomen: **race** (Rennen, Wettrennen)
• figure ['fɪɡə]	Zahl, Ziffer; Person (Gestalt); Figur	

some figures

a hooded figure

figures of eight

! Betonung auf der 1. Silbe: **figure** ['fɪɡə]

210

| p.17 regular ['regjələ] | regelmäßig, normal | Adjektiv: **regular** – our **regular** customers; a **regular** verb |
| | | Adverb: **regularly** – We meet **regularly** every Friday afternoon. |

| not ... at all | überhaupt nicht | |

> **not ... at all**
> John does**n't** use his car **at all**. — John benutzt sein Auto überhaupt nicht.
> They do**n't** have any money **at all**. — Sie haben gar kein/überhaupt kein Geld.
> She did**n't** say anything **at all**. — Sie hat gar nichts/überhaupt nichts gesagt.
> Do you like meat? – **Not at all.** — Magst du Fleisch? – Überhaupt nicht.

cooking ['kʊkɪŋ]	(das) Kochen; Küche, Essen	• my mum's cooking = die Art, wie meine Mutter kocht
		• French cooking = französiche Küche/französisches Essen
general ['dʒenrəl]	allgemein	
record [rɪ'kɔːd]	aufnehmen, aufzeichnen	Our school band is going to ~ a CD.
slide [slaɪd]	Dia, Dia-; Folie *(bei Präsentation m. Computerprogramm)*	

Text

pp. 18–21 and 103–104

swerve [swɜːv]	*(das Auto/Steuer)* herumreißen, *(mit dem Auto)* ausweichen	Suddenly, an animal ran out into the road. I **swerved** and nearly hit a tree.
grandson ['grænsʌn]	Enkel	your child's son
granddaughter ['grændɔːtə]	Enkelin	your child's daughter
ponytail ['pəʊniteɪl]	Pferdeschwanz *(Frisur)*	
chin [tʃɪn]	Kinn	
any ['eni]	irgendein(e, r, s); jede(r) beliebige	

> **any**
> • **in questions:**   **Any** questions?   **Irgendwelche** Fragen?
>   Do we have **any** bread?   Haben wir Brot? *(unübersetzt)*
>
> • **in negative statements:**   I do**n't** have **any** money.   Ich habe **kein** Geld.
>   It was**n't** just **any** car.   Es war **nicht** einfach **irgendein** Auto. / Es war **kein** x-beliebiges Auto.
>
> • **in positive statements:**   You can buy **any** of these bikes, they're all good.   ... **jedes** dieser Räder / **irgendeins** von diesen Rädern ...
>   You can choose **any** DVD you like.   Du kannst **irgendeine** DVD auswählen.
>   **Any** teacher will help you.   **Jede/r** Lehrer/in wird dir helfen.

1 VOCABULARY

•whose [huːz]	wessen	
•his [hɪz]	seiner, seine, seins *(zu „he")*	Is this your bike? – No, it's ~. (Ist dies dein Rad? – Nein, das ist seins.)

Possessivpronomen (Possessive pronouns)

I	**my** dog	**mine**	meiner, meine, meins	we	**our** dog	**ours**	unserer, unsere, unseres
you	**your** dog	**yours**	deiner, deine, deins	you	**your** dog	**yours**	eurer, eure, eures
he	**his** dog	**his**	seiner, seine, seins	they	**their** dog	**theirs**	ihrer, ihre, ihrs
she	**her** dog	**hers**	ihrer, ihre, ihrs				

be up for sth. *(infml)*	bei etwas dabei sein, mitmachen	We're going to the disco tonight. **Are you ~ for it?** (Bist du dabei? / Machst du mit?)
•engine [ˈendʒɪn]	Motor	
•risk [rɪsk]	riskieren, aufs Spiel setzen	Don't ride your bike without a helmet! You're ~ing your life!
clearing [ˈklɪərɪŋ]	Lichtung	
goat [gəʊt]	Ziege	
hitchhiker [ˈhɪtʃhaɪkə]	Anhalter/in, Tramper/in	
•fuel [ˈfjuːəl]	Treibstoff, Kraftstoff	
kind of glamorous	irgendwie glamourös	! **kind =** 1. a **kind of** puzzle (eine Art Rätsel) 2. **kind of** cool (irgendwie cool)
glamorous [ˈglæmərəs]	glamourös	Working as a babysitter isn't ~, but I earn my own money and I'm proud of that!
•nail [neɪl]	Nagel	**fingernail** = Fingernagel
nail polish [ˈneɪl pɒlɪʃ]	Nagellack	
•retell [riːˈtel], retold [riːˈtəʊld], retold	nacherzählen	**Retell** the story. = Tell the story again (in your own words).

! Wenn du den Text auf den Seiten 18–21 gelesen hast, kannst du die folgenden neuen Wörter daraus zusätzlich lernen.

pp. 18–21

°waistcoat [ˈweɪskəʊt]	Weste	
°turn up [tɜːn ˈʌp]	auftauchen, erscheinen	
°familiar [fəˈmɪliə]	vertraut, bekannt	Who's that guy over there? He looks ~, but I can't think of how I might know him.
°threaten [ˈθretn]	(be)drohen	They ~ed him with a knife and he ran away.
°You got it. *(infml)*	Genau! / Du hast es!	

°head west [hed]	Richtung Westen gehen/fahren	After finishing high school, Lucas left home and ~ed west for college.	
°boot [bu:t]	Kofferraum (Auto)		
°appear [əˈpɪə]	auftauchen, erscheinen	appear ◄► disappear (verschwinden)	
°overtake [əʊvəˈteɪk], overtook [əʊvəˈtʊk], overtaken [əʊvəˈteɪkən]	überholen		
°bully [ˈbʊli]	tyrannisieren, mobben		
°counter [ˈkaʊntə]	(Verkaufs-)Schalter, Ladentheke		
°while [waɪl]	Weile	! while = 1. während – while we were waiting 2. Weile – after a while	

Speaking course

p.22 presentation [preznˈteɪʃn]	Referat, Präsentation	! English: give a presentation German: ein Referat halten	
copy [ˈkɒpi]	kopieren, abschreiben		
structure [ˈstrʌktʃə]	Struktur	Nomen: structure Verb: structure (strukturieren, gliedern)	
materials (pl) [məˈtɪəriəlz]	Materialien, Hilfsmittel		
make sure that …	sicherstellen, dass …; darauf achten, dass …; dafür sorgen, dass …	Make ~ that you turn off the lights when you leave the room.	
visuals (pl) [ˈvɪʒuəlz] (kurz für: visual materials)	visuelle Materialien/Hilfsmittel		
p.23 topic [ˈtɒpɪk]	Thema		

Unit 2: Respect

p.30 respect [rɪˈspekt]	Respekt	Verb: respect (respektieren) Nomen: respect	
jealous (of) [ˈdʒeləs]	eifersüchtig (auf), neidisch (auf)	She is ~ of her baby brother because she thinks her parents love him more. You get so much pocket money! I'm really ~.	
delete [dɪˈliːt]	löschen	I ~d the message from my phone. (… die Nachricht auf meinem Telefon …)	
p.31 no big deal	nichts Besonderes, kein Drama	Of course I can help you on Friday. No big ~!	
go away	verschwinden		
ending [ˈendɪŋ]	Endung; Ende (eines Texts, einer Geschichte)	Not every story can have a happy ~. ! English: happy ending – German: Happy End	
cyberbullying [saɪbəˈbʊliɪŋ]	Cybermobbing		
victim [ˈvɪktɪm]	Opfer	No one should be a ~ of cyberbullying.	
bystander [ˈbaɪstændə]	Zuschauer/in, (unbeteiligte/r) Beobachter/in	Lots of ~s saw the man fall, but nobody helped him.	

VOCABULARY

	bully ['bʊli]	tyrannisieren, mobben	
	bully ['bʊli]	Mobber/in, Tyrann/in	
	horrible ['hɒrəbl]	scheußlich, ätzend, gemein	It's ~ to tell those untrue stories about Kim.

Theme 1

p.32	deal with sth. [diːl], dealt [delt], dealt	umgehen mit etwas, mit etwas fertigwerden/klarkommen	We have to ~ with these questions before we can continue. I find it hard to ~ with stress.
	peer pressure ['pɪə preʃə]	Gruppendruck, Gruppenzwang	**pressure** = Druck
	peer [pɪə]	Gleichaltrige/r, Ebenbürtige/r, jemand aus derselben sozialen Gruppe	
	interest ['ɪntrəst]	Interesse	❗ Betonung auf der 1. Silbe: <u>in</u>terest [ˈɪntrəst]
	classmate ['klɑːsmeɪt]	Mitschüler/in	
	influence ['ɪnfluəns]	beeinflussen	Even today, the Beatles still ~ musicians all over the world. Verb: **influence** Nomen: **influence** (Einfluss)
	fit in [fɪt 'ɪn]	dazugehören; hineinpassen	There are some students in my sister's class who just don't ~ in.
	such a … [sʌtʃ]	so ein/e …; solch ein/e …	This is ~ a great shop, and they sell ~ nice sweets. ❗ English: There's **no such thing as** ghosts. German: Es gibt **keine** Gespenster.
	issue ['ɪʃuː]	(Streit-)Frage, Problem, Thema	Bullying is a big ~ at a lot of schools.
	cigarette [sɪgə'ret]	Zigarette	
	shoplifting ['ʃɒplɪftɪŋ]	Ladendiebstahl	Verb: **shoplift** (Ladendiebstahl begehen) Nomen: **shoplifting**
	be/feel comfortable (with) ['kʌmftəbl]	sich wohlfühlen (bei/mit)	❗ **comfortable** = 1. a ~ bed/chair/car (bequem) 2. I don't **feel** ~ **with** big groups of people. (sich wohlfühlen bei/mit)
	agree on sth. [ə'griː]	in etwas übereinstimmen, sich einig sein bei etwas	

agree			
agree on sth.		1. in etwas übereinstimmen, sich einig sein bei etwas	We're good friends, even if we don't **agree on** everything. (… selbst wenn wir nicht in allem übereinstimmen)
		2. sich auf etwas einigen	Talk to your partner about your ideas and **agree on** the best one. (… einigt euch darauf, welches die beste ist / … einigt euch auf die beste)
agree with sb./sth.	jm./etwas zustimmen; mit jm./etwas übereinstimmen		Sue says playing darts is boring, and I **agree with** her. (… und ich stimme ihr zu / stimme mit ihr überein)

p.33	**support** [sə'pɔːt]	unterstützen	Verb: **support** – My parents always ~ my dreams and plans. Nomen: **support** (Unterstützung) – My parents are a great ~.
p.33	**steal** [stiːl], **stole** [stəʊl], **stolen** ['stəʊlən]	stehlen	Where's your bike? – Someone has **stolen** it.
	accept [ək'sept]	akzeptieren, annehmen	I've asked 20 people to my party and 13 have already **~ed** the invitation.
p.34	**lately** ['leɪtli]	in letzter Zeit	Have you seen any good films ~? ❗ **late** = spät; zu spät – **lately** = in letzter Zeit
	(just) the two of us	(nur) wir beide	We met at the station, and then **the two of ~** walked home together.

Theme 2

p.35	**badge** [bædʒ]	Anstecknadel, Button	
	frustrating [frʌ'streɪtɪŋ]	frustrierend	Verb: **frustrate sb.** (jn. frustrieren) Adjektiv: **frustrating**
	discrimination (against) [dɪskrɪmɪ'neɪʃn]	Diskriminierung (von)	❗ *English:* **discrimination against** women/ black people *German:* **Diskriminierung von** Frauen/ Schwarzen
	racism ['reɪsɪzəm]	Rassismus	❗ Betonung auf der 1. Silbe: **ra**cism ['reɪsɪzəm]
	It stops with me.	Bei mir hört's auf. / Ich mache da nicht mit.	
	racist ['reɪsɪst]	rassistisch; Rassist/in	❗ Betonung auf der 1. Silbe: **ra**cist ['reɪsɪst]
	race [reɪs]	Volk, Stamm; Rasse	
	call sb. **names**	jn. beschimpfen	He was really angry. Someone had **called him a racist ~**. (Jemand hatte ihn mit einem rassistischen Wort beschimpft / hatte ihm ein rassistisches Schimpfwort nachgerufen.)
	staff [stɑːf]	Personal, Belegschaft	
	question sb.	jn. befragen, verhören	Nomen: **question** Verb: **question** (befragen, verhören)
	society [sə'saɪəti]	(die) Gesellschaft	❗ *No article:* **in (modern) society** in **der** (modernen) Gesellschaft
	prejudice ['predʒʊdɪs]	Vorurteil, Voreingenommenheit	Some people still have a ~ against girls and think that girls aren't good at maths.
	campaign [kæm'peɪn]	Kampagne	
p.36	**matter** ['mætə]	von Bedeutung sein, wichtig sein	Do you want to see change in our school? Tell us what you think! Your opinion **~s**.
	face sth. [feɪs]	vor etwas stehen *(Problem)*; einer Sache ins Auge sehen, sich einer Sache stellen; einer Sache entgegentreten	Jamie, ~ the facts. You'll never be a professional football player. As a single parent, I have to ~ problems other parents don't have to deal with.

2 VOCABULARY

	entry [ˈentri]	Eintrag (in Wörterbuch/ Tagebuch)	a dictionary ~; a diary ~
	equal [ˈiːkwəl]	gleich(berechtigt)	Everyone gets an ~ number of biscuits! Husband and wife should be ~ partners.
	negativity [negəˈtɪvəti]	negative Einstellung	
	vicinity [vəˈsɪnəti]	Umgebung	The police are looking in the Elm Street ~ for the thief.
	ignorance [ˈɪgnərəns]	Ignoranz, Unwissenheit	❗ Betonung auf der 1. Silbe: **ignorance** [ˈɪgnərəns]
	unity [ˈjuːnəti]	Einheit, (innere) Geschlossenheit	

Focus on language

p. 38	**introduce** sb. **to** sb. [ɪntrəˈdjuːs]	jm. jn. vorstellen, jn. mit jm. bekanntmachen	Can you ~ me **to** your sister, John?
	Don't be a pain. [peɪn]	Nerv nicht. / Geh mir/uns nicht auf die Nerven.	
	pain	Schmerz(en)	
p. 39	**indirect** [ɪndəˈrekt]	indirekt	
	direct [dəˈrekt]	direkt, unmittelbar	**direct** ◄► **indirect**
	exact [ɪgˈzækt]	exakt, genau	❗ Adjektiv: the **exact** time Adverb: **exactly** 12 o'clock
p. 40	**command** [kəˈmɑːnd]	Befehl	
	request [rɪˈkwest]	Wunsch, Bitte; Anfrage	

Text

pp. 41–43 and 115–116

	curtain [ˈkɜːtn]	Vorhang, Gardine	curtains
	warn sb. [wɔːn]	jn. warnen; jn. ermahnen	The teacher ~ed Josie that she had to work harder. *English:* They **warned me not** to go there. *German:* Sie **warnten mich davor, dort hinzugehen.**
	squatter [ˈskwɒtə]	Hausbesetzer/in	Verb: **squat** (*ein Haus/Grundstück besetzen*) Nomen: **squatter**
	candle [ˈkændl]	Kerze	a candle — a hammer
	hammer [ˈhæmə]	hämmern	
	have every right to do sth.	guten Grund / alles Recht haben, etwas zu tun	I **have every** ~ **to** be here. (Es ist mein gutes Recht, hier zu sein.)

right	Recht	
busybody [ˈbɪzibɒdi]	Wichtigtuer/in	
tramp [træmp]	Obdachlose(r), Stadtstreicher/in	
setting [ˈsetɪŋ]	Schauplatz (z.B. Film/ Geschichte)	The ~ of the film is a small village in Cornwall.
plot [plɒt]	Handlung(sverlauf) (z.B. Film/ Geschichte)	the story that a play, book, film tells us
recommendation [rekəmenˈdeɪʃn]	Empfehlung	Verb: **recommend** Nomen: **recommendation**

pp. 41–43

°**spooky** [ˈspuːki]	unheimlich, gruselig	
°**spook** [spuːk]	Geist	Wenn du den Text auf den Seiten 41–43 gelesen hast, kannst du die folgenden neuen Wörter daraus zusätzlich lernen.
°**weed** [wiːd]	(Un-)Kraut	
°**freeze** [friːz], **froze** [frəʊz], **frozen** [ˈfrəʊzn]	(ge)frieren; erstarren	Rivers and lakes sometimes ~ in winter. Suddenly the lights went out, and I **froze**.
°**See for yourself.**	Sieh selbst! / Sehen Sie selbst!	
°**of one's own**	eigene(r, s)	Do you have a room **of your ~?** (= your own room) I don't have a car **of my ~** – I share one with my sister.
°**respectable** [rɪˈspektəbl]	anständig, angesehen, ehrbar	
°**a while** [waɪl]	eine Weile, einige Zeit	First we watched the monkeys for a ~.
°**shake** [ʃeɪk], **shook** [ʃʊk], **shaken** [ˈʃeɪkən]	schütteln	! English: He **shook his** head. German: Er **schüttelte den** Kopf. **shake your head ◄► nod your head**
°**bedtime** [ˈbedtaɪm]	Schlafenszeit	
°**Off you go!**	Dann mal los! / Ab mit dir!	
°**tease** sb. [tiːz]	jn. hänseln, sich über jn. lustig machen	
°**mysterious** [mɪˈstɪəriəs]	geheimnisvoll	! Betonung auf der 2. Silbe: my**ste**rious [mɪˈstɪəriəs]

pp. 115–116

		Wenn du den Text auf den Seiten 115–116 gelesen hast, kannst du die folgenden neuen Wörter daraus zusätzlich lernen.
°**tool** [tuːl]	Werkzeug	
°**keep an eye on** sb./sth.	jn./etwas im Auge behalten, ein (wachsames) Auge haben auf jn./etwas	**Keep an ~** on your little brother, please. I have to make a phone call.
°**magic** [ˈmædʒɪk]	zauberhaft; Zauberei, Magie	
°**shower** [ˈʃaʊə]	Dusche	! English: **have a shower** German: **duschen, sich duschen**
°**Go on.**	Na los, mach(t) schon!	

VOCABULARY

Speaking course

p.44	conversation [kɒnvəˈseɪʃn]	Gespräch, Unterhaltung	
	dos and don'ts [duːz ən ˈdəʊnts]	was man tun und lassen sollte	What are the **dos and ~** in the computer room?
	exchange [ɪksˈtʃeɪndʒ]	(Schüler-)Austausch	
p.45	step by step [step]	Schritt für Schritt	
	by the way	übrigens	"Hi Dad. Yes, Dad, I took out the rubbish. And I did my homework. ... Oh, **by the ~**, Dad, I got a part in the school play today."
	See you around.	Bis dann.	
	sometime [ˈsʌmtaɪm]	irgendwann	❗ • **sometime** = irgendwann: We must meet again **sometime**. • **sometimes** = manchmal: We **sometimes** go to the park after school.
	paraphrase [ˈpærəfreɪz]	umschreiben, mit anderen Worten sagen	Mr Parker, I don't know what Joanna meant. Could you ~ what she said, please?

Unit 3: Looking forward

p.52	college [ˈkɒlɪdʒ]	höhere Schule, Fach(hoch)schule	
	ingredient [ɪnˈɡriːdiənt]	Zutat, Bestandteil	What **~s** do you need to make scones?
	sauce [sɔːs]	Sauce	❗ Aussprache: **sauce** [sɔːs]
	takeaway [ˈteɪkəweɪ]	Essen zum Mitnehmen	If we don't feel like cooking, we often get a Chinese ~.
	pick sth. up [pɪk ˈʌp]	etwas kaufen, etwas (aus einem Geschäft) mitbringen	➡ **pick** • **pick sth. up** = etwas hochheben, aufheben • **pick sth. up** = etwas kaufen, mitbringen (aus Geschäft) • **pick sb. up** = jn. abholen
	vacuum cleaner [ˈvækjuəm kliːnə]	Staubsauger	
	washing machine [ˈwɒʃɪŋ məʃiːn]	Waschmaschine	
	iron [ˈaɪən]	bügeln	Verb: **iron** – Nomen: **iron** (Bügeleisen) ❗ Aussprache – das „r" wird nicht gesprochen: **iron** [ˈaɪən]
	earn [ɜːn]	verdienen *(Geld)*	❗ German „Geld verdienen" = 1. *(Gehalt bekommen)* **earn money** 2. *(Profit machen)* **make money**
	manage [ˈmænɪdʒ]	verwalten, regeln	My brother is too young to ~ his own money.

vacuum cleaner

washing machine

iron

	budget [ˈbʌdʒɪt]	haushalten (sparsam sein)	Verb: **budget** – Nomen: **budget** (Budget, Haushalt) ❗ Betonung auf der 1. Silbe: **bud**get [ˈbʌdʒɪt]
	overspend (on sth.) [əʊvəˈspend], overspent, overspent [əʊvəˈspent]	zu viel Geld ausgeben (für etwas)	= spend too much money
	I often **run out of** money.	Mir geht oft das Geld aus. / Bei mir wird oft das Geld knapp. →	**run out** (knapp werden, zu Ende gehen) • **Time is running out.** (Die Zeit wird knapp.) • **I'm running out of time.** (Ich habe keine Zeit mehr.) • **It was so hot that the shops ran out of cold drinks.** (…, dass den Geschäften die kalten Getränke ausgingen.)
p.53	sb. **can't wait to do** sth.	jd. kann es kaum erwarten, etwas zu tun	I'm so excited. I **can't ~ to** go to Australia!
	skill [skɪl]	Fähigkeit, Fertigkeit	Her computer **~s** are amazing.

Theme 1

p.54	strength [streŋθ]	Stärke, Kraft	One of my ~s is that I speak three languages.
	weakness [ˈwiːknəs]	Schwäche	weak ◄► strong weakness ◄► strength
	work experience [ˈwɜːk ɪkspɪərɪəns]	Praktikum/Praktika; Arbeitserfahrung(en)	
	confident [ˈkɒnfɪdənt]	(selbst)sicher; zuversichtlich	He's very shy. He'd like to become more ~. The interview went very well. I'm ~ I'll get the job.
	energetic [enəˈdʒetɪk]	energisch, energiereich	We need an ~ person for this job.
	enthusiastic [ɪnθjuːziˈæstɪk]	begeistert	Look at those flowers! You can see how ~ Joan is about gardening.
	punctual [ˈpʌŋktʃuəl]	pünktlich	= on time
	reliable [rɪˈlaɪəbl]	zuverlässig, verlässlich	She's a very ~ person. If she says she will do something, then she will really do it.
	criticism [ˈkrɪtɪsɪzəm]	Kritik	❗ German „Kritik" = 1. *(an etwas/jm.)* **criticism** 2. *(Rezension eines Buches/Films usw.)* **review**
p.55	study [ˈstʌdi]	studieren; lernen	She wants to ~ history when she's finished school. I'll stay at home this afternoon and ~ for tomorrow's test.
	university [juːnɪˈvɜːsəti]	Universität	
	solution (**to** a problem) [səˈluːʃn]	Lösung (eines Problems)	❗ *English:* **the solution to** this problem *German:* **die Lösung für** dieses Problem / **die Lösung** dieses Problems
	identity [aɪˈdentəti]	Identität	My native language is part of my ~. (Meine Muttersprache ist Teil meiner Identität.)

VOCABULARY

Theme 2

p. 56	qualify ['kwɒlɪfaɪ]	(sich) qualifizieren	He wants to ~ as a kindergarten teacher next year.
	qualified ['kwɒlɪfaɪd]	qualifiziert; ausgebildet, mit Abschluss	Pete's Pasta Place is looking for a ~ cook.
	(working) hours (pl) ['wɜːkɪŋ 'aʊəz]	Arbeitszeit(en)	Cooks have long working ~ – up to 14 hours a day.
	apply (for) [ə'plaɪ]	sich bewerben (um)	Did your brother ~ for the job? – Yes, but he didn't get it.
	stylist ['staɪlɪst]	Friseur/in; (Mode-)Stylist/in	
	up to	bis (zu)	This tree can get ~ to 35 metres high.

German „bis"

• **zeitlich** meist:	**until**	I had to work **until** ten o'clock last night. We lived in Austria **until** I was eight years old.
• „**bis jetzt**":	**up to now/so far**	**Up to now/So far** everything has been OK.
• „**von ... bis ...**":	**from ... to ...**	We're open **from** Monday **to** Friday **from** 9 **to** 5.
• „**bis zu**" + Menge/Zahl:	**up to**	There'll be **up to** 200 guests. You can earn **up to** £ 60,000 here.
• **räumlich** meist:	**as far as / up to**	Walk **as far as/up to** the school, then turn left.

	CV (= curriculum vitae) [siː 'viː, kərɪkjələm 'viːtaɪ] (BE)	Lebenslauf	
	communication [kəmjuːnɪ'keɪʃn]	Kommunikation, Verständigung	
	pay [peɪ]	Bezahlung, Lohn	Verb: **pay (for)** (bezahlen) – Nomen: **pay**
	trainee [treɪ'niː]	Auszubildende(r), Trainee	
	qualification [kwɒlɪfɪ'keɪʃn]	(Schul-)Abschluss, Qualifikation	What ~s do you need for this job? Verb: **qualify** – Nomen: **qualification**
	30 years of age	30 Jahre alt	My grandmother is 75 **years of age**. (= 75 years old)
	assistant [ə'sɪstənt]	Helfer/in, Assistent/in	❗ Betonung auf der 2. Silbe: as**sis**tant [ə'sɪstənt]
p. 57	care [keə]	Versorgung, Betreuung	**childcare** = Kinderbetreuung **health care** = Gesundheitsversorgung
	shift [ʃɪft]	Schicht (bei der Arbeit)	❗ English: I **work shifts** at a restaurant. German: Ich **arbeite im Schichtdienst** ...
	at all times	jederzeit, ständig	= all the time, always
	duty ['djuːti]	Pflicht, Aufgabe; Dienst	❗ English: **on duty** – German: **im Dienst**
	outdoors [aʊt'dɔːz]	im Freien, draußen	**outdoors** ◄► **indoors**
	quality ['kwɒləti]	Eigenschaft; Qualität	❗ English: **personal qualities** German: **persönliche Eigenschaften**
	adventurous [əd'ventʃərəs]	abenteuerlustig	Nomen: **adventure** – Adjektiv: **adventurous**

Theme 3

p. 58	**dynamic** [daɪˈnæmɪk]	dynamisch	We are looking for ~, energetic people to be salespeople in our downtown store.
	sales assistant [ˈseɪlz əsɪstənt]	Verkäufer/in	**assistant** = Assistent/in; **sales assistant** = Verkäufer/in

sale / sales

for sale (zu verkaufen; zum Verkauf)

sale (Schlussverkauf; Ausverkauf)

She works in sales. (Sie arbeitet im Verkauf.)

	fitting room [ˈfɪtɪŋ ruːm]	Anprobe, Umkleide(kabine)	
	cash desk [ˈkæʃ desk]	Kasse	

fitting rooms / sales assistant / cash desk

	answer the phone	ans Telefon gehen	Can you ~ the phone, please? I'm busy. ❗ English: answer the phone German: ans Telefon gehen English: answer the door German: aufmachen, zur/an die Tür gehen
	flexible [ˈfleksəbl]	flexibel	❗ Betonung auf der 1. Silbe: **flex**ible [ˈfleksəbl]
	key skills *(pl)* [ˈkiː skɪlz]	Schlüsselqualifikationen, Schlüsselkompetenzen	
	key [kiː]	Schlüssel; Schlüssel-	I can't drive home. I've lost my car ~s! The coach plays a ~ role for any sports team.
	education [edʒuˈkeɪʃn]	(Schul-)Bildung	You need a good ~ if you want to get a good job.
	petrol station [ˈpetrəl steɪʃn]	Tankstelle	

a petrol station

	achievement [əˈtʃiːvmənt]	Errungenschaft, Leistung	Learning to play the guitar is quite an ~.

3 VOCABULARY

	keen [kiːn]	(sehr) interessiert, begeistert	Mary is a ~ musician.
	be keen on sth. / **on doing** sth. [kiːn]	an etwas sehr interessiert sein; etwas unbedingt (tun) wollen	She's especially ~ **on** jazz / **on** playing jazz.
	reference [ˈrefrəns]	Referenz, Empfehlung; jd., der eine Referenz erteilt	I listed my coach and my maths teacher as ~**s**.
p.59	**cover letter** [ˈkʌvə letə]	Anschreiben, Begleitschreiben, Motivationsschreiben	
	Dear Sir/Madam [sɜː], [ˈmædəm]	Sehr geehrte Damen und Herren	
	advertisement [ədˈvɜːtɪsmənt] (*infml auch:* **ad** [æd], **advert** [ˈædvɜːt])	Anzeige, Inserat, Annonce	You find job ~**s** in newspapers and on the internet.
	suitable [ˈsuːtəbl]	geeignet, passend	Jeans aren't ~ clothes for a job interview.
	enclose [ɪnˈkləʊz]	beifügen, beilegen (*einem Brief*)	Please ~ a copy of your driving licence.
	Yours faithfully [ˈfeɪθfəli] (BE)	Mit freundlichen Grüßen (Briefschluss)	

> **Beginning and ending formal letters**
>
> | | You start with: | You end with: |
> |---|---|---|
> | • If you <u>know</u> the person's name: | **Dear Ms Jones**
Dear Mr Brown | (BE:) **Yours sincerely**
(AE:) **Sincerely** |
> | • If you <u>don't know</u> the person's name: | **Dear Sir/Madam** | (BE:) **Yours faithfully**
(AE:) **Sincerely** *or* **Sincerely yours** |

	relevant [ˈreləvənt]	relevant, wichtig	❗ Betonung auf der 1. Silbe: **re**levant [ˈreləvənt]

Focus on language

p.60	**be (good) friends with** sb.	mit jm. (gut) befreundet sein	I'm ~ with Joe and Jack. = Joe and Jack are my friends.
	though [ðəʊ]	aber; allerdings; jedoch	She was born in France. She isn't French ~. (= … She isn't French, however.) ❗ Das Adverb **though** steht am Satzende, anders als die deutschen Entsprechungen.
	admire [ədˈmaɪə]	bewundern	We stopped at the lake to ~ the view.
	style [staɪl]	Stil	
	speech [spiːtʃ]	Rede; Sprechweise	I'm nervous when I have to give/make a ~ in front of a lot of people. Clear ~ is important in a presentation. ❗ English: **give/make** a speech German: eine Rede **halten**
	for sure	ganz sicher, ganz bestimmt	❗ English: …, **that's for sure.** German: …, **das ist (ganz) sicher.** English: **One thing is for sure:** … German: **Eins ist sicher:** …
p.61	**send** sth. **out**	etwas verschicken	I **sent** ~ the party invitations last Thursday.

Text

blurb [blɜːb]		Klappentext *(eines Buches)*	the text on the back cover of a book that tells the reader what the book is about
pretend (to be sth.**)** [prɪˈtend]		so tun, als ob (man etwas wäre)	They **~ed to be** ill so that they could miss school.
in order to [ˈɔːdə]		um … zu	We should go early **in ~ to** get good seats.
realize sth. [ˈriːəlaɪz]		etwas erkennen; sich einer Sache bewusst werden	When I got home, I **~d** that I had left my bag on the train.
complicated [ˈkɒmplɪkeɪtɪd]		kompliziert	❗ Betonung auf der 1. Silbe: **com**plicated [ˈkɒmplɪkeɪtɪd]
lie (to sb.**)** [laɪ]		(jn. an)lügen	What he said wasn't true. He **lied to** me. ❗ Schreibung: **lie, lied** – He **lied** to me. aber: **lying** – Stop **lying** to me.
lie [laɪ]		Lüge	lügen = lie *oder* tell a lie/tell lies
put up one's hand		sich melden; seine/die Hand heben	They're putting up their hands.
application form [æplɪˈkeɪʃn fɔːm]		Bewerbungsformular, Antragsformular	**application** = Bewerbung, Antrag **form** = Formular
boardwalk [ˈbɔːdwɔːk]		Steg, Uferpromenade *(aus Holz)*	a boardwalk
program *(AE)* [ˈprəʊɡræm]		Programm; (Fernseh-/Radio-)Sendung	❗ **programme** *(BE)* / **program** *(AE)* = 1. Programm 2. (Fernseh-/Radio-)Sendung
blouse [blaʊz]		Bluse	a blouse a shirt
lipstick [ˈlɪpstɪk]		Lippenstift	lips a lipstick
cheerful [ˈtʃɪəfl]		fröhlich, gut gelaunt	
curly [ˈkɜːli]		lockig	They have curly hair.
neon [ˈniːɒn]		Neon; neonfarbig	

VOCABULARY

can [kæn]	Dose		a can of juice a can of cola a can of tomatoes
half [hɑːf], *pl* **halves** [hɑːvz]	Hälfte		❗ English: **sixteen and a half** German: **sechzehneinhalb**
credit card [ˈkredɪt kɑːd]	Kreditkarte		
fire sb. [ˈfaɪə]	jn. feuern, entlassen		You'll get me **fired**. (Du schaffst es noch, dass ich gefeuert werde.)
kiss [kɪs]	(sich) küssen		Verb: **kiss** – Nomen: **kiss**
pull back	sich zurückziehen, zurückweichen		❗ English: **pull back one's hair** German: **sich die Haare zusammenbinden**
lie [laɪ], **lay** [leɪ], **lain** [leɪn]	liegen		My dog often **lies** on our sofa. ❗ Aber *-ing*-Form: **lying** – Why is your cat **lying** on my bed? ❗ **lie, lay, lain** = liegen **lie, lied, lied** = lügen
act [ækt]	handeln, sich verhalten; so tun, als ob		

> **act**
> - I'm going to **act** in a play.   **Theater spielen; schauspielern**
> - We have to **act** fast!   **handeln**
> - He **acted** very strangely.   **sich verhalten**
> - She sometimes **acts** (= pretends to be) shy, but she's really quite confident.   **so tun, als ob**

it does have …	es hat (ja/wohl) doch/tatsächlich …	She **does** look very tired. We **do** have enough time, you know. But you **did** say six o'clock! ❗ In Aussagesätzen ohne Hilfsverb kannst du **do/does/did** verwenden, um der Aussage des Satzes Nachdruck zu verleihen.

pp. 62–64

°**tenth grader** [ˈgreɪdə]	Zehntklässler/in	❗ Wenn du den Text auf den Seiten 62–64 gelesen hast, kannst du die folgenden neuen Wörter daraus zusätzlich lernen.
°**bakery** [ˈbeɪkəri]	Bäckerei	
°**mention** [ˈmenʃn]	erwähnen, nennen	Thank you! – Don't ~ it. (= You're welcome.)
°**clerk** [klɑːk]	Angestellte(r)	**(front) desk clerk** = Empfangsmitarbeiter/in
°**immediately** [ɪˈmiːdiətli]	sofort	When I call my dog, she comes **immediately**.
°**hand** sb. sth. [hænd]	jm. etwas (an)reichen, aushändigen	Can you ~ (= give) me the sugar, please?
°**on one's own**	allein, selbstständig (*ohne Unterstützung*)	I repaired this **on my** ~ – nobody helped me.

°a friend of Cindy's / of hers / of mine	ein/e Freund/in von Cindy / von ihr / von mir	**a friend of Cindy's / of hers / of mine**
		• Charlotte is **a friend of Cindy's**.
		  (= eine von Cindys Freundinnen)
		• Josie is **Charlotte's friend**.
		  (= Charlottes (beste) Freundin)
		❗ a friend of **mine/his/hers/ours**
		  (nicht: … of ~~me/him/her/us~~)

°several ['sevrəl]	mehrere, einige	
°block [blɒk]	(Häuser-)Block	

°storey (BE) / story (AE) ['stɔːri]	Stock, Stockwerk, Etage	**German „Stock(werk)"**
		• When you want to say <u>where someone lives or works</u>: **floor**
		  Our offices are on the sixth **floor**.
		• When you want to say <u>how high a building is</u>: **storey** (BE) / **story** (AE)
		  The building is 14 **storeys** high.

°unattractive [ˌʌnə'træktɪv]	unattraktiv	attractive ◄► unattractive
°mature [mə'tʃʊə]	reif, vernünftig	
°actually ['æktʃuəli]	eigentlich, tatsächlich	I didn't think I would enjoy the film, but ~ it was fun.
°pumps (pl) [pʌmps]	Pumps (elegante Damenschuhe)	**pumps**
°heel [hiːl]	Absatz (Schuh)	heel
°graveyard ['greɪvjɑːd]	Friedhof	**graveyard shift** (infml) = Nachtschicht
°lady ['leɪdi]	Dame	
°slam [slæm]	(zu-, hin)knallen	**slam down the phone** = den Hörer aufknallen
°shocked [ʃɒkt]	schockiert	
°swimsuit ['swɪmsuːt]	Badeanzug	
°sandals (pl) ['sændlz]	Sandalen	sandals a swimsuit
°foolish ['fuːlɪʃ]	töricht, dumm	Nomen: **fool** – Adjektiv: **foolish**
p.65 **personality** [ˌpɜːsə'næləti]	Persönlichkeit; Charakter	
appearance [ə'pɪərəns]	Erscheinung(sbild), Aussehen	You should have an appropriate ~ at a job interview. Verb: **appear** – Nomen: **appearance**

Speaking course

p.66 **job interview**	Vorstellungsgespräch	
performance [pə'fɔːməns]	Vorstellung, Aufführung	
p.67 **individual** [ˌɪndɪ'vɪdʒuəl]	Einzelne(r), Individuum; Person	

3-4 VOCABULARY

necessary [ˈnesəsəri]	notwendig, nötig, erforderlich	Some changes will be ~. (= Some changes will have to be made.)
candidate [ˈkændɪdət]	Bewerber/in, Kandidat/in	❗ Betonung auf der 1. Silbe: **can**didate [ˈkændɪdət]
approach [əˈprəʊtʃ]	Ansatz, Herangehensweise	This isn't working. Let's try a different ~.
greet [griːt]	begrüßen	
pleased [pliːzd]	froh, erfreut, zufrieden	**Pleased to meet you.** = Freut mich, Sie kennenzulernen.
contact [ˈkɒntækt]	Kontakt aufnehmen zu, sich melden bei	❗ **contact** = 1. Kontakt; 2. Kontakt aufnehmen zu, sich melden bei

Unit 4: Generation *like*

p.74 | **generation** [dʒenəˈreɪʃn] | Generation

Theme 1

p.76	**digital** [ˈdɪdʒɪtl]	digital	❗ Betonung auf der 1. Silbe: **digital** [ˈdɪdʒɪtl]
	average [ˈævərɪdʒ]	durchschnittlich; Durchschnitt	The ~ age of students in our year is 16.5. I practise the piano two hours a day on ~. (= im Durchschnitt, durchschnittich)
	multitask [mʌltiˈtɑːsk]	mehrere Tätigkeiten gleichzeitig ausführen	
	video-chat [ˈvɪdiəʊ tʃæt]	sich per Videokonferenz unterhalten	
	at the same time	zur selben Zeit, gleichzeitig	He chats, reads a magazine and watches TV, all **at the same ~**.
	attraction [əˈtrækʃn]	Attraktion; Anziehungskraft	The British Museum is one of London's biggest tourist ~s.
	media (pl) [ˈmiːdiə]	Medien	It's so much faster to use ~ like the phone or email than to write letters. **social media** = soziale Medien/Dienste
	social [ˈsəʊʃl]	gesellschaftlich, sozial	❗ Betonung auf der 1. Silbe: **social** [ˈsəʊʃl]
	the pros and cons (pl) [prəʊz ənd ˈkɒnz]	das Pro und Kontra; das Für und Wider	What are **the pros and ~** (= the reasons for and against) buying a new car now?
	addicted (to) [əˈdɪktɪd]	süchtig (nach), abhängig (von)	He smokes a lot. He's ~ **to** cigarettes.
p.77	**habit** [ˈhæbɪt]	(An-)Gewohnheit	something you do regularly Smoking is a bad ~.
	focus (on) [ˈfəʊkəs]	sich konzentrieren (auf)	**Focus** on your homework now and later we can go out.
	brain [breɪn]	Gehirn	**brains** (pl) = Verstand, Intelligenz, „Köpfchen": You need a lot of **brains** for this job.
	be a drifter [ˈdrɪftə]	sich treiben lassen (ziellos vor sich hinleben)	I spend a lot of time on the internet. I think **I'm a** digital ~.
	butterfly [ˈbʌtəflaɪ]	Schmetterling	**butterflies**

Theme 2

p.78	**profile** [ˈprəʊfaɪl]	Profil; Beschreibung, Portrait	! Betonung auf der 1. Silbe: **pro**file [ˈprəʊfaɪl]
	standard [ˈstændəd]	normal, üblich, Standard-	! **standard** = 1. normal, üblich, Standard-; 2. Norm, Standard
	basic [ˈbeɪsɪk]	einfach, elementar	• Adjektiv: **basic** We stayed at a cheap, **basic** hotel. • Adverb: **basically** (im Prinzip, grundsätzlich) **Basically** I like your idea. But I'd like to discuss some of the details.
	imaginative [ɪˈmædʒɪnətɪv]	einfallsreich, kreativ	He's a great cook and so ~! He can make anything taste great!
	puppy [ˈpʌpi]	(Hunde-)Welpe	three **puppies**
	creative [kriˈeɪtɪv]	kreativ	! Betonung auf der 2. Silbe: cr**ea**tive [kriˈeɪtɪv]
	search for sth. [sɜːtʃ]	etwas suchen / nach etwas suchen	! English: search the internet **for** sth. German: das Internet **nach** etwas durchsuchen **search** = 1. suchen; 2. Suche
	come up	auftauchen, herauskommen; aufkommen *(Frage)*	Look what **came** ~ when I looked for cute cats on the internet.
	Go ahead. [əˈhed]	Nur zu. / Dann mal los.	Can I use your laptop? – Sure, **go** ~.
p.79	**vain** [veɪn]	eitel	He's so ~. He spends all of his time looking in the mirror and checking his hair.
	critic [ˈkrɪtɪk]	Kritiker/in	! English: **critic** – German: **Kritiker/in** English: **criticism** – German: **Kritik**
	actually [ˈæktʃuəli]	eigentlich, tatsächlich	

actually

Das Wort **actually** kann im Deutschen – je nach Situation – mit **eigentlich, übrigens, tatsächlich** wiedergegeben werden. Manchmal hat es auch überhaupt keine Entsprechung.

Man verwendet **actually**,

• wenn man jemanden höflich darauf hinweisen möchte, dass er/sie etwas Falsches gesagt hat	I'm not English, **actually**: I'm Welsh. **Actually**, London is bigger than Paris.
• wenn man ausdrücken möchte, dass etwas in Wirklichkeit anders ist oder war, als man erwartet hat	I didn't think I would enjoy the party, but it was **actually** fun.
• als entschuldigende Einleitung, wenn man etwas Unangenehmes mitzuteilen hat.	When are you going to give me my ruler back? – **Actually**, I can't. I've lost it.

	post [pəʊst]	posten *(im Internet veröffentlichen)*	
	depressing [dɪˈpresɪŋ]	deprimierend	
	astronaut [ˈæstrənɔːt]	Astronaut/in	an **astronaut** ! Betonung auf der 1. Silbe: **a**stronaut [ˈæstrənɔːt]
	artist [ˈɑːtɪst]	Künstler/in	! English: **artist** Betonung: **a**rtist [ˈɑːtɪst] German: **Künstler/in** (nicht: ~~Artist/in~~)

4 VOCABULARY

self-portrait [ˈpɔːtreɪt]	Selbstporträt	
in other words	mit anderen Worten	
although [ɔːlˈðəʊ] (*kurz auch:* **though** [ðəʊ])	obwohl	We stayed up and watched the late film, **although** we were really tired. (*oder:* …, **though** we were really tired.)
relax [rɪˈlæks]	sich entspannen	
argument [ˈɑːɡjumənt]	Argument; Streit	→ **argument** • Prepare your **arguments** before you start the discussion. (= **Argument**) • Mum and Dad had an **argument** last night. They shouted a lot. (= **Streit**) **!** Betonung auf der 1. Silbe: <u>argument</u> [ˈɑːɡjumənt]
conclusion [kənˈkluːʒn]	Schluss(folgerung)	

Theme 3

p.80	**target** sb. [ˈtɑːɡɪt]	auf jn. zielen *(jn. als Zielgruppe haben/wählen)*, jn. ins Visier nehmen	**!** **target** = 1. zielen auf, ins Visier nehmen: Fashion companies often ~ young adults. 2. Ziel: I am the ~ of a lot of fashion adverts.
	savvy [ˈsævi] *(infml)*	versiert, gewieft	→ **savvy** wird oft an andere Wörter angehängt: **ad-savvy** versiert/gewieft/erfahren im Umgang mit Werbung **media-savvy** versiert/gewieft/erfahren im Umgang mit Medien **net-savvy** interneterfahren **tech-savvy** technikversiert
	one in three	eine/r von drei(en)	**One in three** children in the UK have never climbed a tree. **!** Auf **One in xxx children/teens/cars/…** kann ein Verb im Plural oder im Singular folgen: **One in three** kids **have** never climbed … *oder* **One in three** kids **has** never climbed …
	reduce sth. **(by)** [rɪˈdjuːs]	etwas reduzieren, etwas verringern (um)	Oh look, they have ~d the price.
	advertiser [ˈædvətaɪzə]	Werber/in, Werbetreibende(r)	

adverts and advertising

• **advertise (sth.)** [ˈædvətaɪz]	Werbung machen (für etwas)
• **advertising** [ˈædvətaɪzɪŋ]	Werbung, Reklame
• **advertisement**, *infml auch:* **ad, advert**	Anzeige, Inserat, Annonce
• **advertiser** [ˈædvətaɪzə]	Werber/in, Werbetreibende(r)

design [dɪˈzaɪn]	entwerfen, gestalten, entwickeln	
product [ˈprɒdʌkt]	Produkt	**!** Betonung auf der 1. Silbe: <u>product</u> [ˈprɒdʌkt]

	repeat [rɪˈpiːt]	wiederholen	Could you ~ that, please? (= Could you say/do that again, please?)
p.81	strategy [ˈstrætədʒi]	Strategie	
	irritate [ˈɪrɪteɪt]	(ver)ärgern, irritieren	Pop-up ads ~ me so much!

Focus on language

p.82	gatecrash (a party) [ˈgeɪtkræʃ]	(bei einer Party) ungebeten erscheinen	gatecrasher = uneingeladene Person (die eine Party „sprengt")
	a while [waɪl]	eine Weile, einige Zeit	❗ while = 1. während – while we were waiting 2. Weile – for a while (eine Weile lang)
	reach (sb./a place) [riːtʃ]	(jn./einen Ort) erreichen	If we leave now, we'll ~ London before dinner.
	damage (no pl) [ˈdæmɪdʒ]	Schaden, Schäden	The fire destroyed part of the kitchen, but there was no ~ to the house. (…, aber es gab keine Schäden am Haus / aber das Haus wurde nicht beschädigt.)
	clean-up [ˈkliːn ʌp]	Reinemachen, Hausputz	
	fault [fɔːlt]	Fehler, Schuld	Don't blame me! It wasn't my ~!
	learn a/your lesson	eine/deine Lektion lernen	teach sb. a lesson = jm. eine Lektion erteilen
p.83	straight away [streɪt əˈweɪ]	sofort	When you get home, call Grandma ~ away. It's her birthday.
	type (of) [taɪp]	Art, Sorte, Typ (von)	What ~ of person is she? Quiet? Noisy? Funny? Shy?
	theme park [ˈθiːm pɑːk]	Themenpark (Freizeitpark mit Attraktionen zu einem bestimmten Thema)	
	a shame [ʃeɪm]	ein Jammer; schade	It's a ~ (that) you can't come over! What a ~ you can't come over! (Wie schade, dass …)

Text

pp.84–87 and 136–138	onto [ˈɒntə, ˈɒntu]	auf (… hinauf)	He's jumping onto the box.
	virtual [ˈvɜːtʃuəl]	virtuell	❗ Betonung auf der 1. Silbe: <u>vir</u>tual [ˈvɜːtʃuəl]
	combat [ˈkɒmbæt]	Kampf	
	unwanted [ʌnˈwɒntɪd]	unerwünscht	
	killer [ˈkɪlə]	Mörder/in	
	virus [ˈvaɪrəs], pl viruses [ˈvaɪrəsɪz]	Virus	
	catch sth. [kætʃ]	sich mit etwas anstecken; sich etwas einfangen (Krankheit)	
	realistic [riːəˈlɪstɪk]	realistisch	I want to see all the sights in London. – Come on, be ~. We only have two days.
	the most realistic game ever	das realistischste Spiel, das es je gegeben hat	

VOCABULARY

I haven't eaten **in days.**	Ich habe tagelang nichts gegessen.	
backstreet [ˈbækstriːt]	*(kleinere)* Seitenstraße *(weitab von den Hauptstraßen)*	
rich [rɪtʃ]	reich	**rich ◄► poor**
leave sb. **alone**	jn. in Ruhe lassen	Go away and ~ me alone! ❗ *English:* Leave me **alone**. *German:* Lass mich **in Ruhe**.
finder [ˈfaɪndə]	Finder/in	❗ **Finders keepers, losers weepers.** *etwa:* Was man findet, darf man behalten. (Wer's findet, darf's behalten, wer's verloren hat, muss weinen.)
creep up (on sb.**)** [kriːp], **crept, crept** [krept]	sich heranschleichen (an jn.)	Two men **crept ~ on** me from behind and stole my bag.
drop [drɒp]	fallen; fallen lassen	❗ **drop** = 1. fallen – The glass **dropped** to the floor. 2. fallen lassen – Don't **drop** that glass.
till [tɪl]	bis	= until
idiot [ˈɪdiət]	Idiot/in	❗ Betonung auf der 1. Silbe: **idiot** [ˈɪdiət]
… is bad news.	… ist gefährlich. / … ist (gar) nicht gut.	You can't trust him. He's bad ~.
twins *(pl)* [twɪnz]	Zwillinge	**twin sister/brother** = Zwillingsschwester/-bruder
grin (at sb.**)** [grɪn]	(jn. an)grinsen	Look at him! He's **grinning at** us.
roof [ruːf]	Dach	
fire escape [ˈfaɪər ɪskeɪp]	Feuertreppe, Notausgang	
ladder [ˈlædə]	(die) Leiter	
mobile [ˈməʊbaɪl]	mobil	❗ **mobile** = 1. mobil; 2. mobile (phone) Mobiltelefon, Handy
I can't …, can I?	Ich kann doch nicht …, nicht wahr?	

Question tags (Frageanhängsel)

- This exercise is hard, **isn't it**?
  He teaches maths, **doesn't he**?
  She didn't go home, **did she**?

  Die Sätze links sind keine echten Fragen; die roten „Anhängsel" sind sogenannte **question tags**. Sie helfen, ein Gespräch in Gang zu halten.
  Auf Deutsch sagt man „nicht wahr?", „nicht?" oder „oder?".

- The band **is** great, **isn't** it?

  Wenn der **Aussagesatz bejaht** ist, ist das **Frageanhängsel verneint**.

- Jim **can't** speak Italian, **can** he?

  Wenn der **Aussagesatz verneint** ist, ist das **Frageanhängsel bejaht**.

▶ *Language file 31, p. 203*

pp. 84–87	°**heavyweight** ['heviweit]	Schwergewicht; Schwergewichts-	❗ Wenn du den Text auf den Seiten 84–87 gelesen hast, kannst du die folgenden neuen Wörter daraus zusätzlich lernen.
	°**turn away**	sich abwenden, sich wegdrehen	
	°**spread** sth. [spred], **spread, spread**	etwas verbreiten *(Virus, Krankheit)*	
	°**army** ['ɑːmi]	Armee	
	°**take over**	die Macht übernehmen	
	°**energy** ['enədʒi]	Energie	❗ Betonung auf der 1. Silbe: **en**ergy ['enədʒi]
	°**torture** ['tɔːtʃə]	Folter	
	°**step** [step]	treten *(einen Schritt tun)*	
	°**weapon** ['wepən]	Waffe	
	°**frightened** ['fraɪtnd]	verängstigt	➡ **frighten, frightened, frightening** • **it frightens me** = es macht mir Angst • **be frightened of** sth. = vor etwas Angst haben • **it's frightening** = es ist beängstigend
	°**shake** [ʃeɪk], **shook** [ʃʊk], **shaken** ['ʃeɪkən]	schütteln	❗ *English*: He shook **his** head. *German*: Er schüttelte **den** Kopf. **shake your head** ◄► **nod your head**
	°**leather** ['leðə]	Leder	made of **leather**
	°**no need for** sth. / **no need to do** sth. [niːd]	kein Grund für etwas / kein Grund, etwas zu tun	There's **no ~ for** tears. There's **no ~ to** cry. Everything will be fine.
	°**know** sth. **like the back of your hand**	etwas wie seine Westentasche kennen; etwas in- und auswendig kennen	the **back of your hand**
	°**short cut** ['ʃɔːt kʌt], [ʃɔːt 'kʌt]	Abkürzung	
	°**choice** [tʃɔɪs]	(Aus-)Wahl	Nomen: **choice** – Verb: **choose, chose, chosen**
	°**crash** [kræʃ]	krachen; stürzen	She dropped the glass, and it **~ed** (on)to the floor.
	°**flash** [flæʃ]	(das) (Auf-)Blitzen	**flash a torch** = mit einer Taschenlampe leuchten/blinken
	°**freeze** [friːz], **froze** [frəʊz], **frozen** ['frəʊzn]	(ge)frieren; erstarren	Rivers and lakes sometimes **~** in winter. Suddenly the lights went out, and I **froze**.

Speaking course

p.88	**shocking** ['ʃɒkɪŋ]	schockierend	➡ **shock, shocked, shocking** • **it shocked us** = es hat uns schockiert • **be/look shocked** = schockiert sein/ aussehen • **shocking news** = schockierende Nachrichten

4 VOCABULARY

	vamping [ˈvæmpɪŋ]	spät in der Nacht noch aktiv sein	❗ Das Wort **vamping** kommt von **vampire** [ˈvæmpaɪə] („Vampir") – Vampire sind auch nachtaktiv.
	express [ɪkˈspres]	ausdrücken, zum Ausdruck bringen	"In my opinion" and "I think" are useful phrases to ~ your opinion.
	invention [ɪnˈvenʃn]	Erfindung	I don't think it's true that every ~ makes life easier.
p.89	observer [əbˈzɜːvə]	Beobachter/in	
	moderator [ˈmɒdəreɪtə]	Moderator/in *(z.B. bei Debatten)*	
	speaker [ˈspiːkə]	Sprecher/in; Redner/in	
	point [pɔɪnt]	Argument	→ **point** • **Make your point.** = Sag, wie du darüber denkst. • **That's a good point.** = Das ist ein (gutes) Argument.
	respectful [rɪˈspektfl]	respektvoll	• Adjektiv: **respectful** If you are **respectful** to your teachers, most of them will be **respectful** to you. • Adverb: **respectfully** Speak **respectfully** when you are having a discussion. You will be more successful.

MORE CHALLENGE 1

p.28	°idiom [ˈɪdiəm]	Redewendung	
	°spare room [speə ˈruːm]	Gästezimmer	
	°bark [bɑːk]	bellen	
	°surroundings *(pl)* [səˈraʊndɪŋz]	Umgebung	
	°shower [ˈʃaʊə]	(sich) duschen; Dusche	❗ English: **shower** or **have a shower** or **take a shower** German: **(sich) duschen** English: **have a bath** or **take a bath** German: **baden** *(in der Wanne)*
	°bath [bɑːθ]	Bad, Badewanne	
	°bathtub [ˈbɑːθtʌb]	Badewanne	bathtubs
	°realize sth. [ˈriːəlaɪz]	etwas erkennen, sich einer Sache bewusst werden	
	°cupboard [ˈkʌbəd]	Schrank	❗ Aussprache: **cupboard** [ˈkʌbəd]
	°what …, anyway? [ˈeniweɪ]	was/welche/r … überhaupt?	But you know I don't like fish! **What kind of fish is it, ~?** (Was für eine Art Fisch ist es denn überhaupt?)
	°put sb. at ease [iːz]	jn. beruhigen, jm. die Befangenheit nehmen	My new boss introduced me to everyone and that helped to ~ me at ~.

°chief [tʃiːf]	Haupt-; leitende(r)	I'm the ~ dogwalker at home. (= It's mostly me who walks the dog.)
°poison ['pɔɪzn]	Gift	**poison**
°damage (no pl) ['dæmɪdʒ]	Schaden, Schäden	The fire destroyed part of the kitchen, but there was no ~ to the house. (..., aber es gab keine Schäden am Haus / aber das Haus wurde nicht beschädigt.)
°be/feel uncomfortable [ʌnˈkʌmftəbl]	sich unbehaglich fühlen	Everyone was looking at me. I felt so ~.
°moon [muːn]	Mond	the **moon**

MORE CHALLENGE 2

°keep up (with sb.)	(mit jm.) Schritt halten	He's such a good runner. He can ~ **up with** runners four years older.
°elementary school (AE) [elɪˈmentri skuːl]	Grundschule	= BE **primary school** [ˈpraɪməri skuːl]
°middle school (AE) [ˈmɪdl skuːl]	Mittelschule (für 11- bis 14-Jährige)	
°abroad [əˈbrɔːd]	im/ins Ausland	My friend Emily has never been ~.
°beyond [bɪˈjɒnd]	über ... hinaus, weiter als	Spending some time abroad helped me to see ~ my own culture.
°hardship [ˈhɑːdʃɪp]	Not, Mühsal, harte Umstände	My grandparents experienced lots of ~ when they arrived in New York as teenagers.
°able-bodied [eɪbl ˈbɒdid]	(körperlich) gesund	Some ~-**bodied** people never think about people with disabilities.
°rare [reə]	selten	Wow! That's a ~ kind of bike. Where did you get it?
°condition [kənˈdɪʃn]	Leiden, Erkrankung	Alan has a rare ~ which makes him sleep 15 hours a day.
°properly [ˈprɒpəli]	richtig, ordentlich, korrekt	My mum always says I don't set the table ~.
°display [dɪˈspleɪ]	zeigen, zur Schau stellen	There are always lots of mobile phones ~**ed** in the shop window.
°rather than [ˈrɑːðə]	anstelle von, (an)statt	Olivia prefers to wear trousers ~ **than** dresses.
°taunt [tɔːnt]	Spott, höhnische Bemerkung	
°disabled [dɪsˈeɪbld]	(körper)behindert	My cousin is ~. He has to use a wheelchair.
°confident [ˈkɒnfɪdənt]	selbstbewusst, (selbst)sicher; zuversichtlich	My dad doesn't feel ~ when he has to drive in other countries ...
°admit [ədˈmɪt]	zugeben, (ein)gestehen	... but he would never ~ it!
°cabin [ˈkæbɪn]	Kabine	
°rather [ˈrɑːðə]	ziemlich	He felt ~ sad. (= quite sad)

VOCABULARY

MORE CHALLENGE 3

p. 72	°imagination [ɪmædʒɪˈneɪʃn]	Fantasie, Vorstellungskraft	
	°relationship [rɪˈleɪʃnʃɪp]	Beziehung, Verhältnis *(zu anderen Menschen)*	
	°forever [fərˈevə]	für immer, ewig (lange)	I hope they arrive soon. We can't wait ~.
	°minor character [ˈmaɪnə ˈkærəktə]	Nebenfigur *(in Roman, Film usw.)*	
	°flatmate [ˈflætmeɪt]	Mitbewohner/in	
	°response [rɪˈspɒns]	Antwort, Reaktion	
	°serious [ˈsɪəriəs]	ernst(haft)	She's very funny but always has a ~ face. Jack has had a ~ accident and is in hospital.
	°typical (of) [ˈtɪpɪkl]	typisch (für)	What food is ~ **of** your area?
	°rhyme [raɪm]	(sich) reimen	
p. 73	°umbrella [ʌmˈbrelə]	(Regen-)Schirm	Would you like to share my ~? (Möchtest du mit unter meinen Regenschirm?)

MORE CHALLENGE 4

p. 94	°analysis [əˈnæləsɪs], *pl* analyses [əˈnæləsiːz]	Analyse	
	°location [ləʊˈkeɪʃn]	Ort *(Standort; Einsatzort)*	
p. 95	°exit [ˈeksɪt]	Ausgang; hinausgehen	Nomen: **exit** – The emergency ~ is on the right. Verb: **exit** – Please ~ quickly if there is an emergency.
	°gift [gɪft]	Geschenk	
	°lively [ˈlaɪvli]	lebendig, lebhaft	My grandma is still very ~ at 85. She goes dancing twice a week.
	°get lucky	Glück haben	
	°sell [sel], **sold, sold** [səʊld]	sich verkaufen (lassen)	Beatles songs still ~ quite well, even after all these years.
	°Incredibly [ɪnˈkredəbli], …	Unglaublicherweise … / Es ist kaum zu glauben, aber …	**Incredibly,** my ring was still on my desk five hours after I had left it there.
	°even though	auch wenn, obwohl *(betont)*	**!** English: He's world-famous, **even though** he isn't really an artist. German: … weltberühmt, **und das, obwohl** er gar kein wirklicher Künstler ist.
	°sum [sʌm]	Summe, Betrag	
	°hint [hɪnt]	Hinweis	
	°in fact [ɪn ˈfækt]	eigentlich, um genau zu sein	
	°make sth. up	etwas erfinden, sich etwas ausdenken	a **made-up** character, story, etc. (eine erfundene Figur, Geschichte usw.)
	°entertaining [entəˈteɪnɪŋ]	unterhaltsam	The concert wasn't very ~. I wanted to leave after 20 minutes.
	°aspect [ˈæspekt]	Aspekt	There are many **~s** to think about before you go on a student exchange.

DICTIONARY

English – German ABC

Das **English – German dictionary** enthält den Wortschatz der Bände 1 bis 5 von *Lighthouse*. Wenn du wissen möchtest, was ein englisches Wort bedeutet, wie man es ausspricht oder wie es genau geschrieben wird, dann kannst du hier nachschlagen.

Im **Dictionary** werden folgende **Abkürzungen und Symbole** verwendet:

sb. = somebody   sth. = something   jn. = jemanden   jm. = jemandem
pl = plural (Mehrzahl) BE = British English   AE = American English infml = informal (umgangssprachlich)

° Mit diesem Kringel sind Wörter markiert, die nicht zum Lernwortschatz gehören.

Die **Fundstellenangaben** zeigen, wo ein Wort zum ersten Mal vorkommt. Die Ziffern in Klammern bezeichnen Seitenzahlen:

I = *Lighthouse* Band 1   •   II = *Lighthouse* Band 2   •   III = *Lighthouse* Band 3   •   IV = *Lighthouse* Band 4
V 1 (8) = *Lighthouse* Band 5, Unit 1, Seite 8

Tipps zur Arbeit mit einem Wörterbuch findest du im Skills file auf Seite 163.

A

a [ə] ein, eine I   **a bit** ein bisschen I   **a few** ein paar, einige II   **a little money/time/...** ein bisschen Geld/Zeit/... II   **a lot (of)** viel, viele II   **£ 10 a week** 10 Pfund pro Woche II
able ['eɪbl]: **be able to do sth.** etwas tun können; fähig sein / in der Lage sein, etwas zu tun IV
°**able-bodied** [eɪbl 'bɒdid] (körperlich) gesund
Aboriginal [æbə'rɪdʒənl] Aborigine- (die Ureinwohner/innen Australiens betreffend) V 1 (8)
about [ə'baʊt]:
1. über I
2. ungefähr I
about me über mich I   **I'm sorry about yesterday.** Es tut mir leid wegen gestern. II   **The text is about ...** Der Text handelt von ... III   **What about ...?** Wie wär's mit ...? I   **What about you?** Und du? / Und was ist mit dir? I   **What's special about ...?** Was ist das Besondere an ...? III   **Who is the text about?** Von wem handelt der Text? III   °**do sth. about it** etwas daran tun, etwas dagegen unternehmen
°**above** [ə'bʌv] oben; über, oberhalb (von)
°**abroad** [ə'brɔːd] im/ins Ausland
absolute ['æbsəluːt] absolute(r, s) IV
accent ['æksent] Akzent III
accept [ək'sept] akzeptieren, annehmen V 2 (33)
accident ['æksɪdənt] Unfall II
accommodation [əkɒmə'deɪʃn] Unterkunft III
according to [ə'kɔːdɪŋ] laut, zufolge IV
account [ə'kaʊnt] Account, Konto V 4 (76)

achievement [ə'tʃiːvmənt] Errungenschaft, Leistung V 3 (58)
°**acre** ['eɪkə] britisches Flächenmaß, entspricht 0,405 Hektar
across Dartmoor / the street / the beach [ə'krɒs] über das Dartmoor / die Straße / den Strand II
act [ækt]:
1. handeln, sich verhalten; so tun, als ob V 3 (64)
2. Theater spielen; schauspielern II
°3. aufführen
action ['ækʃn] Action IV   **go into action** einen Einsatz haben V 1 (11)
active ['æktɪv] aktiv II
activity [ək'tɪvəti] Aktivität II
actor ['æktə] Schauspieler/in II
actually ['æktʃuəli] eigentlich, tatsächlich V 4 (79)
ad [æd] *(kurz für:* **advertisement***)* Anzeige, Inserat, Annonce V 3 (59)
°**adapted from** [ə'dæptɪd] (frei) nach
adapter [ə'dæptə] Adapter III
add (to) [æd] hinzufügen (zu) III
addicted (to) [ə'dɪktɪd] süchtig (nach), abhängig (von) V 4 (76)
°**addition** [ə'dɪʃn]:   **in addition** außerdem
address [ə'dres] Adresse, Anschrift I
admire [əd'maɪə] bewundern V 3 (60)
admission [əd'mɪʃn] Eintritt, Eintrittspreis IV
°**admit** [əd'mɪt] zugeben, (ein)gestehen
adopt [ə'dɒpt] adoptieren; *(Tier)* bei sich aufnehmen II
adult ['ædʌlt] Erwachsene(r) II
advantage [əd'vɑːntɪdʒ] Vorteil IV
adventure [əd'ventʃə] Abenteuer I
adventurous [əd'ventʃərəs] abenteuerlustig V 3 (57)
advert ['ædvɜːt] Anzeige, Werbung I
advertise (sth.) ['ædvətaɪz] Werbung machen (für etwas) V 4 (80)

advertisement [əd'vɜːtɪsmənt] Anzeige, Inserat, Annonce V 3 (59)
advertiser ['ædvətaɪzə] Werber/in, Werbetreibende(r) V 4 (80)
advertising ['ædvətaɪzɪŋ] Werbung, Reklame V 4 (80)
advice [əd'vaɪs] Rat(schlag), Ratschläge II   **a piece of advice** ein Rat, ein Ratschlag IV
°**advise** [əd'vaɪz] (be)raten
°**affect** [ə'fekt] beeinflussen, sich auswirken auf
afraid [ə'freɪd]:   **be afraid (of)** Angst haben (vor) IV   **I'm afraid** leider III
Africa ['æfrɪkə] Afrika I
after ['ɑːftə]:
1. nach I
after dinner nach dem Abendessen/Abendbrot I   **after that** danach IV
2. nachdem IV
look after sb. sich um jn. kümmern; auf jn. aufpassen I   **run after sb.** hinter jm. herrennen IV
afternoon [ɑːftə'nuːn] Nachmittag I   **in the afternoon** nachmittags, am Nachmittag I   **on Friday afternoon** freitagnachmittags, am Freitagnachmittag I
again [ə'gen] wieder; noch einmal I
against [ə'genst] gegen III
age [eɪdʒ] Alter I   **30 years of age** 30 Jahre alt V 3 (56)   **at the age of 16** mit 16; im Alter von 16 III
aggressive [ə'gresɪv] aggressiv IV
ago [ə'gəʊ]:   **two years ago** vor zwei Jahren III
agree [ə'griː]:   **agree on sth.** in etwas übereinstimmen, sich einig sein bei etwas V 2 (32)   **agree with sb./sth.** jm./etwas zustimmen; mit jm./etwas übereinstimmen II
agriculture ['ægrɪkʌltʃə] Landwirtschaft IV

235

DICTIONARY

English – German

ahead [ə'hed]: **Go ahead.** Nur zu. / Dann mal los. V 4 (78)
aim [eɪm] Ziel III
air [eə] Luft II
airport ['eəpɔːt] Flughafen III
alarm clock [ə'lɑːm klɒk] Wecker I
alcohol ['ælkəhɒl] Alkohol IV
all [ɔːl]: **all (the)** alle I **all day** den ganzen Tag (lang) I **all over the world** auf der ganzen Welt IV **all right** gut; in Ordnung; OK II **in all** insgesamt III **not ... at all** überhaupt nicht V 1 (17)
allergic (to) [ə'lɜːdʒɪk] allergisch (gegen) V 1 (11)
alligator ['ælɪgeɪtə] Alligator IV
allowed [ə'laʊd]: **be allowed to do sth.** etwas tun dürfen III °**be allowed** erlaubt sein
almost ['ɔːlməʊst] fast, nahezu, beinahe V 1 (15)
alone [ə'ləʊn]: allein II **leave sb. alone** jn. in Ruhe lassen V 4 (85)
along the street [ə'lɒŋ] die Straße entlang II
alphabet ['ælfəbet] Alphabet I
already [ɔːl'redi] schon II
also ['ɔːlsəʊ] auch II
although [ɔːl'ðəʊ] obwohl V 4 (79)
always ['ɔːlweɪz] immer I
am [eɪ'em]: **9 am / 9 a.m.** 9 Uhr morgens/vormittags I
amazing [ə'meɪzɪŋ] erstaunlich III
ambulance ['æmbjələns] Krankenwagen II
American Indian [əmerɪkən 'ɪndɪən] Indianer/in; indianisch IV
among [ə'mʌŋ] zwischen, unter *(mehreren Personen, Tieren, Dingen)* III **among the sheep** zwischen den Schafen, unter den Schafen III
°**amputate** ['æmpjuteɪt] amputieren
an [ən] ein, eine I
°**analyse** ['ænəlaɪz] analysieren, untersuchen
ancient ['eɪnʃənt] (ur)alt; antik IV
and [ænd], [ənd] und I **less and less** immer weniger III **more and more** immer mehr II
angry ['æŋgri] wütend II
animal ['ænɪml] Tier I
announcement [ə'naʊnsmənt] Durchsage, Ansage; Bekanntgabe, Ankündigung IV
°**anonymous** [ə'nɒnɪməs] anonym
another [ə'nʌðə] ein anderer / eine andere / ein anderes; noch ein(e) II
answer ['ɑːnsə]:
1. Antwort I
2. antworten; beantworten II
answer the door aufmachen, zur/an die Tür gehen V 3 (58) **answer the phone** ans Telefon gehen V 3 (58)
anthem ['ænθəm]: **national anthem** Nationalhymne III

°**anti-** ['ænti] Anti-, Gegen- **antivenom** Gegengift
any ['eni]:
1. irgendein(e, r, s); jede(r) beliebige V 1 (19)
2. **Any ideas?** Irgendwelche Ideen? I
3. **we don't have any ...** wir haben kein/e ... II
anybody ['enibʌdi]:
1. **I didn't know anybody.** Ich kannte niemanden. IV
2. *(in Fragen)* (irgend)jemand IV
anyone ['eniwʌn]:
1. **I didn't know anyone.** Ich kannte niemanden. IV
2. *(in Fragen)* (irgend)jemand IV
anything ['eniθɪŋ]:
1. **I can't do anything.** Ich kann nichts machen. II
2. *(in Fragen)* etwas, irgendetwas III **Anything else?** Sonst noch etwas? III
3. **I'll do anything.** Ich werde alles tun. III
anytime ['enitaɪm] jederzeit IV
°**anyway** ['eniweɪ]: **what ... anyway?** was/welche/r ... überhaupt?
anywhere ['eniweə]: **not (...) anywhere** nirgendwo; nirgendwohin III
apartment [ə'pɑːtmənt] Wohnung IV
°**ape** [eɪp] Menschenaffe
app [æp] App V 4 (79)
°**appear** [ə'pɪə] auftauchen, erscheinen
appearance [ə'pɪərəns] Erscheinung(sbild), Aussehen V 3 (65)
apple ['æpl] Apfel I
application [æplɪ'keɪʃn] Bewerbung, Antrag V 3 (62)
application form [æplɪ'keɪʃn fɔːm] Bewerbungsformular, Antragsformular V 3 (62)
apply (for) [ə'plaɪ] sich bewerben (um) V 3 (56)
appointment [ə'pɔɪntmənt] Termin, Verabredung II
°**apprentice** [ə'prentɪs] Lehrling, Auszubildende(r)
°**approach** [ə'prəʊtʃ] Ansatz, Herangehensweise V 3 (67)
appropriate [ə'prəʊpriət] angemessen, passend, geeignet IV
April ['eɪprəl] April I **April 1st joke** Aprilscherz IV
aquarium [ə'kweərɪəm] Aquarium I
archery ['ɑːtʃəri] Bogenschießen II
are [ɑː] bist; sind; seid I **Here you are.** Bitte schön. / Hier, bitte. I **How are you?** Wie geht's? / Wie geht es dir/euch? I **The mobiles are £10.** Die Handys kosten 10 Pfund. I
area ['eəriə] Gebiet, Gegend III
argue [ɑː'gjuː] argumentieren IV
argument ['ɑːgjumənt] Argument, Streit V 4 (79)
arm [ɑːm] Arm II
°**army** ['ɑːmi] Armee

around [ə'raʊnd]:
1. um ... (herum) III
2. in ... umher, durch III
look around sich umsehen III **run around** umherrennen; herumlaufen II **See you around.** Bis dann. V 2 (45) °**be around** da sein, vorhanden sein
°**arrange** [ə'reɪndʒ] arrangieren; anordnen
arrangement [ə'reɪndʒmənt] Vereinbarung II **make an arrangement** eine Vereinbarung treffen; etwas vereinbaren, etwas verabreden
arrest sb. [ə'rest] jn. festnehmen, verhaften IV
arrival [ə'raɪvl] Ankunft III
arrive [ə'raɪv] ankommen II
°**arsehole** ['ɑːshəʊl] *(taboo)* Arschloch
art [ɑːt] Kunst I
article ['ɑːtɪkl] (Zeitungs-)Artikel III
artist ['ɑːtɪst] Künstler/in V 4 (79)
artistic [ɑː'tɪstɪk] künstlerisch; *auch:* künstlerisch begabt V
°**arty** ['ɑːti] *(infml)* (gewollt) künstlerisch
as [æz], [əz]:
1. als, während IV
2. da, weil V 1 (11)
3. **as a footballer/singer/...** als Fußballer/in / Sänger/in / ... III
4. wie III
as much as $80 bis zu 80$; nicht weniger als 80$ IV **as much as you can** so viel, wie du kannst III **the same as ...** der-/die-/dasselbe wie ...; dieselben wie ... I
as soon as [əz 'suːn əz] sobald, sowie III
Asian ['eɪʃn] Asiate/Asiatin; asiatisch IV
ask [ɑːsk] fragen I **ask for sth.** um etwas bitten II **ask questions** Fragen stellen I **ask sb. about sth.** sich bei jm. nach etwas erkundigen II **ask sb. the way** jn. nach dem Weg fragen II **ask sb. to do sth.** jn. bitten, etwas zu tun IV
asleep [ə'sliːp]: **be asleep** schlafen IV **fall asleep** einschlafen IV
assembly [ə'sembli] Schulversammlung, Morgenappell I
°**assess** [ə'ses] beurteilen, bewerten
°**assessor** [ə'sesə] Prüfer/in, Gutachter/in
assistant [ə'sɪstənt] Helfer/in, Assistent/in V 3 (56)
astronaut ['æstrənɔːt] Astronaut/in V 4 (79)
at [æt], [ət]: **at (the age of) 16** mit 16; im Alter von 16 III **at 1 o'clock** um 1 Uhr / um 13 Uhr I **at a restaurant** in einem Restaurant I **at break** in der Pause *(zwischen Schulstunden)* II **at Ellie's house** bei Ellie daheim, bei Ellie zu Hause I **at first** zuerst, am Anfang II **at home** daheim, zu Hause I **at last** schließlich, endlich III **at least** mindestens, wenigstens II **at MARTINS**

236

bei MARTINS I **at night** nachts, in der Nacht I **at school** in der Schule I **at the bottom (of)** unten, am unteren Ende (von) II **at the cinema** im Kino I **at the market** auf dem Markt I **at the moment** im Moment, gerade I **at the same time** zur selben Zeit, gleichzeitig V 4 (76) **at the top (of)** oben; am oberen Ende (von), an der Spitze (von) II **at the weekend** am Wochenende I **at this school** auf/an dieser Schule I **at work** bei der Arbeit, am Arbeitsplatz I
ate [eɪt], [et] *siehe* **eat**
attack [əˈtæk] Angriff II
attic [ˈætɪk] Dachboden IV
°**attitude** [ˈætɪtjuːd] Einstellung, (Geistes-)Haltung
attraction [əˈtrækʃn] Attraktion; Anziehungskraft V 4 (76)
°**attractive** [əˈtræktɪv] attraktiv
audience [ˈɔːdiəns] Publikum; Zuschauer/innen, Zuhörer/innen II
°**audio** [ˈɔːdiəʊ] Audio-, Ton-
August [ˈɔːɡəst] August I
aunt [ɑːnt] Tante I
°**Aussie** [ˈɒzi] *(infml)* Australier/in
author [ˈɔːθə] Autor/in IV
autumn [ˈɔːtəm] Herbst II
available [əˈveɪləbl] erhältlich, verfügbar, *(Stelle)* frei IV **be available** zur Verfügung stehen, Zeit haben V 3 (59)
avatar [ˈævətɑː] Avatar *(virtuelle Figur)* V (78)
avenue [ˈævənjuː] Allee, Prachtstraße *(in den USA oft Teil v. Straßennamen)* IV
average [ˈævərɪdʒ] durchschnittlich; Durchschnitt V 4 (76) **on average** im Durchschnitt, durchschnittlich V 4 (76)
°**avoid** [əˈvɔɪd] (ver)meiden
°**award** [əˈwɔːd] Preis *(Auszeichnung)*
°**aware** [əˈweə]: **be aware of sth.** etwas wissen, sich einer Sache bewusst sein
away [əˈweɪ] weg, fort I **go away** verschwinden V 2 (31)
awesome [ˈɔːsəm] *(AE, infml)* klasse, stark, großartig IV

B

baby [ˈbeɪbi] Baby I
babysitter [ˈbeɪbisɪtə] Babysitter I
back [bæk]:
1. zurück I
2. Rücken; Rückseite II
at the back hinten, im hinteren Teil IV °**know sth. like the back of one's hand** etwas wie seine Westentasche kennen; etwas in- und auswendigkennen °**the back of the hand** der Handrücken
°**back cover** [ˈbæk kʌvə] Umschlagrückseite *(Buch)*

background [ˈbækɡraʊnd] Hintergrund III
backstreet [ˈbækstriːt] *(kleinere)* Seitenstraße *(weitab von den Hauptstraßen)* V 4 (85)
backyard [bækˈjɑːd] *(AE)* Garten *(hinter dem Haus)*, Hinterhof IV
bad [bæd]: schlecht; schlimm I **... is bad news.** ... ist gefährlich. / ... ist (gar) nicht gut. V 4 (85)
badge [bædʒ] Anstecknadel, Button V 2 (35)
bag [bæɡ] Tasche, Beutel I
bagel [ˈbeɪɡl] Bagel IV
baked potato [beɪkt pəˈteɪtəʊ] Ofenkartoffel *(in der Schale gebackene Kartoffel)* II
°**bakery** [ˈbeɪkəri] Bäckerei
ball [bɔːl] Ball I **Pass the ball!** Spiel ab! III
ballroom dancing [ˈbɔːlruːm ˈdɑːnsɪŋ] Standardtanz II
ban [bæn]:
1. **ban (on)** Verbot (von) V 1 (10)
2. verbieten V 1 (10)
be banned verboten sein/werden IV
banana [bəˈnɑːnə] Banane III
band [bænd] Band, (Musik-)Gruppe I
bank [bæŋk] Bank *(Geldinstitut)* II
bar [bɑː] Bar IV **chocolate bar** Schokoriegel III
barbecue [ˈbɑːbɪkjuː] Grillfest, Grillparty II
°**bark** [bɑːk] bellen
barn [bɑːn] Scheune, Stall I
baseball [ˈbeɪsbɔːl] Baseball IV
°**based on** [beɪst] auf der Grundlage von
basic [ˈbeɪsɪk] einfach, elementar V 4 (78) **basically** im Prinzip, grundsätzlich V 4 (78)
basketball [ˈbɑːskɪtbɔːl] Basketball I
bat [bæt] Fledermaus III
°**bath** [bɑːθ] Bad, Badewanne **have/take a bath** baden *(in der Wanne)*
bathroom [ˈbɑːθruːm] Badezimmer, Bad I
°**bathtub** [ˈbɑːθtʌb] Badewanne
be [biː], **was/were, been** sein I
beach [biːtʃ] Strand I **on the beach** am Strand I
bear [beə] Bär I
°**beat** [biːt] (Takt-)Schlag, Rhythmus **on the beat** im Rhythmus
beat [biːt], **beat, beaten** schlagen, besiegen III
beaten [ˈbiːtn] *siehe* **beat**
beautiful [ˈbjuːtɪfl] schön II
became [bɪˈkeɪm] *siehe* **become**
because [bɪˈkɒz] weil I **because of** wegen IV **That's because ...** Das liegt daran, dass ... IV
become [bɪˈkʌm], **became, become** werden III
bed [bed] Bett I

bed and breakfast (B&B) [bed ən ˈbrekfəst] Frühstückspension; Zimmer mit Frühstück III
bedroom [ˈbedruːm] Schlafzimmer I
°**bedtime** [ˈbedtaɪm] Schlafenszeit
bee [biː] Biene III
been [biːn] *siehe* **be**
before [bɪˈfɔː]:
1. vor *(zeitlich)* I
before breakfast vor dem Frühstück I
2. bevor I
before you read bevor du liest I
3. vorher; zuvor II
I've never had a pasty before. Ich habe vorher noch nie / noch nie zuvor eine Pastete gegessen. II
the night before die Nacht zuvor, die Nacht davor III
began [bɪˈɡæn] *siehe* **begin**
begin [bɪˈɡɪn], **began, begun** beginnen, anfangen III
°**beginner** [bɪˈɡɪnə] Anfänger/in
beginning [bɪˈɡɪnɪŋ] Anfang, Beginn III
begun [bɪˈɡʌn] *siehe* **begin**
behave [bɪˈheɪv] sich verhalten, sich benehmen IV
behind [bɪˈhaɪnd] hinter I
believe [bɪˈliːv] glauben III
bell [bel] Glocke; Klingel III
°**bellhop** [ˈbelhɒp] *(AE)* Hotelpage
belly button [ˈbeli bʌtn] *(infml)* Bauchnabel IV
belongings *(pl)* [bɪˈlɒŋɪŋz] Sachen, Hab und Gut II
below [bɪˈləʊ] unten; unter, unterhalb (von) III
bend [bend] Kurve III
beside [bɪˈsaɪd] neben III
best [best] am besten II **Best wishes** Viele Grüße, ... *(Briefschluss)* I **like sth. best** etwas am liebsten mögen II **my best friends** meine besten Freunde/Freundinnen I **the best of both worlds** das Beste von beidem I
best-known [best ˈnəʊn] der/die/das bekannteste; am bekanntesten V 1 (10)
better [ˈbetə] besser II **do better** besser abschneiden II
better-known [betə ˈnəʊn] bekannter V 1 (10)
between [bɪˈtwiːn] zwischen I
°**beyond** [bɪˈjɒnd] über ... hinaus, weiter als
big [bɪɡ]:
1. dick, schwer *(Person)* V 1 (20)
2. groß I
bike [baɪk] Fahrrad I **by bike** mit dem Rad I **go by bike** mit dem Rad fahren I **ride a bike** Rad fahren I
°**billboard** [ˈbɪlbɔːd] *(AE)* Plakatwand, Werbeplakat
bin [bɪn]: **litter bin** Abfalleimer, Mülleimer II

237

DICTIONARY

English – German

°**biography** [baɪˈɒgrəfi] Biografie
bird [bɜːd] Vogel I
birthday [ˈbɜːθdeɪ] Geburtstag I
   It's her birthday. Sie hat Geburtstag.
   I **My birthday is on 5th May.**
   Ich habe am 5. Mai Geburtstag. I
   on my birthday an meinem Geburtstag I **When's your birthday?**
   Wann hast du Geburtstag? I
biscuit [ˈbɪskɪt] Keks, Plätzchen II
bit [bɪt] *siehe* **bite**
bit [bɪt]: **a bit** ein bisschen I
bite [baɪt]:
   1. Biss, (Insekten-)Stich V 1 (12)
   2. bite, bit, bitten beißen II
bitten [ˈbɪtn] *siehe* **bite**
black [blæk] schwarz I
blame sb. (for) [bleɪm] jm. die Schuld geben (an); jm. Vorwürfe machen (wegen) III **Don't blame yourself.** Mach dir keine Vorwürfe. III
blazer [ˈbleɪzə] Blazer *(Jackett, oft Teil der Schuluniform)* I
bled [bled] *siehe* **bleed**
bleed [bliːd], **bled, bled** bluten V 1 (13)
blind [blaɪnd] blind III
°**block** [blɒk] (Häuser-)Block
block of flats [blɒk] Wohnblock, Häuserblock III
blog [blɒg] Blog *(Internet-Tagebuch)* II
blond [blɒnd] blond V 4 (85)
blood [blʌd] Blut IV
blouse [blaʊz] Bluse V 3 (63)
blue [bluː] blau I
blues [bluːz] Blues IV
blurb [blɜːb] Klappentext *(eines Buches)* V 3 (62)
blush [blʌʃ] erröten, rot werden III
BMX [biː em ˈeks] BMX-Rad I
board [bɔːd]:
   1. einsteigen, an Bord gehen IV
   °2. **board sth. up** etwas mit Brettern vernageln/zunageln
boardwalk [ˈbɔːdwɔːk] Steg, Uferpromenade *(aus Holz)* V 3 (62)
boat [bəʊt] Boot III
body [ˈbɒdi] Körper V 1 (14) **body painting** Körperbemalung V 1 (14)
bodybuilder [ˈbɒdibɪldə] Bodybuilder/in V 1 (20)
boil [bɔɪl] kochen; zum Kochen bringen III
bonfire [ˈbɒnfaɪə] *(großes Freuden-)* Feuer II
book [bʊk]:
   1. Buch I
   2. buchen, reservieren III
°**boomerang** [ˈbuːməræŋ] Bumerang
boot [buːt]:
   1. Stiefel II
   °2. Kofferraum *(Auto)*
booth [buːθ] Nische, (Sitz-)Ecke *(im Restaurant)* IV
bored [bɔːd] gelangweilt III
boring [ˈbɔːrɪŋ] langweilig I

born [bɔːn]: **be born** geboren werden/sein V 1 (10)
borrow [ˈbɒrəʊ] (aus)leihen, sich borgen I
bossy [ˈbɒsi] herrisch; rechthaberisch I
both [bəʊθ] beide III **the best of both worlds** das Beste von beidem III
bottle [ˈbɒtl]: **a bottle of …** eine Flasche … I
bottom [ˈbɒtəm] unteres Ende, Unterteil IV **at the bottom (of)** unten, am unteren Ende (von) II
bought [bɔːt] *siehe* **buy**
bowl (of) [bəʊl] eine Schüssel III
bowling [ˈbəʊlɪŋ] Kegeln, Bowling II
box [bɒks] Kasten, Kiste, Kästchen I
box [bɒks] boxen III
boxer [ˈbɒksə] Boxer/in III
boxing [ˈbɒksɪŋ] Boxen III
boy [bɔɪ] Junge I
boycott [ˈbɔɪkɒt]:
   1. Boykott IV
   2. boykottieren IV
boyfriend [ˈbɔɪfrend] (fester) Freund I
°**bracket** [ˈbrækɪt] Klammer
brain [breɪn] Gehirn V 4 (77) **brains** *(pl)* Verstand, Intelligenz, „Köpfchen" V 4 (77)
brave [breɪv] mutig III
bread [bred] Brot II
break [breɪk] Pause I **at break** in der Pause *(zwischen Schulstunden)* II
break [breɪk], **broke, broken** brechen; zerbrechen; kaputt gehen; kaputt machen IV **break down** eine Panne haben, kaputtgehen *(Auto)* V 1 (12)
breakfast [ˈbrekfəst] Frühstück I **have breakfast** frühstücken I
bridge [brɪdʒ] Brücke II
°**brief** [briːf] kurz (gefasst), knapp **be brief** sich kurzfassen
brilliant [ˈbrɪliənt] super, großartig III
bring [brɪŋ], **brought, brought** bringen, mitbringen I
Britain [ˈbrɪtn] *(kurz für:* **Great Britain***)* Großbritannien I
British [ˈbrɪtɪʃ] britisch I
brochure [ˈbrəʊʃə] Broschüre, Prospekt I
broke [brəʊk] *siehe* **break**
broken [ˈbrəʊkn]:
   1. *siehe* **break**
   2. zerbrochen, gebrochen; kaputt III
brother [ˈbrʌðə] Bruder I
brought [brɔːt] *siehe* **bring**
brown [braʊn] braun I
°**buddy** [ˈbʌdi] Freund/in, Kumpel
budget [ˈbʌdʒɪt]:
   1. Budget, Haushalt V 3 (52)
   2. haushalten *(sparsam sein)* V 3 (52)
budgie [ˈbʌdʒi] Wellensittich II
buffalo, *pl* **buffalo** *or* **buffaloes** [ˈbʌfələʊ] Büffel; Bison IV
°**buffet** [ˈbʊfeɪ] Büfett
build [bɪld], **built, built** bauen IV
°**builder** [ˈbɪldə] Bauunternehmer/in

building [ˈbɪldɪŋ] Gebäude III
°**building work** [ˈbɪldɪŋ wɜːk] Bauarbeiten
built [bɪlt] *siehe* **build**
bully [ˈbʊli]:
   1. Mobber/in, Tyrann/in V 2 (31)
   2. tyrannisieren, mobben V 2 (31)
bump into sb. [bʌmp] mit jm. zusammenstoßen IV
burger [ˈbɜːgə] Hamburger II
burn [bɜːn] (ver)brennen V 1 (10)
°**burst** [bɜːst], **burst, burst** stürmen, platzen
bus [bʌs] Bus I **by bus** mit dem Bus I **go by bus** mit dem Bus fahren I **on the bus** im Bus I
bus stop [ˈbʌs stɒp] Bushaltestelle II
bush [bʊʃ] Busch, Strauch III
business [ˈbɪznəs] Geschäft, Firma III
business studies [ˈbɪznəs stʌdiz] Wirtschaftskunde III
busy [ˈbɪzi]:
   1. belebt; verkehrsreich III
   2. **be busy** beschäftigt sein; viel zu tun haben I
   The kitchen is too busy. In der Küche ist zu viel los. I
busybody [ˈbɪzibɒdi] Wichtigtuer/in V 2 (42)
but [bʌt], [bət] aber I
butter [ˈbʌtə] Butter II
butterfly [ˈbʌtəflaɪ] Schmetterling V 4 (77)
buy [baɪ], **bought, bought** kaufen I
by [baɪ]:
   1. **by bus/bike** mit dem Bus/Rad I **go by bus/bike/car** mit dem Bus/Rad/Auto fahren I
   2. **written by** geschrieben von III
   3. **by saying/asking** indem du sagst/fragst IV
   4. **come by** *(AE)* vorbeikommen, vorbeischauen (besuchen) IV
Bye. [baɪ] Tschüs. I
bystander [ˈbaɪstændə] Zuschauer/in, *(unbeteiligte/r)* Beobachter/in V 2 (31)

C

°**cabin** [ˈkæbɪn] Kabine
cable [ˈkeɪbl] Kabel, Drahtseil IV
cafe [ˈkæfeɪ] Café I
cafeteria [kæfəˈtɪəriə] *(AE)* Kantine, Mensa IV
cage [keɪdʒ] Käfig I
cake [keɪk] Kuchen II
calculator [ˈkælkjuleɪtə] Taschenrechner I
calf, *pl* **calves** [kɑːf], [kɑːvz] Kalb IV
Californian [kælɪˈfɔːniən] kalifornisch IV
call [kɔːl] rufen; anrufen; nennen II **call sb. names** jn. beschimpfen V 2 (35) **call sb. a racist name** jn. mit einem rassistischen Wort beschimpfen V 2 (35) **be called** genannt werden, heißen III

calm [kɑːm] ruhig, still III
calves [kɑːvz] *Mehrzahl von* **calf** IV
came [keɪm] *siehe* **come**
camel ['kæml] Kamel V 1 (11)
camera ['kæmərə] Kamera, Fotoapparat II
camp [kæmp]:
1. campen, zelten IV
2. Lager, Camp II
make camp sein Lager/Zelt aufschlagen V 1 (17)
camp fire ['kæmp faɪə] Lagerfeuer IV
campaign [kæm'peɪn] Kampagne V 2 (35)
camper ['kæmpə] Camper/in IV
campground ['kæmpgraʊnd] *(AE)* Campingplatz IV
campsite ['kæmpsaɪt] *(BE)* Campingplatz IV
can [kæn], [kən] können I **I can't do my homework.** Ich kann meine Hausaufgaben nicht machen. I **I can't …, can I?** Ich kann doch nicht …, nicht wahr? V 4 (87)
can [kæn] Dose V 3 (63)
°**cancer** ['kænsə] Krebs *(Erkrankung)*
candidate ['kændɪdət] Bewerber/in, Kandidat/in V 3 (67)
candle ['kændl] Kerze V 2 (42)
candy ['kændi] *(AE)* Süßigkeiten IV
canteen [kæn'tiːn] Kantine, (Schul-)Mensa I
cap [kæp] Mütze, Kappe III
capital ['kæpɪtl] Hauptstadt III
capital letter ['kæpɪtl] Großbuchstabe II
captain ['kæptɪn] Spielführer/in, Anführer/in; Kapitän/in V 2 (39)
caption ['kæpʃn] Bildunterschrift III
car [kɑː] Auto I **by car** mit dem Auto I **go by car** mit dem Auto fahren I
car park ['kɑː pɑːk] Parkplatz II
card [kɑːd] Karte I
care [keə]:
1. Versorgung, Betreuung V 3 (57)
2. Sorgfalt, Vorsicht V 1 (13)
with care vorsichtig, mit Bedacht V 1 (13)
3. **I don't care.** Ich mach mir nichts draus. / Ist mir egal. III
Who cares? Wen interessiert das? / Was soll's? / Na und? IV
°**career** [kə'rɪə] Karriere; (schulischer/beruflicher) Werdegang
careful ['keəfl] vorsichtig II
carefully ['keəfəli]: **drive carefully** vorsichtig fahren II **listen carefully** aufmerksam/genau zuhören II
°**careless** ['keələs] leichtsinnig, unvorsichtig
carnival ['kɑːnɪvl] Karneval IV
°**carpet** ['kɑːpɪt] Teppich **red carpet event** Promi-Veranstaltung mit rotem Teppich

carrot ['kærət] Karotte, Möhre, Mohrrübe II
cart [kɑːt] Wagen, Karren IV
cartoon [kɑː'tuːn] Cartoon *(Zeichentrickfilm; Bilderwitz)* II
cash desk ['kæʃ desk] Kasse V 3 (58)
casino [kə'siːnəʊ] (Spiel-)Kasino IV
castle ['kɑːsl] Burg, Schloss III
cat [kæt] Katze I
catch [kætʃ], **caught, caught** fangen, erwischen II **catch sth.** sich mit etwas anstecken; sich etwas einfangen *(Krankheit)* V 4 (84)
cattle *(pl)* ['kætl] Vieh, Rinder V 1 (16)
cattle station ['kætl steɪʃn] *(AustE)* Rinderfarm V 1 (16)
caught [kɔːt] *siehe* **catch**
°**caution** ['kɔːʃn] Vorsicht
CCTV camera [siː siː tiː 'viː] Überwachungskamera III
CD [siː 'diː] CD I
CD player [siː 'diː pleɪə] CD-Spieler II
celebrate ['selɪbreɪt] feiern II
celebrity [sə'lebrəti] Prominente/r, Promi V 3 (56)
cell phone ['sel fəʊn] *(AE)* Handy IV
Celsius (C) ['selsɪəs] Celsius IV
cent [sent] Cent III
central ['sentrəl] zentral V 1 (10)
central Sydney Sydney Stadtmitte V 1 (10)
centre ['sentə] Zentrum, Center I
°**century** ['sentʃəri] Jahrhundert
cereals *(pl)* ['sɪərɪəlz] Getreideflocken, Frühstücksflocken II
°**certificate** [sə'tɪfɪkət] Urkunde, Bescheinigung
chain [tʃeɪn] Kette II
chair [tʃeə] Stuhl I
challenge ['tʃælɪndʒ] Herausforderung III
°**challenging** ['tʃælɪndʒɪŋ] anspruchsvoll
chance [tʃɑːns] Gelegenheit, Möglichkeit, Chance IV
change [tʃeɪndʒ]:
1. (ver)ändern; sich (ver)ändern II
2. wechseln II
3. sich umziehen IV
4. Veränderung, Wechsel III
channel ['tʃænl] Kanal II
chant [tʃɑːnt] Sprechgesang I
chaotic [keɪ'ɒtɪk] chaotisch IV
°**chapter** ['tʃæptə] Kapitel
character ['kærəktə] Figur, Person *(in Roman, Film usw.)* III
°**characterization** [kærəktəraɪ'zeɪʃn] Charakterisierung
charge [tʃɑːdʒ] (auf)laden *(Batterie, Handy, …)* III
charity ['tʃærəti] Wohltätigkeit, wohltätige Zwecke; Wohlfahrtsorganisation III **charity shop** Geschäft, das gespendete Waren für wohltätige Zwecke verkauft II
chart [tʃɑːt] Diagramm, Tabelle IV

chase sb./sth. [tʃeɪs] jn./etwas jagen; hinter jm./etwas herrennen III
chat [tʃæt]:
1. Unterhaltung; Chat II
2. **chat (with)** chatten (mit); sich unterhalten (mit) II
chatty ['tʃæti] gesprächig; zum Plaudern aufgelegt III
cheap [tʃiːp] billig, preiswert II
check [tʃek]:
1. (über)prüfen, kontrollieren II **check sth. out** *(infml)* sich etwas anschauen, anhören; etwas ausprobieren IV **check the internet** im Internet nachschauen II
2. Kontrolle, Überprüfung IV
cheek [tʃiːk] Wange IV
cheer [tʃɪə] jubeln, *(Sportler/innen)* anfeuern IV
cheerful ['tʃɪəfl] fröhlich, gut gelaunt V 3 (63)
cheerleader ['tʃɪəliːdə] Cheerleader *(Stimmungsanheizer/in bei Sportereignissen)* IV
cheese [tʃiːz] Käse III
cheeseburger ['tʃiːzbɜːgə] Cheeseburger *(Hamburger mit Käsescheibe)* IV
chicken ['tʃɪkɪn] Huhn; (Brat-)Hähnchen I
°**chief** [tʃiːf] Haupt-; leitende/r
child, *(pl)* **children** [tʃaɪld], [tʃɪldrən] Kind I
childcare ['tʃaɪldkeə] Kinderbetreuung V 3 (57)
chill [tʃɪl] *(infml)* relaxen, sich ausruhen II
chin [tʃɪn] Kinn V 1 (18)
chips *(pl)* [tʃɪps]:
1. *(BE)* Pommes frites I
2. *(AE)* Kartoffelchips IV
chocolate ['tʃɒklət] Schokolade II
chocolate bar [bɑː] Schokoriegel III
°**choice** [tʃɔɪs] (Aus-)Wahl
choose [tʃuːz], **chose, chosen** (sich) aussuchen, (aus)wählen IV
chore [tʃɔː] (Haus-)Arbeit, *(lästige)* Pflicht II **do chores** (Haus-)Arbeiten erledigen II
chose [tʃəʊz] *siehe* **choose**
chosen [tʃəʊzn] *siehe* **choose**
Christmas ['krɪsməs] Weihnachten II
church [tʃɜːtʃ] Kirche III
cigarette [sɪgə'ret] Zigarette V 2 (32)
cinema ['sɪnəmə] Kino I
circle ['sɜːkl] Kreis II
circus ['sɜːkəs] Zirkus II
citizen ['sɪtɪzn] Bürger/in V 1 (10)
city ['sɪti] (Groß-)Stadt I
civil rights *(pl)* [sɪvl 'raɪts] Bürgerrechte IV
class [klɑːs]:
1. (Schul-)Klasse I
2. Unterricht; Kurs II
class teacher ['klɑːs tiːtʃə] Klassenlehrer/in I

DICTIONARY

English – German

classmate [ˈklɑːsmeɪt] Mitschüler/in V 2 (32)
classroom [ˈklɑːsruːm] Klassenzimmer I
clean [kliːn]:
1. sauber IV
2. sauber machen, putzen I
clean sth. up etwas aufräumen, sauber machen IV
cleaner [ˈkliːnə] Reinigungskraft V 3 (56)
clean-up [ˈkliːn ʌp] Reinemachen, Hausputz V 4 (82)
clear [klɪə] klar, deutlich, eindeutig III
clearing [ˈklɪərɪŋ] Lichtung V 1 (19)
clearly [ˈklɪəli]: **speak clearly** deutlich sprechen II
°**clerk** [klɑːk] Angestellte(r)
clever [ˈklevə] schlau, klug II
cleverness [ˈklevənəs] Klugheit V 1 (13)
climate [ˈklaɪmət] Klima V 1 (8)
climb [klaɪm] klettern II
close [kləʊz]:
1. schließen, zumachen I
2. sich schließen III
close sth. down etwas schließen, stilllegen (Fabrik, Geschäft) III
°**close on sb.** jm. näher kommen, zu jm. aufholen
close (to) [kləʊs] nahe (bei, an) IV
closed [kləʊzd]:
1. geschlossen IV
2. gesperrt (Straße) V 1 (16)
clothes (pl) [kləʊðz] Kleidung, Kleidungsstücke II
cloud [klaʊd] Wolke II
cloudy [ˈklaʊdi] wolkig II
club [klʌb] Klub I
coach [kəʊtʃ] Trainer/in II
coast [kəʊst] Küste IV **on the coast** an der Küste IV
coat [kəʊt] Mantel III
cocoa [ˈkəʊkəʊ] Kakao II
coffee [ˈkɒfi] Kaffee I
cola [ˈkəʊlə] Cola II
cold [kəʊld]:
1. kalt II
2. Kälte; Erkältung II
collar [ˈkɒlə] Halsband II
collect [kəˈlekt] sammeln II
college [ˈkɒlɪdʒ] höhere Schule, Fach(hoch)schule V 3 (52)
colour [ˈkʌlə] Farbe I
coloured [ˈkʌləd] farbig II
°**colourful** [ˈkʌləfl] farbenfroh, bunt
°**column** [ˈkɒləm] Spalte
combat [ˈkɒmbæt] Kampf V 4 (84)
°**combine** [kəmˈbaɪn] verbinden, kombinieren
come [kʌm], **came, come** kommen I
come by (AE) vorbeikommen, vorbeischauen (besuchen) IV **come home** nach Hause kommen I **come in** hereinkommen II **Come on, Luca!** Na los, Luca! / Komm, Luca! I
come up auftauchen, herauskommen, aufkommen (Frage) V 4 (78)

comedy [ˈkɒmədi] Comedyshow; Komödie II
comfortable [ˈkʌmftəbl] bequem II
be/feel comfortable (with) sich wohlfühlen (bei/mit) V 2 (32)
comic [ˈkɒmɪk] Comic(heft) II
command [kəˈmɑːnd] Befehl V 2 (40)
comment (on) [ˈkɒment]:
1. Kommentar (zu) III
°2. **comment (on sth.)** (etwas) kommentieren
commercial [kəˈmɜːʃl] kommerziell (auf Gewinn ausgerichtet) IV
common [ˈkɒmən] häufig; weit verbreitet IV °**have sth. in common** etwas gemeinsam haben
communicate (with sb.) [kəˈmjuːnɪkeɪt] (mit jm.) kommunizieren; sich (mit jm.) verständigen IV
communication [kəmjuːnɪˈkeɪʃn] Kommunikation, Verständigung V 3 (56)
community [kəˈmjuːnəti] Gemeinschaft, Gemeinde IV
community service [kəˈmjuːnəti sɜːvɪs] gemeinnützige Arbeit, Sozialdienst IV
company [ˈkʌmpəni] Firma, Gesellschaft IV
compare [kəmˈpeə] vergleichen IV
compare (with/to) vergleichbar sein (mit), sich vergleichen lassen (mit) V 1 (10)
compass [ˈkʌmpəs] Kompass II
competition [kɒmpəˈtɪʃn] Wettbewerb III
complain [kəmˈpleɪn] sich beschweren/beklagen III
°**complete** [kəmˈpliːt] vervollständigen
complicated [ˈkɒmplɪkeɪtɪd] kompliziert V 3 (62)
computer [kəmˈpjuːtə] Computer I
concert [ˈkɒnsət] Konzert I
conclusion [kənˈkluːʒn] Schluss(folgerung) V 4 (79)
°**condition** [kənˈdɪʃn] Leiden, Erkrankung
confident [ˈkɒnfɪdənt] (selbst)sicher; zuversichtlich V 3 (54)
confirm [kənˈfɜːm] bestätigen III
connect [kəˈnekt] verbinden IV
cons [kɒnz]: **the pros and cons** (pl) das Pro und Kontra; das Für und Wider V 4 (76)
contact [ˈkɒntækt]:
1. Kontakt III
2. Kontakt aufnehmen zu, sich melden bei V 3 (67)
context [ˈkɒntekst] (Text-)Zusammenhang IV
continent [ˈkɒntɪnənt] Kontinent V 1 (15)
continue [kənˈtɪnjuː] weitergehen, weitermachen, (sich) fortsetzen V 1 (10)
contract [ˈkɒntrækt] Vertrag IV

°**contrast** [kənˈtrɑːst] vergleichen, (einander) gegenüberstellen
control [kənˈtrəʊl]:
1. kontrollieren, beherrschen V 2 (33)
2. regulieren, bestimmen III
conversation [kɒnvəˈseɪʃn] Gespräch, Unterhaltung V 2 (44)
cook [kʊk]:
1. Koch, Köchin I
2. kochen, (Essen) zubereiten I
cooking [ˈkʊkɪŋ] (das) Kochen, Küche, Essen V 1 (17)
cool [kuːl]:
1. cool I
2. kühl II
cool down [kuːl ˈdaʊn] sich abkühlen; sich beruhigen V 1 (12)
°**coolhunter** [ˈkuːlhʌntə] Trendscout (Person, die Trends aufspürt)
°**cope (with)** [kəʊp] zurechtkommen, fertig werden (mit)
copy [ˈkɒpi]:
1. kopieren, abschreiben V 1 (22)
°2. Kopie; Exemplar
corner [ˈkɔːnə] Ecke; (Mund-, Augen-) Winkel IV
correct [kəˈrekt]:
1. korrekt, richtig IV
2. korrigieren, berichtigen II
cost [kɒst], **cost, cost** kosten III
cost a fortune ein Vermögen kosten IV
costs (pl) [kɒsts] Kosten V 3 (56)
costume [ˈkɒstjuːm] Kostüm, Verkleidung II
cottage [ˈkɒtɪdʒ] Häuschen, Hütte II
cotton [ˈkɒtn] Baumwolle IV
°**couch potato** [ˈkaʊtʃ pəteɪtəʊ] Stubenhocker/in; Faulpelz, der ständig vor dem Bildschirm/Fernseher hängt
could [kʊd]:
1. **they could ...** sie konnten ... II
2. **you could ...** du könntest ... II
°**counter** [ˈkaʊntə] (Verkaufs-)Schalter, Ladentheke
country [ˈkʌntri] Land I **country (music)** Country (amerik. Volksmusik) IV **in the country** auf dem Land I
countryside [ˈkʌntrisaɪd] Landschaft, Umgebung, Natur III
couple [ˈkʌpl]: **a couple (of)** ein paar; ein Paar III
°**courage** [ˈkʌrɪdʒ] Mut, Courage
course [kɔːs] Kurs, Lehrgang III
course [kɔːs]: **of course** natürlich, selbstverständlich II
court [kɔːt] Platz, Court (Tennis, Basketball) IV
cousin [ˈkʌzn] Cousin/e I
cover letter [ˈkʌvə letə] Anschreiben, Begleitschreiben, Motivationsschreiben V 3 (59)
cow [kaʊ] Kuh I
°**cowardly** [ˈkaʊədli] feige
crab [kræb] Krebs (Tier) I

cracker ['krækə] (salziger) Keks IV
°**crash** [kræʃ]:
1. einen Unfall haben
2. krachen; stürzen
crash (into) zusammenstoßen (mit)
crazy ['kreɪzi] verrückt III   **go crazy** verrückt werden III
cream [kriːm] Sahne I
°**create** [kri'eɪt] (er)schaffen, kreieren
creative [kri'eɪtɪv] kreativ V 4 (78)
credit card ['kredɪt kɑːd] Kreditkarte V 3 (63)
creep up (on sb.) [kriːp], **crept, crept** sich heranschleichen (an jn.) V 4 (85)
crept [krept] siehe **creep**
crew [kruː] Mannschaft, Team; Clique V 1 (14)
crime [kraɪm] Kriminalität; Verbrechen IV
crime series, pl crime series ['kraɪm sɪəriːz] Krimiserie II
°**criminal** ['krɪmɪnl] kriminell
°**cripple** ['krɪpl] Krüppel (beleidigend)
crisps (pl) [krɪsps] Kartoffelchips II
critic ['krɪtɪk] Kritiker/in V 4 (79)
criticism ['krɪtɪsɪzəm] Kritik V 3 (54)
crocodile ['krɒkədaɪl] Krokodil I
cross [krɒs]:
1. Kreuz II
2. überqueren II
3. **be cross (with)** böse sein (auf), sauer sein (auf) II
crossroads, pl crossroads ['krɒsrəʊdz] (Straßen-)Kreuzung III
crown [kraʊn] Krone IV
cruise [kruːz]:
1. herumfahren (mit dem Auto, ohne festes Ziel) IV
2. Kreuzfahrt IV
cry [kraɪ] weinen II
cucumber ['kjuːkʌmbə] (Salat-)Gurke III
culture ['kʌltʃə] Kultur III
cup [kʌp]:   **a cup (of)** eine Tasse ... I
°**cupboard** ['kʌbəd] Schrank
cupcake ['kʌpkeɪk] Cupcake (kleiner runder Kuchen) II
curly ['kɜːli] lockig V 3 (63)
curtain ['kɜːtn] Vorhang, Gardine V 2 (41)
cushion ['kʊʃn] Kissen I
customer ['kʌstəmə] Kunde/Kundin III
cut [kʌt], **cut, cut** schneiden II   **cut the grass** Rasen mähen II
cute [kjuːt] niedlich, süß I
CV (= curriculum vitae) [siː 'viː], [kərɪkjələm 'viːtaɪ] Lebenslauf V 3 (56)
cyberbullying [saɪbə'bʊliɪŋ] Cybermobbing V 2 (31)
cycle ['saɪkl] Rad fahren, mit dem Rad fahren III   **cycle tour** Radtour III

D

dad [dad] Papa, Vati I
damage ['dæmɪdʒ] (no pl) Schaden, Schäden V 4 (82)

dance [dɑːns]:
1. Tanz III
2. tanzen I
dancer ['dɑːnsə] Tänzer/in III
danger ['deɪndʒə] Gefahr III
dangerous ['deɪndʒərəs] gefährlich I
dark [dɑːk] dunkel II
darkness ['dɑːknəs] Dunkelheit, Finsternis IV
dart [dɑːt] (Wurf-)Pfeil II
dartboard ['dɑːtbɔːd] Dartscheibe II
date [deɪt]:
1. Datum I
2. Verabredung, Date (auch die Person, mit der man ausgeht) IV
daughter ['dɔːtə] Tochter III
day [deɪ] Tag I   **get/have a day off** einen Tag frei bekommen/haben IV   **I haven't eaten in days** ich habe tagelang nichts gegessen V 4 (85)   **in the old days** früher II   **one day** eines Tages, einmal IV
dead [ded] tot IV   °**The phone went dead.** Die Leitung war tot.
deadly ['dedli] tödlich V 1 (11)
deal [diːl]:   **a good deal** ein guter Deal, ein gutes Geschäft, ein gutes Angebot III   **It's a deal!** Abgemacht! II   **make a deal** ein Geschäft abschließen, vereinbaren II   **no big deal** nichts Besonderes, kein Drama V 2 (31)
deal with sth. [diːl], **dealt, dealt** umgehen mit etwas, mit etwas fertigwerden, klarkommen V 2 (32)
dealt [delt] siehe **deal**
Dear ... [dɪə] Liebe/r ... I   **Dear Sir/Madam** Sehr geehrte Damen und Herren V 3 (59)   **Oh dear.** Oje! II
debate [dɪ'beɪt] debattieren, diskutieren IV
December [dɪ'sembə] Dezember I
decide (to do sth.) [dɪ'saɪd] beschließen, (sich) entscheiden (etwas zu tun) IV
°**decorator** ['dekəreɪtə] Tapezierer/in   **painter and decorator** Maler/in und Tapezierer/in
deep [diːp] tief III
definitely ['defɪnətli] auf jeden Fall; ganz bestimmt III
degree [dɪ'griː]:
1. Grad II
°2. **(university) degree** (Universitäts-)Abschluss
delete [dɪ'liːt] löschen V 2 (30)
den [den] Versteck; Hobbyraum II
department [dɪ'pɑːtmənt] Abteilung III
department store [dɪ'pɑːtmənt stɔː] Kaufhaus III
departure [dɪ'pɑːtʃə] Abflug II
°**depending on** [dɪ'pendɪŋ ɒn] abhängig von, je nach(dem)
depressing [dɪ'presɪŋ] deprimierend V 4 (79)

describe [dɪ'skraɪb] beschreiben I
°**description** [dɪ'skrɪpʃn] Beschreibung
desert ['dezət] Wüste IV
°**desert island** [dezət 'aɪlənd] einsame Insel
design [dɪ'zaɪn] entwerfen, gestalten, entwickeln V 4 (80)
desk [desk] Schreibtisch I   **front desk** Rezeption, Empfang (z.B. Hotel) V 3 (62)
°**desk clerk** ['desk klɑːk] Empfangsmitarbeiter/in
dessert [dɪ'zɜːt] Nachtisch, Dessert II
destroy [dɪ'strɔɪ] zerstören IV
detail ['diːteɪl] Detail, Einzelheit IV
detective [dɪ'tektɪv] Detektiv/in III
dialogue ['daɪəlɒg] Dialog I
diary ['daɪəri] Tagebuch; Kalender I
dictionary ['dɪkʃənri] Wörterbuch, (alphabetisches) Wörterverzeichnis I
did [dɪd] siehe **do**   **Did they go?** Sind sie gegangen? / Gingen sie? II   **I didn't have a ...** ich hatte kein/e ... I
°**didgeridoo** [dɪdʒəri'duː] Didgeridoo
die [daɪ] sterben II
difference ['dɪfrəns] Unterschied I
different ['dɪfrənt] verschieden; anders I   **different from** anders als III   **in a different way** anders; auf andere Art und Weise III
difficult ['dɪfɪkəlt] schwierig, schwer I
°**dig** [dɪg], **dug, dug** graben
digital ['dɪdʒɪtl] digital V 4 (76)
diner ['daɪnə] (AE) (kleines, preiswertes) Restaurant IV
dinner ['dɪnə] Abendessen, Abendbrot I   **have dinner** Abendbrot essen, zu Abend essen I
dinosaur ['daɪnəsɔː] Dinosaurier III
direct [də'rekt] direkt, unmittelbar V 2 (39)
direction [də'rekʃn] Richtung IV   **directions** (pl) Wegbeschreibung(en) II
°**director** [də'rektə] Regisseur/in
°**dirty** ['dɜːti] schmutzig
disability [dɪsə'bɪləti] Behinderung IV
°**disabled** [dɪs'eɪbld] (körper-)behindert
disadvantage [dɪsəd'vɑːntɪdʒ] Nachteil IV
disagree (with sb.) [dɪsə'griː] anderer Meinung sein (als jemand); nicht übereinstimmen (mit jm.) III
disappear [dɪsə'pɪə] verschwinden IV
disappoint sb. [dɪsə'pɔɪnt] jn. enttäuschen IV
disappointed (with sb./sth.) [dɪsə'pɔɪntɪd] enttäuscht (von jm./etwas) II
disaster [dɪ'zɑːstə] Katastrophe, Desaster III
discover [dɪ'skʌvə] entdecken; herausfinden III
discrimination (against) [dɪskrɪmɪ'neɪʃn] Diskriminierung (von) V 2 (35)

241

DICTIONARY

English – German

discuss sth. [dɪˈskʌs] über etwas diskutieren; etwas besprechen IV
discussion [dɪˈskʌʃn] Diskussion I
disease [dɪˈziːz] Krankheit V 1 (15)
dish [dɪʃ] Gericht *(Speise)* III
°**dishonest** [dɪsˈɒnɪst] unehrlich
dishwasher [ˈdɪʃwɒʃə] Geschirrspülmaschine, Geschirrspüler II
dislikes [ˈdɪslaɪks]: **likes and dislikes** *(pl)* Vorlieben und Abneigungen IV
°**display** [dɪˈspleɪ] zeigen, zur Schau stellen
disturb [dɪˈstɜːb] stören III
dive [daɪv]:
1. einen Kopfsprung machen I
2. tauchen II
diver [ˈdaɪvə] Taucher/in III
do [duː]: **did, done** machen, tun I **do a paper round** Zeitungen austragen II **do better** besser abschneiden II **do chores** (Haus-)Arbeiten erledigen II **do sport** Sport treiben I **Don't panic.** Keine Panik. / Immer mit der Ruhe. II **dos and don'ts** *(pl)* was man tun und lassen sollte V 2 (44) **I don't like blue.** Ich mag Blau nicht. / Ich mag kein Blau. I **it does have …** es hat (ja/wohl) doch/tatsächlich … V 3 (64) **she doesn't have a …** sie hat kein/keine/keinen … I **What do you think?** Was meinst du? / Was denkst du? I
doctor [ˈdɒktə] Arzt/Ärztin, Doktor II
°**doctor's office** Arztpraxis; Behandlungszimmer
documentary [dɒkjuˈmentri] Dokumentarfilm II
dog [dɒɡ] Hund I **dogs' home** Hundeheim II
dollar ($) [ˈdɒlə] Dollar III
done [dʌn] *siehe* **do** **Well done.** Gut gemacht! I
donkey [ˈdɒŋki] Esel I
door [dɔː] Tür I
dormitory [ˈdɔːmətri] Schlafsaal III
°**dossier** [ˈdɒsieɪ] Mappe
dot [dɒt] Punkt, Pünktchen V 1 (15) **dot painting** Punktmalerei; Punktgemälde V 1 (15)
°**double** [ˈdʌbl] doppelt, Doppel-
down [daʊn]:
1. nach unten; hinunter, herunter I
2. **down this hill** diesen Hügel hinunter I
3. **write sth. down** (sich) etwas aufschreiben III
downside [ˈdaʊnsaɪd] Kehrseite, Nachteil II
downstairs [daʊnˈsteəz] unten; nach unten I
downtown [daʊnˈtaʊn] *(AE)* (im/ins) Stadtzentrum IV
°**dragon** [ˈdræɡən] Drachen

drama [ˈdrɑːmə]:
1. Drama IV
2. Schauspiel, darstellende Kunst I
°**dramatic** [drəˈmætɪk] dramatisch
drank [dræŋk] *siehe* **drink**
dream [driːm]:
1. Traum I
2. **dream (about, of)** träumen (von) IV
°**dreamy** [ˈdriːmi] traumhaft
dress [dres]:
1. Kleid II
2. Kleidung IV
3. sich anziehen, sich kleiden IV
get dressed sich anziehen IV
drifter [ˈdrɪftə]: **be a drifter** sich treiben lassen *(ziellos vor sich hinleben)* V 4 (77)
drink [drɪŋk]:
1. Getränk I
2. **drink, drank, drunk** trinken I
°**drive** [draɪv] (Auto-)Fahrt
drive [draɪv], **drove, driven**:
1. (mit dem Auto) fahren I **drive carefully** vorsichtig fahren II
2. (an)treiben III
driven [ˈdrɪvn] *siehe* **drive**
driver [ˈdraɪvə] Fahrer/in III
driver's license [ˈdraɪvəs laɪsəns] *(AE)* Führerschein, Fahrerlaubnis IV
driving licence [ˈdraɪvɪŋ laɪsəns] *(BE)* Führerschein, Fahrerlaubnis III
drop [drɒp] fallen; fallen lassen V 4 (85)
drove [drəʊv] *siehe* **drive**
drown [draʊn] ertrinken III
drug [drʌɡ] Droge IV
drums *(pl)* [drʌmz] Schlagzeug; Trommeln I **play the drums** Schlagzeug spielen I
drunk [drʌŋk]:
1. *siehe* **drink**
2. betrunken IV
get drunk sich betrinken IV
dry [draɪ]:
1. trocknen III
2. trocken V 1 (16)
duck [dʌk] Ente I
°**due to** [ˈdjuː tə] aufgrund, wegen
°**dug** [dʌɡ] *siehe* **dig**
dull [dʌl] langweilig, trist, öde IV
dump [dʌmp] abladen *(Müll)* III
during [ˈdjʊərɪŋ] während IV
duty [ˈdjuːti] Pflicht, Aufgabe; Dienst V 3 (57) **on duty** im Dienst V 3 (57)
DVD [diːviːˈdiː] DVD I
DVD player [diːviːˈdiː pleɪə] DVD-Spieler II
dynamic [daɪˈnæmɪk] dynamisch V 3 (58)

E

each [iːtʃ] jede(r, s) (einzelne) II
each other einander; sich (gegenseitig) IV
eagle [ˈiːɡl] Adler IV

ear [ɪə] Ohr II
early [ˈɜːli] früh I
earn [ɜːn] verdienen *(Geld)* V 3 (52)
earth [ɜːθ] Erde II **on earth** auf der Erde II
earthquake [ˈɜːθkweɪk] Erdbeben III
°**ease** [iːz]: **put sb. at ease** jn. beruhigen, jm. die Befangenheit nehmen
east [iːst] Osten, nach Osten II
Easter [ˈiːstə] Ostern IV
eastern [ˈiːstən] östlich, Ost- IV
easy [ˈiːzi] einfach, leicht I **Take it easy!** *(infml)* etwa: Reg dich nicht auf. / Bleib mal locker. III
easy-going [iːzi ˈɡəʊɪŋ] gelassen, locker II
eat [iːt], **ate, eaten** essen; fressen I
eaten [ˈiːtn] *siehe* **eat**
°**ecology** [iˈkɒlədʒi] Ökologie
°**economy** [ɪˈkɒnəmi] (Volks-)Wirtschaft
editor [ˈedɪtə] Herausgeber/in; Redakteur/in IV **letter to the editor** Leserbrief IV
education [edʒuˈkeɪʃn] (Schul-)Bildung V 3 (58)
°**effect** [ɪˈfekt] (Aus-)Wirkung, Einfluss, Effekt
e.g. [iː ˈdʒiː] *(aus dem Lateinischen)* z.B. (zum Beispiel) II
egg [eɡ] Ei III
eight [eɪt] acht I
°**either … or …** [ˈaɪðə] entweder … oder …
electric [ɪˈlektrɪk] elektrisch, Elektro- IV
electronics [ɪlekˈtrɒnɪks] Elektronik II
°**elementary school** [elɪˈmentri skuːl] *(AE)* Grundschule
elephant [ˈelɪfənt] Elefant I
elevator [ˈelɪveɪtə] *(AE)* Fahrstuhl, Aufzug, Lift IV
eleven [ɪˈlevn] elf I
else [els]: **Anything else?** Sonst noch etwas? I **everybody else** alle anderen; jede/r andere II **something else** etwas anderes III **What else …?** Was (sonst) noch …? IV
email [ˈiːmeɪl]:
1. E-Mail I
2. **email sb.** jn. anmailen IV
email sth. etwas mailen IV
embarrassed [ɪmˈbærəst] verlegen II
embarrassing [ɪmˈbærəsɪŋ] peinlich IV
emergency [ɪˈmɜːdʒənsi] Notfall II
emergency services *(pl)* [ɪˈmɜːdʒənsi sɜːvɪsɪz] Rettungsdienste II
employee [ɪmˈplɔɪiː] Arbeitnehmer/in, Angestellte(r) III
°**employer** [ɪmˈplɔɪə] Arbeitgeber/in
empty [ˈempti]:
1. leer II
2. leeren II
°**emu** [ˈiːmjuː] Emu
enclose [ɪnˈkləʊz] beifügen, beilegen *(einem Brief)* V 3 (59)

°encourage [ɪnˈkʌrɪdʒ] ermutigen, ermuntern
end [end]:
1. enden, zu Ende gehen IV
2. Ende, Schluss I
in the end schließlich, zum Schluss II
ending [ˈendɪŋ] Endung; Ende *(eines Texts, einer Geschichte)* V 2 (31)
happy ending Happy End II
enemy [ˈenəmi] Feind/in III
energetic [enəˈdʒetɪk] energisch, energiereich V 3 (54)
°energy [ˈenədʒi] Energie
engine [ˈendʒɪn] Motor V 1 (19)
England [ˈɪŋɡlənd] England I
English [ˈɪŋɡlɪʃ] Englisch; englisch I
enjoy [ɪnˈdʒɔɪ] genießen II Enjoy yourself/yourselves. Viel Vergnügen! / Viel Spaß! III
enjoyable [ɪnˈdʒɔɪəbl] angenehm, unterhaltsam IV
enough [ɪˈnʌf] genug II
enter [ˈentə]:
1. sich anmelden (für), teilnehmen (an) *(Wettbewerb)* V 1 (16)
°2. eintreten in, betreten
enthusiastic [ɪnθjuːziˈæstɪk] begeistert V 3 (54)
°entrepreneur [ɒntrəprəˈnɜː] Unternehmer/in
entry [ˈentri]:
1. Eintrag *(in Wörterbuch/Tagebuch)* V 2 (36)
2. Eintritt, Zutritt III
episode [ˈepɪsəʊd] Episode; Folge III
equal [ˈiːkwəl] gleich(berechtigt) V 2 (36)
equipment [ɪˈkwɪpmənt] Ausrüstung III
eraser [ɪˈreɪzə] *(AE)* Radiergummi IV
escalator [ˈeskəleɪtə] Rolltreppe III
escape [ɪˈskeɪp]:
1. entkommen; fliehen IV
2. Flucht V 4 (86)
especially [ɪˈspeʃəli] besonders; vor allem II
etc. [etˈsetərə] *(aus dem Lateinischen)* usw. (und so weiter) II
euro (€) [ˈjʊərəʊ] Euro III
Europe [ˈjʊərəp] Europa III
European [jʊərəˈpiːən] Europäer/in; europäisch IV
even [ˈiːvn] sogar, selbst III not even (noch) nicht einmal IV
evening [ˈiːvnɪŋ] Abend I in the evening abends, am Abend I on Friday evening freitagabends, am Freitagabend I
event [ɪˈvent] Ereignis, Event IV
fund-raising event Event zur Beschaffung von Geld/Spenden IV
ever [ˈevə] jemals, schon mal III
Have you ever …? Hast du schon mal …? / Hast du jemals …? III
Have you ever been to …? Bist du schon mal in … gewesen? III the

most realistic game ever das realistischste Spiel, das es je gegeben hat V 4 (84)
every day/room/… [ˈevri] jeder Tag/jedes Zimmer/… I
everybody [ˈevribɒdi] jeder; alle I
everybody else alle anderen; jede/r andere II
everyone [ˈevriwʌn] jeder; alle II
everything [ˈevriθɪŋ] alles II
everywhere [ˈevriweə] überall II
exact [ɪɡˈzækt] exakt, genau V 2 (39)
exam [ɪɡˈzæm] Prüfung V 1 (11) final (school) exam (Schul-)Abschlussprüfung V 1 (11) take/do an exam eine Prüfung machen V 1 (11)
example [ɪɡˈzɑːmpl] Beispiel I for example zum Beispiel II
excellent [ˈeksələnt] ausgezeichnet, hervorragend IV
except (for) [ɪkˈsept] außer, bis auf IV
exchange [ɪksˈtʃeɪndʒ] (Schüler-)Austausch V 2 (44)
excited [ɪkˈsaɪtɪd] aufgeregt, gespannt I
excitement [ɪkˈsaɪtmənt] Aufregung, Begeisterung IV
exciting [ɪkˈsaɪtɪŋ] aufregend, spannend II
Excuse me, … [ɪksˈkjuːz miː] Entschuldigung, … / Entschuldigen Sie, … I
exercise [ˈeksəsaɪz] Übung, Aufgabe I
exercise book [ˈeksəsaɪz bʊk] Schulheft, Übungsheft I
expect [ɪkˈspekt] erwarten V 1 (12)
°expedition [ekspəˈdɪʃn] Expedition
expensive [ɪkˈspensɪv] teuer I
experience [ɪkˈspɪəriəns]:
1. erfahren, erleben IV
2. Erfahrung, Erlebnis III
in my experience nach meiner Erfahrung V 2 (33)
experiment [ɪkˈsperɪmənt]:
1. Experiment, Versuch II
2. experimentieren III
expert [ˈekspɜːt] Experte, Expertin V 1 (11)
explain sth. (to sb.) [ɪkˈspleɪn] (jm.) etwas erklären, (jm.) etwas erläutern IV
°explode [ɪkˈspləʊd] explodieren
express [ɪkˈspres] ausdrücken, zum Ausdruck bringen V 4 (88)
°expression [ɪkˈspreʃn] Ausdruck
extra [ˈekstrə]:
1. zusätzlich II
°2. (TV) extra Statist/in, Komparse/-in *(Fernsehen)*
extreme [ɪkˈstriːm] extrem IV
extremely [ɪkˈstriːmli] äußerst, höchst IV
eye [aɪ] Auge II °keep an eye on sb./sth. jn./etwas im Auge behalten, ein (wachsames) Auge haben auf jn./etwas
°eyesight [ˈaɪsaɪt] Sehkraft

F

face [feɪs]:
1. Gesicht I
2. face sth. vor etwas stehen; *(Problem)*; einer Sache ins Auge sehen, sich einer Sache stellen; einer Sache entgegentreten V 2 (36)
fact [fækt] Tatsache, Fakt IV
fair [feə] fair, gerecht I
faithfully [ˈfeɪθfəli]: Yours faithfully Mit freundlichen Grüßen *(Briefschluss)* V 3 (59)
fall [fɔːl] *(AE)* Herbst IV
fall [fɔːl], fell, fallen fallen; hinfallen I fall asleep einschlafen IV fall down hinfallen IV °fall in love (with sb.) sich verlieben (in jn.)
fallen [ˈfɔːlən] *siehe* fall
false [fɔːls] falsch I
°familiar [fəˈmɪliə] vertraut, bekannt
family [ˈfæməli] Familie I family name Familienname, Nachname I family tree (Familien-)Stammbaum I
famous (for) [ˈfeɪməs] berühmt (für, wegen) III
fan [fæn] Fan III
fancy [ˈfænsi] schick IV
fantastic [fænˈtæstɪk] fantastisch, wunderschön V 1 (15)
fantasy [ˈfæntəsi] Fantasy *(Film-, Comic-, Romangattung)* IV
far [fɑː] weit (entfernt) II as far as bis *(räumlich)* V 3 (56) so far bis jetzt V 3 (56)
farm [fɑːm]:
1. Bauernhof, Farm I
2. Landwirtschaft betreiben V 1 (15)
farmer [ˈfɑːmə] Farmer; Bauer, Bäuerin III
°farming [ˈfɑːmɪŋ] *(die)* Landwirtschaft
farmyard [ˈfɑːmjɑːd] Hof *(eines Bauernhauses)* III
°fascinate [ˈfæsɪneɪt] faszinieren fascinating faszinierend
fashion [ˈfæʃn] Mode III
fast [fɑːst] schnell I
fast-food restaurant [fɑːst fuːd ˈrestrɒnt] Schnellimbiss V 3 (67)
father [ˈfɑːðə] Vater I
fault [fɔːlt] Fehler, Schuld V 4 (82)
favourite [ˈfeɪvrɪt] Lieblings- favourite colour Lieblingsfarbe I
feather [ˈfeðə] Feder IV
February [ˈfebruəri] Februar I
fed [fed] *siehe* feed
fed up [fed ˈʌp]: feel fed up genervt sein, sauer sein; die Nase voll haben I
feed [fiːd], fed, fed füttern I
feedback [ˈfiːdbæk] Feedback *(Rückmeldung)* V 1 (22)
feel [fiːl], felt, felt sich fühlen; fühlen I feel fed up genervt sein, sauer sein; die Nase voll haben I I don't feel like it. Mir ist nicht danach. II

243

DICTIONARY

English – German

I'm not feeling well. Ich fühle mich nicht gut. II
feeling [ˈfiːlɪŋ] Gefühl I
feet [fiːt] *Mehrzahl von* **foot** IV
fell [fel] *siehe* **fall**
°**fellow student** [ˈfeləʊ] Mitschüler/in
felt [felt] *siehe* **feel**
female [ˈfiːmeɪl] weiblich III
fence [fens] Zaun III
ferry [ˈferi] Fähre II
festival [ˈfestɪvl] Festival, Fest II
few [fjuː]: **a few** ein paar, einige II
field [fiːld] Feld; Weide I **in the field** auf der Weide I
fight [faɪt]:
 1. **Kampf** IV
 2. **fight, fought, fought** kämpfen III; (sich) streiten IV **fight sb.** jn. bekämpfen, gegen jn. kämpfen IV
fighter [ˈfaɪtə] Kämpfer/in V 4 (84)
figure [ˈfɪɡə] Zahl, Ziffer; Person (*Gestalt*); Figur V 1 (16)
°**file** [faɪl] Datei; Ordner, Liste
fill [fɪl] füllen II **fill up** sich füllen IV
°**fill in** ausfüllen, einsetzen
film [fɪlm]:
 1. Film I
 2. filmen II
film set [ˈfɪlm set] Filmset; Filmkulisse IV
film star [ˈfɪlm stɑː] Filmstar III
final [ˈfaɪnl] letzte(r, s) V 1 (11)
finally [ˈfaɪnəli] schließlich; abschließend III
°**finances** (*pl*) [ˈfaɪnænsɪz] Finanzen
°**financial** [faɪˈnænʃl] finanziell
find [faɪnd], **found, found** finden I
 find out about sth. sich über etwas informieren II **find sth. out** etwas herausfinden II
finder [ˈfaɪndə] Finder/in V 4 (85)
 Finders keepers, losers weepers. Was man findet, darf man behalten. (*Redensart*) V 4 (85)
fine [faɪn] gut; in Ordnung I **I'm fine, thanks.** Danke, (es geht mir) gut. I
fine [faɪn]:
 1. Geldstrafe III
 2. **fine sb.** jn. zu einer Geldstrafe verurteilen IV
finger [ˈfɪŋɡə] Finger III
fingernail [ˈfɪŋɡəneɪl] Fingernagel V 1 (20)
finish [ˈfɪnɪʃ] beenden, zu Ende machen II
fire [ˈfaɪə]:
 1. Feuer II
 2. **fire sb.** jn. feuern, entlassen V 3 (63) **you'll get me fired** du schaffst es noch, dass ich entlassen werde V 3 (63)
fire escape [ˈfaɪər ɪskeɪp] Feuertreppe, Notausgang V 4 (86) **fire escape ladder** Feuerleiter V 4 (86)
fire station [ˈfaɪə steɪʃn] Feuerwache I

°**firefighter** [ˈfaɪəfaɪtə] Feuerwehrmann, Feuerwehrfrau
firework [ˈfaɪəwɜːk] Feuerwerkskörper II **fireworks** (*pl*) Feuerwerk II
first [fɜːst]:
 1. erste(r, s) I
 2. zuerst, als Erstes I
 at first zuerst, am Anfang II
first-aid kit [fɜːst ˈeɪd kɪt] Erste-Hilfe-Kasten II
Firstly, ... [ˈfɜːstli] Erstens ... III
fish, *pl* **fish** [fɪʃ] Fisch I
fishing [ˈfɪʃɪŋ] Fischen, Angeln III
fist [fɪst] Faust II
fit [fɪt] fit II
fit in [fɪt ˈɪn] dazugehören; hineinpassen V 2 (32)
fitness [ˈfɪtnəs] Fitness V 1 (13)
fitting room [ˈfɪtɪŋ ruːm] Anprobe, Umkleide(kabine) V 3 (58)
five [faɪv] fünf I
fix sth. [fɪks] (*infml*) etwas in Ordnung bringen IV
flag [flæɡ] Flagge, Fahne II
°**flash** [flæʃ]:
 1. (*das*) (Auf-)Blitzen
 2. **flash a torch** mit einer Taschenlampe leuchten/blinken
flashlight [ˈflæʃlaɪt] (*AE*) Taschenlampe IV
flat [flæt]:
 1. Wohnung I
 2. flach, eben V 1 (10)
°**flatmate** [ˈflætmeɪt] Mitbewohner/in
flew [fluː] *siehe* **fly**
flexible [ˈfleksəbl] flexibel V 3 (58)
flight [flaɪt] Flug III
flood [flʌd] überfluten, überschwemmen IV
°**flooding** [ˈflʌdɪŋ] Flut, Überschwemmung, Hochwasser
floor [flɔː]:
 1. Fußboden IV
 2. Stock(werk) IV
flour [ˈflaʊə] Mehl III
flow [fləʊ] fließen IV
flower [ˈflaʊə] Blume; Blüte II
flown [fləʊn] *siehe* **fly**
flute [fluːt] Querflöte IV
fly [flaɪ], **flew, flown**:
 1. fliegen III
°2. rasen (*z.B. Auto*)
°**focus** [ˈfəʊkəs] Schwerpunkt
focus (on) [ˈfəʊkəs] sich konzentrieren (auf) V 4 (77)
fog [fɒɡ] Nebel II
foggy [ˈfɒɡi] neblig II
follow [ˈfɒləʊ] folgen; verfolgen III
follower [ˈfɒləʊə] Anhänger/in, Fan V 4 (80)
°**follow-up** [ˈfɒləʊ ʌp] Anschluss-, Folge-
food [fuːd] Essen; Lebensmittel; Futter I
fool [fuːl] Dummkopf, Narr/Närrin IV
°**foolish** [ˈfuːlɪʃ] töricht, dumm

foot, *pl* **feet** [fʊt], [fiːt] Fuß IV °**put your foot down** Gas geben (*Auto*)
football [ˈfʊtbɔːl] Fußball I
footballer [ˈfʊtbɔːlə] Fußballspieler/in III
for [fɔː], [fə] für I **for a few minutes** ein paar Minuten (lang) II **for example** zum Beispiel II **for lots of reasons** aus vielen Gründen III **for myself** für mich selbst I **for the last time** zum letzten Mal II **for two months / a week** seit zwei Monaten / einer Woche III **What do you need money for?** Wofür brauchst du Geld? II **What's for homework?** Was haben wir als Hausaufgabe auf? I
force sb. to do sth. [fɔːs] jn. zwingen, etwas zu tun IV
forecast [ˈfɔːkɑːst] (*kurz für:* **weather forecast**) Wettervorhersage II
foreground [ˈfɔːɡraʊnd] Vordergrund III
°**forever** [fərˈevə] für immer, ewig (lange)
forget [fəˈɡet], **forgot, forgotten** vergessen II **forget about sth.** etwas vergessen, nicht mehr an etwas denken II
forgot [fəˈɡɒt] *siehe* **forget**
forgotten [fəˈɡɒtn] *siehe* **forget**
form [fɔːm]:
 1. Form I
 2. Formular V 3 (62)
fortune [ˈfɔːtʃuːn] Vermögen IV **cost a fortune** ein Vermögen kosten IV
forward [ˈfɔːwəd] vorwärts, nach vorn II **look forward to doing sth.** sich darauf freuen, etwas zu tun IV **look forward to sth.** sich auf etwas freuen II
fought [fɔːt] *siehe* **fight**
found [faʊnd] *siehe* **find**
°**founder** [ˈfaʊndə] Gründer/in
four [fɔː] vier I
fox [fɒks] Fuchs II
freak [friːk] Freak; Fan II
°**freak out** [friːk ˈaʊt] (*infml*) ausflippen
free [friː]:
 1. frei I
 2. kostenlos II
 free-time activities Freizeitaktivitäten II
freedom [ˈfriːdəm] Freiheit IV
°**freeze** [friːz], **froze, frozen** (ge)frieren; erstarren
freezing [ˈfriːzɪŋ] eisig, eiskalt II
French [frentʃ] Französisch; französisch I
French fries (*pl*) [frentʃ ˈfraɪz] (*AE*) Pommes frites IV
fresh [freʃ] frisch II
Friday [ˈfraɪdeɪ], [ˈfraɪdi] Freitag I
fridge [frɪdʒ] Kühlschrank IV
fried [fraɪd] gebraten III
friend [frend] Freund/in I **be (good) friends with sb.** mit jm. (gut) be-

244

freundet sein V 3 (60) make friends Freunde finden II °a friend of Cindy's / of hers / of mine ein/e Freund/in von Cindy / von ihr / von mir
friendliness ['frendlinəs] Freundlichkeit V 1 (13)
friendly ['frendli] freundlich I
friendship ['frendʃɪp] Freundschaft IV
fries [fraɪz]: French fries (pl) (AE) Pommes frites IV
°frighten sb. ['fraɪtn] jm. Angst machen
°frightened ['fraɪtnd] verängstigt be frightened of sth. Angst haben vor etwas
°frightening ['fraɪtnɪŋ] beängstigend
frisbee ['frɪzbi] Frisbee(scheibe) II
from [frɒm], [frəm] aus; von I from Monday to Friday von Montag bis Freitag I a text from mum eine SMS von Mama I I'm from Plymouth. Ich bin aus Plymouth. / Ich komme aus Plymouth. I
front [frʌnt] Vorderseite; Fassade; Front IV front wall vordere Wand IV at the front vorn, im vorderen Teil IV in front of vor I
front desk [frʌnt 'desk] Rezeption, Empfang (z.B. Hotel) V 3 (62)
°front desk clerk [frʌnt 'desk klɑːk] Empfangsmitarbeiter/in
°froze [frəʊz] siehe freeze
°frozen ['frəʊzn] siehe freeze
fruit [fruːt] Obst I
fruit tea ['fruːt tiː] Früchtetee II
frustrate [frʌ'streɪt] frustrieren V 2 (35)
frustrating [frʌ'streɪtɪŋ] frustrierend V 2 (35)
fuel ['fjuːəl] Treibstoff, Kraftstoff V 1 (20)
full (of) [fʊl] voll (mit, von) III
full-time job [fʊl taɪm 'dʒɒb] Ganztagsjob, Vollzeitjob IV
fun [fʌn] Spaß I fun run Volkslauf III it's fun es macht Spaß I
fund-raising event ['fʌndreɪzɪŋ ɪvent] Event zur Beschaffung von Geld/Spenden IV
funny ['fʌni] witzig, komisch II
furry ['fɜːri] flauschig; pelzig I
future ['fjuːtʃə] Zukunft II

G

°gadget ['gædʒɪt] Gerät, technischer Krimskrams
°Gaelic ['geɪlɪk] gälisch
°gallery ['gæləri] Galerie
game [geɪm] Spiel II
gamer ['geɪmə] Gamer/in (Computerspieler/in) V 4 (77)
gaming ['geɪmɪŋ] (das) Spielen am Computer V 4 (87)
gang [gæŋ] Gang (Bande) V 4 (86)
°gap [gæp] Lücke

garage ['gærɑːʒ]:
1. Garage I
2. (Auto-)Werkstatt II
garbage ['gɑːbɪdʒ] (AE) (Haus-)Müll, Abfall IV
garden ['gɑːdn] Garten I
°gardening ['gɑːdnɪŋ] Gartenarbeit, Gärtnern
gas [gæs] (AE) Benzin IV
gate [geɪt]:
1. Flugsteig III
2. Tor, Gatter III
gatecrash (a party) ['geɪtkræʃ] (bei einer Party) ungebeten erscheinen V 4 (82)
gatecrasher ['geɪtkræʃə] nicht eingeladene Person (die eine Party sprengt) V 4 (82)
°gather ['gæðə] sammeln
gave [geɪv] siehe give
gear [gɪə] Ausrüstung II
general ['dʒenrəl] allgemein V 1 (17)
generation [dʒenə'reɪʃn] Generation V 4 (74)
geography [dʒi'ɒgrəfi] Geografie, Erdkunde I
German ['dʒɜːmən] Deutsch; deutsch I
Germany ['dʒɜːməni] Deutschland I
get [get], got, got:
1. bekommen I
2. holen, besorgen II
3. get (to) gelangen, (hin)kommen II
4. werden II
get around sich fortbewegen (mobil sein) IV get dressed sich anziehen IV get drunk sich betrinken IV get lost sich verirren, sich verlaufen IV get married heiraten IV get off a plane/bus/train aus einem Flugzeug/Bus/Zug aussteigen III get on (well/badly) together (gut/schlecht) miteinander auskommen, zurechtkommen IV get on a plane/bus/train in ein Flugzeug/einen Bus/einen Zug einsteigen III get out of (a car) (aus einem Auto) aussteigen IV get out (of) herauskommen (aus) III get ready (for) sich fertig machen (für), sich vorbereiten (auf) I get rid of sth. etwas loswerden II get started anfangen III get to do sth. etwas tun können/dürfen; die Möglichkeit haben/bekommen, etwas zutun IV get to know sb./each other jn./sich kennenlernen IV get up aufstehen II get used to sth. sich an etwas gewöhnen IV Do you get it? (infml) Verstehst du? / Kapierst du? III °You got it. (infml) Genau! / Du hast es!
ghost [gəʊst] Gespenst, Geist III
giant ['dʒaɪənt] Riese/Riesin IV
girl [gɜːl] Mädchen I
girlfriend ['gɜːlfrend] (feste) Freundin I

gist [dʒɪst]: the gist (no pl) das Wesentliche; die Kernaussage(n) IV
give [gɪv], gave, given geben II give a talk einen Vortrag halten II give up aufgeben, aufhören IV
given ['gɪvn] siehe give
glamorous ['glæmərəs] glamourös V 1 (20)
glass (of) [glɑːs] Glas III
glasses (pl) ['glɑːsɪz] (eine) Brille II
glove [glʌv] Handschuh II a pair of gloves ein Paar Handschuhe II
go [gəʊ], went, gone gehen; fahren I go away verschwinden V 2 (31) go by bus/bike/car/... mit dem Bus/Rad/Auto/... fahren I go crazy verrückt werden III go for a walk einen Spaziergang machen, spazieren gehen II Go for it, Luca! Nichts wie ran, Luca! II go home nach Hause gehen I go off losgehen (Wecker, Alarm, …) IV go on weiterreden, fortfahren; weitermachen III go out rausgehen, weggehen, ausgehen II go shopping einkaufen gehen I go swimming schwimmen gehen I go to bed ins Bett gehen I go to school zur Schule gehen I Go to sleep! Schlaf jetzt! I go to work zur Arbeit gehen I go with gehören zu, passen zu I go wrong schiefgehen III How's it going? Wie geht's? / Wie läuft's? I I must go. (am Telefon) Ich muss Schluss machen. I I'm going to do some chores. Ich werde ein paar Hausarbeiten erledigen. II What's going on? Was ist los? / Was gibt's? IV °go (a)round to ... zu ... gehen °go by (Zeit) vergehen °Go on. Na los, mach(t) schon!
°goal [gəʊl] Tor (Sport)
goat [gəʊt] Ziege V 1 (20)
God [gɒd] Gott III
gold [gəʊld] Gold IV
gone [gɒn] siehe go be gone weg sein, nicht (mehr) da sein IV
good [gʊd] gut I Good boy. / Good dog. Braver Junge. / Braver Hund. II Good luck. Viel Glück. IV Good morning. Guten Morgen. I be good at sth. etwas gut können; gut in etwas sein II be good with sth. gut mit etwas umgehen können III be no good at sth. etwas nicht gut können; nicht gut in etwas sein II
Goodbye. [gʊd'baɪ] Auf Wiedersehen! I
good-looking [gʊd 'lʊkɪŋ] gut aussehend IV
got [gɒt] siehe get
government ['gʌvənmənt] Regierung; Regierungs- IV
gown [gaʊn] Robe IV
grade [greɪd] (AE) Klassenstufe, Jahrgang IV

°grader ['greɪdə]: **tenth grader** Zehntklässler/in
graduation [grædʒu'eɪʃn] (Schul-, Universitäts-)Abschluss; Abschlussfeier IV
graffiti [grə'fiːti] Graffiti IV
grandad ['grændæd] Opa III
granddaughter ['grændɔːtə] Enkelin V 1 (18)
grandfather ['grænfɑːðə] Großvater I
grandma ['grænmɑː] Oma I
grandmother ['grænmʌðə] Großmutter I
grandpa ['grænpɑː] Opa I
grandparents ['grænpeərənts] Großeltern I
grandson ['grænsʌn] Enkel V 1 (18)
grass [grɑːs] Gras; Rasen **cut the grass** Rasen mähen II
°graveyard ['greɪvjɑːd] Friedhof
°graveyard shift ['greɪvjɑːd ʃɪft] Nachtschicht
great [greɪt] großartig, prima I
Great Britain [greɪt 'brɪtn] Großbritannien II
green [griːn] grün I
greet [griːt] begrüßen V 3 (67)
grew [gruː] siehe **grow**
grey [greɪ] grau I
grin (at sb.) [grɪn] (jn. an)grinsen V 4 (86)
groceries (pl) ['grəʊsəriz] Lebensmittel IV
grocery store ['grəʊsəri stɔː] Lebensmittelgeschäft IV
ground [graʊnd] (Erd-)Boden II
group [gruːp]:
1. Gruppe I
2. gruppieren IV
grow [grəʊ], **grew, grown**:
1. wachsen II
2. anbauen, anpflanzen IV
3. (allmählich) werden IV
grow up aufwachsen; erwachsen werden IV
°growl [graʊl] knurren
grown [grəʊn] siehe **grow**
guess [ges]:
1. raten, erraten I
2. Vermutung IV
Guess what – … Stell dir vor – … III
I guess … Ich nehme an, … / Ich glaube, … IV
guest [gest] Gast III
guide [gaɪd]:
1. Reiseführer (Buch) IV
2. Reiseleiter/in, Fremdenführer/in IV
3. Ratgeber, Einführung IV
guitar [gɪ'tɑː] Gitarre I **play the guitar** Gitarre spielen I
guy [gaɪ] (infml): **guy** Typ, Kerl II
guys (pl) Leute (als Anrede verwendet) I
gym [dʒɪm] Sporthalle, Turnhalle II
gymnastics [dʒɪm'næstɪks] Gymnastik II

H

habit ['hæbɪt] (An-)Gewohnheit V 4 (77)
had [hæd] siehe **have**
hair [heə] Haar, Haare II
hairdresser ['heədresə] Friseur/in II
at the hairdresser's beim Friseur II
hairdryer ['heədraɪə] Föhn, Haartrockner II
half [hɑːf]: **half an hour** eine halbe Stunde II
half, pl **halves** [hɑːf], [hɑːvz] Hälfte V 3 (63) **sixteen and a half** sechzehneinhalb V 3 (63)
hall [hɔːl]:
1. Flur, Diele I
2. Halle II
hallway ['hɔːlweɪ] (AE) Korridor, Gang IV
hammer ['hæmə]:
1. Hammer V 2 (42)
2. hämmern V 2 (42)
hamster ['hæmstə] Hamster I
hand [hænd]:
1. Hand II
on the one hand einerseits III **on the other hand** andererseits III **put up one's hand** sich melden; seine/die Hand heben V 3 (62) °**back of the hand** Handrücken °**know sth. like the back of one's hand** etwas wie seine Westentasche kennen; etwas in- und auswendig kennen
°2. **hand sb. sth.** jm. etwas (an)reichen, aushändigen
°**hand-pass the ball** ['hænd pɑːs] den Ball (mit der Hand) zupassen, zuspielen
handshake ['hændʃeɪk] Händedruck, Handschlag IV
hang [hæŋ], **hung, hung** hängen IV
happen ['hæpən] geschehen, passieren I
happiness ['hæpɪnəs] Glück V 1 (13)
happy ['hæpi] glücklich, froh I
Happy birthday! Herzlichen Glückwunsch zum Geburtstag! I **happy ending** Happy End II °**be happy to do sth.** gerne etwas tun
harbour ['hɑːbə] Hafen I
hard [hɑːd] schwer, schwierig; hart I
Hard luck! Pech (gehabt)! III **rain hard** stark regnen V 1 (17) **try hard** sich sehr bemühen, sich anstrengen IV **work hard** hart arbeiten I
°hardship ['hɑːdʃɪp] Not, Mühsal, harte Umstände
hard-working ['hɑːd 'wɜːkɪŋ] fleißig III
has [hæz], [həz]: **he/she/it has …** er/sie/es hat … I
hat [hæt] Hut II
hate [heɪt] hassen, gar nicht mögen I
have [hæv], **had, had** haben I **Have a good day.** Ich wünsch dir einen schönen Tag. / Schönen Tag noch. I
have a party eine Party feiern I
have breakfast frühstücken I **have dinner** Abendbrot essen, zu Abend essen I **have lunch** (zu) Mittag essen I **have to do sth.** etwas tun müssen II **I have a sore leg.** Mein Bein tut weh. I **I'll have …** Ich nehme … (beim Essen, im Restaurant) II **Let's have a look.** Lass uns nachsehen. III
he [hiː] er I
head [hed]:
1. Kopf I
°2. Leiter/in, Chef/in
3. **head for sth.** auf etwas zugehen/zusteuern IV °**head west** Richtung Westen gehen/fahren
headache ['hedeɪk] Kopfschmerzen II
heading ['hedɪŋ] Überschrift III
headline ['hedlaɪn] Schlagzeile IV
health [helθ] Gesundheit V 1 (15)
health care ['helθ keə] Gesundheitsversorgung V 3 (57)
healthy ['helθi] gesund II
hear [hɪə], **heard, heard** hören II
heard [hɜːd] siehe **hear**
heart [hɑːt] Herz III
heat [hiːt] Hitze, Wärme V 1 (12)
heat stress ['hiːt stres] Hitzestress, Wärmebelastung des Körpers V 1 (12)
heavy ['hevi] schwer III
°heavyweight ['heviweɪt] Schwergewicht; Schwergewichts-
°heel [hiːl] Absatz (Schuh)
°height [haɪt] Höhe, Größe (bei Menschen) **have a (good) head for heights** schwindelfrei sein
held [held] siehe **hold**
helicopter ['helɪkɒptə] Helikopter, Hubschrauber IV
Hello. [hə'ləʊ] Hallo. / Guten Tag. I
helmet ['helmɪt] Helm I
help [help]:
1. helfen I
2. Hilfe I
Help yourselves. Bedient euch! / Greift zu! II
helper ['helpə] Helfer/in II
helpful ['helpfl] hilfsbereit; hilfreich, nützlich IV
her [hɜː], [hə]:
1. sie; ihr I
2. **her dad** ihr Vater I
°herd [hɜːd] Herde
here [hɪə] hier; hierher I **Here you are.** Bitte schön. / Hier, bitte. I
near here hier in der Nähe II
hero, pl **heroes** ['hɪərəʊ] Held/in III
hers [hɜːz] ihre/r, ihrs (zu „she") V 1 (19)
herself [hɜː'self] sich III
Hi. [haɪ] Hallo. I **Say hi to everybody.** Grüß alle. I
hid [hɪd] siehe **hide**
hidden ['hɪdn] siehe **hide**
hide [haɪd], **hid, hidden** verstecken; sich verstecken I
high [haɪ] hoch III

high street [ˈhaɪ striːt] Hauptstraße *(mit vielen Geschäften)* III
Highlands [ˈhaɪləndz]: **the Highlands** *(pl)* das schottische Hochland III
highlight [ˈhaɪlaɪt] Höhepunkt IV
highway [ˈhaɪweɪ] Fernstraße *(in den USA; oft mit vier oder mehr Spuren)* IV
hike [haɪk] wandern IV
hiking [ˈhaɪkɪŋ] Wandern IV
hill [hɪl] Hügel I
hilly [ˈhɪli] hügelig III
him [hɪm] ihn; ihm I
himself [hɪmˈself] sich III
hip hop [ˈhɪp hɒp] Hip Hop II
hire [ˈhaɪə] mieten, leihen III
his [hɪz]:
 1. sein/e I
 2. seiner, seine, seins *(zu „he")* V 1 (19)
history [ˈhɪstri] Geschichte I
hit [hɪt], **hit, hit**:
 1. schlagen IV
 2. treffen II
 3. prallen/stoßen gegen/auf IV
hitchhiker [ˈhɪtʃhaɪkə] Anhalter/in, Tramper/in V 1 (20)
hobby [ˈhɒbi] Hobby I
hockey [ˈhɒki] Hockey III
hold [həʊld], **held, held** halten IV
hole [həʊl] Loch III
hole punch [ˈhəʊl pʌntʃ] Locher I
holiday(s) [ˈhɒlədeɪ] Ferien; Urlaub I **be/go on holiday** in Urlaub sein/fahren III
home [həʊm] Heim, Zuhause I **at home** daheim, zu Hause I **come/go home** nach Hause kommen/gehen I **dogs' home** Hundeheim II
homeless [ˈhəʊmləs] obdachlos IV
homesick [ˈhəʊmsɪk]: **be/feel homesick** Heimweh haben II
hometown [ˈhəʊmtaʊn] Heimatstadt IV
homework [ˈhəʊmwɜːk] Hausaufgabe(n) I **I forgot my homework.** Ich habe meine Hausaufgaben vergessen. I **What's for homework?** Was haben wir als Hausaufgabe auf? I
honest [ˈɒnɪst] ehrlich IV
hood [hʊd] Kapuze III
hood *(AE, infml)* [hʊd] *kurz für* **neighbo(u)rhood** IV
°**hooded** [ˈhʊdɪd]: **a hooded figure** eine Person/Gestalt mit Kapuze
hoodie [ˈhʊdi] Kapuzenpullover, -jacke I
hoover [ˈhuːvə] staubsaugen II
hope [həʊp]:
 1. hoffen I
 2. Hoffnung IV
°**hopeful** [ˈhəʊpfl] hoffnungsvoll
horrible [ˈhɒrəbl] scheußlich, ätzend, gemein V 2 (31)
horror [ˈhɒrə] Horror IV
horse [hɔːs] Pferd V 1 (16)
hospital [ˈhɒspɪtl] Krankenhaus I

hostel [ˈhɒstl] Herberge, Hostel III
hot [hɒt] heiß II
hot dog [ˈhɒt dɒg] Hotdog IV
hot spot [ˈhɒt spɒt] Anziehungspunkt V 1 (11) **tourist hot spot** touristischer Anziehungspunkt V 1 (11)
hotel [həʊˈtel] Hotel III
hour [ˈaʊə] Stunde II **(working) hours** *(pl)* Arbeitszeit(en) V 3 (56) **half an hour** eine halbe Stunde II
house [haʊs] Haus II
how? [haʊ] wie? I **How are you?** Wie geht's? / Wie geht es dir/euch? I **How many ...?** Wie viele ...? II **How much ...?** Wie viel ...? II **How much are ...?** Was (Wie viel) kosten ...? I **How much is ...?** Was (Wie viel) kostet ...? I **how to do sth.** wie man etwas tut / tun kann / tun soll III **How's it going?** Wie geht's? / Wie läuft's? I
however [haʊˈevə] allerdings; jedoch IV
huge [hjuːdʒ] riesig III
hundred [ˈhʌndrəd] **a hundred, one hundred** (ein)hundert I
hung [hʌŋ] *siehe* **hang**
hungry [ˈhʌŋgri] **be hungry** hungrig sein, Hunger haben I
hunt [hʌnt] jagen IV
hurricane [ˈhʌrɪkən] Hurrikan, Orkan IV
hurry [ˈhʌri]:
 1. **Hurry up.** Beeil dich. IV
 2. **be in a hurry** in Eile sein, es eilig haben II
hurt [hɜːt], **hurt, hurt** verletzen; wehtun II **be hurt** verletzt sein II **get hurt** sich verletzen II
husband [ˈhʌzbənd] Ehemann IV

I

I [aɪ] ich I **I'm ... (= I am)** ich bin ... I
ice [aɪs] Eis III
ice cream [aɪs ˈkriːm] (Speise-)Eis II
ice hockey [ˈaɪs hɒki] Eishockey II
ice rink [ˈaɪs rɪŋk] Schlittschuhbahn, Eisbahn IV
ice skating [ˈaɪs skeɪtɪŋ] Schlittschuhlaufen II
ICT (Information and Communication technology) [aɪ siː ˈtiː], [ˌɪnfəmeɪʃn ənd kəmjuːnɪˈkeɪʃn ˈteknəlɒdʒi] Informations- und Kommunikationstechnologie I
idea [aɪˈdɪə] Idee I
ideal [aɪˈdɪəl] ideal III
°**identify** [aɪˈdentɪfaɪ] erkennen, identifizieren **identify with** sich identifizieren mit
identity [aɪˈdentəti] Identität V 3 (55)
°**idiom** [ˈɪdiəm] Redewendung
idiot [ˈɪdiət] Idiot/in V 4 (85)
if [ɪf]:
 1. ob II
 2. wenn, falls II

ignorance [ˈɪgnərəns] Ignoranz, Unwissenheit V 2 (36)
ignore [ɪgˈnɔː] nicht beachten, ignorieren IV
ill [ɪl] krank II
illegal [ɪˈliːgl] illegal III
illness [ˈɪlnəs] Krankheit V 1 (13)
image [ˈɪmɪdʒ] Bild, Abbild; Vorstellung; Image IV
°**imagination** [ɪˌmædʒɪˈneɪʃn] Fantasie, Vorstellungskraft
imaginative [ɪˈmædʒɪnətɪv] einfallsreich, kreativ V 4 (78)
imagine sth. [ɪˈmædʒɪn] sich etwas vorstellen III
°**immediately** [ɪˈmiːdiətli] sofort
immigrant [ˈɪmɪgrənt] Einwanderer/Einwanderin IV
immigration [ˌɪmɪˈgreɪʃn] Einwanderung, Zuwanderung IV
impatient [ɪmˈpeɪʃnt] ungeduldig III
°**import** [ɪmˈpɔːt] importieren
important [ɪmˈpɔːtnt] wichtig I
°**impress** [ɪmˈpres] beeindrucken
impressed [ɪmˈprest] beeindruckt III
°**impression** [ɪmˈpreʃn] Eindruck
improve [ɪmˈpruːv] verbessern IV
in [ɪn] in I **in a different way** anders; auf andere Art und Weise III **in all** insgesamt III **in England** in England I **in English** auf Englisch I **in front of** vor I **in my opinion** meiner Meinung nach II **in other words** mit anderen Worten V 4 (79) **in the 1990s** in den 90er-Jahren (des 20. Jahrhunderts) III **in the afternoon** nachmittags, am Nachmittag I **in the country** auf dem Land I **in the end** schließlich, zum Schluss II **in the evening** abends, am Abend I **in the field** auf dem Feld I **in the middle** in der Mitte I **in the morning** am Morgen, morgens I **in the old days** früher II **in the photo** auf dem Foto I **in the picture** auf dem Bild I **in town** in der Stadt I **I haven't eaten in days** ich habe tagelang nichts gegessen V 4 (85) **one in three** eine/r von drei(en) V 4 (80)
°**include** [ɪnˈkluːd] einschließen
included [ɪnˈkluːdɪd] inbegriffen III
including [ɪnˈkluːdɪŋ] einschließlich; darunter (auch) III
incredible [ɪnˈkredəbl] unglaublich IV
independence [ˌɪndɪˈpendəns] Unabhängigkeit IV
independent [ˌɪndɪˈpendənt] unabhängig III
Indian [ˈɪndiən]: **(American) Indian** Indianer/in; indianisch IV
indigenous (to) [ɪnˈdɪdʒənəs] einheimisch (in) V 1 (15) **indigenous Australian** australische(r) Ureinwohner/in V 1 (15) **indigenous people** Einheimische, Ureinwohner/innen V 1 (15)

DICTIONARY

English – German

indirect [ɪndə'rekt] indirekt V 2 (39)
individual [ɪndɪ'vɪdʒuəl] Einzelne(r), Individuum; Person V 3 (67)
indoors [ɪn'dɔːz] drinnen *(im Haus)* V 3 (57)
industry ['ɪndəstri] Industrie IV
influence ['ɪnfluəns]:
 1. beeinflussen V 2 (32)
 2. Einfluss V 2 (32)
inform sb. [ɪn'fɔːm] jn. informieren IV
information (about) [ɪnfə'meɪʃn] *(no pl)* Information(en) (über) III
ingredient [ɪn'griːdiənt] Zutat, Bestandteil V 3 (52)
inland [ɪn'lænd] landeinwärts, im Landesinneren/ins Landesinnere V 1 (8)
innocent ['ɪnəsnt] unschuldig IV
inside [ɪn'saɪd]:
 1. drinnen; nach drinnen I
 2. **inside sth.** in, innerhalb, im Innern von etwas IV
install [ɪn'stɔːl] installieren, einrichten III
instead [ɪn'sted] stattdessen, dafür III
°**instruction** [ɪn'strʌkʃn] Anweisung
instrument ['ɪnstrəmənt] Instrument I
°**interactive** [ɪntər'æktɪv] interaktiv
interest ['ɪntrəst]:
 1. Interesse V 2 (32)
 °2. **interest sb.** jn. interessieren
interested ['ɪntrəstɪd]: **be interested in** sich interessieren für; interessiert sein an II
interesting ['ɪntrəstɪŋ] interessant I
international [ɪntə'næʃnəl] international III
internet ['ɪntənet] Internet II
interview ['ɪntəvjuː]:
 1. Interview I
 °2. befragen, interviewen
interviewer ['ɪntəvjuːə] Interviewer/in V 3 (61)
intimidating [ɪn'tɪmɪdeɪtɪŋ] beängstigend, einschüchternd IV
into ['ɪntu] in (... hinein) I **into the living room** ins Wohnzimmer (hinein) I °**be into sth.** *(infml)* interessiert sein an etwas, etwas gerne tun
introduce sb. to sb. [ɪntrə'djuːs] jm. jn. vorstellen, jn. mit jm. bekanntmachen V 2 (38)
introduction [ɪntrə'dʌkʃn] Einleitung, Einführung IV
°**invent** [ɪn'vent] erfinden
invention [ɪn'venʃn] Erfindung V 4 (88)
°**invest (in)** [ɪn'vest] investieren (in)
°**investor** [ɪn'vestə] Investor/in
invisible [ɪn'vɪzəbl] unsichtbar IV
invitation (to) [ɪnvɪ'teɪʃn] Einladung (zu, nach) I
invite (to) [ɪn'vaɪt] einladen (zu, nach) I
iron ['aɪən]:
 1. Bügeleisen V 3 (52)
 2. bügeln V 3 (52)

irritate ['ɪrɪteɪt] (ver)ärgern, irritieren V 4 (81)
is [ɪz] *(er/sie/es)* ist I **The calculator is £1.** Der Taschenrechner kostet 1 Pfund. I
island ['aɪlənd] Insel IV
issue ['ɪʃuː] (Streit-)Frage, Problem, Thema V 2 (32)
it [ɪt] er/sie/es I **..., isn't it?** ..., oder? / ..., nicht wahr? III
its [ɪts] sein/seine, ihr/ihre II
itself [ɪt'self] sich III

J

jacket ['dʒækɪt] Jacke, Jackett II
jam [dʒæm] Marmelade I
January ['dʒænjuəri] Januar I
jazz [dʒæz] Jazz IV
jealous (of) ['dʒeləs] eifersüchtig (auf), neidisch (auf) V 2 (30)
jeans *(pl)* [dʒiːnz] Jeans II
jelly ['dʒeli] *(AE)* Marmelade IV
°**jellyfish,** *pl* **jellyfish** ['dʒelifɪʃ] Qualle
°**jigsaw** ['dʒɪgsɔː] Puzzle, Gruppenpuzzle
jingle ['dʒɪŋgl] Jingle *(Werbemelodie, -song)* V 4 (80)
job [dʒɒb] Job, (Arbeits-)Stelle I **on the job** bei der Arbeit IV
job advert ['dʒɒb ædvɜːt] Stellenanzeige V 3 (56)
job interview ['dʒɒb ɪntəvjuː] Vorstellungsgespräch V 3 (66)
jogger ['dʒɒgə] Jogger/in IV
jogging ['dʒɒgɪŋ] Jogging, Joggen II
join a club [dʒɔɪn] sich einem Klub anschließen; in einen Klub eintreten I
joke [dʒəʊk]:
 1. Witz II
 2. Witze machen, scherzen II
journalist ['dʒɜːnəlɪst] Journalist/in IV
journey ['dʒɜːni] Reise, Fahrt IV
judo ['dʒuːdəʊ] Judo II
juice [dʒuːs] Saft I
July [dʒu'laɪ] Juli I
jump [dʒʌmp]:
 1. springen III
 2. zusammenzucken *(vor Schreck)* III
June [dʒuːn] Juni I
°**jungle** ['dʒʌŋgl] Dschungel, Urwald
junk food ['dʒʌŋk fuːd] ungesundes Essen II
just [dʒʌst]:
 1. gerade (eben), soeben II
 2. (einfach) nur, bloß III
 3. einfach (so) IV
 4. **just like Berry** genau wie Berry II

K

°**K** [keɪ]: **£20K** zwanzigtausend Pfund (= £ 20.000)
°**kangaroo** [kæŋgə'ruː] Känguru
keen [kiːn] (sehr) interessiert, begeistert V 3 (58) **be keen on sth./ on doing sth.** an etwas sehr interessiert sein, etwas unbedingt (tun) wollen V 3 (58)
keep [kiːp], **kept, kept:**
 1. halten III
 2. behalten III
 3. aufbewahren IV
 keep away from sb. sich fernhalten von jm. IV **Keep it up.** Mach weiter so! II **Keep me posted.** Halt mich auf dem Laufenden. III °**keep an eye on sb./sth.** jn./etwas im Auge behalten, ein (wachsames) Auge haben auf jn./etwas °**keep up (with sb.)** (mit jm.) Schritt halten
keeper ['kiːpə]: **Finders, keepers, losers, weepers.** Was man findet, darf man behalten. *(Redensart)* V 4 (85)
kept [kept] *siehe* **keep**
kettle ['ketl] (Wasser-)Kessel, Wasserkocher III
key [kiː] Schlüssel; Schlüssel- V 3 (58)
key skills *(pl)* ['kiː skɪlz] Schlüsselqualifikationen, Schlüsselkompetenzen V 3 (58)
kick [kɪk]:
 1. treten, schießen III
 kick *(infml)* (eine Gewohnheit/Handlungsweise) aufgeben, sich befreien von V 2 (36)
 2. Tritt, Stoß, Kick V 2 (36)
kid [kɪd] Kind; Jugendliche(r) I
kidding ['kɪdɪŋ] *(infml)*: **Are you kidding?** Machst du Witze? / Willst du mich auf den Arm nehmen? IV
kill [kɪl] töten II
killer ['kɪlə] Mörder/in V 4 (84)
kilometre (km) ['kɪləmiːtə] Kilometer II °**kilometres per hour (kph)** Kilometer pro Stunde (km/h)
kind [kaɪnd] nett, freundlich II
kind (of) [kaɪnd] Art, Sorte II **kind of glamorous** irgendwie glamourös V 1 (20) **What kind of mistakes ...?** Was für Fehler ...? II
°**kinda stupid** [ndə] *(infml, = kind of)* irgendwie blöd
king [kɪŋ] König III
kingdom ['kɪŋdəm]: **the United Kingdom (the UK)** das Vereinigte Königreich III
kiss [kɪs]:
 1. (sich) küssen V 3 (63)
 2. Kuss V 3 (63)
kitchen ['kɪtʃɪn] Küche I
kitten ['kɪtn] Kätzchen, junge Katze II
knee [niː] Knie II
knew [njuː] *siehe* **know**
knife, *pl* **knives** [naɪf], [naɪvz] Messer III
knock (on) [nɒk] (an)klopfen (an) III
know [nəʊ], **knew, known** wissen; kennen I **get to know each other** sich kennenlernen IV **get to know sb.** jn. kennenlernen IV
known [nəʊn] *siehe* **know** **be well known** bekannt sein IV

°**kph** [keɪ piː ˈeɪt ʃ] (= *kilometres per hour*) Kilometer pro Stunde (km/h)

L

lab [læb] Labor I
°**label** [ˈleɪbl] etikettieren, beschriften
°**lad** [læd] (*infml*) Junge, junger Kerl
°**ladder** [ˈlædə] (*die*) Leiter V 4 (86)
°**lady** [ˈleɪdi] Dame
°**laid** [leɪd] *siehe* **lay**
lain [leɪn] *siehe* **lie**
lake [leɪk] (Binnen-)See II
lamp [læmp] Lampe I
land [lænd]:
  1. Land, Grund und Boden IV
  2. landen III
landowner [ˈlændəʊnə] Grundbesitzer/in IV
landscape [ˈlændskeɪp] Landschaft V 1 (8)
lane [leɪn] Gasse, Weg (*oft als Teil von Straßennamen*) II
language [ˈlæŋgwɪdʒ] Sprache I
°**lapse** [læps]: **time lapse** Zeitraffer (*Film*)
laptop [ˈlæptɒp] Laptop III
large [lɑːdʒ] groß V 1 (10)
lasagne [ləˈsænjə] Lasagne II
last [lɑːst] letzte(r, s) I **at last** schließlich, endlich III **for the last time** zum letzten Mal III
late [leɪt] spät I °**have a late night** lange aufbleiben, spät ins Bett gehen
lately [ˈleɪtli] in letzter Zeit V 2 (34)
later [ˈleɪtə] später I
laugh [lɑːf] lachen I **laugh at** lachen über, sich lustig machen über III
law [lɔː] Gesetz IV
lay [leɪ] *siehe* **lie**
°**lay** [leɪ], **laid, laid** legen
lazy [ˈleɪzi] faul I
lead [liːd] (Hunde-)Leine III
°**lead** [liːd], **led, led** führen, leiten
leader [ˈliːdə] Leiter/in, (an-)Führer/in II
°**league** [liːg] Liga
lean [liːn] sich lehnen; sich beugen IV
learn [lɜːn] lernen I **learn a/your lesson** eine/deine Lektion lernen V 4 (82)
°**learner** [ˈlɜːnə] Lernende/r
°**learner licence** [ˈlɜːnə laɪsns] Führerschein für Begleitetes Fahren
least [liːst] am wenigsten III **at least** mindestens, wenigstens II
°**leather** [ˈleðə] Leder
leave [liːv], **left, left**:
  1. abfahren; (weg)gehen II
  2. verlassen III
  3. zurücklassen II
  leave sb. alone jn. in Ruhe lassen V 4 (85) **leave a message** eine Nachricht hinterlassen III **leave school** von der Schule abgehen III
°**led** [led] *siehe* **lead**
left [left] links; nach links I **on the left** links, auf der linken Seite I
left [left] *siehe* **leave**

leg [leg] Bein I **I have a sore leg.** Mein Bein tut weh. I
lend sb. sth. [lend], **lent, lent** jm. etwas leihen III
lent [lent] *siehe* **lend**
less [les] weniger II **less and less** immer weniger III
lesson [ˈlesn] (Unterrichts-)Stunde I **learn a/your lesson** eine/deine Lektion lernen V 4 (82) **teach sb. a lesson** jm. eine Lektion erteilen V 4 (82)
let [let], **let, let** lassen I **Let's have a look.** Lass uns nachsehen. III **Let's see.** Mal sehen. / Mal abwarten. III
letter [ˈletə]:
  1. Brief I
  letter to the editor Leserbrief IV
  2. Buchstabe II
letter box [ˈletə bɒks] Briefkasten II
liberty [ˈlɪbəti] Freiheit IV
library [ˈlaɪbrəri] Bücherei, Bibliothek IV
°**licence** [ˈlaɪsns] Lizenz, Erlaubnis
lie [laɪ]:
  1. Lüge V 3 (62)
  tell a lie/lies lügen V 3 (62)
  2. **lie (to sb.)** (jn. an)lügen V 3 (62)
lie [laɪ], **lay, lain** liegen V 3 (64)
life, *pl* **lives** [laɪf], [laɪvz] (das) Leben I **way of life** Lebensweise V 1 (15)
lifeguard [ˈlaɪfgɑːd] Rettungsschwimmer/in; Bademeister/in IV
°**life-saving** [ˈlaɪf seɪvɪŋ] lebensrettend, Rettungs-
lift [lɪft] Fahrstuhl, Aufzug, Lift IV
light [laɪt] leicht IV
light [laɪt], **lit, lit** anzünden V 1 (12) **light a fire** (ein) Feuer machen V 1 (12)
lighthouse [ˈlaɪthaʊs] Leuchtturm II
lights (*pl*) [laɪts] Licht; Lampen III
like [laɪk] mögen, gernhaben I **like sth. best** etwas am liebsten mögen II **He doesn't like to be lonely.** Er mag es nicht, allein zu sein. I **I like watching TV.** Ich sehe gern fern. I **I'd like to go home.** (= I would like to ...) Ich würde gern nach Hause gehen. II **What would you like?** Was möchtest du? / Was hättest du gern? II **Would you like some tea/chips?** Möchtest du (etwas) Tee / (ein paar) Pommes frites? II
like [laɪk] wie I **like that** so, auf diese Weise IV **Like what?** Was (denn) zum Beispiel? III **I don't feel like it.** Mir ist nicht danach. II **What's it like?** Wie ist es? / Wie sieht es aus? I
likeable [ˈlaɪkəbl] sympathisch, liebenswert IV
likely [ˈlaɪkli] wahrscheinlich V 1 (11) **be likely to do sth.** wahrscheinlich etwas tun (werden) V 1 (11)
likes and dislikes (*pl*) [ˈdɪslaɪks] Vorlieben und Abneigungen IV
line [laɪn]: Zeile; Linie IV

°**link (to)** [lɪŋk] verbinden (mit)
lion [ˈlaɪən] Löwe IV
lip [lɪp] Lippe V 3 (63)
lipstick [ˈlɪpstɪk] Lippenstift V 3 (63)
list [lɪst]:
  1. auflisten, aufzählen III
  2. Liste II
listen [ˈlɪsn] zuhören I **listen carefully** aufmerksam/genau zuhören II **listen to sb.** jm. zuhören I **listen to sth.** sich etwas anhören I
listener [ˈlɪsənə] Zuhörer/in III
lit [lɪt] *siehe* **light**
litre [ˈliːtə] Liter V 1 (12)
litter [ˈlɪtə] Abfall II
litter bin [ˈlɪtə bɪn] Abfalleimer, Mülleimer II
little [ˈlɪtl]:
  1. klein I
  2. **a little money/time/...** ein bisschen Geld/Zeit/... I
live [lɪv] leben; wohnen I
lives [laɪvz] *Mehrzahl von* **life** I
living room [ˈlɪvɪŋ ruːm] Wohnzimmer I
°**loads (of)** [ləʊdz] (*infml*) eine Menge
lobby [ˈlɒbi] Eingangshalle IV
local [ˈləʊkl] örtlich, Orts-, Lokal- III
locker [ˈlɒkə] Spind, Schließfach IV
°**logical** [ˈlɒdʒɪkl] logisch
logo [ˈləʊgəʊ] Logo V 4 (84)
lonely [ˈləʊnli] einsam I
long [lɒŋ] lang II
look [lʊk]:
  1. schauen, gucken I
  2. aussehen I
  3. **Let's have a look.** Lass uns nachsehen. III
  Look, Adam. Sieh mal, Adam. / Schau mal, Adam. I **look after** sich kümmern um; aufpassen auf I **look around** sich umsehen III **look at sth.** sich etwas anschauen I **look for sth.** etwas suchen II **look forward to doing sth.** sich darauf freuen, etwas zu tun IV **look forward to sth.** sich auf etwas freuen IV **look sth. up** etwas nachschlagen (*Wörter, Informationen*) IV **look up** aufschauen, hochsehen II
°**lorry** [ˈlɒri] Lastwagen, Lkw
lose [luːz], **lost, lost** verlieren II
loser [ˈluːzə] Verlierer/in III **Finders, keepers, losers, weepers.** Was man findet, darf man behalten. (*Redensart*) V 4 (85)
lost [lɒst] *siehe* **lose get lost** sich verirren, sich verlaufen IV **I'm not lost.** Ich habe mich nicht verlaufen/verirrt. I °**Get lost.** Verschwinde(t)!
lot [lɒt]: **a lot (of); lots (of)** viel ..., viele ... I
loud [laʊd] laut III
love [lʌv]:
  1. Liebe III °**fall in love (with sb.)** sich verlieben (in jn.)

DICTIONARY — English – German

2. lieben, sehr mögen I **I'd (= I would) love to come.** Ich komme sehr gern. / Ich würde sehr gern kommen. I **she loves going to ...** sie geht sehr gern zu/nach ...; sie liebt es, zu/nach ... zu gehen II
°**love affair** [əˈfeə] Liebesbeziehung I
love life [ˈlʌv laɪf] Liebesleben III
loveable [ˈlʌvəbl] liebenswert IV
°**lover** [ˈlʌvə]: **animal lover** Tierfreund/in
luck [lʌk]: **Good luck.** Viel Glück. IV **Hard luck!** Pech (gehabt)! III
luckily [ˈlʌkɪli] glücklicherweise; zum Glück III
lucky [ˈlʌki]: **you're lucky** du hast Glück I
lunch [lʌntʃ] Mittagessen I **have lunch** (zu) Mittag essen I
lunch box [ˈlʌntʃ bɒks] Brotdose II
lunchtime [ˈlʌntʃtaɪm] Mittagszeit II

M

machine [məˈʃiːn] Maschine, Gerät III
madam [ˈmædəm] gnädige Frau V 3 (59) **Dear Sir/Madam** Sehr geehrte Damen und Herren V 3 (59)
made [meɪd] siehe **make be made of sth.** aus etwas (gemacht) sein IV
magazine [mægəˈziːn] Zeitschrift, Magazin II
°**magic** [ˈmædʒɪk] zauberhaft; Zauberei, Magie
main [meɪn] Haupt- III
°**majority** [məˈdʒɒrəti] Mehrheit, Mehrzahl
make [meɪk], **made, made** machen, herstellen I **make a deal** ein Geschäft abschließen, vereinbaren II **make an arrangement** eine Vereinbarung treffen; etwas vereinbaren, etwas verabreden II **make friends** Freunde finden II **make money** Geld verdienen II **make notes** (sich) Notizen machen (zur Vorbereitung) III **make sb. do sth.** jn. dazu bringen, etwas zu tun; jn. veranlassen, etwas zu tun IV **make sth. special** etwas zu etwas Besonderem machen III **make sure that ...** sicherstellen, dass ...; darauf achten, dass ...; dafür sorgen, dass ... V 1 (22)
make-up [ˈmeɪkʌp] Make-up II
mall [mɔːl] (kurz für:) **shopping mall** Einkaufszentrum II
man, (pl) **men** [mæn], [men] Mann I
manage [ˈmænɪdʒ] verwalten, regeln V 3 (52)
management [ˈmænɪdʒmənt] Management, Leitung, (Geschäfts-)Führung V 3 (63)
manager [ˈmænɪdʒə] Manager/in; Geschäftsführer/in III
manners (pl) [ˈmænəz] Manieren IV

many [ˈmeni] viele II **How many ...?** Wie viele ...? II
map [mæp] Stadtplan; Landkarte II
March [mɑːtʃ] März I
°**marine** [məˈriːn] Meeres-
mark [mɑːk] kennzeichnen, markieren III
market [ˈmɑːkɪt] Markt I
married (to) [ˈmærɪd] verheiratet (mit) II **get married** heiraten IV
mask [mɑːsk] Maske II
match [mætʃ] Spiel; Wettkampf II
°**match** [mætʃ] passen zu **match with** zuordnen
°**mate** [meɪt] Freund/in, Kumpel
materials (pl) [məˈtɪəriəlz] Materialien, Hilfsmittel V 1 (22)
math [mæθ] (AE) Mathematik IV
maths [mæθs] (BE) Mathematik I
matter [ˈmætə]:
1. von Bedeutung sein, wichtig sein V 2 (36)
It doesn't matter. Es/Das ist egal. II
2. **What's the matter?** Was ist denn? / Was ist los? II
°**mature** [məˈtʃʊə] reif, vernünftig
°**maximum** [ˈmæksɪməm] Höchst-, maximal, Maximum
May [meɪ] Mai I
maybe [ˈmeɪbi] vielleicht I
me [miː] mich; mir I **Me too.** Ich auch. I **It's me.** Ich bin es. I **Not me!** Ich nicht! I
meal [miːl] Mahlzeit III
mean [miːn]:
1. geizig II
2. gemein, fies I
mean [miːn], **meant, meant**:
1. bedeuten III
2. meinen, sagen wollen III
meaning [ˈmiːnɪŋ] Bedeutung IV
meant [ment] siehe **mean**
meat [miːt] Fleisch II
mechanic [mɪˈkænɪk] Mechaniker/in III
media (pl) [ˈmiːdiə] Medien V 4 (76) **social media** soziale Medien/Dienste V 4 (76)
°**mediation** [midiˈeɪʃn] Vermittlung, Sprachmittlung
meet [miːt], **met, met**:
1. kennenlernen; treffen I
2. sich treffen II
Nice to meet you! Freut mich, dich/euch kennenzulernen. I
meeting [ˈmiːtɪŋ] Treffen; Zusammenkunft; Besprechung IV
member [ˈmembə] Mitglied IV
memorial (to sb./sth.) [məˈmɔːriəl] Denkmal (für jn./etwas) IV
men [men] Mehrzahl von **man** I
°**mention** [ˈmenʃn] erwähnen, nennen **Don't mention it.** Bitte, gern geschehen. / Nichts zu danken.
menu [ˈmenjuː] Speisekarte V
mess [mes] Durcheinander, Chaos IV

message [ˈmesɪdʒ]:
1. Nachricht II
2. Botschaft III
take a message (jm.) etwas ausrichten III
°**messaging** [ˈmesɪdʒɪŋ] (Nachrichten-, Bild-)Übermittlung; das Versenden von SMS
messy [ˈmesi] unordentlich I
met [met] siehe **meet**
metal [ˈmetl] Metall IV
metre [ˈmiːtə] Meter I
mice [maɪs] Mehrzahl von **mouse** III
middle [ˈmɪdl] Mitte I **in the middle** in der Mitte I **in the middle of nowhere** etwa: am Ende der Welt III
°**middle school** [ˈmɪdl skuːl] (AE) Mittelschule (für 11- bis 14-Jährige)
midnight [ˈmɪdnaɪt] Mitternacht III
might [maɪt]: **it might help** es hilft vielleicht; es könnte (vielleicht) helfen IV
migrant [ˈmaɪɡrənt] Zuwanderer, Zuwanderin III
mile [maɪl] Meile (ca. 1,6 km) II
milk [mɪlk] Milch II
milkshake [ˈmɪlkʃeɪk] Milchshake II
million [ˈmɪljən] Million III
°**millionaire** [mɪljəˈneə] Millionär/in
mind [maɪnd]: **Do you mind?** Entschuldige mal! / Was fällt dir ein? IV **I don't mind ...** Es macht mir nichts aus ... IV
mine [maɪn] meiner, meine, meins III
°**minor character** [maɪnə ˈkærəktə] Nebenfigur (in Roman, Film usw.)
°**minority** [maɪˈnɒrəti] Minderheit
minus [ˈmaɪnəs] minus II
minute [ˈmɪnɪt] Minute II
mirror [ˈmɪrə] Spiegel I
miss [mɪs]:
1. vermissen I
2. verpassen II
Miss Borowski [mɪs] Frau Borowski (Anrede für unverheiratete Frauen) I
mistake [mɪˈsteɪk] Fehler II
mobile [ˈməʊbaɪl]:
1. mobil V 4 (87)
2. (kurz für: **mobile phone**) Mobiltelefon, Handy
mobile phone [məʊbaɪl ˈfəʊn] (kurz auch: **mobile**) Mobiltelefon, Handy I
model [ˈmɒdl] Fotomodell, Model V 3 (60)
moderator [ˈmɒdəreɪtə] Moderator/in (z.B. bei Debatten) V 4 (89)
modern [ˈmɒdn] modern V 1 (15)
°**modern-day** [mɒdn deɪ] modern, von heute
mom [mɒm], [mɑːm] (AE) Mama, Mutti IV
moment [ˈməʊmənt] Moment, Augenblick I **at the moment** im Moment, gerade I
Monday [ˈmʌndeɪ], [ˈmʌndi] Montag I

money [ˈmʌni] Geld I **make money** Geld verdienen I
monitor [ˈmɒnɪtə] Monitor, Bildschirm III
monkey [ˈmʌŋki] Affe I
monster [ˈmɒnstə] Monster III
month [mʌnθ] Monat I
mood [muːd] Stimmung, Laune IV
°**moon** [muːn] Mond
more [mɔː]: **more and more** immer mehr III **more ideas** mehr Ideen; weitere Ideen II **more popular** beliebter II **more than** mehr als II
morning [ˈmɔːnɪŋ] Morgen I **in the morning** morgens, am Morgen I **on Friday morning** freitagmorgens, am Freitagmorgen I
most [məʊst]: **the most boring ...** der/die/das langweiligste ... II **the most sports** die meisten Sportarten II
mostly [ˈməʊstli] hauptsächlich; meistens II
motel [məʊˈtel] Motel *(Hotel an einer Autobahn)* IV
mother [ˈmʌðə] Mutter I
°**motivate** [ˈməʊtɪveɪt] motivieren
°**motorway** [ˈməʊtəweɪ] Autobahn
motto [ˈmɒtəʊ] Motto III
mountain [ˈmaʊntən] Berg II
mouse, *pl* **mice** [maʊs], [maɪs] Maus III
mouth [maʊθ] Mund I
move [muːv]:
1. (sich) bewegen III
2. **move (to)** umziehen (nach, in) II
movement [ˈmuːvmənt] Bewegung IV
movie [ˈmuːvi] Film IV
Mr Jahn [ˈmɪstə] Herr Jahn I
Mrs Schmidt [ˈmɪsɪz] Frau Schmidt *(Anrede für verheiratete Frauen)* I
Ms Lee [mɪz], [məz] Frau Lee *(allgemeine Anrede für Frauen)* I
much [mʌtʃ] viel II **as much as $80** bis zu 80$; nicht weniger als 80$ IV **How much ...?** Wie viel ...? II **How much is ...? / How much are ...?** Was (Wie viel) kostet ...? / Was (Wie viel) kosten ...? I **miss/like/love sb. so much** jn. so sehr vermissen/mögen/lieben II **Thanks very much.** Danke sehr. / Danke vielmals. II
mud [mʌd] Schlamm, Matsch II
muddy [ˈmʌdi] schlammig, matschig III
muesli [ˈmjuːzli] Müsli III
muffin [ˈmʌfɪn] Muffin III
°**multimillionaire** [mʌltimɪljəˈneə] Multimillionär/in
multitask [mʌltiˈtɑːsk] mehrere Tätigkeiten gleichzeitig ausführen V 4 (76)
mum [mʌm] Mama, Mutti I
°**muscle car** [ˈmʌsl kɑː] Muscle-Car *(Serienmodell, nachgerüstet mit besonders starkem Motor)*
°**muscular dystrophy** [mʌskjələ ˈdɪstrəfi] Muskeldystrophie
museum [mjuːˈzɪəm] Museum III

music [ˈmjuːzɪk] Musik I
musical [ˈmjuːzɪkl] Musical III
musician [mjuːˈzɪʃn] Musiker/in I
must [mʌst]:
1. müssen I
mustn't do nicht tun dürfen II
I must go. *(am Telefon)* Ich muss Schluss machen. I
2. **... is a must.** *(infml)* ... ist ein Muss. IV
my [maɪ] mein/e I
myself [maɪˈself] mich, mir (selbst) I **for myself** für mich selbst I
°**mysterious** [mɪˈstɪəriəs] geheimnisvoll
mystery [ˈmɪstri] Geheimnis II

N

nail [neɪl] Nagel V 1 (20)
nail polish [ˈneɪl pɒlɪʃ] Nagellack V 1 (20)
name [neɪm]:
1. benennen, nennen IV
2. Name I
call sb. a racist name jn. mit einem rassistischen Wort beschimpfen V 2 (35) **call sb. names** jn. beschimpfen V 2 (35) **What's your name?** Wie heißt du? I
narrow [ˈnærəʊ] schmal, eng III
nation [ˈneɪʃn] Nation, Volk IV
national [ˈnæʃnəl] national, National- III
national anthem [ˈnæʃnəl ˈænθəm] Nationalhymne III
national park [ˈnæʃnəl ˈpɑːk] Nationalpark II
native [ˈneɪtɪv]: **Native American** amerikanische/r Ureinwohner/in IV **native animals/plants** (ein)heimische Tiere/Pflanzen V 1 (11)
nature [ˈneɪtʃə] Natur IV
near [nɪə] in der Nähe von, nahe (bei) I **near here** hier in der Nähe II
°**nearby** [nɪəˈbaɪ] in der Nähe
nearest [ˈnɪərɪst]: **the nearest ...** der/die/das nächstgelegene ... V 1 (16)
nearly [ˈnɪəli] fast, beinahe II
necessary [ˈnesəsəri] notwendig, nötig, erforderlich V 3 (67)
need [niːd]:
1. brauchen, benötigen I
need to do sth. etwas tun müssen IV
°2. Bedürfnis
°**children with special needs** Kinder mit besonderen Bedürfnissen / Förderbedarf °**no need for ... / no need to do sth.** kein Grund für ... / kein Grund, etwas zu tun
negative [ˈnegətɪv] negativ II
negativity [negəˈtɪvəti] negative Einstellung V 2 (36)
neighbour [ˈneɪbə] Nachbar/in II
neighbourhood [ˈneɪbəhʊd] Nachbarschaft, Viertel, Gegend II
neighbouring [ˈneɪbərɪŋ] benachbart, Nachbar- IV
neon [ˈniːɒn] Neon; neonfarbig V 3 (63)

nervous [ˈnɜːvəs] nervös, aufgeregt I
net [net] *kurz für* Internet V 4 (76)
network [ˈnetwɜːk] Netz; Wortnetz I
°**networking website** [netwɜːkɪŋ ˈwebsaɪt] Online-Kommunikationsplattform
never [ˈnevə] nie, niemals I **I've never had ...** ich habe (noch) nie ... gehabt II
new [njuː] neu I
New Year [njuː ˈjɪə] Neujahr II
newcomer [ˈnjuːkʌmə] Neuling IV
news [njuːz]:
1. Nachrichten I
2. Neuigkeiten II
... is bad news. ... ist gefährlich. / ... ist (gar) nicht gut. V 4 (85)
newsagent [ˈnjuːzeɪdʒənt] Zeitungshändler/in II **the newsagent's** der Zeitungsladen II
newsletter [ˈnjuːzletə] Mitteilungsblatt, Informationsblatt II
newspaper [ˈnjuːzpeɪpə] *(oft auch kurz:* **paper***)* Zeitung II
next [nekst] nächste(r, s) I **Next ...** Als Nächstes ... II **next time** nächstes Mal II **the next day** am nächsten Tag III
next to [ˈnekst tə] neben I
nice [naɪs] nett, schön I **Nice to meet you!** Freut mich, dich/euch kennenzulernen. I
nickname [ˈnɪkneɪm] Spitzname V 1 (8)
night [naɪt] Nacht I **at night** nachts, in der Nacht I
nine [naɪn] neun I
nineties [ˈnaɪntiːz]: **the 90s** die Neunzigerjahre II
no [nəʊ] nein I
no [nəʊ] kein, keine I **No way!** Auf keinen Fall! III
nobody [ˈnəʊbədi] niemand II
nod (to sb.) [nɒd] (jm. zu)nicken IV
noise [nɔɪz] Geräusch; Lärm I
noisy [ˈnɔɪzi] laut, voller Lärm I
°**nomadic** [nəʊˈmædɪk] nomadisch, Nomaden-
none [nʌn] keine(r, s) II
normal [ˈnɔːml] normal, gewöhnlich I
north [nɔːθ] Norden; nach Norden II
north-east Nordosten; nach Nordosten II **north-west** Nordwesten; nach Nordwesten II
northern [ˈnɔːðən] nördlich, Nord- IV
nose [nəʊz] Nase IV
nosey [ˈnəʊzi] *(auch:* **nosy***)* neugierig IV
not [nɒt] nicht I **not (...) anywhere** nirgendwo; nirgendwohin II **not ... yet** noch nicht I **not even** (noch) nicht einmal IV **Not me!** Ich nicht! I **I can't do anything.** Ich kann nichts machen. II **I'm not a boy.** Ich bin kein Junge. I **we don't have any ...** wir haben kein/e ... II

251

DICTIONARY

English – German

note [nəʊt]:
1. Notiz III
make notes (sich) Notizen machen (zur Vorbereitung) III **take notes** (sich) Notizen machen (beim Lesen oder Zuhören) III
°2. **note sth. down** sich etwas aufschreiben, notieren
nothing [ˈnʌθɪŋ] (gar) nichts I
notice [ˈnəʊtɪs] (be)merken III
notice [ˈnəʊtɪs] Notiz, Aushang, Anzeige III
°**novel** [ˈnɒvl] Roman
November [nəʊˈvembə] November I
now [naʊ]:
1. nun, jetzt I
2. **right now** jetzt gerade; im Augenblick III
nowhere [ˈnəʊweə] nirgendwo; nirgendwohin III **in the middle of nowhere** etwa: am Ende der Welt III
number [ˈnʌmbə]:
1. Anzahl, Zahl III
2. Nummer I
nut [nʌt] Nuss I

O

o'clock [əˈklɒk]: **at 1 o'clock** um 1 Uhr / um 13 Uhr I
observer [əbˈzɜːvə] Beobachter/in V 4 (89)
ocean [ˈəʊʃn] Ozean IV
October [ɒkˈtəʊbə] Oktober I
of [ɒv], [əv] von I **(just) the two of us** (nur) wir beide V 2 (34) **the best of both worlds** das Beste von beidem I **the last day of the holidays** der letzte Tag der Ferien I
of course [əv ˈkɔːs] natürlich, selbstverständlich II
off [ɒf]:
1. **off the seats/the bridge/the bike/...** von den Sitzen/der Brücke/dem Rad/... (herunter) IV
2. **get/have a day off** einen Tag frei bekommen/haben IV
3. **go off** losgehen (z. B. Alarm) IV
start off (as) anfangen (als) V 2 (45)
°**Off you go!** Dann mal los!/Ab mit dir!
offer [ˈɒfə] bieten, anbieten III
office [ˈɒfɪs] Büro III
official [əˈfɪʃl] offiziell, amtlich IV
often [ˈɒfn], [ˈɒftən] oft I
Oh dear. [əʊ ˈdɪə] Oje! II
OK [əʊˈkeɪ] okay, gut, in Ordnung I **I'm OK, thanks.** Danke, (es geht mir) gut. I
old [əʊld] alt I **in the old days** früher II
old-fashioned [əʊld ˈfæʃənd] altmodisch IV
Olympic Games [əlɪmpɪk ˈɡeɪmz] Olympische Spiele III
omelette [ˈɒmlət] Omelette I
on [ɒn] auf I **on 5th May** am 5. Mai I **on earth** auf der Erde II **on Friday**

morning freitagmorgens, am Freitagmorgen I **on Monday** am Montag I **on my birthday** an meinem Geburtstag I **on the beach** am Strand I **on the bus** im Bus I **on the job** bei der Arbeit IV **on the left** links, auf der linken Seite I **on the one hand** einerseits III **on the other hand** andererseits III **on the phone** am Telefon I **on the right** rechts, auf der rechten Seite I **on the Tube** in der (Londoner) U-Bahn III **on the way to ...** auf dem Weg zu/nach ... I **on time** pünktlich II **drive/run/go on** weiterfahren/-laufen/-gehen IV **go on** weiterreden, fortfahren; weitermachen III **straight on** geradeaus (weiter) II **What's going on?** Was ist los? / Was gibt's? IV °**Go on.** Na los, mach(t) schon!
once [wʌns]:
1. einmal III
°**at once** sofort
2. einst, (früher) einmal IV
one [wʌn]:
1. eins I **one day** eines Tages, einmal IV **one way** einfache Fahrt IV
2. **the only one** der/die/das Einzige IV **two lollipops – a green one and a red one** zwei Lutscher – ein grüner und ein roter IV
one-way ticket [wʌn ˈweɪ tɪkɪt] einfache Fahrkarte I
online [ɒnˈlaɪn] online, Online- V 3 (52)
only [ˈəʊnli]:
1. nur, bloß I
2. einzige(r,s) **the only one** der/die/das Einzige IV **the only student** der einzige Schüler / die einzige Schülerin I
onto [ˈɒntə], [ˈɒntu] auf (... hinauf) V 4 (84)
open [ˈəʊpən]:
1. eröffnen IV
2. öffnen II
3. offen, geöffnet II
opinion [əˈpɪnjən] Meinung III **in my opinion** meiner Meinung nach III
opposite [ˈɒpəzɪt] Gegenteil II
option [ˈɒpʃn] Option, (Wahl-)Möglichkeit IV
or [ɔː] oder I **... or something ...** oder so was III
orange [ˈɒrɪndʒ]:
1. orange(farben) I
2. Orange, Apfelsine II
orange juice [ˈɒrɪndʒ dʒuːs] Orangensaft II
orca [ˈɔːkə] Orca, Schwertwal IV
°**orchestra** [ˈɔːkɪstrə] Orchester IV
order [ˈɔːdə]:
1. bestellen IV
2. Bestellung IV
order [ˈɔːdə] Reihenfolge III
order [ˈɔːdə]: **in order to** um ... zu V 3 (62)

organic apples/vegetables/... [ɔːˈɡænɪk] Bio-Äpfel/Gemüse/... III
organize [ˈɔːɡənaɪz] organisieren IV
original [əˈrɪdʒənəl] Original-, ursprünglich; Original IV
other [ˈʌðə] andere(r, s) I **each other** einander; sich (gegenseitig) IV **in other words** mit anderen Worten V 4 (79) **the other day** neulich III
our [ˈaʊə] unser/e I
ours [ɑːz], [ˈaʊəz] unsere/r, unseres V 1 (19)
ourselves [aʊəˈselvz] wir/uns selbst III
out of ... [ˈaʊt əv] aus ... (heraus/hinaus) II °**two out of five** zwei von fünf
°**outback** [ˈaʊtbæk]: **the outback** das Hinterland (Australien)
outdoor [aʊtˈdɔː ʃɒp]: **outdoor shop** Geschäft für Outdoor-Bekleidung und -Ausrüstung III
outdoors [aʊtˈdɔːz] im Freien, draußen V 3 (57)
outfit [ˈaʊtfɪt] Outfit (Kleidung, Ausstattung) III
outside [aʊtˈsaɪd]:
1. außerhalb, vor III
2. draußen; nach draußen I
over [ˈəʊvə]:
1. über III
all over the world auf der ganzen Welt IV **walk/come/... over to sb.** zu jm. hinübergehen/-kommen/... IV
2. **over 300** über 300, mehr als 300 III
3. **be over** vorbei sein, zu Ende sein IV
over there [əʊvə ˈðeə] da drüben, dort drüben V 1 (13)
overspend [əʊvəˈspend], **overspent, overspent (on sth.)** zu viel Geld ausgeben (für etwas) V 3 (52)
overspent [əʊvəˈspent] siehe **overspend**
°**overtake** [əʊvəˈteɪk], **overtook, overtaken** überholen
°**overtaken** [əʊvəˈteɪkən] siehe **overtake**
°**overtook** [əʊvəˈtʊk] siehe **overtake**
own [əʊn]: **your own card/text/...** deine eigene Karte / dein eigener Text / ... III °**of one's own** eigene(r, s)
°**on one's own** allein, selbstständig (ohne Unterstützung)
owner [ˈəʊnə] Eigentümer/in, Besitzer/in II

P

p [piː]: **50p** 50 Pence I
pack [pæk] packen, einpacken II
packet (of) [ˈpækɪt] Packung, Päckchen, Schachtel II
page [peɪdʒ] Seite I **What page is it?** Auf welcher Seite sind wir? I
paid [peɪd] siehe **pay**
pain [peɪn]:
1. Schmerz(en) V 2 (38)
2. **Don't be a pain.** Nerv nicht. / Geh mir/uns nicht auf die Nerven. V 2 (38)

252

What a pain! etwa: So ein Mist. / Es nervt! III
paint [peɪnt] lackieren, (be)malen, (mit Farbe) streichen V 1 (14)
painter [ˈpeɪntə] Maler/in V 1 (14)
°**painter and decorator** Maler/in und Tapezierer/in
painting [ˈpeɪntɪŋ] Gemälde, (gemaltes) Bild; Malerei V 1 (14) **body painting** Körperbemalung V 1 (14)
pair [peə] Paar I **a pair of gloves** ein Paar Handschuhe I
palace [ˈpæləs] Palast III
panic [ˈpænɪk] in Panik geraten IV **Don't panic.** Keine Panik. / Immer mit der Ruhe. II
pants (pl) [pænts] (AE) Hose IV
paper [ˈpeɪpə]:
1. Papier I
2. Zeitung II
do a paper round Zeitungen austragen II
parade [pəˈreɪd] Parade, Umzug IV
paradise [ˈpærədaɪs] Paradies IV
paragraph [ˈpærəgrɑːf] Absatz (im Text) III
paraphrase [ˈpærəfreɪz] umschreiben, mit anderen Worten sagen V 2 (45)
parents (pl) [ˈpeərənts] Eltern I
park [pɑːk] Park I
park [pɑːk] parken III
part [pɑːt] Teil II **take part in sth.** an etwas teilnehmen, bei etwas mitmachen III
partner [ˈpɑːtnə] Partner/in I
part-time job [pɑːt taɪm dʒɒb] Halbtagsjob, Teilzeitjob IV
party [ˈpɑːti] Party I **have a party** eine Party feiern I
party-goer [ˈpɑːti gəʊə] Partygast V 4 (82)
pass [pɑːs] Pass, Ausweis IV **visitor pass** Besucherausweis IV
pass [pɑːs]:
1. **pass sth./sb.** an etwas/jm. vorbeigehen, vorbeifahren V
2. **Pass the ball!** Spiel ab! III
passenger [ˈpæsɪndʒə] Passagier/in, Fahrgast II
passive [ˈpæsɪv] Passiv IV
past [pɑːst] Vergangenheit II
past the shop [pɑːst] am Laden vorbei II
pasta [ˈpæstə] Pasta; Nudeln III
pasty [ˈpæsti] Pastete mit Fleisch- und/oder Gemüsefüllung II
patient [ˈpeɪʃnt] geduldig IV
pattern [ˈpætn] Muster II
pavement [ˈpeɪvmənt] (BE) Gehweg, Bürgersteig II
pay [peɪ]:
1. Bezahlung, Lohn V 3 (56)
2. **pay (for sth.), paid, paid** (etwas) bezahlen III

it doesn't pay very well es wird nicht besonders gut bezahlt IV
PE (physical education) [piː ˈiː], [ˌfɪzɪkl edʒuˈkeɪʃn] (Schul-)Sport I
peanut [ˈpiːnʌt] Erdnuss II
peanut butter [ˈpiːnʌt] Erdnussbutter II
peer [pɪə] Gleichaltrige/r, Ebenbürtige/r, jemand aus derselben sozialen Gruppe V 2 (32)
peer pressure [ˈpɪə preʃə] Gruppendruck, Gruppenzwang V 2 (32)
pen [pen] Kugelschreiber, Stift, Füller I
pence [pens] Pence I
pencil [ˈpensl] Bleistift I
pencil case [ˈpensl keɪs] Federmäppchen I
pencil sharpener [ˈpensl ʃɑːpnə] Bleistiftanspitzer I
penfriend [ˈpenfrend] Brieffreund/in II
people [ˈpiːpl] Leute, Menschen I
pepper [ˈpepə] Pfeffer V 1 (11)
per cent (%) [pəˈsent] (AE usually: **percent**) Prozent II
per person/day/... [pɜː], [pə] pro Person/Tag/... IV
perfect [ˈpɜːfɪkt] perfekt, ideal II
°**perform** [pəˈfɔːm] aufführen, durchführen **perform well/badly** eine gute/schlechte Leistung zeigen
performance [pəˈfɔːməns] Vorstellung, Aufführung V 3 (66)
perhaps [pəˈhæps] vielleicht IV
person [ˈpɜːsn] Person I
personal [ˈpɜːsnl] persönlich V 1 (16)
personal computer [ˌpɜːsnl kəmˈpjuːtə] PC IV
personality [ˌpɜːsəˈnæləti] Persönlichkeit; Charakter V 3 (65)
°**perspective** [pəˈspektɪv] Perspektive
°**persuade** [pəˈsweɪd] überreden, überzeugen
pet [pet] Haustier I
petrol [ˈpetrəl] Benzin IV
petrol station [ˈpetrəl steɪʃn] Tankstelle V 3 (58)
°**pharmacist** [ˈfɑːməsɪst] Apotheker/in
°**pharmacy** [ˈfɑːməsi] Apotheke
phone [fəʊn]:
1. anrufen I
phone for an ambulance einen Krankenwagen rufen V 1 (12)
2. Telefon I
answer the phone ans Telefon gehen V 3 (58) **on the phone** am Telefon I
°**The phone went dead.** Die Leitung war tot.
phone call [ˈfəʊn kɔːl] (oft auch kurz: **call**) (Telefon-)Anruf I
phone number [ˈfəʊn nʌmbə] Telefonnummer I
photo [ˈfəʊtəʊ] Foto I **in the photo** auf dem Foto I **take photos** fotografieren, Fotos machen II
photographer [fəˈtɒgrəfə] Fotograf/in IV

phrase [freɪz] Ausdruck, (Rede-)Wendung I
piano [piˈænəʊ] Klavier, Piano I **play the piano** Klavier spielen I
pick [pɪk]:
1. (aus)wählen, aussuchen II
2. **pick sb. up** jn. abholen III
3. **pick sth. up** etwas aufheben (vom Boden), etwas hochheben II
pick up kaufen, (aus einem Geschäft) mitbringen V 3 (52) °**pick sth. out** etwas auswählen, heraussuchen
°**pick on sb.** auf jm. herumhacken, jn. drangsalieren
pickpocket [ˈpɪkpɒkɪt] Taschendieb/in III
picnic [ˈpɪknɪk] Picknick I
picture [ˈpɪktʃə] Bild I **in the picture** auf dem Bild I
piece [piːs]: **a piece of ...** ein Stück ... IV **a piece of advice** ein Rat, ein Ratschlag IV
piercing [ˈpɪəsɪŋ] Piercing II
pig [pɪg] Schwein I
°**pilot** [ˈpaɪlət] Pilot/in
pink [pɪŋk] pink, rosa I
°**piss off** [pɪs ˈɒf] (taboo) sich verpissen
pizza [ˈpiːtsə] Pizza II
place [pleɪs] Ort, Platz, Stelle I
plan [plæn]:
1. Plan II
2. planen I
plane [pleɪn] Flugzeug III
plant [plɑːnt] Pflanze I
plastic [ˈplæstɪk] Plastik, Kunststoff II **plastic bag** Plastiktüte I
plate (of) [pleɪt] Teller III
platform [ˈplætfɔːm] Bahnsteig, Gleis II
play [pleɪ]:
1. spielen I
2. Theaterstück II
play the guitar/the piano/the drums Gitarre/Klavier/Schlagzeug spielen I
player [ˈpleɪə] Spieler/in III
playground [ˈpleɪgraʊnd] Spielplatz IV
please [pliːz] bitte I
pleased [pliːzd] froh, erfreut, zufrieden V 3 (67) **Pleased to meet you.** Freut mich Sie kennenzulernen. V 3 (67)
°**pledge** [pledʒ] Gelöbnis, Versprechen **take a pledge** ein Gelöbnis ablegen
plot [plɒt] Handlung(sverlauf) (z.B. Film/Geschichte) V 2 (43)
Plus, ... [plʌs] Und außerdem ... IV
pm [piːˈem] **5 pm/5 p.m.** 5 Uhr nachmittags/abends; 17 Uhr I
pocket [ˈpɒkɪt] Tasche (Manteltasche, Hosentasche, etc.) I
pocket money [ˈpɒkɪt mʌni] Taschengeld II
poem [ˈpəʊɪm] Gedicht I
point [pɔɪnt]:
1. Argument V 4 (89)
good point gutes Argument V 4 (89)
make a point ein Argument vortra-

DICTIONARY

English – German

gen V 4 (89) **make your point** sagen, wie du darüber denkst V 4 (89) **2. Punkt** III
point of view Standpunkt III
1.6 million (one point six million) 1,6 Millionen (eins Komma sechs Millionen) IV
point (to sb./sth.) [pɔɪnt] (auf jn./ etwas) zeigen, deuten II
°**poison** [ˈpɔɪzn] Gift
police (pl) [pəˈliːs] Polizei II
police officer [pəˈliːs ˈɒfɪsə] Polizist/in II
police station [pəˈliːs ˈsteɪʃn] Polizeiwache, -revier IV
policy [ˈpɒləsi] Politik, Richtlinie(n), Bestimmung(en) III
polite [pəˈlaɪt] höflich IV
°**politics** [ˈpɒlətɪks] Politik
pond [pɒnd] Teich I
pony [ˈpəʊni] Pony I **ride a pony** auf einem Pony reiten I
ponytail [ˈpəʊniteɪl] Pferdeschwanz (Frisur) V 1 (18)
poor [pɔː], [pʊə] arm II **poor Ellie** (die) arme Ellie II
°**pop** [pɒp] (infml) Papa, Vati
popcorn [ˈpɒpkɔːn] Popcorn II
popular [ˈpɒpjələ] beliebt, populär II
population [pɒpjuˈleɪʃn] Bevölkerung, Einwohner(zahl) IV
porch [pɔːtʃ] (AE) Veranda IV
port [pɔːt] Hafen; Hafenstadt III
portrait [ˈpɔːtreɪt] Porträt V 4 (79)
position [pəˈzɪʃn] Position, Stelle, Platz IV
positive [ˈpɒzətɪv] positiv II
possible [ˈpɒsəbl] möglich III
post [pəʊst] posten (im Internet veröffentlichen) V 4 (79)
post office [ˈpəʊst ˈɒfɪs] Postamt II
postcard [ˈpəʊstkɑːd] Postkarte II
posted [ˈpəʊstɪd]: **Keep me posted.** Halt mich auf dem Laufenden. III
poster [ˈpəʊstə] Poster I
postman/-woman [ˈpəʊstmən, -wʊmən] Briefträger/in III
potato, pl **potatoes** [pəˈteɪtəʊ] Kartoffel II
pound (£) [paʊnd] Pfund (britische Währung) I
°**powerful** [ˈpaʊəfl] kräftig, stark, mächtig
practice [ˈpræktɪs]:
1. (AE) üben; trainieren IV
2. Übung; Training IV
practise [ˈpræktɪs] (BE) üben; trainieren IV
prefer sth. (to sth.) [prɪˈfɜː] etwas (einer anderen Sache) vorziehen II
I'd (= I would) prefer ... ich würde ... vorziehen; ich würde lieber ... III
prefer to do sth. etwas lieber tun IV
prejudice [ˈpredʒʊdɪs] Vorurteil, Voreingenommenheit V 2 (35)

prepare [prɪˈpeə] vorbereiten; sich vorbereiten III **prepare for sth.** sich auf etwas vorbereiten III
preposition [prepəˈzɪʃn] Präposition IV
present [ˈpreznt]:
1. Gegenwart II
2. gegenwärtig V 3 (58)
present [ˈpreznt] Geschenk I
°**present** [ˈpreznt] vorhanden; anwesend
present sth. (to sb.) [prɪˈzent] (jm.) etwas präsentieren, (jm.) etwas vorstellen IV
presentation [preznˈteɪʃn] Referat, Präsentation V 1 (22) **give a presentation** ein Referat halten V 1 (22)
°**presenter** [prɪˈzentə] Referent/in
president [ˈprezɪdənt] Präsident/in III
°**press** [pres] drücken
pressure [ˈpreʃə] Druck V 2 (32)
pretend (to be sth.) [prɪˈtend] so tun, als ob (man etwas wäre) V 3 (62)
pretty [ˈprɪti]:
1. hübsch II
°**2.** ziemlich
price [praɪs] (Kauf-)Preis I
pride [praɪd] Stolz III **pride (in sth.)** Stolz (auf etwas) IV
°**primary school** [ˈpraɪməri skuːl] Grundschule
prince [prɪns] Prinz III
princess [prɪnˈses] Prinzessin III
principal [ˈprɪnsəpl] Rektor/in, Schulleiter/in I
°**print** [prɪnt] Druck-, gedruckt
prison [ˈprɪzn] Gefängnis IV **put sb. in prison** jn. ins Gefängnis sperren V 1 (15)
prize [praɪz] Preis, Gewinn III
probably [ˈprɒbəbli] wahrscheinlich III
problem [ˈprɒbləm] Problem I
product [ˈprɒdʌkt] Produkt V 4 (80)
professional [prəˈfeʃnl] professionell, Profi- IV
profile [ˈprəʊfaɪl] Profil; Beschreibung, Portrait V 4 (78)
profit [ˈprɒfɪt] Gewinn, Profit III
program [ˈprəʊɡræm] (AE) Programm V 3 (62)
programme [ˈprəʊɡræm] (Fernseh-)Sendung I
project [ˈprɒdʒekt] Projekt II
promise [ˈprɒmɪs] versprechen IV
°**properly** [ˈprɒpəli] richtig, ordentlich, korrekt
pros [prəʊz]: **the pros and cons** (pl) das Pro und Kontra; das Für und Wider V 4 (76)
°**prosthetic leg** [prɒsˈθetɪk leɡ] Beinprothese
protect (from) [prəˈtekt] (be)schützen (vor) V 1 (13)
protest [prəˈtest] protestieren IV
proud (of) [praʊd] stolz (auf) I
pub [pʌb] Kneipe, Lokal III
pull [pʊl] ziehen IV **pull back** sich zurückziehen, zurückweichen V 3 (63)

pull back your hair sich die Haare zusammenbinden V 3 (63) **pull in** anhalten, an den Straßenrand fahren IV
°**pull over** anhalten, an den Straßenrand fahren
pullover [ˈpʊləʊvə] Pullover I
°**pumps** (pl) [pʌmps] Pumps (elegante Damenschuhe)
punctual [ˈpʌŋktʃuəl] pünktlich V 3 (54)
puppy [ˈpʌpi] (Hunde-)Welpe V 4 (78)
purple [ˈpɜːpl] violett; lila I
push [pʊʃ] schieben, stoßen, drücken IV
put [pʊt], **put, put** (etwas wohin) tun, legen, stellen II **put sth. in** etwas einsetzen, eingeben II **put sth. on** etwas anziehen (Kleidung); etwas aufsetzen (Hut, Brille) II **put up one's hand** sich melden; seine/die Hand heben V 3 (62)
puzzle [ˈpʌzl] Rätsel IV
pyjamas (pl) [pəˈdʒɑːməz] Schlafanzug II

Q

quad [kwɒd] Quad (vierrädriges Motorrad) III
qualification [kwɒlɪfɪˈkeɪʃn] (Schul-)Abschluss, Qualifikation V 3 (56)
qualified [ˈkwɒlɪfaɪd] qualifiziert; ausgebildet, mit Abschluss V 3 (56)
qualify [ˈkwɒlɪfaɪ] (sich) qualifizieren V 3 (56)
quality [ˈkwɒləti] Eigenschaft; Qualität V 3 (57) **personal qualities** persönliche Eigenschaften V 3 (57)
queen [kwiːn] Königin III
question [ˈkwestʃən]:
1. Frage I
ask questions Fragen stellen I
2. question sb. jn. befragen, verhören V 2 (35)
questionnaire [kwestʃəˈneə] Fragebogen IV
quick [kwɪk] schnell II
quiet [ˈkwaɪət] ruhig, still, leise I
quite [kwaɪt] ziemlich II
quiz [kwɪz] Quiz, Ratespiel I

R

rabbit [ˈræbɪt] Kaninchen I
race [reɪs]:
1. (Wett-)Rennen V 1 (16)
2. rasen, schnell fahren V 1 (16)
race [reɪs] Volk, Stamm; Rasse V 2 (35)
racing [ˈreɪsɪŋ] Rennsport V 1 (16)
racism [ˈreɪsɪzəm] Rassismus V 2 (35)
racist [ˈreɪsɪst]:
1. Rassist/in V 2 (35)
2. rassistisch V 2 (35)
radio [ˈreɪdiəʊ] Radio III
rain [reɪn]:
1. Regen II
2. regnen II
rainy [ˈreɪni] regnerisch II
°**rally** [ˈræli] Rallye

ran [ræn] *siehe* **run**
rang [ræŋ] *siehe* **ring**
ranger ['reɪndʒə] Ranger/in; (Park-)Aufseher/in II
°**rank** [ræŋk] einstufen, anordnen
rap [ræp]:
1. Rap *(rhythmischer Sprechgesang)* I
2. rappen I
rapper ['ræpə] Rapper/in I
°**rare** [reə] selten
rat [ræt] Ratte I
°**rather** ['rɑːðə] ziemlich **rather than** anstelle von, (an)statt
reach (sb./a place) [riːtʃ] (jn./einen Ort) erreichen V 4 (82)
react (to) [ri'ækt] reagieren (auf) III
°**reaction (to)** [ri'ækʃn] Reaktion (auf)
read [riːd], **read, read** lesen I °**read out** (laut) vorlesen
reader ['riːdə] Leser/in III
ready ['redi] bereit, fertig III **get ready (for)** sich fertig machen (für), sich vorbereiten (auf) I
real [rɪəl] echt, wirklich I
realistic [riːə'lɪstɪk] realistisch V 4 (84)
reality [ri'ælti] Wirklichkeit, Realität II
reality show [ri'ælti ʃəʊ] Realityshow II
realize sth. ['riːəlaɪz] etwas erkennen, sich einer Sache bewusst werden V 3 (62)
really ['riːəli], ['rɪəli] wirklich I
reason ['riːzn] Grund III **for lots of reasons** aus vielen Gründen II
recently ['riːsntli] in letzter Zeit; vor Kurzem III
receptionist [rɪ'sepʃənɪst] Empfangschef/in III
recipe ['resəpi] (Koch-)Rezept I
recommend sth. (to sb.) [rekə'mend] (jm.) etwas empfehlen IV
recommendation [rekəmen'deɪʃn] Empfehlung V 2 (43)
record [rɪ'kɔːd] aufnehmen, aufzeichnen V 1 (17)
recycle [riː'saɪkl] wiederverwerten II
red [red] rot I
°**redial** [riː'daɪəl] die Wahlwiederholung betätigen
redness ['rednəs] Rötung, Röte V 1 (13)
reduce (by) [rɪ'djuːs] reduzieren, verringern (um) V 4 (80)
reef [riːf] Riff V 1 (9)
reference ['refrəns] Referenz, Empfehlung; jd., der eine Referenz erteilt V 3 (58)
°**refresh** [rɪ'freʃ] (sich) erfrischen
reggae ['regeɪ] Reggae II
°**region** ['riːdʒən] Region, Gegend
regular ['regjələ] regelmäßig, normal V 1 (17)
°**relationship** [rɪ'leɪʃnʃɪp] Beziehung
relax [rɪ'læks] sich entspannen V 4 (79)
relaxing [rɪ'læksɪŋ] entspannend, beruhigend II

relevant ['reləvənt] relevant, wichtig V 3 (59)
reliable [rɪ'laɪəbl] zuverlässig, verlässlich V 3 (54)
°**remain** [rɪ'meɪn] (ver)bleiben
remember [rɪ'membə]:
1. daran denken; sich merken I
2. sich erinnern (an) I
remind sb. (of sth.) [rɪ'maɪnd] jn. (an etwas) erinnern IV
°**remote** [rɪ'məʊt] entlegen, abgelegen
rent [rent] mieten, leihen IV
repair [rɪ'peə] reparieren V 1 (16)
repeat [rɪ'piːt] wiederholen V 4 (80)
°**replace** [rɪ'pleɪs] ersetzen, austauschen
report [rɪ'pɔːt]:
1. Bericht IV
2. **report (on sth.)** (über etwas) berichten IV
reporter [rɪ'pɔːtə] Reporter/in III
represent [reprɪ'zent] repräsentieren, vertreten III
request [rɪ'kwest] Wunsch, Bitte; Anfrage V 2 (40)
rescue ['reskjuː] Rettung(sdienst) IV
°**research** [rɪ'sɜːtʃ] Forschung(en), Recherche(n) **do research** recherchieren
reservation [rezə'veɪʃn] Reservierung III
°**resource** [rɪ'sɔːs] (Hilfs-)Mittel, Ressource
respect [rɪ'spekt]:
1. Respekt V 2 (30)
2. respektieren, achten III
°**respectable** [rɪ'spektəbl] anständig, angesehen, ehrbar
respectful [rɪ'spektfl] respektvoll V 4 (89)
°**respond** [rɪ'spɒnd] antworten, reagieren
°**response** [rɪ'spɒns] Reaktion, Antwort
responsible [rɪ'spɒnsəbl] verantwortungsbewusst; verantwortlich IV
rest [rest] (Erholungs-)Pause IV
°**take a rest** Pause machen
restaurant ['restrɒnt] Restaurant I
restroom ['restruːm] *(AE)* Toilette, WC IV
result [rɪ'zʌlt] Ergebnis, Resultat III
retell [riː'tel], **retold, retold** nacherzählen V 1 (21)
retold [riː'təʊld] *siehe* **retell**
°**return** [rɪ'tɜːn] zurückkehren, zurückkommen
°**revenge** [rɪ'vendʒ] Rache
review [rɪ'vjuː] Rezension, Besprechung, Kritik III
revision [rɪ'vɪʒn] Wiederholung (des Lernstoffs) III
°**rhyme** [raɪm] (sich) reimen
rich [rɪtʃ] reich V 4 (85)
rid [rɪd]: **get rid of sth.** etwas loswerden II
ridden ['rɪdn] *siehe* **ride**
ride [raɪd] Fahrt; Fahrgeschäft *(auf Volksfest, in Vergnügungspark)* III

ride [raɪd], **rode, ridden**:
1. fahren IV
2. reiten I
ride a bike Rad fahren I **ride a pony** auf einem Pony reiten I
right [raɪt]:
1. rechts; nach rechts I
2. richtig I **all right** gut; in Ordnung; OK IV **on the right** rechts, auf der rechten Seite I **You're right. Du hast Recht.** III
3. **right now** jetzt gerade; im Augenblick III
right [raɪt] Recht V 2 (42) **civil rights** *(pl)* Bürgerrechte IV **have every right to do sth.** guten Grund / alles Recht haben, etwas zu tun V 2 (42)
ring [rɪŋ], **rang, rung**:
1. anrufen III
2. läuten, klingeln I
ringtone ['rɪŋtəʊn] Klingelton III
°**rip current** ['rɪp kʌrənt] Brandungsrückstrom *(gefährliche Strömung an Küsten)*
risk [rɪsk]:
1. Risiko III
take risks Risiken eingehen III °**at (your) own risk** auf eigene Gefahr
2. riskieren, wagen V 1 (19)
risky ['rɪski] riskant V 2 (32)
river ['rɪvə] Fluss II
road [rəʊd] Straße *(zwischen Orten, aber auch in Orten)* I
road trip ['rəʊd trɪp] Autoreise IV
°**roadside** ['rəʊdsaɪd] (am) Straßenrand
rock [rɒk]:
1. Fels, Felsen II
2. Rock(musik) II
rock band ['rɒk bænd] Rockband II
°**rocket** ['rɒkɪt] rasen, schießen
rode [rəʊd] *siehe* **ride**
°**role** [rəʊl] Rolle
role model ['rəʊl mɒdl] Vorbild III
°**role-play** ['rəʊl pleɪ] Rollenspiel
roll [rəʊl] rollen IV **roll sth. down** etwas herunterrollen IV **roll sth. up** etwas aufrollen, hochrollen, aufkrempeln IV °**roll as one** gemeinsam vorankommen
°**roller skating** ['rəʊlə skeɪtɪŋ] Rollschuhlaufen
romance [rəʊ'mæns] Romanze IV
romantic [rəʊ'mæntɪk] romantisch; Liebes- IV
roof [ruːf] Dach V 4 (86)
room [ruːm], [rʊm] Raum, Zimmer I
round [raʊnd]:
1. rund II
2. **do a paper round** Zeitungen austragen II
route [ruːt] Strecke, Route IV
routine [ruː'tiːn] Routine IV
rubber ['rʌbə] Radiergummi I

DICTIONARY

English – German

rubbish [ˈrʌbɪʃ] (Haus-)Müll, Abfall II
 That's rubbish. (infml) Das ist Unsinn. / Das ist Quatsch. III
rucksack [ˈrʌksæk] Rucksack II
rude [ruːd] unhöflich, frech III
rug [rʌg] Teppich, Läufer I
rugby [ˈrʌgbi] Rugby III
rule [ruːl] Regel II
ruler [ˈruːlə] Lineal I
run [rʌn], **ran, run** rennen, laufen II
 run a business / a hotel eine Firma / ein Hotel leiten, führen III **run after sb.** hinter jm. herrennen IV **run around** umherrennen; herumlaufen II **run out** knapp werden V 3 (52)
 I often run out of money. Mir geht oft das Geld aus. / Bei mir wird oft das Geld knapp. V 3 (52)
rung [rʌŋ] siehe **ring**
runner [ˈrʌnə] Läufer/in III
°**Rural Fire Service** [ˈruərəl] Buschbrandfeuerwehr

S

°**sacred** [ˈseɪkrɪd] heilig
sad [sæd] traurig II
sadness [ˈsædnəs] Traurigkeit V 1 (13)
safe [seɪf] sicher; in Sicherheit III
safety [ˈseɪfti] Sicherheit II
said [sed] siehe **say**
salad [ˈsæləd] Salat (als Gericht oder Beilage) I
salami [səˈlɑːmi] Salami II
°**salary** [ˈsæləri] Lohn, Gehalt
sale [seɪl] Verkauf; Schlussverkauf I
 sales (pl) Verkauf V 3 (58) **for sale** zu verkaufen; zum Verkauf V 3 (58)
sales assistant [ˈseɪlz əsɪstənt] Verkäufer/in V 3 (58)
salesperson [ˈseɪlzpɜːsn] Verkäufer/in III
salt [sɔːlt] Salz V 1 (11)
same [seɪm]: **be the same** gleich sein II **the same** derselbe/dieselbe/dasselbe; dieselben I
°**sample** [ˈsɑːmpl] Muster, Probe(exemplar)
°**sandals** (pl) [ˈsændlz] Sandalen
sandwich [ˈsænwɪtʃ], [ˈsænwɪdʒ] Sandwich I
sang [sæŋ] siehe **sing**
°**sank** [sæŋk] siehe **sink**
sat [sæt] siehe **sit**
Saturday [ˈsætədeɪ], [ˈsætədi] Samstag, Sonnabend I
sauce [sɔːs] Sauce V 3 (52)
sausage [ˈsɒsɪdʒ] Wurst, Würstchen II
save [seɪv]:
 1. retten III
 2. sparen (Geld, Zeit) II
savvy [ˈsævi] (infml) versiert, gewieft V 4 (80)
saw [sɔː] siehe **see**
°**saxophone** [ˈsæksəfəʊn] Saxofon
say [seɪ], **said, said** sagen I **Say hi to everybody.** Grüß alle. I

scan a text [skæn] einen Text schnell nach bestimmten Wörtern/Informationen absuchen IV
scare sb. [skeə] jn. erschrecken, jm. Angst machen II
scared [skeəd]: **be scared (of)** Angst haben (vor) II
scarf, pl **scarves** [skɑːf], [skɑːvz] Schal II
scary [ˈskeəri] unheimlich, gruselig II
scene [siːn] Szene II
school [skuːl] Schule I **leave school** von der Schule abgehen III
school bag [ˈskuːl bæg] Schultasche I
school subject [ˈskuːl sʌbdʒɪkt] Schulfach III
school yard [ˈskuːl jɑːd] Schulhof II
science [ˈsaɪəns] Naturwissenschaft I
science fiction [saɪəns ˈfɪkʃn] Sciencefiction IV
scissors (pl) [ˈsɪzəz] Schere I
scone [skɒn] kleines rundes Milchbrötchen, leicht süß, oft mit Rosinen I
scrambled eggs [skræmbld ˈegz] Rührei IV
scream [skriːm] schreien II
screen [skriːn] Leinwand; Bildschirm IV
screenager [ˈskriːneɪdʒə] Screenager (Jugendliche/r, der/die sehr viel Zeit vor dem Bildschirm verbringt) V 4 (76)
screenshot [ˈskriːnʃɒt] Screenshot (Bildschirmabbild) V 4 (81)
sea [siː] Meer I
sea lion [ˈsiː laɪən] Seelöwe IV
seagull [ˈsiːgʌl] Möwe I
search [sɜːtʃ]:
 1. Suche V 4 (78)
 2. **search for sth.** etwas suchen / nach etwas suchen V 4 (78)
 search the internet for sth. das Internet nach etwas durchsuchen V 4 (78)
season [ˈsiːzn] Jahreszeit II
°**seasonal** [ˈsiːzənl] Saison-, saisonal
seat [siːt] (Sitz-)Platz I
second [ˈsekənd]:
 1. Sekunde IV
 2. zweite(r, s) I
second-hand [sekənd ˈhænd] gebraucht, aus zweiter Hand II
Secondly, … [ˈsekəndli] Zweitens … III
secret [ˈsiːkrət]:
 1. geheim V 1 (15)
 2. Geheimnis V 1 (15)
security [sɪˈkjʊərəti] Sicherheit; Sicherheits- III
see [siː], **saw, seen** sehen I **See you around.** Bis dann. V 2 (45) **See you. / See you later.** Bis dann. / Bis später. I **I see.** Ach so. / Aha. / Verstehe. II **Let's see.** Mal sehen. / Mal abwarten. III °**See for yourself.** Sieh selbst! / Sehen Sie selbst!
°**seek shade** [siːk], **sought, sought** Schatten (auf)suchen

seem [siːm] scheinen (anscheinend sein) IV
seen [siːn] siehe **see**
segregation [segrɪˈgeɪʃn] Trennung (nach Rasse/Religion/Geschlecht) IV
selfie [ˈselfi] Selfie (Schnappschuss von sich selbst) V 4 (79)
self-portrait [self ˈpɔːtreɪt] Selbstporträt V 4 (79)
°**self-respect** [self rɪˈspekt] Selbstachtung
sell [sel], **sold, sold** verkaufen III
send [send], **sent, sent** schicken, senden I **send sth. out** etwas verschicken V 3 (61)
sent [sent] siehe **send**
sentence [ˈsentəns] Satz II
September [sepˈtembə] September I
series, pl **series** [ˈsɪəriːz] (Sende-)Reihe, Serie II
°**serious** [ˈsɪəriəs] ernst(haft) **Are you serious?** Meinst du das ernst?
serve [sɜːv] servieren (Essen, Getränke); bedienen (Kunden) III
service [ˈsɜːvɪs] Dienst, Service II
set the table [set], **set, set** den Tisch decken I
setting [ˈsetɪŋ] Schauplatz (z.B. Film/Geschichte) V 2 (43)
°**settings** (pl) [ˈsetɪŋz] Einstellungen, Settings
settle [ˈsetl] sich niederlassen, sich ansiedeln V 1 (10)
settler [ˈsetlə] Siedler/in IV
seven [ˈsevn] sieben I
°**several** [ˈsevrəl] mehrere, einige
shade [ʃeɪd] Schatten (vor der Sonne geschützt) V 1 (12)
shadow [ˈʃædəʊ] Schatten (Umriss) V 1 (12)
°**shake** [ʃeɪk]
 1. Schüttelbewegung
 2. **shake, shook, shaken** schütteln **shake your head** den Kopf schütteln **He shook his head.** Er schüttelte den Kopf.
°**shaken** [ˈʃeɪkən] siehe **shake**
shame [ʃeɪm]: **a shame** ein Jammer; schade V 4 (83)
shampoo [ʃæmˈpuː] Shampoo, Haarwaschmittel IV
share [ʃeə]: **share a room with …** sich ein Zimmer mit … teilen I
 °**Would you like to share my umbrella?** Möchtest du mit unter meinen Regenschirm?
shark [ʃɑːk] Hai I
she [ʃiː] sie (Singular) I
sheep, pl **sheep** [ʃiːp] Schaf I
°**sheep station** [ˈʃiːp steɪʃn] (AustE) Schaffarm (in Australien)
°**sheet** [ʃiːt] Blatt (Papier)
shelf, (pl) **shelves** [ʃelf], [ʃelvz] Regal I

shift [ʃɪft] Schicht *(bei der Arbeit)* V 3 (57) **work shifts** im Schichtdienst arbeiten V 3 (57)
shine [ʃaɪn], **shone, shone** scheinen (Sonne) III
ship [ʃɪp] Schiff III
shirt [ʃɜːt] Hemd I
shock [ʃɒk] schockieren V 4 (88)
shocked [ʃɒkt] schockiert V 4 (88)
shocking [ˈʃɒkɪŋ] schockierend V 4 (88)
shoe [ʃuː] Schuh I
shone [ʃɒn] *siehe* **shine**
°**shook** [ʃʊk] *siehe* **shake**
shop [ʃɒp] Geschäft, Laden I
shoplift [ˈʃɒplɪft] Ladendiebstahl begehen V 2 (32)
shoplifting [ˈʃɒplɪftɪŋ] Ladendiebstahl V 2 (32)
shopper [ˈʃɒpə] (Ein-)Käufer/in IV
shopping [ˈʃɒpɪŋ]: **do the shopping** Einkäufe erledigen, einkaufen gehen V 3 (52) **go shopping** einkaufen gehen I
shopping centre [ˈʃɒpɪŋ sentə] Einkaufszentrum I
shopping mall [ˈʃɒpɪŋ mɔːl] *(oft auch kurz:* **mall**) Einkaufszentrum III
short [ʃɔːt]:
1. klein *(Person)* II
2. kurz II
°**short cut** [ʃɔːt ˈkʌt] Abkürzung II
short story [ʃɔːt ˈstɔːri] Kurzgeschichte V 3 (62)
shorts *(pl)* [ʃɔːts] Shorts, kurze Hose IV
shot [ʃɒt] Schuss III
should [ʃʊd]: **What should I do?** Was sollte ich tun? II
shoulder [ˈʃəʊldə] Schulter I
shout [ʃaʊt]:
1. Ruf IV
2. rufen II
°**shout sth. out** etwas herausrufen
show [ʃəʊ] Show II
show [ʃəʊ], **showed, shown**:
1. zeigen II
2. sich zeigen, sichtbar sein V 2 (36)
°**shower** [ˈʃaʊə]
1. (sich) duschen
2. Dusche
have/take a shower (sich) duschen
shown [ʃəʊn] *siehe* **show**
Shut up! [ʃʌt] *(infml)* Halt den Mund! I
shy [ʃaɪ] schüchtern, scheu II
sick [sɪk] krank V 1 (12) **I'm/I feel sick.** Mir ist schlecht/übel. V 1 (12)
side [saɪd] Seite III **side by side** Seite an Seite IV
sidewalk [ˈsaɪdwɔːk] *(AE)* Gehweg, Bürgersteig IV
sight [saɪt]:
1. Anblick III
°2. sichten
sights *(pl)* [saɪts] Sehenswürdigkeiten III

sightseeing tour [ˈsaɪtsiːɪŋ] Rundfahrt *(zur Besichtigung der Sehenswürdigkeiten)* III
sign [saɪn]:
1. Schild; Zeichen I
2. unterschreiben IV
signal [ˈsɪgnəl] Signal III
°**silent** [ˈsaɪlənt] still, lautlos
silence [ˈsaɪləns] Stille, Schweigen IV
silly [ˈsɪli] albern; blöd II **Silly me!** Bin ich blöd! I
similar (to sth./sb.) [ˈsɪmələ] (etwas/jm.) ähnlich IV
simple [ˈsɪmpl] einfach, simpel V 1 (15)
since [sɪns]:
1. seit III
since August / 12 o'clock seit August / 12 Uhr III
2. seitdem, seither V 1 (11)
sincerely [sɪnˈsɪəli]: **Sincerely yours** *(AE)* Mit freundlichen Grüßen *(Briefschluss)* V 3 (59) **Yours sincerely ...** *(BE)* / **Sincerely, ...** *(AE)* Mit freundlichen Grüßen *(Briefschluss)* IV
sing [sɪŋ], **sang, sung** singen I
singer [ˈsɪŋə] Sänger/in I
single [ˈsɪŋgl] ledig, alleinstehend II **single parent** Alleinerziehende(r) IV **single ticket** einfache Fahrkarte IV
°**sink** [sɪŋk], **sank, sunk** sinken **sink down in your seat** auf dem Sitz zusammensinken, nach unten rutschen
sir [sɜː] gnädiger Herr V 3 (59) **Dear Sir/Madam** Sehr geehrte Damen und Herren V 3 (59)
°**sis** [sɪs] *(infml)* Schwester *(kurz für:* sister)
sister [ˈsɪstə] Schwester I
sit [sɪt], **sat, sat** sitzen; sich setzen I **sit down** sich hinsetzen III °**sit up** sich aufsetzen, sich gerade hinsetzen
site [saɪt] *(kurz für:* **website**) Website IV
situation [sɪtʃuˈeɪʃn] Situation V 3 (57)
six [sɪks] sechs I
size [saɪz] Größe IV
skateboard [ˈskeɪtbɔːd] Skateboard fahren I
skating [ˈskeɪtɪŋ]:
1. (= *ice skating*) Schlittschuhlaufen V 2 (40)
2. (= *roller skating*) Rollschuhlaufen V 2 (40)
ski [skiː] Ski laufen, Ski fahren II
skier [ˈskiːə] Skiläufer/in III
skill [skɪl] Fähigkeit, Fertigkeit V 3 (53)
°**skills file** [ˈskɪlz faɪl] Anhang mit Lern- und Arbeitstechniken
skim a text [skɪm] einen Text überfliegen *(um den Inhalt grob zu erfassen)* III
skin [skɪn] Haut IV
skinny [ˈskɪni] *(infml)* mager, dürr III
skirt [skɜːt] Rock I

skive [skaɪv] *(infml)* schwänzen *(Schule)* II
sky [skaɪ] Himmel IV **in the sky** am Himmel IV
skyline [ˈskaɪlaɪn] Skyline IV
skyscraper [ˈskaɪskreɪpə] Wolkenkratzer IV
°**slam** [slæm] (zu-, hin)knallen **slam down the phone** den Hörer aufknallen
°**slap on a hat** [slæp ˈɒn] *(infml)* einen Hut/eine Mütze aufsetzen
slave [sleɪv] Sklave/Sklavin IV
slavery [ˈsleɪvəri] Sklaverei III
sleep [sliːp]:
1. Schlaf II
Go to sleep! Schlaf jetzt! I
2. **sleep, slept, slept** schlafen I
sleeping bag [ˈsliːpɪŋ bæg] Schlafsack I
sleepover [ˈsliːpəʊvə] Schlafparty I
sleepy [ˈsliːpi] schläfrig III
slept [slept] *siehe* **sleep**
°**slid** [slɪd] *siehe* **slide**
slide [slaɪd] Dia, Folie V 1 (17)
°**slide on some sunglasses** [slaɪd ˈɒn], **slid, slid** eine Sonnenbrille aufsetzen
°**slip on a T-Shirt** [slɪp ˈɒn] (sich) ein T-Shirt überziehen
slogan [ˈsləʊgən] Slogan V 4 (84)
°**slop on some suncream** [slɒp ˈɒn] *(infml)* Sonnencreme auftragen
slow [sləʊ] langsam II
small [smɔːl] klein I
smart [smɑːt] schick, smart; schlau, clever IV
smartphone [ˈsmɑːtfəʊn] Smartphone V 4 (76)
smell [smel]:
1. Geruch, Gestank IV
2. riechen II
smile [smaɪl]:
1. lächeln III
2. *(das)* Lächeln II
smoke [sməʊk] rauchen IV
smoothie [ˈsmuːði] Smoothie *(Getränk aus Fruchtpüree, evtl. mit Milchprodukten)* II
snack [snæk] Snack, Imbiss II
snake [sneɪk] Schlange I
sneaker [ˈsniːkə] *(AE)* Turnschuh IV
snow [snəʊ] Schnee II
°**snowboard** [ˈsnəʊbɔːd] Snowboard fahren
snowy [ˈsnəʊi] schneebedeckt; verschneit II
so [səʊ]:
1. also; deshalb, daher II
2. **so boring/tired/...** so langweilig/müde/... I
so far bis jetzt V 3 (56) **so that** sodass, damit IV
3. **I don't think so.** Das glaube/denke ich nicht. III
I think so. Ich glaube ja. III

soap [səʊ] Seife; *(infml auch:)* Seifenoper II
soccer ['sɒkə] Fußball IV
social ['səʊʃl] gesellschaftlich, sozial V 4 (76)
social media *(pl)* [səʊʃl 'miːdiə] soziale Medien/Dienste V 4 (76)
society [sə'saɪəti] (die) Gesellschaft V 2 (35)
sock [sɒk] Socke, Strumpf I
sofa ['səʊfə] Sofa II
°**soft drink** ['sɒft drɪŋk] alkoholfreies Getränk
sold [səʊld] *siehe* **sell**
soldier ['səʊldʒə] Soldat/in IV
solution (to a problem) [sə'luːʃn] Lösung (eines Problems) V 3 (55)
some [sʌm], [səm] einige, ein paar; etwas I **Would you like some tea/chips?** Möchtest du (etwas) Tee / (ein paar) Pommes frites? II
somebody ['sʌmbədi] jemand II
someone ['sʌmwʌn] jemand II
someplace ['sʌmpleɪs] irgendwo(hin) IV
something ['sʌmθɪŋ] etwas I **something else** etwas anderes III **… or something** … oder so was III
sometime ['sʌmtaɪm] irgendwann V 2 (45)
sometimes ['sʌmtaɪmz] manchmal I
somewhere ['sʌmweə] irgendwo; irgendwohin III
son [sʌn] Sohn III
song [sɒŋ] Lied, Song I
soon [suːn] bald I **as soon as** sobald, sowie III
°**sophomore** ['sɒfəmɔː] *(AE)* High-School-Schüler/in im 2. Jahr (= 10. Klasse)
sore [sɔː 'θrəʊt]: **a sore throat** Halsschmerzen I **I have a sore leg.** Mein Bein tut weh. I
sorry ['sɒri]: **Sorry. / I'm sorry.** Tut mir leid. / Entschuldigung. I **I'm sorry about yesterday.** Es tut mir leid wegen gestern. II **say sorry** sich entschuldigen V 3 (54)
°**sought** [sɔːt] *siehe* **seek**
sound [saʊnd]:
1. Geräusch; Klang, Laut; Ton I
2. klingen, sich *(gut/schrecklich/…)* anhören III
soup [suːp] Suppe I
south [saʊθ] Süden; nach Süden II **south-east** Südosten; nach Südosten II **south-west** Südwesten; nach Südwesten II
southern ['sʌðən] südlich, Süd- IV
°**souvenir** ['guːdnɪŋ] Andenken, Souvenir
space [speɪs] Platz I
°**spare room** [speə 'ruːm] Gästezimmer
speak [spiːk], **spoke, spoken** sprechen I **speak clearly** deutlich sprechen II

speaker ['spiːkə] Sprecher/in; Redner/in V 4 (89)
special ['speʃl] besondere(r, s) I **make sth. special** etwas zu etwas Besonderem machen III **What's special about …?** Was ist das Besondere an …? III
special offer [speʃl 'ɒfə] Sonderangebot I
speech [spiːtʃ] Rede; Sprechweise V 3 (60) **give/make a speech** eine Rede halten V 3 (60)
°**speech bubble** ['spiːtʃ bʌbl] Sprechblase
spell [spel] buchstabieren I
spelling ['spelɪŋ] Rechtschreibung; Schreibweise IV
spend time/money (on) [spend], **spent, spent** Zeit verbringen (mit); Geld ausgeben (für) II
spent [spent] *siehe* **spend**
spider ['spaɪdə] Spinne V 1 (11)
spirit ['spɪrɪt] Geist, Stimmung IV **school spirit** Schulklima, Gemeinschaftsgefühl IV **team spirit** Teamgeist, Mannschaftsgeist IV
spoke [spəʊk] *siehe* **speak**
spoken [spəʊkən] *siehe* **speak**
°**spook** [spuːk] Geist
°**spooky** ['spuːki] unheimlich, gruselig
sport [spɔːt] Sport; Sportart I **do sport** Sport treiben II
sports car ['spɔːts kɑː] Sportwagen IV
sports hall ['spɔːts hɔːl] Sporthalle I
sportsman/-woman ['spɔːtsmən, -wʊmən] Sportler/in III
sporty ['spɔːti] sportlich II
spot [spɒt]:
1. entdecken IV
2. Stelle, Ort; Fleck V 1 (11)
°**spread sth.** [spred], **spread, spread** etwas verbreiten (Virus, Krankheit)
spring [sprɪŋ] Frühling II
square [skweə] Platz *(in Stadt oder Dorf)* III
squat [skwɒt] (ein Haus/Grundstück) besetzen V 2 (41)
squatter ['skwɒtə] Hausbesetzer/in V 2 (41)
stadium ['steɪdiəm] Stadion II
staff [stɑːf] Personal, Belegschaft V 2 (35)
stairs *(pl)* [steəz] Treppe; Treppenstufen IV
stamp [stæmp] Stempel II
stand [stænd], **stood, stood** stehen; sich (hin)stellen III **stand out (from)** sich abheben (von), herausragen (aus) III **stand up** aufstehen IV
standard ['stændəd]:
1. Norm, Standard V 4 (78)
2. normal, üblich, Standard- V 4 (78)
stank [stæŋk] *siehe* **stink**

star [stɑː]:
1. Star III
2. Stern IV
stare [steə] starren IV
start [stɑːt]:
1. anfangen, beginnen I
2. Start II
start a business ein Geschäft/eine Firma gründen III **start off (as)** anfangen (als) V 2 (45) **get started** anfangen III **To start with, …** Erstens …; Zunächst …; Zuerst einmal … IV
state [steɪt] Staat IV
statement ['steɪtmənt] Aussage II
station ['steɪʃn] Bahnhof II
statistics *(pl)* [stə'tɪstɪks] Statistik IV
statue ['stætʃuː] Statue IV
°**status** ['steɪtəs] Status
stay [steɪ]:
1. Aufenthalt III
2. bleiben I
steal [stiːl], **stole, stolen** stehlen V 2 (33)
step [step]:
1. Schritt II
step by step Schritt für Schritt V 2 (45)
2. Stufe IV
°3. treten *(einen Schritt tun)*
stepbrother ['stepbrʌðə] Stiefbruder I
stepdad ['stepdæd] Stiefvater I
step-dancing ['stepdɑːnsɪŋ] Stepptanz IV
stepfather ['stepfɑːðə] Stiefvater I
stepmother ['stepmʌðə] Stiefmutter I
stepmum ['stepmʌm] Stiefmutter I
stepsister ['stepsɪstə] Stiefschwester I
°**stick** [stɪk] Stock
stick, stuck, stuck [stɪk]: **stick together** zusammenhalten III °**stick with sth.** bei etwas bleiben
still [stɪl]:
1. immer noch, noch immer II
2. still, ruhig V 1 (12)
sting [stɪŋ]:
1. (Insekten-)Stich V 1 (11)
2. **sting, stung, stung** stechen *(Insekt)*; brennen V 1 (11)
°**stinger** ['stɪŋə] Würfelqualle *(giftige Qualle)*
stink [stɪŋk], **stank, stunk** stinken IV
stole [stəʊl] *siehe* **steal**
stolen ['stəʊlən] *siehe* **steal**
stomach ['stʌmək] Magen, Bauch IV
stomach ache ['stʌmək eɪk] Magenschmerzen IV
stone [stəʊn] Stein IV
stood [stʊd] *siehe* **stand**
stop [stɒp]:
1. anhalten III
2. stoppen II
3. Halt, Haltestelle IV
stop sth. mit etwas aufhören; etwas stoppen II **It stops with me.** Bei

mir hört's auf. / Ich mache da nicht mit. V 2 (35)
store [stɔː] Geschäft, Laden III
°**storey** [ˈstɔːri] Etage
story [ˈstɔːri]:
1. Geschichte, Erzählung I
°2. *(AE)* Etage
straight away [streɪt əˈweɪ] sofort V 4 (83)
straight on [streɪt ˈɒn] geradeaus (weiter) II
strange [streɪndʒ] seltsam, sonderbar II
strategy [ˈstrætədʒi] Strategie V 4 (81)
strawberry [ˈstrɔːbəri] Erdbeere IV
street [striːt] Straße *(in Orten)* I
strength [streŋθ] Stärke, Kraft V 3 (54)
stress [stres] Stress, Belastung V 1 (12)
  heat stress Hitzestress, Wärmebelastung des Körpers V 1 (12)
stressed [strest] gestresst III
stressful [ˈstresfl] anstrengend, stressig IV
strict [strɪkt] streng I
°**strike** [straɪk] streiken
stroke [strəʊk] streicheln I
strong [strɒŋ] stark III
structure [ˈstrʌktʃə]:
1. Struktur V 1 (22)
2. strukturieren, gliedern III
stuck [stʌk] *siehe* **stick**
°**stud** [stʌd] (Ohr-/Nasen-)Stecker
student [ˈstjuːdnt] Schüler/in; Student/in I
studio [ˈstjuːdiəʊ] Studio I
study [ˈstʌdi] studieren; lernen V 3 (55)
stuff [stʌf] *(infml)* Zeug, Kram II
stung [stʌŋ] *siehe* **sting**
stunk [stʌŋk] *siehe* **stink**
stupid [ˈstjuːpɪd] dumm, blöd I
style [staɪl] Stil V 3 (60)
stylist [ˈstaɪlɪst] Friseur/in; (Mode-)Stylist/in V 3 (56)
subject [ˈsʌbdʒɪkt]:
1. Schulfach III
2. Thema; *(in E-Mails)* Betreff II
subway [ˈsʌbweɪ] *(AE)* U-Bahn IV
°**success** [səkˈses] Erfolg
successful [səkˈsesfl] erfolgreich III
such (a) [sʌtʃ] so(lch) (ein/e) V 2 (32)
  there's no such thing as … es gibt kein/e … V 2 (32)
such as [ˈsʌtʃ əz] wie zum Beispiel V 1 (11)
suck [sʌk] *(infml)*: **It sucks!** Es nervt! / Es ist Mist! III
suddenly [ˈsʌdənli] plötzlich, auf einmal II
suffer (from) [ˈsʌfə] leiden (an), erleiden V 1 (11)
sugar [ˈʃʊɡə] Zucker II
sugary [ˈʃʊɡəri] süß(lich); zuckerhaltig II
suggest sth. (to sb.) [səˈdʒest] (jm.) etwas vorschlagen III
°**suggestion** [səˈdʒestʃən] Vorschlag

suitable [ˈsuːtəbl] geeignet, passend V 3 (59)
sum sth. up [sʌm ˈʌp] etwas zusammenfassen III **To sum up, …** Um (es) zusammenzufassen, … / Zusammenfassend kann man sagen, … V 2 (33)
summarize [ˈsʌməraɪz] zusammenfassen IV
summary [ˈsʌməri] Zusammenfassung III
summer [ˈsʌmə] Sommer I
sun [sʌn] Sonne II
suncream [ˈsʌnkriːm] Sonnencreme, Sonnenschutzmittel II
Sunday [ˈsʌndeɪ], [ˈsʌndi] Sonntag I
sung [sʌŋ] *siehe* **sing**
sunglasses *(pl)* [ˈsʌnɡlɑːsɪz] (eine) Sonnenbrille II
°**sunk** [sʌŋk] *siehe* **sink**
sunlight [ˈsʌnlaɪt] Sonnenlicht IV
sunny [ˈsʌni] sonnig II
sunshine [ˈsʌnʃaɪn] Sonnenschein IV
°**suntan** [ˈsʌntæn] Sonnenbräune
supermarket [ˈsuːpəmɑːkɪt] Supermarkt I
support [səˈpɔːt]:
1. unterstützen V 2 (32)
2. Unterstützung V 2 (32)
sure [ʃʊə], [ʃɔː] sicher I **for sure** ganz sicher, ganz bestimmt V 3 (60)
make sure that … sicherstellen, dass …; darauf achten, dass …; dafür sorgen, dass … V 1 (22)
surf [sɜːf] surfen, wellenreiten IV
surfer [ˈsɜːfə] Surfer/in, Wellenreiter/in IV
surfing [ˈsɜːfɪŋ] Surfing, Wellenreiten IV
surprise [səˈpraɪz]:
1. überraschen V 1 (11)
2. Überraschung I
surprised [səˈpraɪzd] überrascht II
surprising [səˈpraɪzɪŋ] überraschend V 1 (11)
°**surroundings** *(pl)* [səˈraʊndɪŋz] Umgebung
survey [ˈsɜːveɪ] Umfrage II
°**survive** [səˈvaɪv] überleben
suspension bridge [səˈspenʃn brɪdʒ] Hängebrücke IV
suspicious [səˈspɪʃəs] verdächtig IV
swam [swæm] *siehe* **swim**
swamp [swɒmp] Sumpf IV
°**swap** [swɒp] tauschen
sweat [swet] Schweiß IV
sweatshirt [ˈswetʃɜːt] Sweatshirt I
sweet [swiːt] süß IV
sweets *(pl)* [swiːts] Süßigkeiten I
swerve [swɜːv] herumreißen, *(mit dem Auto)* ausweichen V 1 (18)
swim [swɪm], **swam, swum** schwimmen I
swimmer [ˈswɪmə] Schwimmer/in III
swimming pool [ˈswɪmɪŋ puːl] Schwimmbad, Schwimmbecken I

°**swimsuit** [ˈswɪmsuːt] Badeanzug
switch sth. on/off [swɪtʃ] etwas ein-/ausschalten III
swum [swʌm] *siehe* **swim**
symbol [ˈsɪmbl] Symbol III

T

table [ˈteɪbl]:
1. Tisch I
°2. Tabelle
table tennis [ˈteɪbl tenɪs] Tischtennis II
tablet [ˈtæblət] Tablet(-PC) V 4 (76)
°**tackle** [ˈtækl] angreifen *(Fußball)*; fassen, packen *(Rugby, American Football)*
tae kwon do [taɪ kwɒn ˈdəʊ] Taekwondo I
tail [teɪl] Schwanz II
take [teɪk], **took, taken**:
1. nehmen; mitnehmen II
2. (weg-, hin)bringen IV
3. dauern, *(Zeit)* brauchen III
take a message (jm.) etwas ausrichten II **Take it easy!** *(infml)* etwa: Reg dich nicht auf. / Bleib mal locker. III **take notes** (sich) Notizen machen *(beim Lesen oder Zuhören)* III **take part in sth.** an etwas teilnehmen, bei etwas mitmachen III **take photos** fotografieren, Fotos machen II **take risks** Risiken eingehen III **take sth. on** etwas annehmen, übernehmen V 1 (15) **I'll take it.** Ich nehme es (ihn, sie). *(beim Einkaufen)* I °**take a test** einen Test/eine Prüfung machen °**take over** die Macht übernehmen °**take turns** sich abwechseln
takeaway [ˈteɪkəweɪ] Essen zum Mitnehmen V 3 (52)
taken [ˈteɪkən] *siehe* **take**
°**take-off** [ˈteɪk ɒf] Start *(Flugzeug)*
talent [ˈtælənt] Talent, Begabung III
talk [tɔːk]:
1. Vortrag, Rede; Gespräch II
2. **talk (to sb.)** sprechen, reden (mit jm.) I
  give a talk einen Vortrag halten II
talker [ˈtɔːkə] Redner/in III
tall [tɔːl] groß *(Person)*; hoch *(Gebäude, Baum)* II °**stand tall** aufrecht stehen, den Kopf hoch tragen
°**tap** [tæp] tippen (auf), leise klopfen
target [ˈtɑːɡɪt]:
1. Ziel V 4 (80)
2. **target sb.** auf jn. zielen *(jn. als Zielgruppe haben/wählen)*, jn. ins Visier nehmen V 4 (80)
task [tɑːsk] Aufgabe II
tattoo [təˈtuː] Tattoo, Tätowierung III
taught [tɔːt] *siehe* **teach**
°**taunt** [tɔːnt] Spott, höhnische Bemerkung
taxi [ˈtæksi] Taxi II

DICTIONARY

English – German

tea [tiː] Tee I
teach [tiːtʃ], **taught, taught** unterrichten, lehren III **teach sb. a lesson** jm. eine Lektion erteilen V 4 (82)
teacher [ˈtiːtʃə] Lehrer/in I
team [tiːm] Team, Mannschaft I **the under-18s team** das Team der unter 18-Jährigen V 3 (58)
team spirit [ˈtiːm spɪrɪt] Teamgeist, Mannschaftsgeist IV
teamwork [ˈtiːmwɜːk] Teamarbeit V 3 (55)
tear [tɪə] Träne IV
°**tease sb.** [tiːz] jn. hänseln, sich über jn. lustig machen
°**technique** [tekˈniːk] Methode, Technik
technology [tekˈnɒlədʒi] Technik, Technologie I
teen [tiːn] Teenager III
teen talk [ˈtiːn tɔːk] *etwa:* Teenagergespräche II
teenage [ˈtiːneɪdʒ]: **a teenage girl** ein Mädchen im Teenageralter V 2 (35)
teenager [ˈtiːneɪdʒə] Teenager I
teeth [tuːθ] *Mehrzahl von* **tooth** IV
telephone [ˈtelɪfəʊn] Telefon V 3 (58)
tell (about) [tel], **told, told** erzählen (von), berichten (über) II **tell sb. (not) to do sth.** jn. auffordern, etwas (nicht) zu tun; jm. sagen, dass er/sie etwas (nicht) tun soll IV **tell sb. the way** jm. den Weg beschreiben II
temperature [ˈtemprətʃə] Temperatur; Fieber II **have a temperature** Fieber haben II **take sb.'s temperature** (bei jm.) Fieber messen V 1 (13)
°**temple** [ˈtempl] Tempel
ten [ten] zehn I
tennis [ˈtenɪs] Tennis I
tent [tent] Zelt II
term [tɜːm] Trimester III
terrible [ˈterəbl] schrecklich, fürchterlich I
territory [ˈterətri] Gebiet, Territorium IV
°**terrorism** [ˈterərɪzəm] Terrorismus
terrorist [ˈterərɪst] terroristisch, Terror-; Terrorist/in IV
test [test]:
1. Test; Klassenarbeit II
2. (*kurz für:* **driving test**) Fahrprüfung, Führerscheinprüfung IV
°**take a test** einen Test/eine Prüfung machen
tester [ˈtestə] Tester/in V 4 (87)
text [tekst]:
1. SMS; Text I
2. **text a friend** einem Freund / einer Freundin eine SMS schicken I
text message [ˈtekst mesɪdʒ] (*kurz auch:* **text**) SMS I
than [ðən]: **more than** mehr als III **older than me** älter als ich I
thank you [ˈθæŋk juː] danke (schön) IV

Thanks. [θæŋks] Danke. I **Thanks very much.** Danke sehr. / Danke vielmals. II
Thanksgiving [ˈθæŋksˈɡɪvɪŋ] Erntedankfest (*amerikanischer Feiertag am vierten Donnerstag im November*) IV
that [ðæt], [ðət]:
1. das (dort) I
that field das Feld (dort), jenes Feld I **that morning/afternoon/evening** an jenem Morgen/Nachmittag/Abend III **That's £159.** Das macht 159 Pfund. I **That's because …** Das liegt daran, dass … IV **That's us.** Das sind wir. IV **That's why …** Deshalb …, Darum … II
2. der, die, das; die (*Relativpronomen*) III
3. dass IV
so that sodass, damit IV **they think that …** sie glauben, dass … I
the [ðə], [ði] der, die, das; die I **the 90s** die Neunzigerjahre II
theatre [ˈθɪətə] Theater I
their [ðeə] ihr/e (*Plural*) I
theirs [ðeəz] ihre/r, ihrs (*zu „they"*) V 1 (19)
them [ðem], [ðəm] sie; ihnen I
theme [θiːm] Thema I
theme park [ˈθiːm pɑːk] Themenpark (*Freizeitpark mit Attraktionen zu einem bestimmten Thema*) V 4 (83)
themselves [ðəmˈselvz] sich III
then [ðen] dann, danach I
°**theory** [ˈθɪəri] Theorie
there [ðeə] da, dort; dahin, dorthin I **there are …** es sind … / es gibt … I **there's …** es ist … / es gibt … I **over there** da drüben, dort drüben V 1 (13)
these [ðiːz] die, diese (hier) II
they [ðeɪ] sie (*Plural*) I
thin [θɪn] dünn IV
thing [θɪŋ] Ding, Sache I
think [θɪŋk], **thought, thought** denken, meinen, glauben I **think of sth.** an etwas denken, sich etwas ausdenken III **think of/about** halten von, denken über III **I don't think so.** Das glaube/denke ich nicht. III **I think so.** Ich glaube ja. III
third [θɜːd] dritte(r, s) I
Thirdly, … [ˈθɜːdli] Drittens … III
thirsty [ˈθɜːsti]: **be thirsty** durstig sein, Durst haben I
this [ðɪs] diese(r, s) I **This is …** Dies ist … / Das ist … I **this morning/afternoon/evening** heute Morgen/Nachmittag/Abend II
those CDs [ðəʊz] die CDs dort; jene CDs II
though [ðəʊ]:
1. aber; allerdings; jedoch V 3 (60)
2. obwohl V 4 (79)
thought [θɔːt] *siehe* **think**

thousand [ˈθaʊznd] tausend III
°**threaten** [ˈθretn] (be)drohen
three [θriː] drei I
threw [θruː] *siehe* **throw**
throat [θrəʊt] Hals II **a sore throat** Halsschmerzen II
through [θruː] durch I
throw [θrəʊ], **threw, thrown** werfen III
thrown [θrəʊn] *siehe* **throw**
Thursday [ˈθɜːzdeɪ], [ˈθɜːzdi] Donnerstag I
ticket [ˈtɪkɪt]:
1. Eintrittskarte I
2. Fahrkarte III
one-way ticket einfache Fahrkarte IV
ticket office [ˈtɪkɪt ɒfɪs] Kartenschalter II
tidy [ˈtaɪdi]:
1. ordentlich, aufgeräumt III
2. aufräumen II
tidy (sth.) up (etwas) aufräumen III
tie [taɪ] Krawatte I
tiger [ˈtaɪɡə] Tiger I
tights (*pl*) [taɪts] Strumpfhose I
till [tɪl] bis V 4 (85)
time [taɪm]:
1. Zeit; Uhrzeit I
at all times jederzeit, ständig V 3 (57) **on time** pünktlich II **What's the time?** Wie spät ist es? I
2. Mal II
for the last time zum letzten Mal III
timetable [ˈtaɪmteɪbl] Stundenplan I
tip [tɪp] Tipp II
tired [ˈtaɪəd] müde I
title [ˈtaɪtl] Titel, Überschrift IV
to [tu], [tə]:
1. (*örtlich*) zu, nach I
to the cinema ins Kino I
2. bis I
from Monday to Friday von Montag bis Freitag I
3. um zu II
To start with, … Erstens …; Zunächst …; Zuerst einmal … II
4. **He doesn't like to be lonely.** Er mag es nicht, allein zu sein. I
toast [təʊst] Toast I
today [təˈdeɪ] heute I
together [təˈɡeðə] zusammen I
toilet [ˈtɔɪlət] Toilette I
toilet roll [ˈtɔɪlət rəʊl] Rolle Toilettenpapier II
told [təʊld] *siehe* **tell**
tomato, *pl* **tomatoes** [təˈmɑːtəʊ] Tomate III
tomorrow [təˈmɒrəʊ] morgen II
tongue [tʌŋ] Zunge IV
tonight [təˈnaɪt] heute Nacht, heute Abend III
too [tuː]:
1. auch I
from Berlin too auch aus Berlin I **Me too.** Ich auch. I
2. **too old/big/…** zu alt/groß/… I

took [tʊk] siehe **take**
°**tool** [tuːl] Werkzeug
tooth, *pl* **teeth** [tuːθ], [tiːθ] Zahn IV
toothpaste ['tuːθpeɪst] Zahnpasta IV
top [tɒp] obere Ende, Oberteil IV **at the top (of)** oben; am oberen Ende (von), an der Spitze (von) II
topic ['tɒpɪk] Thema V 1 (23)
torch [tɔːtʃ] Taschenlampe; Fackel III °**flash a torch** mit einer Taschenlampe leuchten/blinken
tornado [tɔːˈneɪdəʊ] Tornado IV
°**torture** ['tɔːtʃə] Folter
°**total** ['təʊtl] Gesamt-; total, völlig
°**touch** [tʌtʃ] berühren, anfassen
tough [tʌf] (knall)hart IV
tour [tʊə] Tour III **a tour of the school** ein Rundgang durch die Schule I
tourist ['tʊərɪst] Tourist/in II
tourist office ['tʊərɪst ɒfɪs] Touristeninformation; Fremdenverkehrsbüro III
towards sb./sth. [təˈwɔːdz] auf jn./ etwas zu IV
towel ['taʊəl] Handtuch III
tower ['taʊə] Turm III
town [taʊn] Stadt I **in town** in der Stadt I
toy [tɔɪ] Spielzeug II
track [træk]:
 1. Pfad, (Feld-)Weg III
 °**stay on track** auf dem richtigen Weg bleiben
 °**2.** Stück (z.B. auf einer CD)
tractor ['træktə] Traktor III
tradition [trəˈdɪʃn] Tradition IV
traditional [trəˈdɪʃənl] traditionell V 1 (14)
traffic ['træfɪk] Verkehr III
traffic lights (*pl*) ['træfɪk laɪts] Verkehrsampel II
trail [treɪl] Weg, Pfad IV
train [treɪn] Zug II
train sb. [treɪn] jn. trainieren, ausbilden III
trainee [treɪˈniː] Auszubildende(r), Trainee V 3 (56)
trainer ['treɪnə] Trainer/in III
trainers (*pl*) ['treɪnəz] Turnschuhe I
training ['treɪnɪŋ] Training, Ausbildung I
tramp [træmp] Obdachlose(r), Stadtstreicher/in V 2 (42)
transport ['trænspɔːt] Verkehrsmittel; Transport(wesen) III
trapped [træpt] gefangen (*in einer Falle*) IV
trash [træʃ] (*AE*) Abfall, Müll IV
travel ['trævl]:
 1. reisen; fahren, sich fortbewegen III
 2. (*das*) Reisen V 3 (56)
 travel costs (*pl*) Reisekosten V 3 (56)
°**travel agency** ['trævl eɪdʒənsi] Reisebüro
Travelcard ['trævlkɑːd] *Ein- oder Mehrtagesfahrkarte (London)* III

travelsick ['trævlsɪk] reisekrank III
tree [triː] Baum I
trend [trend] Trend V 4 (80)
tribe [traɪb] (Volks-)Stamm IV
trick [trɪk] Trick, Kunststück III
°**tricky** ['trɪki] knifflig, schwierig
trip [trɪp] Ausflug; Reise II
trouble ['trʌbl]: **be in trouble** in Schwierigkeiten sein; Ärger kriegen I **get sb. into trouble** jn. in Schwierigkeiten bringen V 2 (32)
trousers (*pl*) ['traʊzəz] Hose I
truck [trʌk] Lastwagen; LKW IV
true [truː] wahr I
trust [trʌst] trauen, vertrauen IV
truth [truːθ] Wahrheit IV
try [traɪ] probieren, ausprobieren I **try hard** sich sehr bemühen, sich anstrengen IV
T-shirt ['tiː ʃɜːt] T-Shirt I
tsunami [tsuːˈnɑːmi] Tsunami IV
tube [tjuːb]: **on the Tube** in der (Londoner) U-Bahn III **the Tube** die U-Bahn (in London) III
Tuesday ['tjuːzdeɪ], ['tjuːzdi] Dienstag I
°**turbocharged engine** ['tɜːbəʊtʃɑːdʒd] Turbomotor
turn [tɜːn]:
 1. sich umdrehen III
 turn sth. etwas umdrehen V 3 (62)
 turn around sich umdrehen IV
 turn over (sich) umdrehen; (*Auto*) sich überschlagen V 1 (16) **turn right/left** (nach) rechts/links abbiegen II °**turn away** sich abwenden, sich wegdrehen °**turn up** auftauchen, erscheinen
 2. **It's your turn.** Du bist dran. / Du bist an der Reihe. I
 °**take turns** sich abwechseln
turning point ['tɜːnɪŋ pɔɪnt] Wendepunkt IV
°**turtle** ['tɜːtl] (Wasser-)Schildkröte
TV [tiːˈviː] Fernsehen, Fernsehgerät I
twelve [twelv] zwölf I
twice [twaɪs] zweimal III
twig [twɪg] (kleiner) Zweig IV
twin sister/brother [twɪn] Zwillingsschwester/-bruder V 4 (85)
twins (*pl*) [twɪnz] Zwillinge V 4 (85)
two [tuː] zwei I
type (of) [taɪp] Art, Sorte, Typ (von) V 4 (83)
°**typical (of)** ['tɪpɪkl] typisch (für)
tyre ['taɪə] Reifen V 1 (16)

U

°**umbrella** [ʌmˈbrelə] (Regen-)Schirm **Would you like to share my umbrella?** Möchtest du mit unter meinen Regenschirm?
°**unattractive** [ʌnəˈtræktɪv] unattraktiv
uncle ['ʌŋkl] Onkel I

°**uncomfortable** [ʌnˈkʌmftəbl]: **be/feel uncomfortable** sich unbehaglich fühlen
uncool [ʌnˈkuːl] uncool II
under ['ʌndə] unter I **the under-18s team** das Team der unter 18-Jährigen V 3 (58)
underground ['ʌndəɡraʊnd]: **the underground** die U-Bahn III
°**underline** [ʌndəˈlaɪn] unterstreichen
understand [ʌndəˈstænd], **understood, understood** verstehen I
understood [ʌndəˈstʊd] siehe **understand**
unemployed [ʌnɪmˈplɔɪd] arbeitslos III
unfit [ʌnˈfɪt] nicht fit II
unforgettable [ʌnfəˈɡetəbl] unvergesslich IV
unfriendly [ʌnˈfrendli] unfreundlich II
unhappy [ʌnˈhæpi] unglücklich I
unhealthy [ʌnˈhelθi] ungesund II
uniform ['juːnɪfɔːm] (Schul-)Uniform I
uninteresting [ʌnˈɪntrəstɪŋ] uninteressant II
unit ['juːnɪt] Kapitel, Lektion I
united [juˈnaɪtɪd]: **the United Kingdom (the UK)** das Vereinigte Königreich III
unity ['juːnəti] Einheit, (innere) Geschlossenheit V 2 (36)
university [juːnɪˈvɜːsəti] Universität V 3 (55)
unknown [ʌnˈnəʊn] unbekannt IV
unless [ənˈles] es sei denn; außer (wenn) IV
unsure [ʌnˈʃʊə], [ʌnˈʃɔː] unsicher II
until [ənˈtɪl] bis (*zeitlich*) II
°**unusual** [ʌnˈjuːʒʊəl] ungewöhnlich
unwanted [ʌnˈwɒntɪd] unerwünscht V 4 (84)
unwelcome [ʌnˈwelkəm] unerwünscht, unwillkommen II
up [ʌp]: **up the hill/wall/...** den Hügel/die Mauer/... hinauf III **be up for sth.** (*infml*) bei etwas dabei sein, mitmachen V 1 (19)
up to ['ʌp tə] bis (zu) V 3 (56)
upside ['ʌpsaɪd] gute Seite, Vorteil III
upside down [ʌpsaɪd ˈdaʊn] verkehrt herum, auf dem/den Kopf V 1 (16)
upstairs [ʌpˈsteəz] oben; nach oben I
us [ʌs], [əs] uns I
use [juːz] benutzen, verwenden I
used to ['juːst tə]:
 1. **be used to sth.** an etwas gewöhnt sein IV
 get used to sth. sich an etwas gewöhnen IV
 2. **where he used to play** wo er früher (immer) gespielt hat IV
useful ['juːsfl] nützlich III
usual ['juːʒʊəl] gewöhnlich, üblich III
usually ['juːʒʊəli] meistens, normalerweise I

DICTIONARY

English – German

V

vacation [vəˈkeɪʃn], [veɪˈkeɪʃn] (AE) Ferien, Urlaub IV
vacuum cleaner [ˈvækjuəm kliːnə] Staubsauger V 3 (52)
vain [veɪn] eitel V 4 (79)
valley [ˈvæli] Tal IV
value [ˈvæljuː] Wert I **It's good value.** Es ist sein Geld wert. I
vamping [ˈvæmpɪŋ] spät in der Nacht noch aktiv sein V 4 (88)
vampire [ˈvæmpaɪə] Vampir V 4 (88)
van [væn] Transporter, Lieferwagen III
vegetables (pl) [ˈvedʒtəblz] Gemüse I
vehicle [ˈviːəkl] Fahrzeug III
°**venom** [ˈvenəm] Gift
°**verse** [vɜːs] Vers, Strophe (Lied)
version [ˈvɜːʃn] Fassung, Version IV
very [ˈveri] sehr I **Thanks very much.** Danke sehr. / Danke vielmals. II
vicinity [vəˈsɪnəti] Umgebung V 2 (36)
victim [ˈvɪktɪm] Opfer V 2 (31)
video [ˈvɪdiəʊ] Video II
video-chat [ˈvɪdiəʊ tʃæt] sich per Videokonferenz unterhalten V 4 (76)
view [vjuː] Blick, Aussicht IV **point of view** Standpunkt III
village [ˈvɪlɪdʒ] Dorf I
violence [ˈvaɪələns] Gewalt; Gewalttätigkeit IV
violent [ˈvaɪələnt] gewalttätig; gewaltsam III
virtual [ˈvɜːtʃuəl] virtuell V 4 (84)
virus, pl **viruses** [ˈvaɪrəs], [ˈvaɪrəsɪz] Virus V 4 (84)
°**visa** [ˈviːzə] Visum
visit [ˈvɪzɪt]:
1. Besuch IV
2. besuchen I
visitor [ˈvɪzɪtə] Besucher/in; Gast I
visitor pass [ˈvɪzɪtə pɑːs] Besucherausweis IV
visuals (pl) [ˈvɪʒuəlz] (kurz für: **visual materials**) visuelle Materialien/Hilfsmittel V 1 (22)
vlog [vlɒg] VLog (Video-Blog) V 4 (80)
vlogger [ˈvlɒgə] Vlogger/in (Video-Blogger/in) V 4 (80)
vocabulary [vəˈkæbjələri] Wörterverzeichnis, Vokabelverzeichnis I
voice [vɔɪs] Stimme II
°**voice-over** [ˈvɔɪs əʊvə] Filmkommentar, Off-Stimme
volleyball [ˈvɒlibɔːl] Volleyball II
°**voluntary** [ˈvɒləntri] freiwillig, ehrenamtlich
volunteer [vɒlənˈtɪə]:
1. freiwillig/ehrenamtlich arbeiten (unbezahlt) IV
2. Freiwillige(r), Ehrenamtliche(r) IV
vote [vəʊt] abstimmen III **vote for sb.** für jn. stimmen II

W

°**waistcoat** [ˈweɪskəʊt] Weste

wait (for) [weɪt] warten (auf) II **sb. can't wait to do sth.** jd. kann es kaum erwarten, etwas zu tun V 3 (53)
waiter [ˈweɪtə] Kellner III
waiting room [ˈweɪtɪŋ ruːm] Wartezimmer IV
waitress [ˈweɪtrəs] Kellnerin III
wake [weɪk], **woke, woken**:
1. wecken I
2. **wake up** aufwachen III
°**wake-up call** [ˈweɪk ʌp kɔːl] Weckruf
walk [wɔːk]:
1. (zu Fuß) gehen I **walk around** umhergehen; herumlaufen II **walk the dog** mit dem Hund rausgehen, den Hund ausführen IV
2. Spaziergang II **go for a walk** einen Spaziergang machen, spazieren gehen II
walker [ˈwɔːkə] Spaziergänger/in; Wanderer/Wanderin III
walking boots (pl) [ˈwɔːkɪŋ buːts] Wanderstiefel II
wall [wɔːl] Wand; Mauer II
want sth. [wɒnt] etwas (haben) wollen I **want to do sth.** etwas tun wollen I **We want you to go to …** Wir möchten/wollen, dass du nach … gehst. III
war [wɔː] Krieg IV
wardrobe [ˈwɔːdrəʊb] Kleiderschrank I
warm [wɔːm] warm II
warn sb. [wɔːn] jn. warnen, jn. ermahnen V 2 (41)
warning [ˈwɔːnɪŋ] Warnung IV
was [wɒz], [wəz]: **I/he/she/it was** Vergangenheitsform von **be** I
wash [wɒʃ] waschen II **wash up** abwaschen I
washing machine [ˈwɒʃɪŋ məʃiːn] Waschmaschine V 3 (52)
waste [weɪst] Verschwendung III
watch sth. [wɒtʃ] sich etwas anschauen; etwas beobachten I **watch TV** fernsehen I
water [ˈwɔːtə]:
1. Wasser I
2. gießen, (be)wässern IV
water sports [ˈwɔːtə spɔːts] Wassersport III
waterproof [ˈwɔːtəpruːf] wasserdicht, wasserfest, wasserundurchlässig V 1 (16)
wave [weɪv] Welle IV
wave (to sb.) [weɪv] (jm. zu)winken IV
way [weɪ]:
1. Weg I
way of life Lebensweise V 1 (15)
ask sb. the way jn. nach dem Weg fragen II **by the way** übrigens V 2 (45) **on the way to …** auf dem Weg zu/nach … I **one way** einfache Fahrt IV **one-way ticket** einfache Fahrkarte IV **tell sb. the way** jm. den Weg beschreiben II

2. Art und Weise III
in a different way anders; auf andere Art und Weise IV **in some ways** in mancher Hinsicht IV **No way!** Auf keinen Fall! III
3. **it's way cooler than …** (infml) es ist viel cooler als … III
we [wiː] wir I
weak [wiːk] schwach III
weakness [ˈwiːknəs] Schwäche V 3 (54)
°**weapon** [ˈwepən] Waffe
wear [weə], **wore, worn** tragen, anhaben (Kleidung) II
weather [ˈweðə] Wetter II
weather forecast [ˈweðə fɔːkɑːst] Wettervorhersage II
Wednesday [ˈwenzdeɪ], [ˈwenzdi] Mittwoch I
°**weed** [wiːd] (Un-)Kraut
week [wiːk] Woche I
weekend [wiːkˈend] Wochenende I **at the weekend** am Wochenende I
weeper [ˈwiːpə]: **Finders, keepers, losers, weepers.** Was man findet, darf man behalten. (Redensart) V 4 (85)
°**weightlifting** [ˈweɪtlɪftɪŋ] Gewichtheben
welcome [ˈwelkəm]:
1. **welcome sb. (to)** jn. begrüßen (in), jn. willkommen heißen (in) III **Welcome to Plymouth.** Willkommen in Plymouth. I
2. **You're welcome.** Bitte, gern geschehen. / Nichts zu danken. I
Well, … [wel] Nun, … / Also, … / Na ja, … I
well [wel]: **Well done.** Gut gemacht! I **well paid** gut bezahlt IV **be well known** bekannt sein IV **I'm not feeling well.** Ich fühle mich nicht gut. II **work/speak/… well** gut funktionieren/sprechen/… I
well-known [wel ˈnəʊn] bekannt V 1 (10)
went [went] siehe **go**
were [wɜː], [wə]: **we/you/they were** Vergangenheitsform von **be** I
west [west] Westen; nach Westen II
western [ˈwestən] westlich, West- IV
wet [wet] nass I
whale [weɪl] Wal IV
what [wɒt]:
1. was I
2. welche(r, s) I
What a pain! etwa: So ein Mist. / Es nervt! III **What about …?** Wie wär's mit …? I **What about you?** Und du? / Und was ist mit dir? I **What do you need money for?** Wofür brauchst du Geld? II **What else …?** Was (sonst) noch …? I **What kind of mistakes …?** Was für Fehler …? II **What page is it?** Auf welcher Seite sind wir? I **What would you like?** Was möchtest du? / Was hättest du gern? II **What's for homework?** Was haben wir als

Hausaufgabe auf? I **What's going on?** Was ist los? / Was gibt's? IV **What's it like?** Wie ist es? / Wie sieht es aus? I **What's special about …?** Was ist das Besondere an …? III **What's the time?** Wie spät ist es? I **What's your name?** Wie heißt du? (wörtlich: Was ist dein Name?) I **What's the matter?** Was ist denn? / Was ist los? II **Like what?** Was (denn) zum Beispiel? III
wheel [wiːl] Rad IV
wheelchair [ˈwiːltʃeə] Rollstuhl I
wheels (pl) [wiːlz] (infml) ein fahrbarer Untersatz (Auto) IV
when [wen]:
1. wann I
2. wenn I
3. als II
When's your birthday? Wann hast du Geburtstag? I
where [weə] wo; wohin I
°**whether** [ˈweðə] ob
which [wɪtʃ]:
1. **Which club?** Welcher Klub? II
2. der, die, das; die (Relativpronomen) V 1 (11)
while [waɪl]:
1. während IV
2. **a while** eine Weile, einige Zeit V 4 (82)
whisper [ˈwɪspə] flüstern II
whistle [ˈwɪsl] (Triller-)Pfeife II
white [waɪt] weiß I
who [huː]:
1. wer I
Who are you? Wer bist du? / Wer seid ihr? I
2. wen II
Who did Adam meet? Wen hat Adam getroffen? / Wen traf Adam? II
3. wem II
Who did Mia talk to? Mit wem hat Mia gesprochen? / Mit wem sprach Mia? II **Who is the text about?** Von wem handelt der Text? II
4. der, die, das; die Relativpronomen III
whole [həʊl] ganze(r, s), gesamte(r, s) IV
whose [huːz] wessen V 1 (19) **Whose are these?** Wem gehören die (hier)? V 1 (19)
why [waɪ] warum I **that's why** deshalb, darum II
wide [waɪd] breit, weit V 1 (14)
wife, pl **wives** [waɪf], [waɪvz] Ehefrau IV
wild [waɪld] wild; wild lebend I
will [wɪl]: **I'll have …** Ich nehme … (beim Essen, im Restaurant) II **it won't rain (= it will not rain)** es wird nicht regnen II **the weather will be good** das Wetter wird gut sein II **We'll find him.** Wir werden ihn finden. II
win [wɪn], **won, won** gewinnen I
wind [wɪnd] Wind II

window [ˈwɪndəʊ] Fenster I
windy [ˈwɪndi] windig II
winner [ˈwɪnə] Gewinner/in II
winter [ˈwɪntə] Winter II
wish [wɪʃ]: **I wish I could tell you …** Ich wünschte, ich könnte dir erzählen, … IV
wishes [ˈwɪʃɪz]: **Best wishes** Viele Grüße, … (Briefschluss) I
witch [wɪtʃ] Hexe II
with [wɪð] mit I **with Ellie** mit Ellie; bei Ellie I
without [wɪˈðaʊt] ohne II
wives [waɪvz] Mehrzahl von **wife** IV
woke [wəʊk] siehe **wake**
woken [ˈwəʊkən] siehe **wake**
woman, pl **women** [ˈwʊmən], [ˈwɪmɪn] Frau II
won [wʌn] siehe **win**
wonder [ˈwʌndə] sich fragen; gern wissen wollen III
won't [wəʊnt]: **it won't rain (= it will not rain)** es wird nicht regnen II
wood [wʊd] Holz; Wald III
word [wɜːd] Wort I
word building [ˈwɜːd bɪldɪŋ] Wortbildung III
word field [ˈwɜːd fiːld] Wortfeld II
wore [wɔː] siehe **wear**
work [wɜːk]:
1. Arbeit I
2. arbeiten; funktionieren I
work hard hart arbeiten I **work on sth.** arbeiten an etwas V 1 (22) **work sth. out** etwas herausfinden, etwas herausarbeiten IV **working hours** (pl) Arbeitszeit(en) V 3 (56)
work experience [ˈwɜːk ɪkspɪəriəns] Praktikum/Praktika; Arbeitserfahrung(en) V 3 (54)
°**work placement** [ˈwɜːk pleɪsmənt] Praktikum
worker [ˈwɜːkə] Arbeiter/in III
workshop [ˈwɜːkʃɒp] Workshop; Seminar I
world [wɜːld] Welt I **the best of both worlds** das Beste von beidem I
worn [wɔːn] siehe **wear**
worried (about) [ˈwʌrid] beunruhigt, besorgt (wegen) I
worry (about) [ˈwʌri] sich Sorgen machen (wegen, um) I
worse (than) [wɜːs] schlechter, schlimmer (als) III
worst [wɜːst] am schlechtesten, am schlimmsten III
worth [wɜːθ] wert V 1 (16) **The film is worth watching.** Es lohnt sich, den Film anzuschauen. V 1 (16)
would [wʊd]: **Would you like some tea/chips?** Möchtest du (etwas) Tee / (ein paar) Pommes frites? II
I'd (= I would) like to go home. Ich würde gern nach Hause gehen. II
I'd (= I would) love to come. Ich

komme sehr gern. / Ich würde sehr gern kommen. I **I'd (= I would) prefer …** ich würde … vorziehen; ich würde lieber … III **What would you like?** Was möchtest du? / Was hättest du gern? II
write [raɪt], **wrote, written** schreiben I **write sth. down** (sich) etwas aufschreiben III
writer [ˈraɪtə] Schreiber/in; Schriftsteller/in III
written [ˈrɪtn] siehe **write written by …** geschrieben von … III
wrong [rɒŋ] falsch I **go wrong** schiefgehen III **You're wrong.** Du hast Unrecht. III
wrote [rəʊt] siehe **write**

Y

yard [jɑːd] (AE) Garten IV **school yard** Schulhof II
year [jɪə] Jahr I
yellow [ˈjeləʊ] gelb I
yes [jes] ja I
yesterday [ˈjestədeɪ] gestern II
yet [jet]:
1. (in Fragen) schon IV
Have you had dinner yet? Hast du schon zu Abend gegessen? IV
2. **not … yet** noch nicht II
yogurt [ˈjɒɡət] Jogurt III
you [ju], [juː]:
1. du; ihr; Sie I
2. dich; dir; euch; Sie; Ihnen I
young [jʌŋ] jung I
your [jɔː], [jə] dein/e; euer/eure; Ihr/e I
yours [jɔːz]:
1. deiner, deine, deins I
2. eurer, eure, eures III
Yours sincerely, … [jɔːz sɪnˈsɪəli] Mit freundlichen Grüßen (Briefschluss) IV
yourself [jɔːˈself], [jəˈself] dich III
°**See for yourself.** Sieh selbst! / Sehen Sie selbst!
yourselves [jɔːˈselvz], [jəˈselvz] euch III
youth [juːθ] Jugend, Jugend- III
yummy [ˈjʌmi] (infml) lecker II

Z

°**Zap off.** [zæp ˈɒf] (infml) Hau ab!
zoo [zuː] Zoo I

IRREGULAR VERBS

infinitive	simple past	past participle	
be	I/he/she/it **was**; you/we/you/they **were**	been	sein
beat	beat	beaten	schlagen, besiegen
become	became	become	werden
begin	began	begun	beginnen, anfangen
bite [aɪ]	bit [ɪ]	bitten [ɪ]	beißen
bleed	bled	bled	bluten
break	broke	broken	brechen; zerbrechen
bring	brought	brought	bringen, mitbringen
build	built	built	bauen
buy	bought	bought	kaufen
catch	caught	caught	fangen, erwischen
choose [uː]	chose [əʊ]	chosen [əʊ]	(sich) aussuchen, (aus)wählen
come	came	come	kommen
cost	cost	cost	kosten
creep up (on)	crept	crept	sich heranschleichen (an)
cut	cut	cut	schneiden; (Rasen) mähen
deal with	dealt [e]	dealt [e]	umgehen mit, fertigwerden/klarkommen mit
do	did	done [ʌ]	tun, machen
drink	drank	drunk	trinken
drive [aɪ]	drove	driven [ɪ]	(mit dem Auto) fahren; (an)treiben
eat	ate [et, eɪt]	eaten	essen
fall	fell	fallen	fallen, hinfallen
feed	fed	fed	füttern
feel	felt	felt	fühlen; sich fühlen
fight	fought	fought	kämpfen; bekämpfen
find	found	found	finden
fly	flew	flown	fliegen
forget	forgot	forgotten	vergessen
freeze	froze [əʊ]	frozen [əʊ]	(ge)frieren; erstarren
get	got	got	bekommen; holen, besorgen; werden; gelangen, (hin)kommen
give	gave	given	geben
go	went	gone [ɒ]	gehen
grow	grew	grown	wachsen; anbauen, anpflanzen; (allmählich) werden
hang	hung	hung	hängen
have	had	had	haben
hear [ɪə]	heard [ɜː]	heard [ɜː]	hören
hide [aɪ]	hid [ɪ]	hidden [ɪ]	verstecken; sich verstecken
hit	hit	hit	schlagen; treffen; prallen/stoßen gegen/auf
hold	held	held	halten
hurt	hurt	hurt	verletzen; wehtun
keep	kept	kept	behalten; halten; aufbewahren
know [nəʊ]	knew [njuː]	known [nəʊn]	wissen; kennen
leave	left	left	abfahren; (weg)gehen; verlassen; zurücklassen
lend sb. sth.	lent	lent	jm. etwas leihen
let	let	let	lassen
lie [aɪ]	lay	lain	liegen
light	lit	lit	anzünden
lose [uː]	lost [ɒ]	lost [ɒ]	verlieren

infinitive	simple past	past participle	
make	made	made	machen
mean [iː]	meant [e]	meant [e]	bedeuten; meinen, sagen wollen
meet	met	met	treffen; sich treffen; kennenlernen
overspend (on)	overspent	overspent	zu viel Geld ausgeben (für)
overtake	overtook	overtaken	überholen
pay	paid	paid	bezahlen
put	put	put	*(etwas wohin)* tun, legen, stellen
read [iː]	read [e]	read [e]	lesen
retell	retold	retold	nacherzählen
ride [aɪ]	rode	ridden [ɪ]	reiten; *(Rad)* fahren
ring	rang	rung	läuten, klingeln; anrufen
run	ran	run	rennen, laufen
say [eɪ]	said [e]	said [e]	sagen
see	saw	seen	sehen
sell	sold	sold	verkaufen
send	sent	sent	schicken, senden
set the table	set	set	den Tisch decken
shake	shook	shaken [eɪ]	schütteln
shine	shone [ɒ]	shone [ɒ]	scheinen *(Sonne)*
show	showed	shown	zeigen
shut up	shut	shut	den Mund halten
sing	sang	sung	singen
sit	sat	sat	sitzen
sleep	slept	slept	schlafen
speak	spoke	spoken	sprechen
spend	spent	spent	ausgeben *(Geld)*; verbringen *(Zeit)*
spread	spread	spread	verbreiten *(z.B. Krankheit)*
stand	stood	stood	stehen; sich (hin)stellen
steal	stole	stolen	stehlen
stick together	stuck	stuck	zusammenhalten
sting	stung	stung	stechen *(Insekt)*; brennen
stink	stank	stunk	stinken
swim	swam	swum	schwimmen
take	took	taken	nehmen; mitnehmen; (weg-, hin)bringen; dauern, *(Zeit)* brauchen
teach	taught	taught	unterrichten, lehren
tell	told	told	erzählen, berichten
think	thought	thought	denken
throw	threw	thrown	werfen
understand	understood	understood	verstehen
wake	woke	woken	wecken
wear [eə]	wore [ɔː]	worn [ɔː]	tragen, anhaben *(Kleidung)*
win	won [ʌ]	won [ʌ]	gewinnen
write	wrote	written	schreiben

LIST OF NAMES

First names (Vornamen)
Aaron [ˈeərən]
Adam [ˈædəm]
Akira [əˈkiːrə]
Alex [ˈælɪks]
Aliyah [əˈliːə]
Amanda [əˈmændə]
Amelia [əˈmiːliə]
Amy [ˈeɪmi]
Andrew [ˈændruː]
Angie [ˈændʒi]
Ant [ænt]
Arnold [ˈɑːnəld]
Asif [æˈsiːf]
Ava [ˈɑːvə], [ˈeɪvə]
Bella [ˈbelə]
Ben [ben]
Bibi [ˈbɪbi]
Billie [ˈbɪli]
Blake [bleɪk]
Cal [kæl]
Cara [ˈkɑːrə]
Carl [kɑːl]
Carol [ˈkærəl]
Catherine [ˈkæθrɪn]
Charlotte [ˈʃɑːlət]
Chloe [ˈkləʊi]
Chris [krɪs]
Cindy [ˈsɪndi]
Craig [kreɪg]
Cynthia [ˈsɪnθiə]
Daisy [ˈdeɪzi]
Dan [dæn]
Dana [ˈdɑːnə], [ˈdeɪnə]
Danny [ˈdæni]
Dave [deɪv]
David [ˈdeɪvɪd]
Devon [ˈdevən]
Dixie [ˈdɪksi]
Don [dɒn]
Dylan [ˈdɪlən]
Ella [ˈelə]
Elli [ˈeli]
Emily [ˈemɪli]
Emma [ˈemə]
Eric [ˈerɪk]
Erin [ˈerɪn]
Ethan [ˈiːθən]
Faye [feɪ]
Finn [fɪn]
Gemma, Gem [ˈdʒemə], [dʒem]
Geoff [dʒef]
Gorodema [gɒrəˈdiːmə]
Grace [greɪs]
Harry [ˈhæri]
Hermione [hɜːˈmaɪəni]
Hugh [hjuː]
Jack [dʒæk]
Jacob [ˈdʒeɪkəb]
Jamie [ˈdʒeɪmi]
Jane [dʒeɪn]
Jay [dʒeɪ]
Jess [dʒes]
Jessica [ˈdʒesɪkə]
Jimmy [ˈdʒɪmi]
Johnny [ˈdʒɒni]
Joshua [ˈdʒɒʃuə]
Julia [ˈdʒuːliə]
Julie [ˈdʒuːli]
Justin [ˈdʒʌstɪn]
Kai [kaɪ]
Karen [ˈkærən]
Kat [kæt]
Kathryn [ˈkæθrɪn]
Kelly [ˈkeli]
Kirsty [ˈkɜːsti]
Kumar [kʊˈmɑːr]
Kyle [kaɪl]
Laura [ˈlɔːrə]
Leah [ˈliːə]
Leo [ˈliːəʊ]
Lily [ˈlɪli]
Lois [ˈləʊɪs]
Lynn [lɪn]
Maggie [ˈmægi]
Marek [ˈmɑːrek]
Mark [mɑːk]
Matt [mæt]
Max [mæks]
Megan, Meg [ˈmegən], [meg]
Michael [ˈmaɪkl]
Michelle [mɪˈʃel]
Mike [maɪk]
Milly [ˈmɪli]
Mohammed [məʊˈhæmɪd]
Munny [ˈmʌni]
Natasha, Tasha [nəˈtæʃə], [ˈtæʃə]
Neil [niːl]
Nemo [ˈniːməʊ]
Nika [ˈniːkə]
Nikki [ˈnɪki]
Ollie [ˈɒli]
Oscar [ˈɒskə]
Owen [ˈəʊɪn]
Patrick [ˈpætrɪk]
Phillip [ˈfɪlɪp]
Poppy [ˈpɒpi]
Rani [ˈrɑːni]
Ratib [ˈrɑːtɪb], [ˈreɪtɪb]
Reeko [ˈriːkəʊ]
Riya [ˈraɪə]
Rob [rɒb]
Robert [ˈrɒbət]
Ron [rɒn]
Rosie [ˈrəʊzi]
Ruby [ˈruːbi]
Sam [sæm]
Scarlett [ˈskɑːlət]
Scott [skɒt]
Shaz [ʃæz]
Sheila [ˈʃiːlə]
Simon [ˈsaɪmən]
Simone [sɪˈməʊn]
Sophie [ˈsəʊfi]
Steve [stiːv]
Tammy [ˈtæmi]
Tess [tes]
Tessa [ˈtesə]
Thomas [ˈtɒməs]
Tia [ˈtiːə]
Todd [tɒd]
Tommy [ˈtɒmi]
Wayne [weɪn]
William [ˈwɪljəm]
Zee [ziː]

Family names / Surnames (Familiennamen)
Bond [bɒnd]
Bradford [ˈbrædfəd]
Chamberlain [ˈtʃeɪmbəlɪn]
Davis [ˈdeɪvɪs]
Duggan [ˈdʌgən]
Eyers [ˈeɪəz]
Fisher [ˈfɪʃə]
Goodes [gʊdz]
Gwynne [gwɪn]
Hughes [hjuːz]
Karpinsky [kɑːˈpɪnski]
Li [liː]
Loundes [laʊndz]
McCarthy [məˈkɑːθi]
Metzger [ˈmetsgə]
Moffat [ˈmɒfət]
Potter [ˈpɒtə]
Rayban [ˈreɪbən]
Rooney [ˈruːni]
Smalley [ˈsmɔːli]
Smith [smɪθ]
Thomson [ˈtɒmpsən]
Twycross [ˈtwaɪkrɒs]
Watson [ˈwɒtsən]
Whincup [ˈwɪnkʌp]
Zuckerberg [ˈzʌkəbɜːg]

Place names (Ortsnamen)
Adelaide [ˈædəleɪd]
Alice Springs [ˌælɪs ˈsprɪŋz]
Arctic Avenue [ˌɑːktɪk ˈævənjuː]
Atlantic City [ətˌlæntɪk ˈsɪti]
Ayr [eə]
Bedworth [ˈbedwəθ]
Berowra [bəˈraʊrə], [bəˈrəʊrə]
Brain [breɪn]
Brisbane [ˈbrɪzbən]
Broadwater Farm Estate [ˌbrɔːdwɔːtə fɑːm ɪˈsteɪt]
Broken Hill [ˌbrəʊkən ˈhɪl]
Broome [bruːm]
Burdekin [ˈbɜːdəkɪn]
Cairns [keənz]
California [kæləˈfɔːniə]
Collingwood [ˈkɒlɪŋwʊd]
Coober Pedy [ˌkuːbə ˈpiːdi]
Cornwall [ˈkɔːnwɔːl]
Crocosaurus Cove [krɒkəˈsɔːrəs ˈkəʊv]
Darwin [ˈdɑːwɪn]
down under [ˌdaʊn ˈʌndə]
EU (= European Union) [ˌiː ˈjuː], [ˌjʊərəpiːən ˈjuːniən]
Frenshaw Avenue [ˌfrenʃɔː ˈævənjuː]
Great Barrier Reef [ˌgreɪt bæriə ˈriːf]
Harvard [ˈhɑːvəd]
Heron Island [ˌherən ˈaɪlənd]
Hollywood [ˈhɒliwʊd]
Hong Kong [ˌhɒŋ ˈkɒŋ]
Kakadu National Park [ˌkækədu næʃnəl ˈpɑːk]
Kalbarri [kælˈbɑːri]
Kimberley [ˈkɪmbəli]
Los Angeles [lɒs ˈændʒəliːz]
Louisiana [luiːziˈænə]
Manchester [ˈmæntʃɪstə]
Melbourne [ˈmelbən]
Mindil Beach [ˌmɪndl ˈbiːtʃ], [ˌmaɪndɪl ˈbiːtʃ]
Montgomery [məntˈgʌməri]
New Jersey [ˌnjuː ˈdʒɜːzi]
Oz [ɒz]
Paris [ˈpærɪs]
Perth [pɜːθ]
Port Augusta [ˌpɔːt ɔːˈgʌstə]
Queensland [ˈkwiːnzlənd]
Seashell Motel [ˌsiːʃel məʊˈtel]
Sydney [ˈsɪdni]
Tasmania [tæzˈmeɪniə]
Tottenham [ˈtɒtnəm]
West Thames College [ˌwest temz ˈkɒlɪdʒ]
Wollongong, Gong [ˈwʊləŋgɒŋ], [gɒŋ]
Yulara [jʊˈlɑːrə]
Yunta [ˈjʊntə]

Other names
(Andere Namen)
Anangu [ˈʌnʌŋu]
Black Caviar [blæk ˈkæviɑː]
Brothablack [brʌðəˈblæk]
Chandlers [ˈtʃɑːndləz]
Darling [ˈdɑːlɪŋ]
Destroy [dɪˈstrɔɪ]
Elite Stylists
 [eɪliːt ˈstaɪlɪsts],
 [ɪliːt ˈstaɪlɪsts]
Ford [fɔːd]
Gaelic [ˈgeɪlɪk]
Ghan [gæn], [gɑːn]
Holden Monaro
 [həʊldən məˈnɑːrəʊ]
Hulu [ˈhuːlu]
Incredible
Hulk [ɪnkredəbl ˈhʌlk]
Marn Grook [mɑːn ˈgrʊk]
Mercedes [məˈseɪdiːz]
Pixar [ˈpɪksɑː]
Royal Flying Doctor
Service [rɔɪəl flaɪɪŋ ˈdɒktə sɜːvɪs]
Rugby Union
 [rʌgbi ˈjuːniən]
Seabreeze Festival
 [ˈsiːbriːz ˈfestɪvl]
Stuart Highway
 [stjuːət ˈhaɪweɪ]
Synapse Drinks
 [ˈsaɪnæps drɪŋks],
 [ˈsɪnæps drɪŋks]
Terra nullius [terə ˈnʌliəs]
Thunderbolt [ˈθʌndəbəʊlt]
Trillium [ˈtrɪliəm]
Typhoon [taɪˈfuːn]
Uluru [ˈuːləruː]
V8 [viː ˈeɪt]
X-factory [ˈeks fæktri]
Zing [zɪŋ]

English sounds

[iː]	green, he, sea	[əʊ]	old, no, road, yellow	[j]	yes, you, uniform
[ɑː]	ask, class, car, park	[aʊ]	now, house	[f]	family, after, laugh
[ɔː]	or, ball, door, four, morning	[eə]	where, pair, share, their	[v]	very, seven, have
[uː]	ruler, blue, too, two, you	[ʊə]	tour	[s]	six, poster, yes
[ɜː]	early, her, girl, work, T-shirt			[z]	zoo, quiz, his, music, please
[ɪ]	in, big, expensive	[b]	bike, table, verb	[ʃ]	she, station, English
[e]	yes, bed, again, breakfast	[p]	pen, paper, shop	[ʒ]	usually, revision, garage
[æ]	animal, apple, black, cat	[d]	day, window, good	[tʃ]	child, teacher, watch
[ʌ]	mum, bus, colour	[t]	ten, letter, at	[dʒ]	job, German, project, orange
[ɒ]	song, on, dog, what	[g]	go, again, bag	[θ]	thing, three, bathroom, both
[ʊ]	book, good, pullover	[k]	kitchen, car, back	[ð]	the, father, with
[ə]	again, today, a sister	[m]	man, remember, mum	[h]	house, who, behind
[i]	happy, monkey	[n]	no, one, ten		
		[ŋ]	wrong, young, uncle, thanks		
[eɪ]	name, eight, play, great	[l]	like, old, small		
[aɪ]	I, time, right, my	[r]	ruler, friend, sorry		
[ɔɪ]	boy, toilet, noise	[w]	we, where, one		

The English alphabet

a	[eɪ]	g	[dʒiː]	m	[em]	s	[es]	y	[waɪ]
b	[biː]	h	[eɪtʃ]	n	[en]	t	[tiː]	z	[zed]
c	[siː]	i	[aɪ]	o	[əʊ]	u	[juː]		
d	[diː]	j	[dʒeɪ]	p	[piː]	v	[viː]		
e	[iː]	k	[keɪ]	q	[kjuː]	w	[ˈdʌbljuː]		
f	[ef]	l	[el]	r	[ɑː]	x	[eks]		

ENGLISH-SPEAKING COUNTRIES

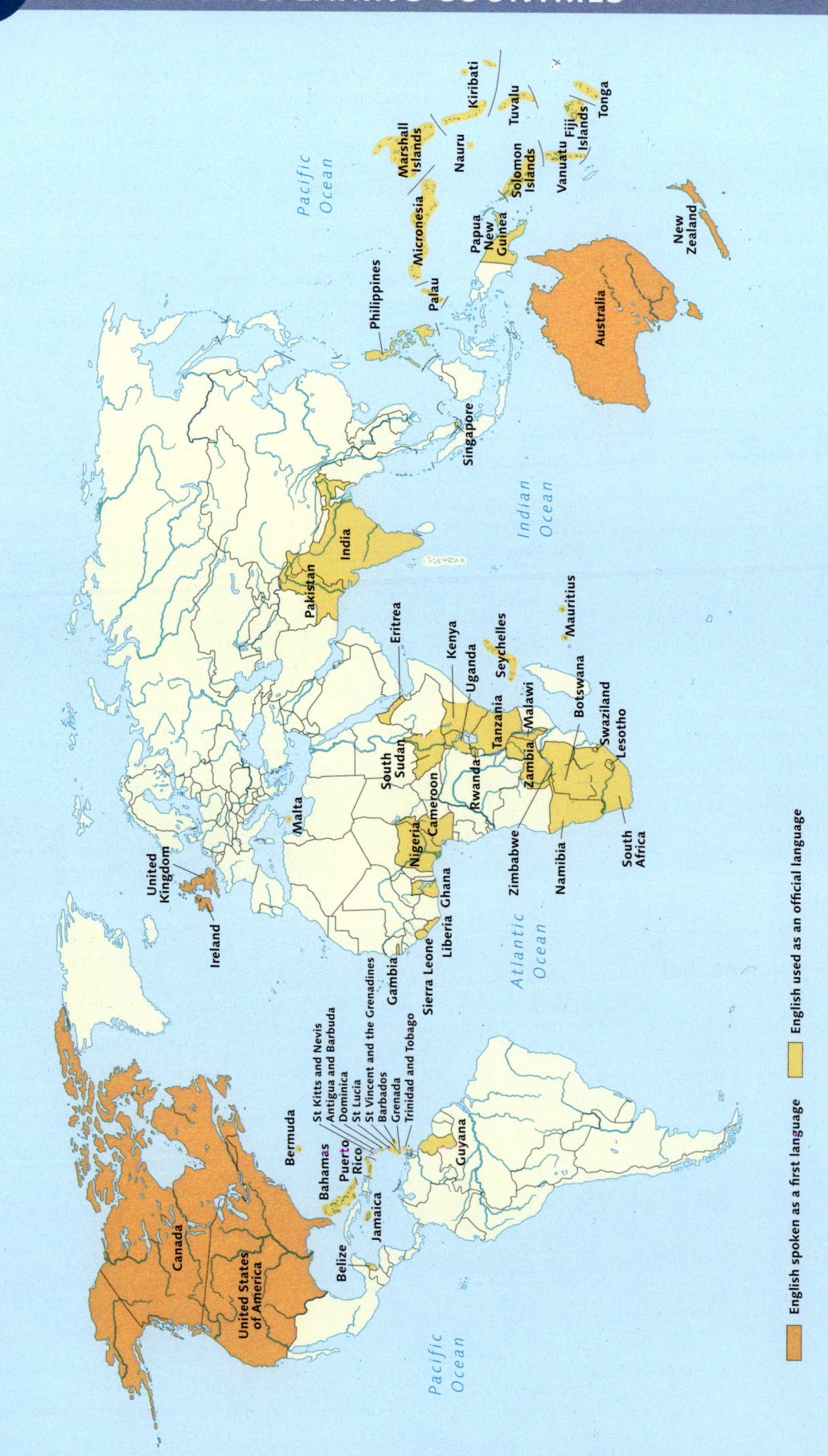

- English spoken as a first language
- English used as an official language

COUNTRIES AND CONTINENTS

Country/Continent	Adjective	Person	People
Afghanistan [æfˈgænɪstæn] *Afghanistan*	Afghan [ˈæfgæn]	an Afghan	the Afghans
Africa [ˈæfrɪkə] *Afrika*	African [ˈæfrɪkən]	an African	the Africans
America [əˈmerɪkə] *Amerika*	American [əˈmerɪkən]	an American	the Americans
Asia [ˈeɪʃə, ˈeɪʒə] *Asien*	Asian [ˈeɪʃn, ˈeɪʒn]	an Asian	the Asians
Australia [ɒˈstreɪliə] *Australien*	Australian [ɒˈstreɪliən]	an Australian	the Australians
Austria [ˈɒstriə] *Österreich*	Austrian [ˈɒstriən]	an Austrian	the Austrians
Belgium [ˈbeldʒəm] *Belgien*	Belgian [ˈbeldʒən]	a Belgian	the Belgians
Bosnia [ˈbɒzniə] *Bosnien*	Bosnian [ˈbɒzniən]	a Bosnian	the Bosnians
Brazil [brəˈzɪl] *Brasilien*	Brasilian [brəˈzɪliən]	a Brasilian	the Brasilians
Bulgaria [bʌlˈgeəriə] *Bulgarien*	Bulgarian [bʌlˈgeəriən]	a Bulgarian	the Bulgarians
Canada [ˈkænədə] *Kanada*	Canadian [kəˈneɪdiən]	a Canadian	the Canadians
China [ˈtʃaɪnə] *China*	Chinese [tʃaɪˈniːz]	a Chinese	the Chinese
Croatia [krəʊˈeɪʃə] *Kroatien*	Croatian [krəʊˈeɪʃn]	a Croatian	the Croatians
the Czech Republic [tʃek rɪˈpʌblɪk] *Tschechien, die Tschechische Republik*	Czech [tʃek]	a Czech	the Czechs
Denmark [ˈdenmɑːk] *Dänemark*	Danish [ˈdeɪnɪʃ]	a Dane [deɪn]	the Danes
England [ˈɪŋglənd] *England*	English [ˈɪŋglɪʃ]	an Englishman/-woman	the English
Europe [ˈjʊərəp] *Europa*	European [jʊərəˈpiːən]	a European	the Europeans
Finland [ˈfɪnlənd] *Finnland*	Finnish [ˈfɪnɪʃ]	a Finn [fɪn]	the Finns
France [frɑːns] *Frankreich*	French [frentʃ]	a Frenchman/-woman	the French
Germany [ˈdʒɜːməni] *Deutschland*	German [ˈdʒɜːmən]	a German	the Germans
(Great) Britain [ˈbrɪtn] *Großbritannien*	British [ˈbrɪtɪʃ]	a Briton [ˈbrɪtn]	the British
Greece [griːs] *Griechenland*	Greek [griːk]	a Greek	the Greeks
Holland [ˈhɒlənd] *Holland, die Niederlande*	Dutch [dʌtʃ]	a Dutchman/-woman	the Dutch
Hungary [ˈhʌŋgəri] *Ungarn*	Hungarian [hʌŋˈgeəriən]	a Hungarian	the Hungarians
India [ˈɪndiə] *Indien*	Indian [ˈɪndiən]	an Indian	the Indians
Iran [ɪˈrɑːn] *Iran*	Iranian [ɪˈreɪniən]	an Iranian	the Iranians
Ireland [ˈaɪələnd] *Irland*	Irish [ˈaɪrɪʃ]	an Irishman/-woman	the Irish
Italy [ˈɪtəli] *Italien*	Italian [ɪˈtæliən]	an Italian	the Italians
Japan [dʒəˈpæn] *Japan*	Japanese [dʒæpəˈniːz]	a Japanese	the Japanese
Lebanon [ˈlebənən] *Libanon*	Lebanese [lebəˈniːz]	a Lebanese	the Lebanese
the Netherlands [ˈneðələndz] *die Niederlande, Holland*	Dutch [dʌtʃ]	a Dutchman/-woman	the Dutch
New Zealand [njuːˈziːlənd] *Neuseeland*	New Zealand [njuːˈziːlənd]	a New Zealander	the New Zealanders
Norway [ˈnɔːweɪ] *Norwegen*	Norwegian [nɔːˈwiːdʒən]	a Norwegian	the Norwegians
Pakistan [pækɪˈstæn] *Pakistan*	Pakistani [pækɪˈstæni]	a Pakistani	the Pakistani
Poland [ˈpəʊlənd] *Polen*	Polish [ˈpəʊlɪʃ]	a Pole [pəʊl]	the Poles
Portugal [ˈpɔːtʃʊgl] *Portugal*	Portuguese [pɔːtʃuˈgiːz]	a Portuguese	the Portuguese
Romania [ruˈmeɪniə] *Rumänien*	Romanian [ruˈmeɪniən]	a Romanian	the Romanians
Russia [ˈrʌʃə] *Russland*	Russian [ˈrʌʃn]	a Russian	the Russians
Scotland [ˈskɒtlənd] *Schottland*	Scottish [ˈskɒtɪʃ]	a Scotsman/-woman, a Scot [skɒt]	the Scots, the Scottish
Serbia [ˈsɜːbiə] *Serbien*	Serbian [ˈsɜːbiən]	a Serb [sɜːb]	the Serbs
Slovakia [sləˈvækiə] *die Slowakei*	Slovak [ˈsləʊvæk]	a Slovakian [sləˈvækiən]	the Slovakians
Slovenia [sləˈviːniə] *Slowenien*	Slovene [ˈsləʊviːn]	a Slovenian [sləˈviːniən]	the Slovenians
Somalia [səˈmɑːliə] *Somalien*	Somali [səˈmɑːli]	a Somali	the Somali
Spain [speɪn] *Spanien*	Spanish [ˈspænɪʃ]	a Spaniard [ˈspænɪəd]	the Spaniards
Sweden [ˈswiːdn] *Schweden*	Swedish [ˈswiːdɪʃ]	a Swede [swiːd]	the Swedes
Switzerland [ˈswɪtsələnd] *die Schweiz*	Swiss [swɪs]	a Swiss	the Swiss
Syria [ˈsɪriə] *Syrien*	Syrian [ˈsɪriən]	a Syrian	the Syrians
Tunisia [tjuːˈnɪziə] *Tunesien*	Tunisian [tjuːˈnɪziən]	a Tunisian	the Tunisians
Turkey [ˈtɜːki] *die Türkei*	Turkish [ˈtɜːkɪʃ]	a Turk [tɜːk]	the Turks
the United Kingdom (the UK) [juːnaɪtɪd ˈkɪŋdəm, juːˈkeɪ] *das Vereinigte Königreich (Großbritannien und Nordirland)*	British [ˈbrɪtɪʃ]	a Briton [ˈbrɪtn]	the British
the United States of America (the USA) [juːnaɪtɪd steɪts əv əˈmerɪkə, juː es ˈeɪ] *die Vereinigten Staaten von Amerika*	American [əˈmerɪkən]	an American	the Americans
Wales [weɪlz] *Wales*	Welsh [welʃ]	a Welshman/-woman	the Welsh
Zimbabwe [zɪmˈbɑːbwi] *Zimbabwe*	Zimbabwean [zɪmˈbɑːbwiən]	a Zimbabwean	the Zimbabweans

QUELLENVERZEICHNIS

Titelbild
Shutterstock/Ralph Loesche

Illustrationen
Carlos Borrell, Berlin (Umschlaginnenseite 1, S. 152; Umschlaginnenseite 3); **Michael Fleischmann**, Waldegg (S. 52; S. 53; S. 68; S. 81; S. 96 unten; S. 208; S. 210; S. 212; S. 221; S. 223; S. 224); **Jeongsook Lee**, Heidelberg (More challenge icon); **David Norman**, Meerbusch (S. 13 Bild C (u. 26); S. 14; S. 18 (u. 103 unten); S. 19 oben u. unten (u. 104); S. 20 (u. 104 u. 162); S. 34; S. 38; S. 39; S. 40; S. 41; S. 42; S. 43; S. 49 unten; S. 64 (u. 124); S. 84 (u. 136); S. 85 (u. 136 u. 137); S. 86 (u. 137 u. 138); S. 87; S. 113; S. 115; S. 116; S. 148; S. 149; S. 150; S. 216)); **Dorina Teßmann**, Berlin (S. 13 unten; S. 26 oben; S. 29; S. 32; S. 37; S. 45; S. 49 oben A–D; S. 96 oben; S. 100);

Bildquellen
action press, Hamburg (S. 24 unten li.: Rex Features Ltd.; S. 60 1. v. oben: Everett Collection/Warner Bros, 2. v. oben: Rex Features Ltd.; S. 75 I: Everett Collection, K: Everett Collection, O: Rex Features; S. 79 A: NASA/REX; S. 152 oben: theoceancleanup/ Exclusivepix Medaction press; S. 153 oben: theoceancleanup/Exclusivepix Medaction press); **akg-images**, Berlin (S. 147 Founding of Australia: Erich Lessing); **Bridgeman Art Library**, Berlin (S. 79 C: BRIDGEMANART.COM); **The Burdekin Crew, Smugglers of Light Foundation**, Desert Pea Media (S. 4 oben li.; S. 14 oben u. unten); **CartoonStock**, Bath (S. 203: Dan Reynolds); **Clip Dealer** (S. 27 unten: Wavebreak Media LTD); **Corbis**, Düsseldorf (S. 6 unten li.: Hero Images; S. 10 Uluru: Jim Holmes/Design Pics; S. 35 unten: MediaServicesAP/Demotix; S. 47 A: Ted Horowitz; S. 60 4. v. oben: Johns PKI/Splash News; S. 76: Hero Images; S. 82 unten: I Love Images; S. 83: I Love Images; S. 94 oben: Ricardo Maynard/Demotix, unten re.: Mike Kemp; S. 154 oben re.: Corbis/Paul Martinka/Splash News); **www.colourbox.com** (S. 93 oben: Monkey Business Images); **dpa Picture Alliance**, Frankfurt/Main (S. 60 3. v. oben: AP Photo; S. 70: dpa; S. 95: dpa; S. 147: dpa); **Frank Donoghue**, Nenagh (S. 156 oben li., Mitte, Mitte li. u. re.); **F1 Online**, Frankfurt/Main (S. 6 unten re.: Maskot; S. 90: Maskot); **Fotofinder.com** (S. 13 Bild A: images.de/ Robert Harding; S. 27 1: images.de/Robert Harding); **Fotolia** (S. 6 oben re. 3. v. li. (u. 55): olgavolodina; S. 8 unten: travel-ing.de; S. 10 passport: instinia.com; S. 10 oben re.: Bernd Leitner; S. 15 boomerang: FPWing; S. 16 D: cirkoglu; S. 25: Aleksandar Mijatovic; S. 27 2: Mingis; S. 40 tablet (M): koosen; S. 47 C: VadimGuzhva, S. 51 Mitte: olly, unten: djtaylor; S. 56 1 apply button: valentint; S. 57 5: Dasha Petrenko; S. 58: Felix Pergande; S. 62 li. (u. 123): Alexander Raths; S. 68: hartphotography; S. 69: Marcin Sadlowski; S. 73 oben: www.delightimages. com, unten: Dmitry Berkut; S. 74 D: Chrispo, G: BlueSkyImages, H: Jurijs Korjakins, like/dislike: bahram7; S. 75 J: danr13, L: Axel Bueckert, M: berc, R: underworld; S. 78 2. v. oben: lev dolgachov, 3. v. oben: szefei, 4. v. oben: Waldemar Dąbrow, 5. v. oben: virinaflora, 6. v. oben: Vitalinka 17762, 7. v. oben: Jenifoto1; S. 79 B: loreanto; S. 80 unten: stockasso; S. 92 A: Texelart, B: Leksiy Mark, C: Cobalt, D: sdecoret, F: sdecoret; S. 93 unten li.: kotoyamagami; S. 135: Kakigori Studio; S. 145 working abroad: gustavofrazao, laboratory: Alexander Raths, factory: industrieblick, hospital: Robert Kneschke; S. 146 map (orange), opera, kangaroo, flag, currency, population, government: a7880ss; S. 154 oben li.: Eléonore H; S. 156 oben re.: cybrflower; 157 oben: Mark Higgins; S. 158 oben: TONO BALAGUER; S. 160: WavebreakMediaMicro; S. 166: Monkey Business; S. 168: lev dolgachov; S. 171: JPC-PROD; S. 180 talking icon u. listening icon: mihey33av, two paper icons (M): jacartoon, glasses icon: IconWeb; S. 181 unten: www.miriamdoerr.com; S. 208 spiders: Henrik Larsson, salt and pepper: markobe; S. 210 horses: photographixx; S. 211: Coka; S. 215 re.: Michael Burrell; S. 216: timonko; S. 218 vacuum cleaner: Nikolai Sorokin); **Glow Images**, München (S. 41: Djavid Lundberg Akvari; S. 47 B: CulturaRF); **Image Source**, Köln (S. 63 (u. 123): Rick Becker-Leckrone; S. 71 li.: Maskot Bildbyrå AB, re.: Per Levander; S. 75 N: Claire Keeley; S. 77: Rick Becker-Leckrone; S. 82 oben: Rick Becker-Leckrone; S. 97: Stefano Gilera; S. 157 unten: Image Source/ Haris Artemis; **Indigineous Advisory Council/ Australian Human Rights Commission** (S. 36); **INTERFOTO**, München (S. 27 3: David Wall); **klein und halm**, Berlin (S. 48 A–E: Steffen Schönbrunn); **LAIF**, Köln (S. 8 Bild A (u. 167): COLIN Matthieu/ Hemispheres Images; S. 9 Bild F: Jean-Daniel Sudres/ hemis.fr); Lyon Photography 2012 (S. 50); **mauritius images**, Mittenwald (S. 8 Bild C: Alamy/Marc Anderson; S. 9 Bild D: Steffan Hill/Alamy, Bild E: Bluegreen Pictures; S. 11 oben li.: Christine Osborne Pictures/Alamy; S. 16 C: doug steley/Alamy; S. 18 (u. 162): martin berry/Alamy; S. 24 oben re.: Gerry Pearce/Alamy; S. 24 unten re.: iconotec; S. 57 6: Greg Bajor/Alamy; S. 62 re. (u. 123): Ian Dagnall/ Alamy; S. 64 (u. 124): PFMIX/Alamy; S. 74 A: United Archives, B: Alvey & Towers Picture Library/Alamy, E: incamerastock/Alamy; S. 75 P: Fancy, Q: AKP Photos/ Alamy; S. 80 oben billboard (M): Jeff Morgan 15/ Alamy; S. 153 Mitte re.: FLPA/Alamy; S. 154 unten: Tom Hanley/Alamy; S. 158 unten: Stephen Barnes/ Public Transport/Alamy; S. 170 unten: Image Source; S. 179: Onoky; S. 180: Ubanimages/Alamy); **Reuters**, Berlin (S. 15 dance: Paul Mathews; S. 74 F: Brendan McDermi); **Rockfinch/Claire Cunningham**, Dublin (S. 22; S. 30; S. 31; S. 44; S. 54; S. 66 unten; S. 88; S. 140); **Royal Flying Doctor Service, Brisbane, Australia** (S. 12 oben: Cameron Laird, logo); **Schule ohne Rassismus – Schule mit Courage**, Berlin (S. 48 unten); **Shutterstock** (S. 4 unten li. teenagers: SpeedKingz; S. 6 oben li. (u. 72): AeChan, oben re. 1. v. li. (u. 55): Golden Pixels LLC, oben re. 2. v. li. (u. 55): Monkey Business Images; S. 8 Bild B (M) road: Totajla, sign (M): max blain, map: Pjasha; S. 10 flag: Steve Allen, girl: tmcphotos; S. 11 unten: Ethan Daniels; S. 13 Bild B: Chet Mitchell; S. 15 painting: dedoma; S. 16 A: Niels Quist, B: Martin Smith; S. 19 map (M) (u. 24 u. 103): Alison1414; S. 24 oben li.: Lev Kropotov; S. 27 4: Visual society, 5: Michael Leslie; S. 35 oben: SpeedKingz; S. 51 oben:

Vikulin; S. 55 Charlotte: Monkey Business Images, Tom: Volt Collection; S. 56 1 boy: Kalinovsky Dmitry, 2: Falcon Eyes, 3: CandyBox Images, 4: Olesia Bilkei; S. 66 oben: leungchopan; S. 74 C: Featureflash; S. 78 1. v. oben: Helga Esteb; S. 80 oben boy (M): Kamenetskiy Konstantin; S. 89 oben: VIGE.CO; S. 92 E: RealVector; S. 93 unten re.: mypokcik; S. 94 unten li.: GTS Productions; S. 114: CREATISTA; S. 131: Benjavisa Ruangvaree; S. 142: Monkey Business Images; S. 143: PathDoc; S. 146 map (climate) of Australia: Rainer Lesniewski, plane icon: Dmitry Fokin, weather icon: bluelela; S. 147 A: Filipe Frazao, B: Stanislav Fosenbauer, C: Bildagentur Zoonar GmbH, D: Photo Image, E: Taras Vyshnya; S. 152/153 background plastic: archetype, plastic bottle caps: cici_2012, plastic bottle: Picsfive; S. 153 oben plastic bottle: Picsfive, plastic bag: photka, buoy: BW Folsom, bottle: Mariyana M, fishing line: Ad Oculos, cup: M. Unal Ozmen, drink holder: You Touch Pix of EuToch; S. 154 notebook paper: teacept; S. 155 oben: Dana Nalbandian, unten: JStone; S. 161: Paul Vasarhelyi; S. 165: Lorelyn Medina; S. 170: Jesus Sanz; S. 172: Tharakorn; S. 175: Monkey Business Images; S. 181 oben: Artisticco; S. 210 cattle: Dariusz Gora; S. 215 li.: Adem Demir; S. 218 washing machine: Sashkin, iron: Chimpinski; S. 221: Worldpics; S. 223 oben: TZIDO SUN, blouse: Karkas, shirt: Jiang Zhongyan, lips: Trifonenko Ivan. Orsk, lipstick: Picsfive, unten: ostill; S. 225 pumps: GG Studios Austria, sandals: Adisa, swimsuit: Michael Kraus; S. 226: suns07butterfly; S. 227 oben: Viorel Sima, unten: NikoNomad; S. 228: Laura Gangi Pond; S. 229 oben: Snap2Art, unten li.: Crevis, unten re.: nanami7; S. 230 li.: Sam Aronov, re.: Annette Shaff; S. 231 oben: mkkmc, unten: ags1973; S. 232 li.: nanD_Phanuwat, re.: lynea; S. 233 oben: Arcady, unten: Ricardo Reitmeyer; S. 235: Robert Spriggs); **vario images**, Bonn (S. 15 didgeridoo: RHPL); **Silvia Wiedemann**, Berlin (S. 156 unten)

Textquellen

S. 14 A and B *Eyes wide open* from The Burdekin Crew, Smugglers of Light Foundation, Desert Pea Media, used by permission; **S. 16 A** *Living in the Kimberley*, reproduced with minor modification by permission of the Australian Broadcasting Corporation - Library Sales © ABC - Joanna Koeyers; **S. 16 B** *I'm a mud racer*, reproduced with minor modification by permission of the Australian Broadcasting Corporation - Library Sales © ABC - Ashlee Modr; **S. 18–21 and S. 103–104** *Swerve* adapted from Phillip Gwynne: Swerve, Penguin Australia, used by permission; **S. 28** *The Spare Room* adapted from Kathryn Lomer: The Spare Room, University of Queensland Press, used by permission; **S. 41–43 and S. 115–116** *Natasha's side of the story* and *Matt's side of the story* adapted from Chloe Rayban: Watching You, Watching Me, Harper Collins Publishers, London 1999, used by permission; **S. 50** *The kid in a wheelchair*, reproduced with permission of Teen Ink and TeenInk.com © Britain R. All rights reserved; *A fashion model and a role model* from Theo Merz: Jack Eyers: My dream is to be seen as a good model, not a sob story, in: The Telegraph, used by permission; **S. 62–64 and S. 123–124** *Seashell Motel* adapted from Lois Metzger: Working days. Short stories about teenagers at work, Persea Books New York, reproduced with minor modification by permission © 1997 Lois Metzger. All rights reserved; **S. 84–87 and S. 136–138** *Gamer* adapted from Chris Bradford: Gamer, Barrington Stoke Ltd., used by permission; **S. 148–151** *Riot* from David Fermer, Cornelsen English Library, used by permission;
S. 160 *My first real job* excerpt from 'Climbing the Golden Arches' by Marissa Nunez reprinted with permission from 'Starting With I' (Persea Books) © 1997 by Youth Communication/New York Center, Inc. (www.youthcomm.org).

271

TYPICAL INSTRUCTIONS IN TESTS AND EXAMS

General / Allgemein

Read the tasks carefully.	Lies die Aufgaben sorgfältig.
You now have 60 seconds to read the tasks.	Du hast ab jetzt 60 Sekunden zum Lesen der Aufgaben.
Now do the tasks.	Nun bearbeite die Aufgaben.
Tick the correct box / the three correct boxes.	Setze ein Häkchen (✓) in das / die richtige(n) Kästchen.
Tick the right statements. (There's only one possible answer per statement.)	Setze ein ✓ bei den korrekten Aussagen. (Pro Aussage ist nur eine Antwort möglich.)
Complete the sentences (with not more than three words per gap / … than two words each).	Vervollständige die Sätze (mit bis zu drei Wörtern pro Lücke / mit je bis zu zwei Wörtern).
Fill in the information / the missing words.	Füge die Information / die fehlenden Wörter ein.
Fill in suitable words / the correct numbers.	Füge passende Wörter / die korrekten Zahlen ein.
Fill in only one detail per box.	Füge nur ein Detail pro Kästchen ein.
Complete these sentences.	Vervollständige diese Sätze.
There is only one possible answer.	Es gibt nur eine mögliche Antwort.
There are two more words than you need.	Es gibt zwei Wörter mehr als du benötigst.
Choose the correct options and fill in the blanks.	Wähle die korrekten Varianten und fülle die Lücken aus.
Mark *true* or *false*.	Markiere (z.B. mit einem ✗) *wahr* oder *falsch*.
There is an example at the beginning.	Am Anfang steht ein Beispiel.
You have a choice here. Choose one of the following tasks: …	Hier hast du die Wahl. Wähle eine der folgenden Aufgaben aus: …

Listening / Hörverstehen

You are going to hear a story / an interview about …	Du wirst eine Geschichte / ein Interview über … hören.
Listen to the interview.	Höre dir das Interview an.
Listen to these people talking about … Who thinks what? Tick the correct letters.	Höre dem Gespräch dieser Personen über … zu. Wer denkt was? Setze ein ✓ bei den korrekten Buchstaben.
You will hear five short conversations.	Du wirst fünf kurze Gespräche hören.
You will hear each conversation twice.	Du wirst jedes Gespräch zweimal hören.
While you are listening, tick the correct box / …	Während du zuhörst, setze ein ✓ in das richtige Kästchen.
At the end you will hear the story / interview again.	Am Ende hörst du die Story / das Interview nochmal.
Now listen to the story and do the tasks.	Höre dir jetzt die Geschichte an und löse die Aufgaben.
Which word group completes the sentence best?	Welche Wortgruppe vervollständigt den Satz am besten?
Mark the correct option to complete the sentences.	Markiere die jeweils korrekte Vervollständigung der Sätze.
Complete the table using one to five words.	Vervollständige die Tabelle mit zwei bis fünf Wörtern.

Reading and Writing / Leseverstehen und Schreiben

First read the text. Then read the sentence beginnings and tick the correct ending.	Lies zuerst den Text. Dann lies die Satzanfänge und setze ein ✓ beim jeweils korrekten Satzende.
First read the information about the people, then look at the job / holiday / … offers. In each case find two options the person could choose.	Lies zuerst die Informationen über die Personen, dann schau dir die Job-/ Ferien-/ …-Angebote an. Finde für jede Person zwei Möglichkeiten, die sie wählen könnte.
You need not write complete sentences.	Du musst keine vollständigen Sätze schreiben.
Quote from the text.	Zitiere aus dem Text.
Find the correct parts of Mr Miller's quote.	Finde die korrekten Teile aus Mr. Millers Zitat.
Match each of these headings with a suitable paragraph from the text. (Some paragraphs don't match.)	Ordne jede dieser Überschriften einem passenden Textabsatz zu. (Zu einigen Absätzen passt keine Überschrift.)
Match the correct sentence parts. (Write down the letter in the box.)	Ordne die passenden Satzteile einander zu. (Schreibe den Buchstaben in das Kästchen.)
Match 1–4 to the information given in A–G. Some information doesn't fit.	Ordne 1–4 den Informationen in A–G zu. Einige Informationen lassen sich nicht zuordnen.
Answer the questions below. Give short answers.	Beantworte die unten stehenden Fragen kurz.
Answer the questions in complete sentences.	Beantworte die Fragen mit vollständigen Sätzen.
You can't find the answers to the following questions directly in the text.	Du wirst auf die folgenden Fragen keine direkten Antworten im Text finden.
The following words have more than one meaning. Which of the meanings is the one used in the text?	Die folgenden Wörter haben mehr als eine Bedeutung. Welche Bedeutung ist im Text gemeint?
Write down the German meaning as used in the text.	Schreibe die im Text gemeinte deutsche Bedeutung auf.
Complete the following sentences with suitable phrases from the text (with not more than five to seven words per gap).	Vervollständige die folgenden Sätze mit passenden Wendungen aus dem Text (max. fünf bis sieben Wörter pro Lücke).
Finish the sentences using information from the text.	Beende die Sätze mit Informationen aus dem Text.
Decide whether the following statements are right or wrong.	Entscheide, ob die folgenden Aussagen wahr oder falsch sind.
Find out whether the following statements are true, false or not given in the text. Tick the correct box.	Sind die folgenden Aussagen wahr, falsch oder nicht im Text gegeben? Setze ein ✓ in das korrekte Kästchen.
Scan paragraph A. Name two examples …	Scanne Absatz A. Nenne zwei Beispiele …